ON
THE POETRY OF
KEATS

E. C. PETTET

ON THE POETRY OF KEATS

CAMBRIDGE
AT THE UNIVERSITY PRESS
1957
REPRINTED
1970

Published by the Syndics of the Cambridge University Press
Bentley House, 200 Euston Road, London, N.W. 1
American Branch: 32 East 57th Street, New York, N.Y. 10022

PUBLISHER'S NOTE

Cambridge University Press Library Editions are re-issues of out-of-print standard works from the Cambridge catalogue. The texts are unrevised and, apart from minor corrections, reproduce the latest published edition.

Standard Book Number: 521 07780 x

First published 1957
Reprinted 1970

First printed in Holland by Joh. Enschedé en Zonen
Reprinted in Great Britain by John Dickens & Co. Ltd, Northampton

CONTENTS

FOREWORD

HAD they been available at the time, I should certainly have profited considerably from several admirable studies of Keats that have appeared since 1956. However, I doubt whether they would have much affected my general attitude to his poetry or the main views I was attempting to advance.

Probably the chief limitation of this book, as the reviewers confirmed, is its scant treatment of *Hyperion*, including the Induction. I should now be inclined to think this limitation arose not only from what was probably an injudicious use of space but from my uncertainties about interpretation of the poem. After thirteen years I believe—if mistakenly—that I have a firmer understanding of it; and I hope to rectify my ommission in the not too-distant future.

Since, wrongly or not, I devoted so much space to *Endymion*, I have been slightly disappointed by my apparent failure to modify the prevailing interpretation. Not that I ever imagined one small, though long-drawn out, trumpet blast would bring down all the high, imposing walls of allegory and metaphysics. But I was hopeful that subsequent critics would perhaps be more sceptical about their substance.

As the present method of reprinting precludes any alteration of text, I can only indicate some of the misprints and minor slips—the (at least consistent) blunder of entitling F. R. Leavis's *Revaluation* as *Revaluations,* the continual mis-spelling of *Mrs Radcliffe* as Radcliff, the spelling of Carey for *Cary* (p. 203 and 217), Gregson for *Grigson* (p. 58), Mabbot for *Mabbott* (note, p. 32), the failure to record Mrs Owen's initials correctly as F. M. (p. 143), and the inexcusable oversight of "Shelly" and "Spencer" at the bottom of p. 143. A more serious mistake than any of these is the printing of "throughly" for "through" (p. 114) in the quotation of l. 109 from *The Eve of St. Agnes.*

E.C.P.

May 1969

PREFACE

THIS book deals with some important aspects of Keats's poetry that I happen to find of particular interest. The obvious danger of such a volume is that it will turn out to be a shapeless collection of miscellaneous essays. I hope I have avoided most of this risk, for I have certainly intended a good deal of interconnexion between the various studies; and in several instances the interests and writing of one led directly to another. There are even moments when I fancy that the book may have some degree of shape.

Though I have not aimed at a comprehensive examination of Keats's poetry, I have in fact brought most of it under consideration—and from several different points of view. I have also in the concluding chapter hazarded some comment and judgment on Keats's work as a whole. There are of course obvious omissions, the two chief ones arising from my very brief discussions of the ode *To Autumn* and the Induction to *The Fall of Hyperion*. It may also seem that I have devoted undue space to *Endymion*.

So far as the omissions are concerned, I am tempted to say of the ode *To Autumn* that, for all its resonant depth, it is so direct and sure in its effect that it puts interpretative criticism out of business. I have no excuse to offer for my superficial treatment of the Induction to *The Fall of Hyperion* except limitations of space that I might perhaps have used to better advantage.

The extensive study of *Endymion* I would justify on several grounds: that this poem, the great divide between the early and later Keats, is more deserving of attention—and to some extent of praise—than many past critics have believed; that it has been much used as a base by a number of recent critics who wish to represent the Keats of the 1819 poems as a deeply metaphysical writer; and that I have attempted both to demolish an interpretation of it that has been widely current for the last fifty years and to suggest an alternative way of reading it.

In spite of the inevitable formality of the phrase I should like to acknowledge my sincere gratitude to the Syndics of the Cambridge University Press for their advice on my MS. in its original state; to Mrs Betty Haigh for her valuable interest in Chapter III when it was in a very rudimentary condition; to the Editor of the *Review of English Studies* for permission to reprint an article that forms part of Chapter I and to the Library of Harvard College for permission to include two photostat copies of parts of the manuscript of *The Eve of St Agnes*; to Mr J. H. Preston of the Keats Memorial House for his ready answers to my enquiries; and to Miss Dickson, the Librarian of Goldsmiths' College, London University, for her unfailing and prompt assistance in procuring necessary reference books.

E. C. P.

August 1956.

CHAPTER I

KEATS AND HIS 'INFLUENCES'

How many bards gild the lapses of time!
A few of them have ever been the food
Of my delighted fancy . . .
Poems (1817), Sonnet IV

IN his essay *Of Myself* Abraham Cowley wrote:

I believe I can tell the particular little chance that filled my head
first with such Chimes of Verse, as have never since left ringing
there: For I remember when I began to read, and to take some
pleasure in it, there was wont to lie in my Mothers Parlour (I
know not by what accident, for she her self never in her life read
any Books but of Devotion) but there was wont to lie Spencers
Works; this I happened to fall upon, and was infinitely delighted
with the Stories of the Knights, and Giants, and Monsters, and
brave houses, which I found every where there: (Though my understanding had little to do with all this) and by degrees with the
tinckling of the Rhyme and Dance of the Numbers, so that I think
I had read him all over before I was twelve years old, and was thus
made a Poet as immediately as a child is made an Eunuch.[1]

It is a curious fact of literary history that this story of a
'particular little chance' was closely repeated in the life of
another and greater poet two hundred years later. One
momentous afternoon in Keats's seventeenth or eighteenth
year his older friend and literary guide, Cowden Clarke, read
him Spenser's *Epithalamion*; when Keats left in the evening he
took home with him *The Faerie Queene*. What happened is
recorded by his later friend, Charles Brown:

Though born to be a poet, he was ignorant of his birthright
until he had completed his eighteenth year. It was the *Faerie
Queene* that awakened his genius. In Spenser's fairy land he was
enchanted, breathed in a new world, and became another being; till
enamoured of the stanza, he attempted to imitate it, and succeeded.*

* Quoted in Sir Sidney Colvin's *Life of John Keats*, p. 20. Brown adds:
'This account of the sudden development of his poetic powers I first
received from his brothers and afterwards from himself.'

I

Yet while Keats's experience was very similar to Cowley's, Brown's record brings out an essential difference. Cowley was one of those poets who 'lisped in numbers'. Keats, on the other hand, appears to have been the much more common sort of schoolboy, fonder of fisticuffs than of books; and he did not start verse-writing till his eighteenth year. All the available evidence goes to show that Brown was speaking literal truth when he talked about Keats becoming 'another being' at this period, and though it would be a mistake to let our ignorance of many unknown factors overstress the significance of the one that is certain, there is every reason to believe that it was chiefly the magic wand of Spenser that brought about the metamorphosis of the eighteen-year-old Keats. It is no exaggeration to say that Spenser became a living presence to him, one of the chief embodiments of that 'overpowering idea of our dead poets'² that almost crazed him with wonder and feverish ambition. And besides this exceptional appeal of the image of a great poet, there was also the unfailing enchantment of the Spenserian world, of its pictorial richness and music, so that even more truly than Cowley he could have said that the chimes of *The Faerie Queene* had never left ringing in his head. Had he never fallen in love with Spenser there would certainly have been no *Eve of St Agnes* as we know it.

However, momentous as the discovery of Spenser was for the young Keats, his earliest poems were by no means exclusively, or even predominantly, influenced by this Elizabethan master. As we read his first volume, *Poems* (1817), we may strip off the layers of 'influences' like skins of an onion; and scholars have shown that the list of echoes and imitations is a very substantial one,* ranging from the poetry of writers like Milton, Wordsworth, Coleridge and Byron, through that of Browne of Tavistock, Thomson, Collins, Campbell, Moore

---

* The opening chapters of C. L. Finney's *The Evolution of Keats's Poetry* contain one of the best examinations into the influences that shaped Keats's early poetry. See also the notes (pp. 387–563) in E. de Selincourt's edition of Keats.

and Leigh Hunt, to verses of nearly forgotten authors like Beattie, Mrs Tighe, and Charlotte Smith.

There is of course nothing singular in the fact that Keats's earliest poems are so derivative and highly synthetic in nature, or that only one, the sonnet *On first looking into Chapman's Homer*, gives any really unmistakable promise of the greatness and originality to come. All young poets, of whatever future attainment, make their first poems largely out of the work of admired models. What is amazing is that in less than three years Keats should have passed from the fumbling imitations of 'I stood tip-toe' or *Calidore* to the great and individual utterance of the odes. Admittedly, even if we dissent from Garrod's opinion—'He ends, save for the Odes, still a conscious imitator of the manner of other poets'*—as an exaggeration, we should be wrong to maintain that Keats had completely found himself as a poet by 1819. But against the Miltonic *Hyperion*, the Byronic *Cap and Bells*,† and the Shakespearean *Otho the Great*, we must set the odes and certain shorter poems like *La Belle Dame Sans Merci*, *Lamia*, the Induction to *The Fall of Hyperion*, and even *The Eve of St Agnes*, all of which owe infinitely more to Keats himself than they do to any other poet. If we bear these poems in mind, his rapid emancipation from his early 'influences' is astounding; and it is doubtful whether any other English poet has ever progressed so swiftly towards self-realization as Keats did between 'I stood tip-toe' and the ode *To Autumn*.

What was it that enabled him to make such an advance? This question is not an unprofitable one to pursue, for besides its particular relevance to Keats's poetry it also has a wider import. Possibly one of the most certain distinctions between 'minor' and 'major' poets is that while all compose their earliest works from an imitation or synthesis of existing poetry,

* H. W. Garrod, *Keats*, p. 64.

† Whether or not we accept Finney's conclusion, 'Keats not only parodied Byron's style but he also satirised Byron himself' (*op. cit.* p. 736), there can be no doubt that Keats was aping the manner of *Don Juan*.

the 'minor' writers, however admirable, never really pass beyond this stage. They may please us, but they contribute nothing to the developing tradition of poetry. Occasional innovations of technique apart, like Surrey's and Wyatt's introduction of the sonnet, or the mid-seventeenth century work of Denham and Waller on the heroic couplet, it is the 'major' poets who are, in the strictest sense of the word, creators.

These generalities may be pointed by comparing Keats with his friend Reynolds. In his earliest verses Reynolds was clearly impelled by the same enthusiasms and admirations* as Keats. More than that, Reynolds's first poems will stand critical comparison with most of what we find in *Poems* (1817). Yet Reynolds never developed into anything more than a competent versifier.

Those who believe unreservedly in the idea of the 'born' poet will have an instant explanation for this difference between Keats and Reynolds: Keats possessed the mysterious x of poetic inspiration, Reynolds did not. No doubt there is plenty of rough truth in such an answer. There is a mysterious x at the heart of the creative process, and there will always be some mystery about Keats's poetic transformation between 1816 and 1819. But that is not to say that we can understand nothing about the causes of this development; and what we do understand is always likely to be of interest, and perhaps help, to future poets.

When we examine the influences in Keats's poetry, especially in his earliest writing, we notice that, compared with the first works of many other poets, his verses do not contain very much verbal echoing—certainly not of a close and unmistakable kind.†

---

* Notably admiration for Wordsworth and Leigh Hunt and for eighteenth century sentimental and romantic poetry based on imitations of Spenser and Milton. (See Finney, *op. cit.* p. 151.)

† Thus E. de Selincourt, from his investigation into Keats's poetic

This fact, and some of the probable implications of it, is clearly demonstrated by Miss Caroline Spurgeon in her book *Keats's Shakespeare*. All readers of *Endymion* must feel, if only as a vague impression, that the poem derives a considerable inspiration from Shakespeare, whom Keats was avidly and intensely reading at the time; and in her study Miss Spurgeon thoroughly examines this impression. Her conclusion supports the general feeling of a strong Shakespearean inspiration behind the work; and she maintains that Keats was particularly under the spell of *A Midsummer Night's Dream* and *The Tempest* while composing it. However, though she gives a long list of text-parallels between these two plays and *Endymion*, most of the reminiscences of phrase and image are remote, as she herself fully admits. For instance, she comments at one point: 'I do not suggest for a moment that there is any plagiarism or imitation on the part of Keats; on the contrary, we are given here a very beautiful example of the creative stimulus and enrichment given by the mature imagination of one poet to the soaring and youthful imagination of another.'*

A study of the two early sonnets, *On the Sea* (April 1817) and *On sitting down to read King Lear once again* (January 1818), leaves exactly the same impression. There is no question about the strong Shakespearean inspiration behind these sonnets: the second expresses this in its substance, while the first is introduced in a letter to Reynolds with the remark: 'the

vocabulary (as single words) concludes: 'Keats's language is not nearly so definitely imitative of single authors as reproductive of a language which the earlier authors held in common and which, therefore, he regarded as his lawful inheritance' (*Poems of John Keats*, p. 571).

* *Keats's Shakespeare*, pp. 10–11. Again, she writes (p. 12): 'the real influence or rather kinship is of quite a different nature. It is almost as if Keats, after living through the magical experiences and sights and sounds of *The Tempest*, was still, when beginning his own poem, so steeped in Shakespearian enchantment that the glamour of it is carried over into the similar adventures of his own hero, who actually sees and hears similar sights and sounds and is stimulated by them to visions of even greater and deeper beauty.' However, it should be added that some close verbal echoes of Shakespeare can be detected elsewhere in Keats's poetry— in *The Eve of St Agnes*, for instance.

passage in Lear—'Do you not hear the sea?'—has haunted me intensely.'[3] Yet in both poems there is hardly anything that can be described as a verbal or image reminiscence of anything Shakespeare has written.

It is also apposite here to consider Keats's classical references and use of classical (mainly Greek) story and mythology—all this, too, outstandingly exemplified in *Endymion*. What is remarkable about all this material in his poetry is not so much its prominence or superficial beauty as the fact that there is so much poetic life in it and that it is rarely used for formal and conventionally acceptable decoration. To put the matter simply, Keats has made these classical allusions and myths authentically his by a power of re-creation. Further, several classical scholars of repute have maintained that somehow, perhaps through his brooding on the Elgin marbles, he has embodied in this re-creation much of the essential Greek spirit;* and the uncompleted *Ode to May* has often been held up as an instance of this re-creative intuition. Yet, unlike Shelley, Keats had only a grammar-school Latin and no Greek, and it is impossible to find in his work verbal echoes from Greek and Latin writers. With Shelley, on the other hand, we can often find a line that is a close—and often, one guesses, conscious—recollection of his wide and continuous classical reading.

What light do such facts as these throw on Keats's amazingly swift discovery of his own poetic voice?†

* But G. Hough (*The Romantic Poets*, p. 159) has entered a just qualification to this common view: 'His vision of Greece really came to him, however, through Elizabethan and seventeenth-century poetry, soaked like all Renaissance literature in Greek myth and allusions, yet luxuriant, disorderly, and mediaevalised.'

† We must, of course, be on our guard against facile answers to such a question. For one thing, we must remember that there are several subtle but quite distinct stages between the extremes of a borrowing that is entirely subconscious and the jackdaw pilfering from other poets to make a poem of one's own. Also, Miss Spurgeon's eagerness to assert that there is no plagiarism or imitation in Keats's reminiscences of Shakespeare must certainly not be taken to imply that major poets are never plagiarists and close imitators in their younger days.

First, it seems highly probable that the comparative rarity of direct verbal echoes in his early poetry points to some fundamental originality or integrity (or both) that restrained him from taking over images and expressions from other poets, even subconsciously, and even from such a master as Shakespeare whom he was continuously reading and re-reading. Such a check may have worked in different ways: he may have possessed a particularly alert awareness about words, so that he immediately recognized any derivative phrase or expression that he was inclined to include in a poem; or, on the other hand, he may have had a poor, or deliberately unexercised, verbal memory of the poetry he had read.

There is an illuminating passage in Stephen Spender's autobiography *World within World* that may bear on some of these possibilities, particularly the last:

One significant difference [between the writer and Auden] was the use to which each put his memory. Auden . . . knew much poetry by heart. I knew almost none. The difference was not just of his good and my bad memory. It was one of our having different attitudes towards remembering. I resisted learning poems by heart, because in recollecting them I did not want to hold them word by word in my mind, in exactly the same form as when I read them. I wanted to remember not the words and the lines, but a line beyond the lines, a sensuous quality which went, as it were, into the lines before they were written by the poet and which remained after I, the reader, had forgotten them. Poetry could thus become in my memory qualities which I could separate from the words themselves. The feeling of a poem which I did not completely remember seemed to put me in touch with the poet's mind in a way which the exactly recollected poem itself could not do. In this way, also, I could relate his poetic impulse to my own, because it was no longer tied to words and a form which, belonging to his time and circumstances, could not apply to mine . . . .

The quality of a poet's memory, and the way in which he uses it, are what chiefly distinguishes him from other poets. There are two main categories of memory: one is what might be called overt and conscious memory, the other is hidden and unconscious. Overt and conscious memory is memory of impressions which at the time of their being experienced have been formulated when they were

7

experienced, so that remembering them is like creating them anew, or like experiencing them for the first time.[4]

This somewhat extensive quotation is given because, from the first-hand experience of a poet (and one who probably belongs to the same essential kind as Keats),* it suggests a second answer to our question that entirely corresponds with the implications of Miss Spurgeon's looser and more lyrical remarks. There is no evidence to show that Keats ever, like Spender, deliberately resisted learning poetry by heart. But it does seem highly probable that what chiefly inspired him in Shakespeare, Spenser—and possibly Leigh Hunt—was not so much admired passages† that lodged in his mind and that he strove to imitate or surpass as what Spender calls a 'sensuous quality' beyond the lines, the 'feeling' of a poem that could not be verbally remembered. This would explain, in the case of Spenser, how the very image of the man, concentrating all the 'feeling' of his poetry, could be such a potent and exciting stimulus. One guesses, from Keats's poems and letters, that he would have thoroughly understood and fully endorsed Spender's remark: 'Poetry could thus become in my memory qualities which I could separate from the words themselves.' In Keats's own terminology this would be part of an 'abstract' idea of poetry. Moreover, if Spender is right in his supposition that the poet lacking in verbal memories is the one most likely to make contact with and feel the essential poetic impulse of an older poet, this would go far to explain the seeming paradox that Miss Spurgeon has demonstrated in *Endymion*: that we are intensely and continuously conscious

* One guesses that a comparison between the poetry of Auden and Spender would show that whereas most of the verbal echoes in Spender's poems are of an oblique and probably subconscious kind, most of those in Auden's poems are deliberate, often in the form of near-quotation or parody.

† Some exceptions to this general observation must be noted: see, for instance, the letter of 22 November 1817 to Reynolds (*Letters of John Keats*, ed. M. B. Forman, p. 65).

of Shakespeare's presence yet can rarely point to any material manifestation of it.

Another answer to our question is suggested by Miss Spurgeon when she reminds us* that the line

> Whose eyelids curtain'd up their jewels dim,[5]

has two apparent Shakespearean origins:

> (i) The fringed curtains of thine eye advance . . .[6]

and (ii) Her eyelids, cases to those heavenly jewels
>> Which Pericles hath lost,
>> Begin to part their fringes of bright gold.[7]

If, as seems most likely, Keats's line is a fusion of these two separate passages, then we may be quite sure that his recollection and combination of them was an entirely subconscious process. We shall return to this matter in more detail a little later on.

Beside the occasional verbal echoes that are to be detected in Keats's early work there are also the imitations—poems or passages, that is to say, where he is deliberately attempting to reproduce the manner of some other poet. Outstanding examples of such imitative writing, taking different forms, are *To Hope* and *Ode to Apollo*, close copies of the dominant late eighteenth-century style of lyrical writing, the epistles with their loose decasyllabic couplets from William Browne's *Britannia's Pastorals*,† and such Hunt-inspired verses as *Calidore* and 'I stood tip-toe', the latter of which Finney rightly describes as Keats's 'most perfect imitation of Hunt's descriptive style'.‡

---

* De Selincourt (*Poems of John Keats*, p. 424) had already noted these Shakespearean echoes.

† However, Finney is right to remind us that Browne's 'heroic couplets are so much like Hunt's that their influence upon Keats's heroic couplets cannot always be distinguished from that of Hunt's' (*The Evolution of Keats's Poetry*, p. 87).

‡ *Op. cit.* p. 160. Bridges appears to have been particularly struck by

However, when we carefully consider this substantial body of imitative poetry, it is not difficult to find evidence of a poet who would in all probability pass rapidly from imitation to original work. For instance, we notice that *Calidore*, doubtless planned as a fairly ambitious work on the scale of Hunt's *Rimini*, was left as a fragment. We have no certain information why Keats never finished this poem, and there may have been several causes at work; but one explanation of his failure to carry it through is almost certainly that he grew tired of a long poem that had no impetus beyond imitation of an admired poet. However facile his talent for imitation may have been, there were evidently, even at the age of twenty, sharp limits to the satisfaction that it afforded him. Two years later the experience of *Calidore* was to be repeated in his attempt to write a Miltonic epic.

Again, as the examples given above, ranging from Browne's technique to Hunt's type of sentiment, clearly show, there was a wide and rich sweep in Keats's imitations. This points to energy, independence, and perhaps a high degree of self-consciousness about what he was doing. Clearly there is a very important distinction to be drawn between a poet who writes varied imitative poetry of the kind we discover in Keats's first volume and one who apes everything—subject, manner and style—in a single admired master.

But what must chiefly strike us about the highly derivative poems that Keats wrote for a year or two is that right from the outset most of them are far more synthetic than imitative. The influences behind the individual pieces of *Poems* (1817) are often almost as varied as those behind the volume as a whole.

Even such an early poetic effort as the *Imitation of Spenser*

Keats's powers of imitation, for he writes of him (*Collected Essays*, Vol. IV, p. 168): 'He was a great deal influenced by other poets, and could reproduce not only the style of any writer whom he imitated, but the mental attitude which informed the style.' But Bridges adds the curious footnote: 'This is not true of his earliest work.'

displays this strong synthetic quality. There is no doubt that
Spenser is present in these lines—in verbal echoes, the easy
mellifluousness, and the undoubted recollection of the Bower
of Bliss; but though some commentators have gone a little too
far in denying the authentic Spenserian note, no one will
quarrel with Colvin's opinion* that Keats was imitating
eighteenth-century Spenserianism, probably from Thomson's
Castle of Indolence, more than he was Spenser himself. Yet the
poem is not simply Thomson out of Spenser, for in his detailed
examination of it, Finney has shown that it is also full of
Miltonic reminiscences.† 'Amber flame', for instance, may well
be an echo of the line in *L'Allegro*,

> Rob'd in flames, and Amber light,[8]

while Keats's description of the swan—

> There saw the swan his neck of arched snow,
> And oar'd himself along with majesty[9]

—almost certainly owes something to a passage in *Paradise
Lost*:

> the Swan with Arched neck
> Between her white wings mantling proudly, Rowes
> Her state with Oarie feet.[10]

Further, Finney suggests that Keats's picture of the king-
fisher—

> There the king-fisher saw his plumage bright
> Vieing with fish of brilliant dye below[11]

—may derive from a poet whom Keats very much admired at
this time, Mary Tighe, whose *Psyche* contains the line,

> The brilliant plumage shines so heavenly bright . . .

Yet even this crude first poem is not merely a confection

---

* '. . . the aforesaid Spenserian stanzas, which in fact echo the cadences
of Thomson's *Castle of Indolence* much more than those of Spenser himself'
(*Life of John Keats*, p. 23).
   † *Op. cit.* pp. 26–33.

from Keats's reading; it also contains some slight hints of the individual voice that is to come. If the bower-image derives from Spenser, it is the first appearance of something that is to be richly and complexly infused with Keats's own sensibility; if the description of the swan has been taken from Milton, the full quotation shows that Keats is already capable of making his own contribution to anything he borrowed; words like 'verdant', 'verdure', 'voluptuously', 'dyes' are soon to be given the stamp of Keats's own currency; and above all 'gushes'* in the line

> Silv'ring the untainted gushes of its rill,

manifests that vigorous, vital sensuousness, occasionally productive of vulgarities, that is to contribute so much to the individuality, power, and attraction of Keats's poetry. In that highly characteristic word 'gushes' we may detect, unmistakably, the sensibility that is to express itself in

> Thou watchest the last oozings hours by hours,[12]

and in

> whose strenuous tongue
> Can burst Joy's grape against his palate fine.[13]

This synthetic rather than imitative quality of so much of Keats's early writing probably goes far to explain why he was soon writing his own original poetry. Nothing can come of straightforward imitations like the *Ode to Apollo* but dim copies of an original. In synthesis, on the other hand, there is always the chance that, given also the mysterious x in the poet himself, the various elements will interact and combine to produce something new and significant. We have seen this very impressively in our own time in the development of T. S. Eliot's poetry, though of course the synthesis of Eliot's early work was much more deliberately contrived than that of Keats ever was.

* For further early uses of this word see *To George Felton Mathew* (l. 78) and *To some Ladies* (l. 7).

Another significant fact about Keats's relation to his poetic models is that generally speaking the influences to which he submitted himself were chosen with an instinctive rightness. It is as though some force were at work in him directing him towards the kind of inspiration that would be most beneficial to his own development. And what he took from other poets was in the main truly assimilated, without poetic indigestion.

His attention to Spenser is an outstanding instance of this entirely appropriate choice of models. Certainly, since the influence of Spenser came so early and decisively, it is hard—and perhaps impossible—to distinguish between what we might call the essential Keats and the Keats who was largely formed by a rhapsodic reading of *The Faerie Queene*. But if we may ignore this distinction, at least there is every reason for feeling, as we read Keats's early poems, that they were produced by a sensibility that in many ways resembled Spenser's, and that most of Spenser's chief poetic qualities—his sensuous, and especially pictorial, richness, his soft, lulling melody, and smooth, gracious but sometimes grave rhythms—were merely drawing out Keats's own inclinations in poetry. In the necessary cliché phrase Keats had found in Spenser a kindred spirit; and the consequence of this is that, even when his delight in Spenser's faery world of love and chivalry was waning, there remained in his poetry, including the great odes, a quality that is recognizably Spenserian. This is not to question the originality of the odes or of poems like *The Eve of St Agnes* and *Lamia*. It simply means that his reading of Spenser stimulated and sustained his own authentic utterance, and that anything he owed to Spenser, over and above such encouragement, was perfectly assimilated into his own writing.

An 'influence' of this kind, in which the work of one important poet serves to release vital and kindred forces in another—like that of Herbert on Vaughan, or Donne on the poets of the second quarter of this century—can never be anything but highly beneficial. But a strong sympathetic

attraction felt by one poet towards another will be dangerous
if the influence of the older writer tends to stimulate inherent and kindred weaknesses in the younger. We are
reminded of this when we consider Keats's relation to the
other principal master of his apprenticeship, Leigh Hunt,
for the harmful effect of Hunt's verse was not so much that
it was generally inferior as that many of Hunt's faults of
taste and sensibility appear to have been ones to which Keats
himself was constitutionally prone. This is proved by the fact
that *Lamia*, written when he had completely outgrown his
early admiration for Hunt, is seriously marred by the same
Huntian blemishes as had appeared in *Poems* (1817). Further,
he himself came very near to confessing kindred weaknesses
with Hunt when, commenting on his draft Preface for *Endymion*, he wrote: 'Since you all agree that the thing is bad, it
must be so—though I am not aware there is anything like
Hunt in it, (and if there is, it is my natural way, and I have
something in common with Hunt).'[14]

On the other hand, if a choice of models and inspiration
based on an instinctive sympathy failed Keats with Hunt, he
displayed an admirable sense of what was needed when he
swung away from Hunt to Haydon, the furious champion
of the 'heroic' and the 'grand style'—of Homer and the Elgin
Marbles, Dante and Raphael, Shakespeare and Milton. It is
easy enough to laugh at the absurdities of Haydon's creed, as,
for instance, when we find him writing: 'My tea was so good
and my cups so large that they always used to say: "We'll have
tea at Haydon's in the grand style." '[15] Again, though Middleton Murry sometimes over-states his case with an unnecessary
denigration of Milton, he is almost certainly right in his sustained contention that Milton and the composition of *Hyperion*
deflected Keats's from the course of his own native genius.
Yet if we consider the poetry that Keats was writing in 1816
(and in most of 1817) we must surely admit that Haydon's
artistic creed, even in its extravagance, was just the sort of
antidote Keats needed to expel from his system the infection

of Hunt's kind of poetry, with its trivialities, effeminate sentimentalities, and cult of the pretty-pretty. *Endymion*, which still contained much of Hunt's manner in spite of Keats's rapidly declining estimation of his old master, was followed by *Hyperion*, which undoubtedly owed something to those conceptions of the 'heroic' that Haydon had no doubt ceaselessly dinned into Keats.* After these two extreme oscillations Keats found his own poetic self and utterance, though even in 1819 he was not entirely assured in his own manner.

Many of the suggestions we have been offering about Keats's reactions to the influences that went to shape and colour his early poetry are endorsed by what he himself says in that interesting sonnet 'How many bards'.

This begins with an acknowledgement of the debt he owes to certain poets who have provided essential nourishment for his 'fancy'. Primarily of course he is confessing the delight these poets have afforded him as a reader; but he would undoubtedly have regarded his 'delighted fancy' as an essentially active and creative faculty, and this, combined with the reference to 'brooding', and the subsequent development of the poem, makes it clear that he is recognizing in these bards a powerful stimulus to his own poetic composition:

> How many bards gild the lapses of time!
> A few of them have ever been the food
> Of my delighted fancy,—I could brood
> Over their beauties, earthly, or sublime.

* 'It is proper that lovers of Keats—who, because they are that, find it hard to love Haydon—should remember this heroical fashion of his mind; for it was not without its influence in directing the genius of Keats towards large conceptions' (Garrod, *Keats*, p. 152). See also Finney (*The Evolution of Keats's Poetry*, pp. 183–4) who writes of Haydon 'instilling in him a conception of poetry which prepared him for his rejection of Hunt's poetic system. With his enthusiasm for the Bible, Greek sculpture, Shakespearian plays and Milton's *Paradise Lost*, Haydon inspired Keats with an understanding of the grand style of the heroic art of the past. He painted huge historical pictures in the grand style and he encouraged Keats to undertake the composition of a great poem, a romance or an epic.'

A detail of this passage that should certainly be noticed is the phrase 'a few of them', for though this may be a confession that he has not yet read very widely, it may also be an assertion of firm and critical discrimination in his enthusiasms. Again, while the personification of poetry into bards may be simply a convenient mode of poetic expression, there may be in these lines (and in what follows) a hint of the exciting inspiration that he derived from his sense of the living presence of poets like Spenser and Shakespeare.

In the next two lines of the sonnet Keats explicitly admits the inspiration of these bards in the actual process of composition:

> And often, when I sit me down to rhyme,
> These will in throngs before my mind intrude . . .

Reading these words we may believe that Keats at least was a poet who wrote his early works in the manner advocated by Virginia Woolf in her *Letter to a Young Poet*:

> Think of yourself rather as something much humbler and less spectacular, but to my mind far more interesting—a poet in whom live all the poets of the past, from whom all poets in time to come will spring. You have a touch of Chaucer in you, and something of Shakespeare; Dryden, Pope, and Tennyson—to mention only the respectable among your ancestors—stir in your blood and sometimes move your pen a little to the right or to the left.[16]

However, much more significant than Keats's sense of tradition tempering the desire for experiment and innovation is his statement about the nature of this intrusion in his mind. He is not, as some other youthful poet might be, tugged helplessly hither and thither by conflicting impulses, hesitations, and confusions. Somehow there is an easy order and harmony in his inspirations:

> But no confusion, no disturbance rude
> Do they occasion; 'tis a pleasing chime.

Since this is a poem, not a close prose analysis like the passage we have earlier quoted from Spender, we must not be disappointed that Keats offers no overt explanation why the influence of his few chosen bards is such a satisfying and beneficial one. But the phrase 'pleasing chime' is probably a direct pointer to his conclusion, and in spite of the danger of reading too much into the poem, it seems reasonable to believe that these bards were 'pleasing music, and not wild uproar' partly because their work corresponded with Keats's own essential needs and poetic constitution, and partly because they were themselves an harmonious company,* not a conflicting, heterogeneous collection of enthusiasms. At any rate the sestet, which contains one of the best lines of *Poems* (1817)—'the great bell that heaves With solemn sound'— confirms through its imagery the impression that this stimulus from other poets was good because its working in Keats was easy, spontaneous, and somehow natural:

> So the unnumber'd sounds that evening store;
> > The songs of birds—the whisp'ring of the leaves—
> The voice of waters—the great bell that heaves
> > With solemn sound,—and thousand others more,
> That distance of recognizance bereaves,
> > Make pleasing music, and not wild uproar.

The suggestion of faint remote sounds, emerging into explicit statement in the line,

> That distance of recognizance bereaves,

may appear to complicate, or even contradict, some of our earlier interpretation, for the sestet might conceivably be read as an assertion that the inspiration from other poets should be a distant, barely conscious one. But the most likely explanation of this apparent contradiction is that, embarking on a descriptive passage, Keats was carried away by his peculiar sensibility for soft and far-off sounds.† If we are to attach any

---

* In spite of Keats's perhaps not very well chosen word 'throngs' in l. 6.

† See Ch. II, 'Some Characteristic Imagery and "Sensations" of Keats's Poetry', pp. 76–7.

context significance to the penultimate line, we might read it either as a concurrence with Spender's belief that we are more intimately in relation with a poet's essential impulse when the words of his poem are forgotten or else as an expression of something that any young poet who has not an exceptional verbal memory is likely to feel—a sense that this or that phrase, image, or cadence is derived from some predecessor, though he cannot precisely identify its origin.

It is interesting to turn from the sonnet to *The Eve of St Agnes* —a poem that is filled with subconscious inspirational echoes of Scott's *The Lay of the Last Minstrel*.*

For an outstanding example of Keats's reminiscence of Scott's poem we may go straight to what is probably the most famous stanza of *The Eve of St Agnes*, the description of the stained-glass casement (stanza XXIV):

> A casement high and triple-arch'd there was,
> All garlanded with carven imag'ries
> Of fruits, and flowers, and bunches of knot-grass,
> And diamonded with panes of quaint device,
> Innumerable of stains and splendid dyes,
> As are the tiger-moth's deep-damask'd wings;
> And in the midst, 'mong thousand heraldries,
> And twilight saints, and dim emblazonings,
> A shielded scutcheon blush'd with blood of queens and kings.

Placing this stanza beside the description of the east oriel in

---

* The connexion between these two poems does not appear to have been noticed, except by J. C. Jordan in his article '*The Eve of St Agnes* and *The Lay of the Last Minstrel*', *M.L.N.* XLIII (1928), pp. 38–40. But this is a very short study and merely touches on two points of resemblance—the window description, and the line, 'Clasp'd like a missal where swart Paynims pray'. I indicate in the following notes wherever Jordan has anticipated the parallel to which I draw attention.

Beside those of Scott we must of course take into account the echoes of Shakespeare and possibly of Burton and Mrs Radcliff. There are also the effects of Keats's visit to Chichester at the time of composing the poem— notably of Mrs Lacy's medieval premises and Stansted Chapel—that R. Gittings so suggestively explores in *John Keats: The Living Year*, pp. 64–82.

The Lay of the Last Minstrel, we cannot miss a resemblance that is too striking to be dismissed as coincidence:*

> The moon on the east oriel shone
> Through slender shafts of shapely stone,
>   By foliaged tracery combin'd;
> Thou would'st have thought some fairy's hand
> 'Twixt poplars straight the ozier wand,
>   In many a freakish knot, had twin'd;
> Then fram'd a spell, when the work was done,
> And chang'd the willow-wreaths to stone.
> The silver light, so pale and faint,
> Shew'd many a prophet, and many a saint,
>   Whose image on the glass was dyed;
> Full in the midst, his Cross of Red
> Triumphant Michael brandished,
>   And trampled the Apostate's pride.
> The moon-beam kiss'd the holy pane,
> And threw on the pavement a bloody stain.[17]

The general similarity of these two passages is remarkable enough: in both we have an elaborate description of a stained-glass window in a medieval building; in both the moonlight is streaming through the window and casting a dominant red light†—in the *The Lay* the 'bloody stain' that marks the position of the tomb of Michael Scott, and in *The Eve of St Agnes*

---

* Gittings (*op. cit.* pp. 79–81) makes a convincing case for a recollection in stanza XXIV of the north-west windows of Stansted Chapel, which Keats must have contemplated during the two to three hours when he was present at the consecration service (25 January 1819). But few of the similarities to which Gittings draws attention would rule out the echoes of *The Lay* suggested in the following pages, and it seems highly probable that Keats's casement is a fusion of his experience at Stansted and his reading of Scott. It may be that it was the Stansted Chapel window that brought back the description in *The Lay* to his mind.

† Colvin (*Life of John Keats*, pp. 400–1) has pointed out the inaccuracy of this: 'Observation, I believe, shows that moonlight has not the power to transmit the separate hues of painted glass as Keats in this celebrated passage represents it, but fuses them into a kind of neutral or indiscriminate opaline shimmer.' Presumably Keats was following Scott in this error.

Gittings, on the other hand, (*op. cit.* p. 80) maintains that Keats was thinking of the sunlight that he had seen flashing through the Stansted Chapel windows.

the 'shielded scutcheon blush'd with blood of queens and kings' and the 'warm gules' and 'rose-bloom' thrown on Madeline. But the correspondence runs much closer than this general parallel. For one thing, each stanza is built on the same pattern: in each there is a description of the stone-work of the window followed by a description of the coloured glass. Further, it will be noticed that in his description of the masonry—

> A casement high and triple-arch'd there was,
> All garlanded with carven imag'ries.
> Of fruits, and flowers, and bunches of knot-grass . . .

Keats employs a vegetal sort of imagery resembling that of Scott in the first eight lines of his stanza.* Certainly this Baudelairean *correspondance* between architecture and vegetation was always a marked characteristic of Keats's native sensibility;† nor does the substance of his image in the first three lines of stanza XXIV owe anything to Scott's foliage, ozier wand, and poplars, or to the conceit in which these details are woven—unless, as a very remote verbal association, Scott's 'freakish knot' suggested his own 'knot-grass'. On the other hand, his 'carven imag'ries Of fruits, and flowers, and bunches of knot-grass' may very well have been a subconscious memory of four lines in *The Lay* that occur just three stanzas before the picture of the oriel window:‡

> Spreading herbs, and flowerets bright,
> Glisten'd with the dew of night;
> Nor herb, nor floweret, glisten'd there,
> But was carv'd in the cloister-arches as fair.[18]

Besides these there are probably several further echoes of *The Lay* in Keats's description of the casement. Perhaps the

---

* Gittings (*op. cit.* p. 77) suggests that these 'imag'ries' are a recollection of wood-carvings by Grinling Gibbons seen by Keats during his visit to Stansted House.

† See Ch. II, 'Some Characteristic Imagery and "Sensations" of Keats's Poetry', p. 60, and G. Wilson Knight's *The Starlit Dome*, pp. 258–307, *passim*.

‡ Jordan (*art. cit.*) makes this suggestion.

most revealing is the phrase 'twilight saints', reminding us of Scott's reference to 'many a saint';* for while the images of saints are perfectly appropriate to the window of a chapel in Melrose Abbey, they are less fitting†—and somewhat un-expected—in a young lady's bedroom window in a feudal castle, however pious Keats intended his Madeline to be. There is also a common use, and in each instance for the purpose of rhyme, of 'dyed' and 'dyes', a word that is not an obvious one in this context of stained glass; while Keats's 'shielded scutcheon', a phrase that he employed in his earliest draft of the stanza, though in a different place, may very well have been a recollection of the word from the stanza imme-diately preceding Scott's oriel window:

> Full many a scutcheon and banner riven,
> Shook to the cold night-wind of heaven,‡

Finally, it is just possible that the elaboration of the 'blushed with blood' metaphor that Keats attached to his 'shielded scutcheon' in his final version of the stanza owed something to the association of the 'bloody stain' of light on the chapel floor, especially as the image of blood is insistent in this part of Scott's poem—again in

> Slow mov'd the Monk to the broad flag-stone
> Which the bloody Cross was trac'd upon . . .'[19]

and a little later in

> Often had William of Deloraine
> Rode through the battle's bloody plain.[20]

* Noted by Jordan (*art. cit.*).

† There is no mention of 'twilight saints' in the cancelled opening of H, the autograph MS.

‡ *The Lay of the Last Minstrel*, II, x (Logie Robertson's edition of Scott's poems, 1926). Jordan thinks that something of this may have gone into Keats's 'dim emblazonings': 'Scott, it will be noticed, has "full many a scutcheon", which, with the banners that "shook to the cold night-wind" to the light of "the dying lamps" and "the scrolls that teach thee to live and to die" (mentioned in the first section of Canto II) may be what Keats remembered as "dim emblazonings"' (*art. cit.* p. 39).

None of these latter details in Keats's description, considered in isolation, can be accepted as conclusive proof of a subconscious recollection of Scott; but taken together and along with the other correspondences we have noted, they do suggest a very strong reminiscence of *The Lay of the Last Minstrel*. Nor should the undistinguished quality of Scott's writing be raised as an objection to the probability that this passage had impressed itself indelibly on Keats's imagination, for if Scott's phrasing is not at all memorable, the subject of the window, to which a long and entire stanza is devoted, certainly remains for most readers as a chief memory of Canto II.

There are several further correspondences between *The Eve of St Agnes* and the second canto of *The Lay of the Last Minstrel* that are certainly striking in their cumulative effect.

First, there is Keats's prologue and epilogue figure of the ancient Beadsman.* If, from the evidence of the corresponding window-descriptions, we may assume that this passage in *The Lay* dealing with the opening of Michael Scott's tomb made a particularly sharp impression† on Keats, is it not likely that something of the Monk of St Mary's aisle also went into the creation of the Beadsman? Like the Monk of St Mary's aisle the Beadsman is a figure of prayer and penance, and though he takes no part in the action of the poem, he dies soon afterwards as the Monk dies after the midnight excitement about Michael Scott's tomb:

> The Monk return'd him to his cell,
> And many a prayer and penance sped;
> When the convent met at the noon-tide bell—
> The Monk of St Mary's aisle was dead![21]

> His was harsh penance on St Agnes' Eve:
> Another way he went, and soon among

---

* In view of the very strong case that W. W. Beyer (*Keats and the Daemon King*, pp. 147–91) makes for the influence of Wieland's *Oberon* on the narrative of *The Eve of St Agnes* it is probable that the Beadsman is also to be connected with the hermit of *Oberon*.

† Was this the reason why the Baron's dreams (*The Eve of St Agnes*, stanza XIII) are of such a sepulchral kind?

> Rough ashes sat he for his soul's reprieve,
> And all night kept awake, for sinners' sake to grieve.[22]

> The Beadsman, after thousand aves told,
> For aye unsought for slept among his ashes cold.[23]

Again, there may have been in Keats's Beadsman some subconscious fusion of the Monk of St Mary's aisle with the Minstrel who tells the story, for not only are the Minstrel and Beadsman both used as prologue figures, but the Minstrel, whom Scott depicts for us through the impact of those opening lines,

> The way was long, the wind was cold,
> The Minstrel was infirm and old;
> His wither'd cheek, and tresses gray,
> Seem'd to have known a better day . . .[24]

very much resembles Keats's Beadsman—in the image of shrunken, decrepit age, and in the surrounding atmosphere, so much more intense in Keats of course, of cold and rigorous weather.*

Nor perhaps is Scott's influence on the opening of *The Eve of St Agnes* confined to the genesis of the Beadsman. Keats's graphic account of the monuments of old knights in the chapel aisle—

> Knights, ladies, praying in dumb orat'ries,
> He passeth by; and his weak spirit fails
> To think how they may ache in icy hoods and mails[25]

—may very well have been stimulated by two passages in *The Lay of the Last Minstrel*, by the stanza (IV) in the first canto describing how ten of the Lady of Buccleuch's knights lived perpetually—and most uncomfortably, one would imagine—in armour, and by a verse in the *Harold* ballad:

* We should also note Keats's description of the Beadsman as 'this aged man and *poor*' (l. 21). Unless rhyme had taken control, there was no reason for stressing the Beadsman's poverty. But if in composing the opening stanzas Keats was stimulated by a subconscious memory of the Introduction of *The Lay*, the epithet 'poor' might easily have come spontaneously to him.

> Seem'd all on fire that chapel proud,
>   Where Roslin's chiefs uncoffin'd lie,
> Each baron, for a sable shroud,
>   Sheath'd in his iron panoply[26]

What makes Keats's echoing of Scott here more probable is an obscurity in his own lines. We have been given to understand that he is describing mere monuments of knights and ladies, the 'sculptur'd dead'. Yet in the last line of the stanza he writes as though these knights and ladies are actually, and painfully, inside their 'icy hoods and mails'. This is all rather puzzling, but at least the abrupt transition of Keats's ideas is explained if we surmise that he was carried away by a suggestion of the verse from the *Harold* ballad where the knights were indeed buried in their armour.

To return to the second canto of *The Lay of the Last Minstrel*: when the porter leads William of Deloraine to the Monk of St Mary's aisle, Scott gives us this picture of the knight's passage:

> The *arched cloister*, far and wide,
> Rang to the warrior's clanking stride,
> Till, *stooping low his lofty crest*,
> He enter'd the cell of the ancient priest.[27]

Both of the images combined in these lines—the 'arched cloister' or 'pillar'd arches'[28] and the 'lofty crest' or 'waving plume'—[29] are strongly impressed on us in this first part of the second canto. Now it happens that in the two opening lines of stanza XIII of *The Eve of St Agnes* we find these two same images in a picture that, without the 'clanking stride' (inappropriate anyway in Keats's context), closely resembles Scott's:

> He follow'd through a *lowly arched way*,
> Brushing the cobwebs *with his lofty plume**

---

* *St Agnes*, ll. 109–10. M. R. Ridley (*Keats's Craftsmanship*, pp. 127–9) suggests that Mrs Radcliff's novels were the source of the imagery in these lines. It must also be admitted that the panache always appears to have held a special fascination for Keats: for example, the Induction to *Calidore*, 1–2. But this *Calidore* image may have been impressed on him by a reading of Scott's romances in the first place.

A further possible link between this part of *The Eve of St Agnes* and the second canto of *The Lay* is that just as Sir William of Deloraine immediately passes into the Monk's cell, so Porphyro straightway enters

> a little moonlight room,
> Pale, lattic'd, chill, and silent as a tomb.[30]

In the second part of Canto II Scott switches our attention from his gothic horror-tale of the midnight opening of Michael Scott's tomb to his other, Romeo and Juliet motif—the meeting of the young lovers Margaret and Lord Cranstoun against a background of relentless family feud. The transition to this meeting is well managed in a stanza (xxv) that, if tricked out with poetic cliché, gives a welcome breath of freshness and the open air. Margaret is introduced in an emphatic association of roses and violets:

> And peeped forth the violet pale,
>   And spread her breast the mountain rose.
> And lovelier than the rose so red,
>   Yet paler than the violet pale,
> She early left her sleepless bed,
>   The fairest maid of Teviotdale.[31]

Were these lines, we may wonder—or some hint of them—obscurely running in Keats's head when he described the consummation of his own lovers?

> Into her dream he melted, as the rose
>   Blendeth its odour with the violet.[32]

The parallel cannot, of course, be closely pressed, but it should be noted, as some further evidence for the possibility that Keats may have been unconsciously echoing Scott, that the two passages have a common association (in Keats's poem implied) with the lady's bed.

Later, when Margaret and Lord Cranstoun are suddenly alarmed, Scott tells us how

Fair Margaret through the hazel grove,
Flew like the startled cushat-dove.[33]

The simile is an obvious one no doubt. But it is interesting to observe that Keats twice[34] likens his Madeline to a frightened dove, and once in these similes describes her as a ring-dove. 'Cushat-dove' is a rare dialect synonym for ring-dove, and it is possible that the trouble that Keats may have taken to ascertain its meaning when he first read *The Lay of the Last Minstrel* lodged the comparison in his mind with particular firmness.

But if there must be some hesitation over these last two parallels, there can be little doubt that Keats's description of the flight of Madeline and Porphyro owes something to the meeting of Margaret and Cranstoun in the second canto of *The Lay*. Describing Margaret's movements as she leaves the bed-chamber, Scott writes:

Why does she stop, and look often around,
     As she glides down the secret stair;
And why does she pat the shaggy bloodhound,
     As he rouses him up from his lair;
And, though she passes the postern alone,
Why is not the watchman's bugle blown?*

Madeline and Porphyro, too, make a 'darkling way' 'down the wide stairs'[35], and later encounter just such a porter and a bloodhound:†

They glide, like phantoms, into the wide hall;
Like phantoms, to the iron porch, they glide;
Where lay the Porter, in uneasy sprawl,
With a huge empty flaggon by his side:
The wakeful bloodhound rose, and shook his hide,
But his sagacious eye an inmate owns.‡

* *The Lay*, II, xxvi. The details of these lines are repeated in the following stanza.
† Another common source in the mastiff watch dog of *Christabel*?
‡ *St Agnes*, ll. 361–6. The 'iron porch' may be a memory of the Minstrel's entry into Newark tower:

After the second canto of *The Lay of the Last Minstrel* there is little of the Margaret-Cranstoun story—at least as far as it parallels that of Madeline and Porphyro—until the last canto, with the betrothal ceremony and the festivity in Branksome Hall. The main significance of this for Keats's poem seems to be that the sustained description of revelry in the castle, along with the account of the earlier entertainment of the English army before the combat between Musgrave and William of Deloraine, suggested to him the idea of setting his elopement story against a background of baronial banqueting. That this is not to be dismissed as a vague hypothesis is indicated by one striking correspondence of detail. In the main description of the festivities Scott tells us how

> from the lofty balcony
> Rung trumpet, shalm, and psaltery.[36]

In his description of the entertainment at the opening of *The Eve of St Agnes* Keats mentions only the trumpet, but his lines are very close indeed to Scott's:

> Soon, up aloft,
> The silver, snarling trumpets 'gan to chide.[37]

However, apart from a possible echo of

> And on her head a crimson hood,
> With pearls embroider'd and entwin'd . . .[38]

in Keats's 'Of all its wreathed pearls her hair she frees',[39] Canto VI of *The Lay of the Last Minstrel* does not appear to have stimulated much in *The Eve of St Agnes*.

> The embattl'd portal arch he pass'd,
> Whose ponderous grate and massy bar
> Had oft roll'd back the tide of war,
> But never closed the *iron door*
> Against the desolate and poor.   (Introduction, 32–6)

Is there in both Scott and Keats a common echo of *Christabel*, l. 127—'The gate that was ironed within and without'?

Of the handful of slight, and no doubt largely coincidental, correspondences* that remain the most interesting is that between

'For Paynim countries I have trod' . . .[40]

and

Clasp'd like a missal where swart Paynims pray,†

for there may be more of reminiscence in Keats's line than his repetition of the word 'Paynim', which he might have picked up from *The Faerie Queene*. One detail of Scott's supernatural story in *The Lay of the Last Minstrel* that is likely to stick in the reader's mind is William Scott's magic book, the book that had the property of closing itself and that Cranstoun's Goblin Page found so baffling to open. This being so, it is not impossible, through the devious process of mental associations, that the magic book suggested to Keats one of his two similes for describing Madeline asleep in all her purity and beauty:

Clasp'd‡ like a missal . . .

Needless to say, with all these parallels, there is never any doubt of the immense superiority of Keats's poem to Scott's. In almost every single instance he has transformed the homespun of his reading into the richest and loveliest cloth of gold. Further—as has been implied—the nature of Keats's echoes of Scott is such that his recollection was certainly a subconscious one, inseparable from the general creative process that produced his poem. But it does seem fairly certain that *The Eve of St Agnes* owes a good deal to *The Lay of the Last Minstrel*,§

* For example *The Lay*, I, xii and *St Agnes*, ll. 201–2; II, xxii and ll. 176–7; VI, xxv and l. 297.

† *St Agnes*, l. 241. Jordan (*art. cit.*, p. 40) observes this parallel, but does not make my point concerning the simile.

‡ 'Shut' in Keats's first version.

§ Though Scott's poetry was not admired in the Hunt circle, we may gather from Keats's letters that he had read Scott's poetry and was inclined—sometimes at any rate—to admire it considerably. See *Letters* pp. 256–7: 'We have seen three literary Kings in our Time—Scott—Byron —and then the scotch novels.'

and the most likely explanation of the fact that Scott's poem came into Keats's subconscious mind at the time is that the Romeo and Juliet motif of his own work carried with it the associated memory of an impressive poem that embodied, though along with much else, the same theme. That this was the association at work in his creative imagination appears proved by the significant fact that most of his echoes originate from Scott's account of the secret meeting of Cranstoun and Margaret—from the part of *The Lay of the Last Minstrel*, that is to say, that runs closest to his own tale. As we should expect, the more martial cantos of *The Lay* appear to have stirred no recollections at all.

Another poem of singular interest for our present purposes is *La Belle Dame Sans Merci*. On the one hand, measured by its direct and immediate impact, this ballad must always impress us as a highly individual, seamless, and self-contained poem, quite unlike anything else in Keats's writing. On the other, there can be little doubt that a good deal of recollection and subconscious synthesis went into its creation.*

Among its other features *La Belle Dame Sans Merci* reminds us, much more than *The Eve of St Agnes* does, of the organic continuity of Keats's poetry—of the remarkable extent to which his own work always constituted one of his principal influences. The title probably came back to him from *The Eve of St Agnes*, since this poem had passed through his hands a day or two before, when he had given it to Woodhouse for copying;† but this is a detail of little consequence, for though the title was borrowed from Chartier's allegory of the same name, Keats owes nothing to this old French work or to the

---

* R. Gittings in his most interesting investigation into the genesis of the poem (*John Keats: The Living Year*, pp. 113–23) writes: 'No other poem that Keats ever wrote shows so clearly the coming-together of the mingled elements of the life he was leading—experience, reading, thought and emotion' (p. 116).

† Gittings (*op. cit.* p. 116) draws attention to Keats's probable recent perusal of the MSS. of these two poems.

pseudo-Chaucerian translation of it. However, another poem
that he had handed to Woodhouse for copying had been *The
Eve of St Mark*, and it is possible that the early descriptive
passage in this poem—

> Of unmatured green vallies cold,
> Of the green thorny bloomless hedge,
> Of rivers new with spring-tide sedge,
> Of primroses by the shelter'd rills,
> And daisies on the aguish hills[41]

—provided some inspiration for the setting of *La Belle Dame*—
for the general atmosphere of cold desolation and for details
like 'The sedge has wither'd from the lake' and 'On the cold
hill's side'.*

Again, though Reynolds's parody of *Peter Bell*, which he
reviewed for *The Examiner* the same day as he wrote *La Belle
Dame*, may have stimulated his consciousness of the 'inveterate
cadence' of Wordsworth's ballad metres,† it is much more
likely that the metrical form of his poem was suggested by his
own 'Ah! ken ye what I met the day', which he had almost
certainly glanced over during the past week.‡ The only
formal difference—though of course a vital one—between the
two poems is that whereas 'Ah! ken ye' is shortened to two
speaking stresses in the second and fourth lines, the two-stress
cadence is reserved in *La Belle Dame* to the fourth line. On
the other hand, Keats cannot have owed much to his Scottish
poem beyond the metrical suggestion,§ apart possibly from

---

* Gittings also points out (*op. cit.* p. 116) that 'sidelong' (*La Belle Dame*,
l. 23) also occurs in *The Eve of St Mark*, l. 42.

† Gittings, *op. cit.* p. 118. The 'same day' was 2 April 1819, and
'inveterate cadence' occurs in the *Letters*, p. 329.

‡ 'Ah! ken ye' was contained in Keats's letter to Tom of 14 July 1818.
On 15 April 1819, Keats had collected Tom's papers from their old lodgings
(see *Letters*, p. 319), and it is fairly certain that the letter of 14 July was one
of the records of the Scottish tour that he sent with his first journal letter to
George and Georgiana (see *Letters*, p. 409).

§ In spite of the footnote to 'Ah! ken ye' in the *Letters* (p. 180)—
'Keats's first approach to the . . . sentiment of *La Belle Dame*.'

the mood of the last lines, where, as the joyful wedding party disappears, the poet is left in a sad solitude:

> Ah! Marie they are all gone hame
> Fra happy wedding,
> Whilst I—Ah is it not a shame?
> Sad tears am shedding.

One part of the description of the Knight in *La Belle Dame*—

> I see a lilly on thy brow,
> With anguish moist and fever dew

—is curiously reminiscent of some lines spoken by Glaucus in *Endymion*:

> O Dis, even now,
> A clammy dew is beading on my brow,
> At mere remembering her pale laugh, and curse.[42]

The similarity here may be entirely coincidental. On the other hand, even if there was no recollection of the Circe episode in *Endymion*, even at a subconscious level of Keats's mind, while he was composing the ballad, it may well be that the imaginative experience of writing one story of a baneful love-enchantment had predisposed him to write in certain ways when he came to compose another. At any rate, verbal echoes or not, *La Belle Dame* is certainly to be connected with the Circe episode, for the chief impulse behind the ballad is Keats's preoccupation with the destructiveness of love, particularly as it is symbolized by the Romantic image of the Fatal Woman.*

If in these respects Keats was himself one of the main influences in the composition of *La Belle Dame*, he was also synthesizing, with a perfect fusion, elements from other poems. It is true that a wide range of sources has been suggested for the ballad; but though some of these suggestions are far-fetched, they should not all be dismissed as cancelling one

---

* See Ch. VI, '*La Belle Dame Sans Merci*', *passim*.

another out and as another example of the scholar's folly of source-hunting.* The basic narrative of *La Belle Dame* is an archetypal one, and it is not surprising therefore that many different analogues have been suggested.

The most convincing influence is again Sir Walter Scott, not this time as an original poet but as the collector of the *Ballad of Thomas of Ercildoune†* in his *Minstrelsy of the Scottish Border*; and this old ballad may very well have been part of a wider complex of memories and associations in which Sir Walter Scott, the Scottish holiday, and 'Ah! ken ye what I met the day' all fitted. To begin with, there is the setting of *La Belle Dame*, the two chief constituents of which are a lake and a hillside. It cannot be pretended that there is any close resemblance between this and anything in *Thomas of Ercildoune*. But the old ballad opens with

> True Thomas lay on Huntlie bank,

and if Keats had read Scott's continuation of this ballad (Part II) he would have encountered some lines where Huntlie bank

---

* I cannot see anything in Praz's suggestion (*The Romantic Agony*, p. 274, note 17) of Coleridge's *Introduction to the Tale of a Dark Lady* and Dante's *Inferno*, Canto v (Cary's translation), though the latter was certainly involved with Keats's thoughts of love's fatality at this time and influenced his Paolo and Francesca sonnet. J. Livingston Lowes (*T.L.S.* 3 May 1934) also suggested this Dante influence, and in *M.L.N.* 1945, pp. 270–2, Mary Thayer drew attention to Coleridge's *Love*. Gittings (*op. cit.*) believes that the Spenser influence came from certain Florimel passages (*F.Q.* III, vii and viii) rather than from the Phaedria-Cymocles episode (II, vi); Beyer (*Keats and the Daemon King*, pp. 249–50) stresses Wieland's *Oberon;* and T. O. Mabbot (*N. and Q.* Vol. 197, pp. 472–3) refers to Cowper's *Anti-Thelyphthora* and reminds us of Amy Lowell's suggestion of *Palmerin of England*.

I have not attempted here a thorough investigation of Keats's sources, and for a fairly comprehensive list of the suggestions that have been made the reader should consult Kenneth Muir's note in *Essays in Criticism*, Vol. IV, 4, pp. 432–5.

† Colvin (*Life of John Keats*, p. 350) hints at some connexion between the two poems and C. Longworth Chambrun drew attention to *Thomas of Ercildoune* in a letter to the *T.L.S.* of 28 March, 1952. Wasserman (*The Finer Tone*, pp. 68–9) suggests an alternative version of the *Thomas Rymer* ballad printed by Jamieson in his *Popular Ballads* (1806).

is associated with water and an awakening from visionary
dream:

> When seven years were come and gane,
>   The sun blink'd fair on pool and stream;
> And Thomas lay on Huntlie Bank,
>   Like one awaken'd from a dream.

Further, Scott's prose note to *Thomas the Rhymer*, Part 1, strongly
associates the old bard with water.*

The first stanza of *Thomas of Ercildoune* continues:

> A ferlie he spied wi' his ee;
> And there he saw a ladye bright,
> Come riding down by the Eildon Tree.

Later, in reply to Thomas's salutation, this 'ladye bright'
declares herself to be 'the Queen of fair Elfland'. In *La Belle
Dame* it is the Knight, not the Lady, who is mounted; but,
apart from this, the opening of the Knight's story is not unlike
that of *Thomas of Ercildoune:*

> I met a lady in the meads,
>   Full beautiful—a faery's child,
> Her hair was long, her foot was light,
>   And her eyes were wild.

It is by kissing the Queen of Elfland that Thomas places
himself irresistibly under her spell—

> 'And if ye dare to kiss my lips,
>   Sure of your bodie I will be',

—and once the Queen has him in her power she rides away
with him on her steed:

---

* 'The Eildon Tree, from beneath the shade of which he delivered his
prophecies, now no longer exists; but the spot is marked by a large stone,
called Eildon Tree Stone. A neighbouring rivulet takes the name of
Bogle Burn (Goblin Brook) from the Rhymer's supernatural visitants.'
Gittings, who thinks that Keats owed more in this poem to *The Anatomy
of Melancholy* than to *The Faerie Queene*, reminds us of the following remarks
of Burton on men of a melancholic disposition: 'They are much given to
weeping, and delight in waters, ponds, pools, rivers...' (quoted *op. cit.* p. 117).

> She mounted on her milk-white steed!
> She's ta'en true Thomas up behind:
> And aye, whene'er her bridle rung,
> The steed flew swifter than the wind.

In *La Belle Dame* we have the comparable lines,

> I set her on my pacing steed,
> And nothing else saw all day long,

and though this episode occurs before the Knight's complete enchantment, it is also a kiss that completes the spell:

> And there I shut her wild, wild eyes
> With kisses four.

The 'ferlies three' that Thomas beholds and his excursion into 'Elflyn Land' have nothing at all in common with the Knight's dream, but there is one further striking similarity between the two poems: in both the vision is preceded by lulling, amorous dalliance. In *Thomas of Ercildoune* we read:

> 'Light down, light down, now, true Thomas,
> And lean your head upon my knee;
> Abide and rest a little space,
> And I will show you ferlies three.'

In *La Belle Dame* the Lady takes the Knight to her elfin grot:

> And there she lulled me asleep,
> And there I dream'd . . .

Many of the words of *Thomas of Ercildoune*—'ladye', 'steed', 'rosy' (as 'rose'), 'lily', 'Elflyn', 'prince'—also recur in *La Belle Dame*. Not too much should be made of this point of course, since most of these words are stock ballad diction. So too Keats could have picked up the conventional forms of expression he uses like 'kisses four' and 'wild, wild eyes' from any reading of the old ballads. But if, as seems highly probable, *Thomas of Ercildoune* was running in his head while he was composing *La Belle Dame*, he would have been encouraged in the

34

use of these expressions by such phrases as 'ferlies three', and 'braid braid road' and 'mirk mirk night'.

Another likely reminiscence, to which Finney, following De Selincourt, has drawn attention,* is the Cymocles-Phaedria episode in *The Faerie Queene* (II, vi). Besides the general similarity of situation, in which a knight encounters a lady of 'light behaviour and loose dalliaunce', is taken away to her secret retreat and lulled through sensual pleasure into sleep (Phaedria is of course not a baleful enchantress like La Belle Dame), there are several striking correspondences of detail, some of these possibly involving verbal echoes in Keats's poem. The setting of the story is a lake, and we know that this image of an island-retreat in a lake, suggested also by the Bower of Bliss canto, had strongly impressed itself on Keats's poetry from the time of his *Imitation of Spenser*. In his description of Phaedria's bowery island Spenser particularly stresses the singing of birds—

> No braunch whereon a fine bird did not sitt;
> No bird but did her shrill notes sweetely sing;
> No song but did containe a lovely ditt[43]

—and this may be the reason that Keats gives us the line 'And no birds sing' as a descriptive detail of the Knight's desolate disenchantment. Spenser also makes much of singing as one of his 'wanton Damsell's' enticements,† and we have a similar touch in Keats's lines,

> For sidelong would she bend, and sing
> A faery's song.

Among other 'vaine toys' of Phaedria's 'fantastic wit' was her decking of herself with flowers:

* De Selincourt, *Poems of John Keats*, pp. 526–7; Finney, *The Evolution of Keats's Poetry*, pp. 594 ff.
† See especially stanza xv.

35

> Sometimes her head she fondly would aguize
> With gaudy girlonds, or fresh flowrets dight
> About her necke, or rings of rushes plight.*

This is remarkably close to Keats's

> I made a garland for her head,
>   And bracelets too, and fragrant zone.

Again, the line in *La Belle Dame*,

> And there she lulled me asleep,

has an obvious parallel in Spenser's

> By this she had him lulled fast asleepe;⁴⁴

while, if Spenser's description of Phaedria charming Cymocles to sleep contributed nothing to the detail of the similar episode in *La Belle Dame*, its spirit is much the same:

> And her sweete selfe without dread or disdayn
> She sett beside, laying his head disarmd
>   In her loose lap, it softly to sustayn,
>   Where soone he slumbred fearing not be harmd:
> The whils with a love lay she thus him sweetly charmd.⁴⁵

If, in the ways we have indicated, *La Belle Dame* does derive something both from *Thomas of Ercildoune* and a canto of *The Faerie Queene*, it furnishes a most interesting example, first, of a perfect fusion from diverse elements in Keats's reading, and secondly of a creative process that must have been effortless and entirely subconscious. Further, many other items of Keats's reading may have gone into the crucible of his imagination besides the two poems we have examined—Wieland's *Oberon* for instance, as Beyer firmly maintains, and perhaps even the hoax 'Amena' love-letters to Tom Keats, which were much in Keats's mind at the time when he wrote *La Belle Dame*. Keats believed that this cruel deception of love had helped to

---

* Stanza VII. As a source for Keats's lines Gittings prefers III, vii, 17:
    Girlonds of flowres sometimes for her fair hed
    He fine would dight.

36

kill his brother, and Gittings has reminded us* of one passage in the 'Amena' letters that appears to have a particularly close bearing on *La Belle Dame:*

> . . . Noble Virtuous Knight onward with thee I'd travel cheering thy heart with Melody of Voice and with Guitarr well strung by Cupid God of Love would lull thy restless heart into a melodious slumber and when that Cloyd I from my breast would take a reeden Pipe and whistle the sweet tunes and lulabies to thy sore Love oppressed heart.†

Besides these more general influences, there are probably several small and random verbal echoes like 'no birds sing' from William Browne's *Britannia's Pastorals* (II, i, 245), 'wild wild eyes' from Wordsworth ('Her eyes are wild', or *Tintern Abbey*, l. 120), and—one that does not appear to have been noticed in print—'honey wild, and manna dew' from Coleridge's 'For he on honey-dew hath fed' (*Kubla Khan*, l. 53).‡

The more we examine *La Belle Dame* the more it reveals a mystery and paradox of poetic creation; and in this respect it very much resembles *The Ancient Mariner*. Its narrative, of spell and awakened disenchantment, is archetypal; it takes its impulse from one of Keats's profoundest imaginative preoccupations; its inspiration is dream-like and subconscious, and it probably makes its chief effect on the reader at the same level. It is singularly flawless, unified, and entire—the kind of work we are inclined to speak of as 'pure' poetry. Yet, with all these qualities, it is highly derivative and synthetic.

There is no occasion here to pursue this paradox further. For our present inquiry what chiefly matters is the nature of

---

* *John Keats: The Living Year*, pp. 120–3. Gittings throws a strong stress on these 'Amena' letters. See the journal letter to George and Georgiana under the date of 15 April 1819: 'I have been looking over the correspondence of the pretended Amena and Wells this evening' etc. (*Letters*, p. 325).

† Quoted by Gittings (*op. cit.* p. 121).

‡ Gittings (*op. cit.* p. 116) draws attention to the fact that while composing l. 268 of *The Eve of St Agnes* Keats had written 'manna wild'. But as this phrase was scored through it is not likely that the words caught his eye in any re-reading of the poem. For other examples of this honey-dew association see 'Had I a man's fair form', ll. 10–11, and *Endymion*, II, 7.

Keats's achievement—the effortless and complete assimilation of his reading into his poetry, the harmonious blending of diverse recollections, and, out of a synthesis to which his own sensibility and imaginative experience made the chief contribution, the emergence of something that is quite new and distinctive.

So far, in attempting to explain Keats's exceptionally swift development from highly derivative verse-writing to original utterance, we have thrown our chief emphasis on subconscious and instinctive processes in his creative imagination. But that is only part of the story, and no less important than this was his possession and exercise of a first-rate critical intelligence. C. D. Thorpe, in his book *The Mind of John Keats*, constantly stresses this point. For instance, he writes: 'I had not proceeded far before I became convinced that the key to the young poet's remarkable advance in power during the brief span of his working years could be traced largely to a natural reaction to his own serious thought on the nature of art and poetry.* Leavis, thinking particularly of the early Hunt environment, expresses much the same conclusion. Commenting on the 'marvellous vitality' of Keats's art and the 'perfection attained within a limiting aestheticism', he adds: 'Remarkable intelligence and character are implied in that attainment, especially when we consider the starting point and surrounding influences.'†

This critical intelligence, which is another mark of the major poet who grows out of derivative writing to original creation, vigorously manifested itself in several directions. In the first place, as his letters show, Keats was constantly and deeply thinking about the general nature of poetry, its technical problems, and the poetic character. This fact is the more

---

* Preface, p.v. See also p. 26. Thorpe also draws attention to the fact that, excluding the sonnets, 7 out of 13 poems in the 1817 volume deal with poetic theory.

† F. R. Leavis, *Revaluations*, p. 264.

striking in that the central conception of poetry during the Romantic period did not encourage poets to critical thought, except perhaps along broadly philosophic lines; and the acuity of Keats's ideas, which it would be out of place to examine here, has received a striking tribute from T. S. Eliot, whose own attitude to poetry would certainly not predispose him in Keats's favour. In some remarks in *The Use of Poetry and the Use of Criticism* Eliot wrote: 'There is hardly one statement of Keats about poetry, which, when considered carefully, and with due allowance for the difficulties of communication, will not be found to be true; and what is more, true for greater and more mature poetry than anything that Keats ever wrote.'*

From this vital core of speculation about the nature of poetry sprang, continuously and from the beginning, an alert critical consideration of those poets he admired and to whose influence he submitted himself. Exposed to criticism, some of his early enthusiasms soon shrivelled up. His admiration for Hunt's poetry did not last for more than eighteen months, and though it is not till December 1818 that we meet such blunt criticism as 'He has lately publish'd a Pocket-Book call'd The literary Pocket-Book—full of the most sickening stuff you can imagine',[46] his letters during the composition of *Endymion*, in 1817, show a rapid decline in his regard for Hunt as a master. In particular, if he was still prepared to allow Hunt's verse some merit,[47] he was discovering that the poetry he wished to write was not to be confined by Hunt's poetic principles. For instance, commenting to his brothers (January 1818) on Hunt's objections to Book i of *Endymion*, he writes: 'He says the conversation is unnatural and too high-flown·for Brother and Sister—says it should be simple, forgetting do ye mind that they are overshadowed by a Supernatural Power, and of force could not speak like Franchesca in the Rimini. He must first prove that Caliban's poetry is unnatural.'[48] These remarks,

* P. 101.

apart from their conscious disassociation from Hunt's familiar, colloquial style, are particularly interesting since they show clearly how his critical consideration of his own work was reinforced by his ponderings upon poetry generally.

The letter that refers to Hunt's 'sickening stuff' also contains a significant remark about two other enthusiasms of his early days: 'Mrs Tighe and Beattie once delighted me—now I see through them and can find nothing in them—or weakness—and yet how many they still delight!'[49] This sentence is significant not only for the development in critical taste that it reflects but for Keats's strength to detach himself from the fashions of the time. There is a similar change, if less pronounced, in his attitude to Byron—from his youthful tribute to the poet of 'pleasing woe'[50] to the stricture of 'Oh! this is a paltry originality, which consists in making solemn things gay, and gay things solemn, and yet it will fascinate thousands, by the very diabolical outrage of their sympathies.'[51]

But the most striking proof of Keats's vigorously critical attitude to the poets who influenced him is furnished by his observations on Milton and Wordsworth. It would take us too far from our present subject to discuss the justice of his criticisms of these two poets (that of Milton is certainly highly controversial ground) or to trace the interesting and significant fluctuations in his response. But no one who reads his letters can fail to see, even if he considers some of the comment misguided, that Keats's admiration for these two poets was always crossed and complicated by the liveliest kind of doubt and questioning. There was never any chance of either of these poets smothering his own poetic identity for very long, and both of them are subjected to some searching criticism of enduring worth. Of all Keats's idols only Shakespeare—and, by the implication of silence, Spenser—remained objects of unqualified regard;* and apart from the Shakespearean influence on his dramatic experiments, so overwhelming that

---

* Possibly the sonnet *On sitting down to read King Lear once again* can be taken as at least a temporary dissatisfaction with the 'Queen of far-away'.

it is extremely unlikely that he would ever have written great poetic drama, neither of these poets was likely to cramp poetic individuality.

Finally, running steadily through the letters, from his observations on *Endymion* to his remarks on his narrative poems,[52] and beyond, there is a keenly critical regard to his own poetry. What impresses us most about this self-criticism is not so much the modesty or the dissatisfaction with what he had achieved— though this is genuine and notable—as the incentive of highest standards, the soundness and penetration of his judgments (so that we usually find him to have anticipated most of the strictures we are inclined to pass on his poems), and perhaps, above all, his conviction that although poetic creation can derive little force from critical or aesthetic principles, it must for its development be combined with an alert and critical self-consciousness: 'The Genius of Poetry must work out its own salvation in a man: It cannot be matured by law and precept, but by sensation and watchfulness in itself.'*

One particular and striking manifestation of Keats's critical awareness of his own poetry was his sense of direction, which is revealed continuously from his earliest letters and the manifesto of *Sleep and Poetry* to such a passage from his 1819 letters as the following: 'The little dramatic skill I may as yet have however badly it might show in a Drama would I think be sufficient for a Poem. I wish to diffuse the colouring of St Agnes eve throughout a Poem in which Character & Sentiment would be the figures to such drapery. Two or three such Poems, if God should spare me, written in the course of the next six years, would be a famous gradus ad Parnassum altissimum. I mean they would nerve me up to the writing of a few fine Plays—my greatest ambition—when I do feel ambitious.'[53]

---

* *Letters*, pp. 222–3. Keats was justifying his assertion of independence from Hunt and his circle. He continues: 'That which is creative must create itself.' But he did not advocate creating blindly. Besides the 'watchfulness' there must be judgment: 'I may write independently, and with judgment hereafter.'

We must not exaggerate Keats's self-knowledge and fore-sight. This statement was followed not by a poem comparable with *The Eve of St Agnes* but by *Cap and Bells*, while it is highly possible that he was mistaken in believing that either his own powers or the climate of his age would allow the writing of any really important poetic drama. Further, it is arguable that, unless in the Induction to *The Fall of Hyperion*, he never ful-filled his intention of writing a poetry

> Where I may find the agonies, the strife
> Of human hearts.

But if he never really achieved his ambitions and aspirations, they were of the loftiest kind, hard to grasp, and he certainly came remarkably close to them in three short years; also they were consciously and clearly formulated, and helped to give his poetry an impressive sense of purpose and direction. Moreover, this consciousness of direction in his thought about his poetry is paralleled by the exceptional homogeneity of the poetry itself: as some of the following essays may help to show, poem grows out of poem in a quite remarkable way, and the more important ones are usually rich in cross-references. Considered together the poems leave an impression, as per-haps only Wordsworth's work among the other Romantic poets does, of one steadily evolving whole. We can perhaps appreciate this quality of Keats's poetry best by placing it beside Shelley's, which, great as it is, reveals a chaotic, zig-zag, and often random development. One of the chief reasons for this difference between these two poets may very well be that Shelley was inferior to Keats in critical self-awareness.

It is always easy—and very tempting—to be wise after the event. But as we ponder Keats's reactions to the poets he read and admired—his instinctive sense of his own most vital needs, his bent towards synthesis rather than imitation, the easy and complete assimilation of his influences, their har-mony, his subconscious and re-creative processes of recollection (including his own work), his fine critical intelligence—it is hard to resist the conclusion that he had everything to bring him in three short years from the halting imitation of 'I stood tip-toe', hardly above the level of Reynolds's apprentice verses, to the assured, original self-utterance of the odes. At all events his development should always be of particular interest to young poets who are struggling to find their feet.

CHAPTER II

SOME CHARACTERISTIC IMAGERY AND 'SENSATIONS' OF KEATS'S POETRY

But, finding in our green earth sweet contents,
There livest blissfully . . .
Endymion

I stood upon a shore, a pleasant shore,
Where a sweet clime was breathed from a land
Of fragrance, quietness, and trees, and flowers.
Full of calm joy it was, as I of grief;
Too full of joy and soft delicious warmth.
Hyperion

In the main Keats was a poet who was, on every morrow,

wreathing
A flowery band to bind us to the earth,[1]

and for this reason the world evoked by his poetry is quite
different from that of Shelley, who was singularly fascinated
by all the celestial phenomena of winds, clouds, rainbows,
lightning, storms, sun and moon, and the remote stars. But the
contrast must not be pressed too far, for, especially in his earliest work, Keats's landscapes often include pictures of the sky.
He was particularly entranced by the beauty of 'Cynthia's
face, the enthusiast's friend',[2] and Endymion's confession of
how he had been enraptured by the sight of the moon from
earliest boyhood[3] is certainly Keats's as well. So it is that the
image that appears in the very early sonnet to Byron (1814)—

As when a cloud the golden moon doth veil,
  Its sides are ting'd with a resplendent glow,
Through the dark robe oft amber rays prevail,
  And like fair veins in sable marble flow[4]

44

—is the beginning of a sequence that may be traced continuously through the early poems to the first appearance of the Moon in *Endymion:*

> And lo! from the opening clouds, I saw emerge
> The loveliest moon, that ever silver'd o'er
> A shell for Neptune's goblet.[5]

Each of these passages reveals a feature that is common to most of Keats's moon descriptions—the first, his fondness for the effect of moonlight filtering and streaming through surrounding cloud, the second, his particular attention to the moon as it first swims into sight.*

Very similar to this early picture of the moon, which disappears after *Endymion,* is his outstanding sky image, that of feathery or fleecy clouds (sometimes of dawn but more frequently of evening) tinged with sunlight.† The first instance of this is to be found in the opening of one of the 1816 sonnets:

> Oh! how I love, on a fair summer's eve,
> When streams of light pour down the golden west . . .

There are other examples in both the sonnet and epistle, *To My Brother George,*[6] and in *Endymion,* the most sustained being Peona's description of her fancies as she contemplates the sunset sky:

> before the crystal heavens darken,
> I watch and dote upon the silver lakes
> Pictur'd in western cloudiness, that takes
> The semblance of gold rocks and bright gold sands,
> Islands, and creeks, and amber-fretted strands.‡

* For examples of one or both of these features see the sonnet *To My Brother George,* 10–11; the epistle *To My Brother George,* 59–60; *To Charles Cowden Clarke* l. 94; and 'I stood tip-toe', 113–15. It will be noticed that the surrounding clouds give rise to a variety of conceits—dress, curtains, bed, etc.

† The 'midday fleece of clouds' in *The Fall of Hyperion,* l. 454 is quite exceptional.

‡ I, 739–43. Miss Caroline Spurgeon (*Keats's Shakespeare*) finds a reminiscence in this of Prospero's great speech in *The Tempest,* IV, i. For further *Endymion* examples see I, 95–7; I, 364–5; III, 44.

Later, in *Hyperion*, there are the lines,

> And let the clouds of even and of morn
> Float in voluptuous fleeces o'er the hills;[7]

and finally—the perfection achieved from four years of rough sketches—we have the line in *To Autumn*, one of the loveliest of that flawless ode:

> While barred clouds bloom the soft-dying day.

However, while images of the kind we have been noticing add to the richness and variety of the Keatsian world, they are sporadic; and the initial contrast that we made between Keats and Shelley stands. Keats is predominantly of the earth; and the earth that he conjures up in his poetry is unmistakably his own individual creation, whatever he may have owed to Leigh Hunt and other writers in the beginning.

Above all else—and often to an overwhelming degree—his world is a teeming, fertile one of luxuriant vegetation, lush grass, fruits and flowers. This is the realm of Flora and old Pan; and in *Sleep and Poetry*, one of his first poems of any consequence, he stakes out his claim to it as the kingdom of his fancy's choice:

> a bowery nook
> Will be elysium—an eternal book
> Whence I may copy many a lovely saying
> About the leaves, and flowers—about the playing
> Of nymphs in woods, and fountains . . .

> First the realm I'll pass
> Of Flora, and old Pan: sleep in the grass,
> Feed upon apples red, and strawberries,
> And choose each pleasure that my fancy sees;
> Catch the white-handed nymphs in shady places,
> To woo sweet kisses from averted faces . . .

> Another, bending o'er her nimble tread,
> Will set a green robe floating round her head,
> And still will dance with ever varied ease,
> Smiling upon the flowers and the trees:

> Another will entice me on, and on
> Through almond blossoms and rich cinnamon;
> Till in the bosom of a leafy world
> We rest in silence, like two gems upcurl'd
> In the recesses of a pearly shell.[8]

But if we do choose to describe these lines as the staking out of a poetic claim, we must hasten to add that the act was largely a formality, for by late 1816 Keats was already in full possession of the realm of Flora and old Pan. Among the few contemporary readers of *Poems* (1817) Reynolds at least sympathetically appreciated the main direction of Keats's sensibilities: 'we find in his poetry', he wrote,* 'the glorious effect of summer days and leafy spots on rich feelings, which are in themselves a summer.'

Endymion, which absorbed almost the whole of Keats's poetic energies in 1817, is the record of his royal and leisurely progress through this poetic kingdom of his first choice. After this work the world of his poetry perceptibly changes to some extent, and we may see the beginning of this change most clearly in some of the letters he wrote during his 1818 walking tour in Scotland, notably perhaps in some observations he set down for his brother Tom: 'What astonishes me more than anything is the tone, the colouring, the slate, the stone, the moss, the rock-weed; or, if I may say so, the intellect, the countenance of such places. The space, the magnitude of mountains and waterfalls are well imagined before one sees them; but this countenance or intellectual tone must surpass every imagination and defy remembrance. I shall learn poetry here . . .'[9] As is hinted in these remarks, the transformation of Keats's aesthetic sensibility was part of a deeper poetic impulse—away from the poesy of 'luxuries' and, however gradually, towards 'the agonies, the strife of human hearts'. There was also, accounting for the changing impres-

---

* From a review of *Poems* (1817), quoted by Finney, *The Evolution of Keats's Poetry*, p. 188. See also, for the same strain of metaphor, Reynolds's sonnet *On reading Keats's Sonnet on Chaucer*.

sion of his poetry of 1818 and 1819, the imitation of Milton's architectural and sculptural splendours in *Hyperion*,* and the composition of two long poems, *The Eve of St Agnes* and *Lamia*, that have mainly interior settings. Nevertheless, it is only the beginning of a possible transformation of Keats's world that is to be discerned in the poetry of late 1818 and 1819: if he was led into Miltonic—and possibly Blakean†—regions of empyreal remoteness in the first two books of *Hyperion*, he emphatically returned to his own familiar country in the third, while the realm of Flora and old Pan is as richly reflected in the odes as it is in the 'green tangle' of *Endymion*.

One or two further general impressions of this profusely vegetative and sylvan world, so abundant in fruits and flowers,‡ of Keats's poetry may perhaps be added at this point. It is a world that is much more Southern and Mediterranean than English—this not only because the long *Endymion*, which does so much to create it, is set in the isle of Latmos, but because of Keats's singular fondness for the more exotic, sub-tropical kind of flora—grape vines, myrtles, laburnums, palms, cinnamon, cassia and almond trees. A southern world too in its warm, genial climate, for we live in a perpetual spring and early summer (the season, incidentally, when Keats himself always felt in the best vein for poetry-writing). Yet while the air is

---

* It is interesting to note that both in the original composition of *Hyperion* and the later re-casting of it Keats was much exercised in suppressing imagery that must have come most naturally to him. However, in the Induction to *The Fall of Hyperion*, he was able to use the realm of Flora and old Pan to symbolize the state of unreflective, sensuous enjoyment. There are (ll. 19–40) the old familiar trees and fountains; roses and an arbour of vines and blooms; and a rich 'feast of summer fruits'.

† See an interesting article by B. Blackstone, '*Poetical Sketches* and *Hyperion*', *Cambridge Journal*, VI, No. 3.

‡ The curious reader will have no difficulty in compiling a list of Keats's favourite flowers, which would include violets, roses, hyacinths and bluebells, foxgloves, marigolds, lilies, honeysuckle, and jasmine. The roses and violets probably owed something to Hunt's taste, while the passage that Keats had marked in *Midsummer Night's Dream* (II, i, 249–52), with its references to woodbine, musk-roses, eglantine, and violets, seems to have lodged itself in his mind with an exceptional tenacity.

summery, it is never blazing or oppressive: there is always green shade, cool soft breezes ('zephyr' being a favourite word in Keats's vocabulary), and above all we are almost invariably close to springs and fountains, streams* and rivers. Now and then, especially in *Endymion*, we are afforded an enchanting prospect of the sea; and occasionally—for Keats had read and admired Wordsworth and had been deeply impressed by Claude's 'Sacrifice to Apollo', with its background of wooded mountains—we may catch a glimpse of mountains, in *Endymion*, and in odd lines like

> The bowery shore
> Went off in gentle windings to the hoar
> And light blue mountains.[10]

The 'green hill' shrouded by April rain in the *Ode on Melancholy* has, like so many of the images in the 1819 odes, a substantial history in Keats's earlier poetry.† Yet though there are these fugitive prospects of seas and mountains, Keats had none of the contemporary relish for the wilder features of nature, and the world of his poetry remains predominantly and characteristically a sheltered inland one of lowlands and lush valleys. Finally—though there are again some notable exceptions to be marked—it is a world created out of sensuous delight rather than such exact observation as we find in Wordsworth, Tennyson, Hardy, or Hopkins.

From these general impressions we may turn now to certain details of the Keatsian world, concentrating our attention on a number of images and sensations that are particularly characteristic of the poet, that are often curious and fascinating, and that sometimes (so one may believe) take us into the depths of his personality.

One of the most striking and recurrent of these sensations is

---

* Keats has, significantly, a wide range of synonyms for 'stream.'

† For example: *Sleep and Poetry*, l. 77 and l. 134; *Endymion, passim*; 'Hence Burgundy', l. 12.

best introduced by a curious phrase that he uses in his dedicatory sonnet to *Poems* (1817):

> *I feel a free*
> *A leafy luxury*, seeing I could please
> With these poor offerings, a man like thee.*

To any reader coming to Keats for the first time this 'leafy luxury' (whatever it may mean) that can be felt intensely enough to take away all regret for the passing of the lovely pagan world of Pan and nature-worship must seem hopelessly vague or obscure. Yet once we have become familiar with Keats's poetry we shall recognize that 'leafy luxury' is in reality an admirable definition of one of its main impressions. All that flowery and fruitful vegetation that he so richly and persistently conjures up in his poems is not simply present as a visual background. Through his poetic 'I', or through the characters of his poems, we are brought into the closest sort of physical contact with what he is describing: the foliage and flowers brush against us, and we are often smothered and buried in them. This is the effect produced by that passage in *Sleep and Poetry*[11] that we have already quoted; and *Endymion* (where there is nothing odd in the hero's resolution to woo his goddess ''mid fresh leaves'[12]) is also full of it:

> There came upon my face, in plenteous showers,
> Dew-drops, and dewy buds, and leaves, and flowers,
> Wrapping all objects from my smothered sight.

> In harmless tendril they each other chain'd,
> And strove who should be smother'd deepest in
> Fresh crush of leaves.[13]

Very commonly this sensation of 'leafy luxury' is concentrated in a recognizable 'bower' or 'arbour' image, this constituting the most widely recurrent one in all Keats's poetry.

---

* Ll. 12–14. Finney has reminded us of the interesting fact that 'leafy luxuries' occurs in the Preface to Hunt's *Nymphs*.

Nowhere is it more prominent than in *Endymion*, where most of the main episodes have a bower setting. It is in his sister's island bower[14] that the hero first unfolds the story of his sorrow, and all three of the visitations of Cynthia have some sort of arbour connexion.[15] In the second book Endymion's adventures come to their climax in the discovery of the sleeping Adonis, and, instinctively at any rate, Keats gives this great vegetation myth its fullest poetic effect by placing the god in one of his most sumptuously and elaborately described bowers:

> Above his head,
> Four lily stalks did their white honours wed
> To make a coronal; and round him grew
> All tendrils green, of every bloom and hue,
> Together intertwin'd and trammel'd fresh:
> The vine of glossy sprout; the ivy mesh,
> Shading its Ethiop berries; and woodbine
> Of velvet leaves and bugle-blooms divine . . .[16]

The complement to this episode is the first embrace of Endymion and Cynthia, and this—as by now we have almost come to expect—takes place in a 'greenest nook', 'a jasmine bower'.* Such a continuously bowery setting has the love-making between Glaucus and Circe in Book III that Glaucus can fitly summarize the enchantress as 'my arbour queen', while—as a final example of the image—we have Endymion's attempt to entice the Indian Maid with the vision of a home that is bowered in ivy and yew trees.[17]

Never again is this bower image quite so prominent in Keats's poetry. But it remains a common one. Lorenzo and Isabella, for instance, meet 'close in a bower of hyacinth and musk',[18] and in the *Ode to a Nightingale* an entire stanza is devoted to a description of the embowered poet. In the *Ode to Psyche* we first see the sleeping god and goddess of love in a setting that is highly reminiscent of the numerous dalliances in *Endymion*:

---

* See II, 663–71 for the full description.

> couched side by side
> In deepest grass, beneath the whisp'ring roof
> Of leaves and trembled blossoms;[19]

and in the last part of the poem the imaginary shrine that the poet builds for Psyche is unmistakably one of his old and favourite arbours:

> And in the midst of this wide quietness
> A rosy sanctuary will I dress
> With the wreath'd trellis of a working brain,
>   With buds, and bells, and stars without a name.[20]

Finally, there is the arbour in *The Fall of Hyperion:*

> with a drooping roof
> Of trellis vines, and bells, and larger blooms,
> Like floral censers swinging light in air.[21]

This major image in Keats's poetry may have been inspired from several sources, including possibly contemporary gardening. It may have started as a seed blown from *The Faerie Queene*, and it is certainly interesting to find a reference to 'woven boughs' in the early *Imitation of Spenser*. The poetry of Moore may have served as another inspiration.* But it is probable that the chief stimulus was Leigh Hunt, a line from whose *Rimini* stands as a revealing epigraph to 'I stood tip-toe':

> Places of nestling green for Poets made.†

---

* See the testimony of *Don Juan*, I, civ:

> Julia sate within as pretty a bower
> As e'er held houri in that heathenish heaven
> Described by Mahomet, and Anacreon Moore . . .

† In his sonnet on *The Story of Rimini* Keats describes it as a 'bower' for the spirit, while in the sonnet written on Hunt's release from prison there is the fancy of his friend escaped from gaol into

> bowers fair
> Culling enchanted flowers.

Above all, some of the earliest bower-images, like the distressing reference in 'I stood tip-toe' to a 'tasteful nook' sound suspiciously like recollections of Hunt.

However, the provenance of the image does not greatly matter. Wherever Keats derived it from, he made it entirely his own, and it became the embodiment of one of his deepest impulses.*

Closely associated with this image, indeed frequently forming part of it, there is another characteristically Keatsian sensation that brings us into exceptionally close sensuous contact with his 'leafy world'. This is the sensation stimulated by the widespread image of the poet, or one of his personages, pillowed in grass or flowers. There are many examples of this in *Poems* (1817), in lines like:

> Who is more happy, when, with heart's content,
> Fatigued he sinks into some pleasant lair
> Of wavy grass?[22]

Endymion, too, abounds in this sensation.† For instance, one of the hero's chief pangs in the deathly underworld is that he

> nor felt, nor prest
> Cool grass,[23]

a longing that later produces the outcry:

> Oh think how I should love a bed of flowers;[24]

and even under the sea, far away from familiar grass and flowers, he on one occasion characteristically lays his head 'upon a tuft of straggling weeds'![25] He reclines on 'living flowers'[26] as he listens to the story of Venus and Adonis, and in this tale the goddess too is pictured lying lovelorn 'on the pleasant grass'.[27] Similarly the Indian Maid (later compared to a 'muskrose upon new-made hay'[28]) is first seen

> panting in the forest grass.[29]

After *Endymion* this sensation is rarer in Keats's poetry. But

---

* See Ch. VIII, 'The *Ode to a Nightingale*', pp. 265–8.
† There are at least twenty examples of this sensation in *Poems* (1817) and *Endymion*.

it returns in the odes, in the glimpse of Cupid and Psyche 'couched side by side In deepest grass',[30] and in the *Ode on Indolence* with the picture of the poet himself,

> cool-bedded in the flowery grass.[31]

As we have already said, this verdant world that Keats's poetry evokes is a cool, murmuring one of springs and fountains, brooks and rivers, pools and lakes. For instance—to be factual about an impression that is usually, and most happily, subconsciously taken—only two of the six 1819 odes are without some reference to streams or rivers. This impression is again particularly strong in *Endymion*, where the prominent fountain image of the first two books comes to a climax in the river myth of Alpheus and Arethusa, and where (to give a later example) the 'crystal rill' is such an outstanding feature of the earthly paradise that Endymion paints for the enticement of the Indian Maid.[32] It is also interesting to notice how these water-images sometimes prompt Keats's incidental similes and metaphors. Thus, when invoking inspiration to describe one of the embraces of Endymion and Cynthia, he writes:

> O fountain'd hill! Old Homer's Helicon!
> That thou wouldst spout a little streamlet o'er
> These sorry pages;[33]

and twenty lines later we read:

> and then there ran
> Two bubbling springs of talk from their sweet lips.[34]

However, this water and verdure are not two separate features of the country of Keats's imagination. On the contrary, one of the most characteristic and abiding impressions it leaves is that of moisture as a necessary condition of all its green lushness. That is why we feel there is a sensation uniquely Keatsian in lines like:

> Upon the sides of Latmos was outspread
> A mighty forest; for the moist earth fed
> So plenteously all weed-hidden roots
> Into o'er-hanging boughs, and precious fruits.[35]

Such a sensation as this is by no means confined to the early poems. For example, the main passage of flower description in *To Fancy* concludes with,

> And every leaf, and every flower
> Pearled with the self-same shower,[36]

while the *Ode on Melancholy* contains the memorable image of the

> weeping cloud,
> That fosters the droop-headed flowers all,
> And hides the green hill in an April shroud.[37]

In particular Keats seems to have had an exceptionally strong sense of moisture nourishing the roots of things. This will be noticed in the last *Endymion* quotation, with which passage we may compare the following metaphor in one of Endymion's speeches:

> essences,
> Once spiritual, are like muddy lees,
> Meant but to fertilize my earthly root,
> And make my branches lift a golden fruit
> Into the bloom of heaven.[38]

'I stood tip-toe' has the characteristic lines:

> And let long grass grow round the roots to keep them
> Moist, cool and green;[39]

and the 'hush'd, *cool-rooted* flowers' of the *Ode to Psyche* grow from a moist earth through which flows 'a brooklet, scarce espied'.[40]

One simple example, particularly noticeable in Keats's earliest poetry, of this conjunction of water and verdure is his fondness for the image of a green island, most commonly set in the middle of a lake. This image first emerges in the *Imitation of Spenser*,* and we find it later in *Calidore*, *Sleep and Poetry*, and in *Endymion*,[41] where Peona's 'bowery island', lying somewhere across what must be a broad river, is the setting for the story that the hero has to tell of his first dream-visitations from Cynthia. After *Endymion* we do not see much of this island, but we certainly glimpse it again in *Hyperion* where Clymene is describing the strange beautiful music she had heard

> from a bowery strand
> Just opposite, an island of the sea.[42]

This is the verdurous island of Delos, 'chief isle of the embowered Cyclades', which is more fully described for us in the next book of the poem, with

> olives green,
> And poplars, and lawn-shading palms, and beech . . .
> And hazels thick, dark-stemm'd beneath the shade.[43]

However, while this particular image deserves notice, the impression we are trying to indicate, of moist verdure, is usually created in more subtle and unobtrusive ways. For instance, there is Keats's exceptional love all through his poetry for the word 'dew' (or for one of its derivatives). Little need be said about this since most of his references to the dewy appearance of things are brief and fugitive, and often commonplace and conventional. So far as we form the impression of a fresh, dew-drenched world the image comes to us subconsciously and cumulatively—mainly from the mere iteration of the word. But there is one interesting point of detail to be marked. This is Keats's fondness for the image of the dewy rose, for though he frequently uses it cliché-wise, out

---

* One is tempted to believe that this island first caught Keats's fancy when he read of the abodes of Phaedria and Acrasia in *The Faerie Queene*. It may have been further impressed on his mind by Claude's 'Enchanted Castle'; and in his verse-epistle *To J. H. Reynolds* we find that his description of this picture includes the lines 'You know the clear lake, and the little Isles' (35) and 'Into the verdurous bosoms of those Isles' (58).

of his conventional tracings ultimately came that lovely and individual line in the *Ode to a Nightingale*,

> The coming musk-rose, full of dewy wine.

For this reason it is extremely interesting to study some of Keats's earlier sketches, the closest one to that in the *Ode to a Nightingale* occurring in the sonnet 'Had I a man's fair form':

> Sweeter by far than Hybla's honied roses
> When steep'd in dew rich to intoxication.[44]

Along with this impression of dewiness in the Keatsian world we may notice an even more marked fascination for moss,* that most striking form of moist vegetation. It spreads everywhere in his poetry—from its first appearance, in the *Imitation of Spenser*, as the 'mossy bed' out of which the rill springs, the 'enmossed realms' of Pan and the mossy rocks and stones in *Endymion*, to the 'mossy winding ways' of the *Ode to a Nightingale* and the 'moss'd cottage trees' of *To Autumn*. Keats's moss is like the actual plant: once our eyes are open to it we begin to notice it everywhere. Mostly it is something small that he describes as covered with moss—stones, a bird's nest, roots of a tree, or a patch of ground where he or one of his personages lies reclined; but in *To J. H. Reynolds* we find Claude's 'Enchanted Castle' described boldly and generally as a 'mossy palace', and though we may usually assume that it is the green lichen that he has in mind, his eye had obviously observed other colourations, for in *Endymion* he alludes to

> a jasmine bower, all bestrown
> With golden moss.[45]

This is an interesting little point of detail since Keats's near contemporary, Samuel Palmer, was also much attracted by moss, in such pictures as his 'Cow-lodge with a mossy Roof'

---

* Bridges noted this: 'he is as fond of moss and eagles as Shelley was' (*Collected Essays*, vol. IV, p. 152). But moss is not such an obvious detail in Shelley's poetry.

and 'A Barn with a mossy Roof'. In many instances Keats's 'mossy', like his epithet 'dewy', passes with little or no effect, but occasionally, as when in 'I stood tip-toe' he writes of the 'quaint mossiness of aged roots', he gives us a word-picture that is comparable with some of Palmer's studies. Further, behind this parallel there is, as Gregson reminds us in his book on this painter, a widespread romantic taste for the strange and minute beauties of lichens as part of the 'picturesque':

> Moss and lichens had impinged, less violently, on the eyes of Crabbe (one of the poets whom Palmer enjoyed), and the Words-worths, and Southey. And before much of this living physique of nature came into poetry and painting, naturalists had begun to peer into natural detail. James Sowerbury, in the seventeen-nineties, had painted golden lichens for his *English Botany*, and Gilpin, the archbishop of the picturesque, had written in 1791, in his *Remarks on Forest Scenery*, a commendation of lichens (he includes lichen in the term 'moss') to the artist's attention: 'In coloured landscape, it is surely a very beautiful object of imitation.'*

It is extremely unlikely that Keats had ever read Gilpin, but his eye may have been caught by some of these illustrations in the books of the naturalists of the time, while his poems are proof that he would certainly have concurred with Gilpin's commendation. If nothing else, this love of moss thoroughly justified his description of himself as 'an old Stager in the picturesque'.†

---

* *Samuel Palmer*, p. 91. See also Edward Ferrars's remarks on the Devon-shire landscape in Jane Austen's *Sense and Sensibility*: 'I can easily believe it to be full of rocks and promontories, grey moss and brushwood, but these are all lost on me. I know nothing of the picturesque' (Ch. 18).

† *Letters*, p. 365. Another example of Keats's taste for the picturesque was his early relish in 'gothic' landscape—woodland, the ruined tower or chapel, a suggestion of loneliness or desolation. (See especially *Calidore*, 35ff, and *To George Felton Mathew*, 31–52.) There are some remarks in the letters to Fanny Brawne (July–August 1819) that suggest a growing dis-satisfaction with the 'picturesque'—for example, 'I am getting a great dislike of the picturesque' (*Letters*, p. 370). It would be wrong to make too much of these remarks, but they clearly have some connexion with the change that was coming over the world of Keats's poetry in 1819.

Even more subtly pervasive than these references to dew and moss in creating an impression of moist, lush growth is Keats's instinctive habit of immediately coupling an allusion to water with some form of vegetation that it nourishes. 'Long grass which hems A little brook', 'cold springs had run To warm their chilliest bubbles in the grass', 'lush-leav'd rill', 'where its pool Lay, half asleep, in grass and rushes cool'[46]— phrases of this sort can be noticed by an attentive reader everywhere in Keats's poetry. He will also remark in these quotations a characteristic linkage of streams and pools with grass. However, much more striking than this is Keats's association of water (in various forms) with flowers: first, because this connexion occurs so frequently, almost to the point of monotony, and secondly, because it appears to constitute a curious, compulsive linkage in the poet's subconscious mind. There are, it is true, many passages in which flowers, like grass, are logically and directly connected with water in one self-contained descriptive item.* But often it seems that a reference to water in one descriptive item subconsciously prompts Keats to a reference to flowers in a separate one, or vice-versa. A single illustration of this would not be very convincing, so we print here a selection of these discrete, latent associations, choosing examples that are varied in nature and cover the whole range of Keats's work:

> . . . the silvery stems
> Of delicate birch trees, or long grass which hems
> A little *brook*. The youth had long been viewing
> These pleasant things, and heaven was bedewing
> The mountain *flowers*.[47]

> . . . sweeter than the *rill*
> To its cold channel, or a swollen *tide*
> To margin sallows, were the leaves he spied,
> And *flowers*, and wreaths . . .[48]

> From vale to vale, from wood to wood, he flew,
> Breathing upon the *flowers* his passion new,
> And wound with many a *river* to its head.[49]

* For example, *To some Ladies*, 7–8.

> . . . while thy hook
> Spares the next swath and all its twined *flowers*:
> And sometimes like a gleaner thou dost keep
> Steady thy laden head across a *brook*.*

There are two other marked features of Keats's poetry that show how spontaneous and intense was his imaginative identity with this world of trees, fruits, and flowers. The first, admirably discussed by G. Wilson Knight in *The Starlit Dome*,† is his fondness for transforming the inorganic into living, vegetal forms. The most familiar instance of this occurs in *The Eve of St Agnes*, in the description of the casement,[50] beside which we may set the description of the fountains and streams changing into 'crystal vines' and 'weeping trees' in the Book II of *Endymion*[51] and—for a more extensive example—the picture of Lamia's magic palace:

> Fresh carved cedar, mimicking a glade
> Of palm and plantain, met from either side,
> High in the midst, in honour of the bride:
> Two palms and then two plantains, and so on,
> From either side their stems branch'd one to one
> All down the aisled place; and beneath all
> There ran a stream of lamps straight on from wall to wall. . .
> Between the tree-stems, marbled plain at first,
> Came jasper pannels; then, anon, there burst
> Forth creeping imagery of slighter trees,
> And with the larger wove in small intricacies.[52]

Secondly, we may observe an instinctive tendency in Keats all through his poetry to turn to vegetal life for his incidental metaphors and similes—sometimes with an unexpected and

---

* *To Autumn*, ll. 17–20. For further examples see *To Emma*, ll. 1–3: 'O Solitude', l. 5: *To G. F. Mathew*, ll. 40–3 and 76–8: 'Hadst thou liv'd', ll. 31–3: *Calidore*, Induction, ll. 67–8: *To C. C. Clarke*, ll. 30–3: 'I stood tip-toe', ll. 41–3: *Endymion*, I, 15–16 and 48–50; II, 52–6, 91–5, 285–6, 945–6; III, 971–2; IV, 641–2: *Hyperion*, III, 33–5: *The Eve of St Mark*, ll. 10–12: *Psyche*, ll. 10–13. There are other passages where it is wisest to remain content with speculation—for example, the third stanza of *La Belle Dame* and *Endymion*, II, 944–6.

† See Ch. IV, *passim*.

arresting effect. *Endymion* contains several outstanding examples of this sort of figure like:

> Her soft arms were entwining me, and on
> Her voice I hung like fruit among green leaves:
> Her lips were all my own, and—ah, ripe sheaves
> Of happiness! ye on the stubble droop,
> But never may be garner'd;[53]

and, even more remarkable:

> Delicious symphonies, like airy flowers,
> Budded, and swell'd, and, full-blown, shed full showers
> Of light, soft, unseen leaves of sounds divine.[54]

Possibly such figures as these are to be expected in the poem that is Keats's chief and richest expression of 'leafy luxury'. But this same kind of figurative imagery is to be found continually in the rest of his work—from such lines as these in *The Eve of St Agnes*,

> Sudden a thought came like full-blown rose,
> Flushing his brow,*

to these in *Lamia:*

> How to entangle, trammel up and snare
> Your soul in mine, and labyrinth you there
> Like the hid scent in an unbudded rose.†

This green leafy world of Keats's imagination is also a richly fruitful one—particularly of apples, pears, plums, strawberries, and clustered grapes. As we should expect from a poet so sharply responsive in all his senses,‡ these fruits do

---

* 136–7. Note also the cancelled l. 65: 'Her anxious lips mouth full pulp'd with rosy thoughts'; and ll. 320–2.

† II. 52–4. See also *Hyperion* I, 209–12. Even the writing in the much maligned *Otho the Great* often has this unmistakable Keatsian quality (II, i, 27–31; II, ii, 133–7; III, ii, 134–9).

‡ Wilson Knight (*The Starlit Dome*, p. 259) reminds us of the exceptional diversity of sense impressions in Keats's poetry: 'Visual imagery is not over-emphasized . . . but rather you tend to touch, to smell, to taste, to feel the living warmth of one object after another.'

not always evoke the same sensation. Sometimes, ripe, luscious, pulpy, they are used for the suggestion of taste: such
are the 'juicy pears' and the 'bunch of blooming plums Ready
to melt between an infant's gums'[55] that are offered to Endymion as he listens to the tale of Venus and Adonis, and
such—most memorable of all—the grapes in the *Ode on
Melancholy*.[56] Sometimes, again, these fruits are described with
a sensitive tactile awareness, and it is interesting to observe
how the lines,

> and here, undimm'd
> By any touch, a bunch of blooming plums . . .[57]

re-appear two years later in

> It is as if the rose should pluck herself,
> Or the ripe plum finger its misty bloom,

and also in the line,

> And the ripe plum still wears its dim attire.[58]

But, most characteristically of all, these fruits are delightedly
cherished in Keats's poetry for their full, rounded shapes.
That is why expressions like 'night-swollen mushrooms',[59]
'wealth of globed peonies',[60] and those lines in *To Autumn*—

> To swell the gourd, and plump the hazel shells
> With a sweet kernel[61]

—strike us as so essentially Keatsian. It will also be noticed that,
with all the leafy, florescent nature of his world, Keats had an
exceptionally appreciative eye for the rounded, swelling forms
of buds in leaves and flowers, and it is typical that the lines
just quoted from *To Autumn* are followed by,

> to set budding more,
> And still more, later flowers for the bees.*

* Ll. 8–9. For earlier examples see 'After dark vapours', ll. 9–10; and
l. 33, *To Fancy*, repeated several months later in *Ode to Psyche*, l. 61.

Similarly his descriptions of the human form almost always concentrate on the rounded shape. The most beautiful illustration of this aspect of his sensibility is undoubtedly his picture of the sleeping Adonis in *Endymion:*

> And coverlids gold-tinted like the peach,
> Or ripe October's faded marigolds,
> Fell sleek about him in a thousand folds—
> Not hiding up an Apollonian curve
> Of neck and shoulder, nor the tenting swerve
> Of knee from knee, nor ankles pointing light;
> But rather, giving them to the filled sight
> Officiously. Sideway his face repos'd
> On one white arm, and tenderly unclos'd,
> By tenderest pressure, a faint damask mouth
> To slumbery pout; just as the morning south
> Disparts a dew-tipp'd rose.[62]

Here it will be noticed how the various incidental details—the thousand folds of the coverlids, the peach, the marigolds, the rose just opening from its bud—all reinforce the impression of curved and rounded forms; and this effect is strongly maintained in the lines that follow, by the intertwining 'tendrils green' and 'virgin's bower, trailing airily', and by the shapes of convolvulus and 'bugle-blooms' of woodbine.

With this passage we may compare, for similar effects, the picture of Georgiana Wylie in 'Had'st thou lived in days of old', though the writing here is of course much inferior. The elaborate description of Georgiana's

> dark hair that extends
> Into many graceful bends . . .[63]

is very characteristic, since curled or waving hair seems to have held a particular fascination for Keats.* So, too, is the 'dainty bend' of Georgiana's eyebrows: round or 'orbed'

---

* There are three such references in *Sleep and Poetry* alone—l. 150, l. 180, and l. 334. See also the description of Endymion's 'dark curls blown vagrant in the wind' (ii, 562) and of Hermes in *Lamia* (i, 25–6).

brows appear in several other poems, and it is significant that in imagining what his beloved Spenser looked like he should have written, 'Spenser! thy brows are arch'd'.[64] The portrait of Georgiana does not include that common image* of a rounded (usually pearl—or shell-like) ear that at last finds perfect expression in Psyche's 'soft-conched ear'; but it does go on to describe what, whether we set it down as a cockney vulgarism or not, is certainly another recurrent example of his love of the rounded form—Georgiana's 'ivory breast'.†

The material objects that appear in his poetry also share this characteristic quality of roundedness. Apart from the dominant moon-image, already discussed, his early poems in particular are filled with numerous references to shells and conchs, pearls, pebbles, and goblets, two of them, *To some Ladies* and *On receiving a Curious Shell*, being directly inspired by a 'shell from the bright golden sands of the ocean'. Usually these objects appear as fugitive descriptive details that we barely notice at the time; but they have a cumulative effect on us, especially in *Endymion*, which is replete with them, while sometimes they do create a memorable and typical image, as in

> Till in the bosom of a leafy world
> We rest in silence, like two gems upcurl'd
> In the recesses of a pearly shell.[65]

Of this group of rounded forms perhaps the most interesting and individual are the pebbles, for though so much less obviously poetic than 'fancifullest' and 'crimson mouthed' shells[66] or 'precious goblets that make rich the wine',[67] they occur with an extraordinary persistency in the early poems. They are especially prominent in *Endymion*: not only do we find them in the under-sea descriptions of

---

* For example 'Cynthia's pearl-round ears' (*Endymion*, 1, 616).

† It is surprising that Keats was not more sensitive to the breastlike configuration of the earth. There are some hints of this in his poetry, but they are not striking: for example, 'the swell of turf and slanting branches' (*Endymion*, 1, 83–4) and 'Or from your swelling downs' (*Ibid*. 1, 201).

gold sand impearl'd
With lily shells, and pebbles milky white,[68]

but the earthly streams and fountains of Latmos also have
their 'bedded pebbles' and 'pebbly margin',[69] while it is
notable that when Endymion is painting the paradise that he
will create for the Indian Maid he says of the rill that runs
through it,

> Its bottom will I strew with amber shells,
> And pebbles blue from deep enchanted wells.[70]

The aesthetic effect produced by these various rounded
objects is intensified by numerous allusions to certain hollow
shapes—urns and vases, caves and grottos, domed or vaulted
spaces—that often suggest curved, flowing lines. Of these
descriptive items the most outstanding are the caves and
grottos,* and it is significant that in one of his invocations to
sleep Keats should write of it as a great key to

> bespangled caves,
> Echoing grottos, full of tumbling waves
> And moonlight.[71]

We meet these grottos and caves in several of the *Poems* (1817)†
but it is not till *Endymion*, especially in the Book of the Underworld, where caves and jetting fountains (another recurrent
curved form) constitute the main group of images, that we
find Keats writing about them with the imaginative power of
lines like:

> It was a sounding grotto, vaulted vast,
> O'er studded with a thousand, thousand pearls,

---

* Severn's account of landing near Lulworth Cove with Keats on their
journey to Italy is interesting: 'He was in a part that he already knew, and
showed me the splendid caverns and grottos with a poet's pride, as though
they had been his by birthright' (quoted by De Selincourt, *Poems of
John Keats*, p. 551).

† See *On receiving a Curious Shell*; the letter and sonnet *To My Brother
George*; *Sleep and Poetry*.

And crimson mouthed shells with stubborn curls,
Of every shape and size.*

After *Endymion* some of Keats's fascination for caves seems to have diminished; but it was certainly not exhausted, as we may see from the 'elfin grot' in *La Belle Dame Sans Merci* and the Naiad of the 'pure grot' in the second sonnet *On Fame*. On the other hand, while two of his most important poems of 1819 were written around the subject of Grecian urns, he paid no attention at all to their shape, concentrating, so far as sensuous response was concerned, entirely on the pictures they displayed. This pedestrian fact is worth mentioning if only to prevent some psychologist, or psychologically-minded critic, exaggerating the uterine symbolism of this group of images.

It is not only the various rounded objects we have been describing that create an impression of rondure and graciously curving lines in Keats's world. For one thing there is his fondness for gently curving stems and branches and the delicately drooping heaviness of leaf- and flower-bud:

> the sweet buds that with a modest pride
> Pull droopingly, in slanting curve aside,
> Their scantly leaved, and finely tapering stems.[72]

'Drooping', and particularly 'slanting',† are favourite words with Keats, and this same effect is to be discerned in the odes, in the 'droop-headed flowers' of the *Ode on Melancholy* and in the line,

> To bend with apples the moss'd cottage trees,

in *To Autumn*. Again, closely connected with this impression

---

* ii, 878–81. A particularly interesting passage for the intense impression of curved and rounded forms.

† Though 'slanting' normally signifies an oblique straight line, in Keats's usage it most frequently suggests bending and bowing and is a near synonym of 'drooping'. See the context above and *To Charles Cowden Clarke*, l. 3.

there is Keats's evident delight in the waving plumes of the knight's helmet,

> Not like the formal crest of latter days:
> But bending in a thousand graceful ways:*

which reappears in a passage full of suggestion of curved and rounded shapes in *The Eve of St Agnes:*

> He follow'd through a lowly arched way,
> Brushing the cobwebs with his lofty plume.[73]

The poems also contain a number of descriptive passages suggestive of wavy or curving motion, one of the loveliest being the lines that follow the hymn to Pan in *Endymion:*

> A shout from the whole multitude arose,
> That lingered in the air like dying rolls
> Of abrupt thunder, when Ionian shoals
> Of dolphins bob their noses through the brine†

Among the 'posey of luxuries' in 'I stood tip-toe' there is the characteristic image of minnows

> Staying their wavy bodies 'gainst the streams,[74]

and of sweet-peas with

> taper fingers catching at all things,
> To bind them all about with tiny rings;[75]

while, for a less common example of wavy, curving movement, we may instance the lines:

> For as delicious wine doth, sparkling, dive
> In nectar'd clouds and curls through water fair,

---

* *Calidore*, Induction ll. 3–4. See also the 'flowing hair' of the horse's mane (*Calidore*, l. 110) and 'the visor arch'd so gracefully Over a knightly brow' (ll. 130–1).

† 1, 308–11. This passage recalls the description of the fountain in the epistle *To My Brother George* (ll. 49–52). Note also in this poem the 'wavy grass', 'the waviness of whitest clouds', and the ship with 'bright silver curling round her prow'.

So from the arbour roof down swell'd an air
Odorous and enlivening.[76]

In much the same sort of way Keats will describe the swelling air of sound:

> a faint breath of music, which e'en then
> Fill'd out its voice, and died away again.
> Within a little space again it gave
> *Its airy swellings, with a gentle wave,*
> To light-hung leaves.*

So far our emphasis has fallen rather more on images than sensations in Keats's poetry and—as the various quotations have implied—on images commoner in the early poems than the late. It is time now to look at some predominant sensations that, occurring continually through the entire range of his work, contribute in an exceptional degree to its individuality.

No one who reads Keats with any attention can fail to notice his addiction to the word 'soft',† which indeed often degenerates into one of his most obvious clichés. He employs the word in a variety of contexts, and sometimes quite generally, but in the main it is confined to three particular sensations.

First, there is his exceptional sensitiveness to bland air and soft breezes‡—a sensation that may be traced continuously through his poetry from such an early example as:

---

* *Endymion*, I, 115–19. This seems as convenient a place as any to mention another recurrent image that I have been unable to weave into the pattern of this chapter. I refer to the censer and its wreath of incense. See dedicatory sonnet to *Poems* (1817), ll. 3–4: 'I stood tip-toe', ll. 197–8: 'Hadst thou liv'd', ll. 21–3: *Endymion*, II, 390: *Hyperion*, I, 167–8: *The Eve of St Agnes*, ll. 6–7: *Ode to Psyche*, ll. 32–3 and 46–7: *Lamia*, II, 179–81: *The Fall of Hyperion*, l. 27.

† 'Soft' occurs three times in *To Autumn*, and the *Ode to Psyche*, twice in the *Ode to a Nightingale*, and once in the *Ode on a Grecian Urn*, the *Ode on Melancholy*, and the *Ode on Indolence*.

‡ This was probably why the soft-sounding word 'zephyr' appealed to him so much, in spite of its unfortunately overworn poetic currency.

Softly the breezes from the forest came,
Softly they blew aside the taper's flame,[77]

to the perfect onomatopoeia of *To Autumn*:

Thy hair soft-lifted by the winnowing wind.[78]

Secondly, there is his sense of the softness of flesh—of lips, breasts, hands; and here it is particularly interesting to notice how the many references* to soft hands in his early poems dealing with imaginary women are paralleled in the 1819 poems written to the living Fanny Brawne.†

The third chief context of his favourite 'soft' is sleep— 'soft closer of our eyes',[79] 'soft embalmer of the still midnight'.[80] No poet has written more than him about or in praise of sleep, itself one of the major sensations of his poetry;‡ and his descriptions of sleep almost invariably include some reference to its luxurious softness. In this respect sleep is closely connected in his poetry—as it is in the common complex of human sensibility—with the breast. We can see this particularly clearly in the 'Bright star' sonnet:

Pillow'd upon my fair love's ripening breast,
To feel for ever its soft fall and swell . . .[81]

while our vision of Cupid and Psyche is of two lovers both embracing each other and embraced by 'soft-handed slumber'.[82]

* For example, the second sonnet on *Woman*, l. 2. In *Endymion* both Peona and the Indian Maid have soft hands, and the Indian Maid's is described by the vile word 'softling' (IV, 316). For a more familiar, later example see the *Ode on Melancholy*, l. 19.

† The *Ode to Fanny* and 'The day is gone' contain the phrase 'soft hand'; 'I cry your mercy' has a straight reference to Fanny's hands; and while there is no explicit allusion in 'What can I do to drive away', this second *Ode to Fanny* has the even more pregnant and revealing general reflection, 'Touch has a memory'.

‡ Wilson Knight (*The Starlit Dome*, p. 261) rightly draws attention to the 'amazing emphasis on sleep' in Keats's poetry. It will be noticed that a large number of Keats's passages on sleep contain references to poppies. But 'poppied sleep' is such a conventional metaphor that it is doubtful whether we can consider the association in Keats's poetry as in any way significantly characteristic.

With this sensation of softness there is a no less pervasive one of coolness—but not coldness, which usually has for Keats some association with death.* Indeed, so intense and continuous is his feeling for coolness that one wonders whether, as an early symptom of the disease that killed him, he suffered from spells of feverish heat that made him exceptionally appreciative of its assuagement. At any rate, it is certainly to be observed that several of these evocations of coolness in his poetry are linked with sickness and fever, most strikingly perhaps in some lines from that curious passage that concludes 'I stood tip-toe':

> The breezes were ethereal, and pure,
> And crept through half closed lattices to cure
> The languid sick; it cool'd their fever'd sleep,
> And soothed them into slumbers full and deep.[83]

Again, the characteristic line in the sonnet 'After dark vapours'—

> The eyelids with the passing coolness play[84]

—interesting, incidentally, as an example of the delicacy of Keats's response to coolness—follows close upon a reference to the 'sick heavens', while in *Isabella* there is another such association, curiously remote from the immediate subject:

> Until sweet Isabella's untouched cheek
>   Fell sick within the rose's just domain,
> Fell thin as a young mother's, who doth seek
>   By every lull to cool her infant's pain.[85]

Much of this sensation of coolness that Keats's poetry communicates is of course indirect—a persistent suggestion evoked by his world of streams, fountains, deep grass and green, leafy shade.† It also owes much to the delicate insinuation of innumerable short phrases like 'cloister'd among cool and bunched leaves', 'fingers cool as aspen leaves',

---

* See *Endymion*, II, 260–338, *passim*; *The Eve of St Agnes*, especially the opening stanzas; *The Fall of Hyperion*, ll. 109–33.

† For example, *The Fall of Hyperion*, I, 19–23.

'cool-rooted flowers', 'in cool mid-forest',[86] and so on. But what is most typical of Keats's writing is the sense it so frequently conveys of direct physical contact with the sources of coolness, of the relief of those bodily heats that the poet goes on to describe in the passage quoted above from 'I stood tip-toe'.

> Soon they awoke clear-eyed: nor burnt with thirsting,
> Nor with hot fingers, nor with temples bursting.[87]

'Nor with temples bursting.'—From that first occasion when the young Keats-Calidore 'bares his forehead to the cool blue sky'[88] how many times do we not read of some feverous or burning forehead that is refreshed by one of the soft breezes that waft so deliciously through the Keatsian world. In the underworld it is one of Endymion's most excruciating deprivations that he

> nor felt, nor prest
> Cool grass, nor tasted the fresh slumberous air,[89]

and a few moments after these reflections, in another vision of his lost delights, he cries out to Diana:

> O woodland Queen,
> What smoothest air thy smoother forehead woos?[90]

As late as *King Stephen* we find Gloucester giving voice to this old and deeply felt sensation:

> Now may we lift our bruised visors up,
> And take the flattering freshness of the air.[91]

So with the phrase 'nor burnt with thirsting', for Keats's poetry is filled with references to the drinking of cool liquors. In particular it is interesting to observe that his numerous descriptions of wine, like

> Let the red wine within the goblet boil,
> Cold as a bubbling well,[92]

almost always contain some explicit mention of coolness or coldness. Again, in connexion with the phrase 'hot fingers' (which, in one antithesis, produced that delectable simile 'fingers cool as aspen leaves') we may recall several character-istic passages in *Endymion*—Proserpine dabbling her tender hands 'on the cool and sluicy sands',[93] Endymion at his old boyhood sport of bubbling up water through a reed and sailing chip-boats,* or stemming the 'upbursting cold' of a spring with 'feverous fingering',[94] or entreating Diana to soothe his burning fever:

> Dost thou now lave thy feet and ankles white?
> O think how sweet to me the freshening sluice![95]

Lamia was not written till two years later, but remembering these passages in *Endymion*, we may well believe that neither the recollection of the ceremonial custom of foot-washing in this later Grecian tale nor the peculiar tone of the description were accidental:

> When in an antichamber every guest
> Had felt the cold full sponge to pleasure press'd,
> By minist'ring slaves, upon his hands and feet.[96]

To say nothing of the expression 'to pleasure', how Keatsian that 'cold, *full* sponge' is: in it we have not only the suggestion of an abundance of cool water but the hint of a form that is rounded and, for all its solid-seeming, pleasurably soft.

Finally, as a marginal note to these sensations of coolness, we may notice a somewhat curious conceit that appears several times in the early poems. In this conceit the very streams are represented as seeking coolness. The image is presented twice in 'I stood tip-toe'[97] and re-appears in *Endymion* as

> clear rills
> That for themselves a cooling covert make
> 'Gainst the hot season.[98]

'Soft' also occurs frequently through another outstanding feature of Keats's world—the singular hush that pervades it.

---

* 1, 880–4. Doubtless a recollection of Keats's own boyish sports.

As with the impression of coolness, this hush is to a large extent a continuous and indirect suggestion, the inevitable effect on us of the numerous brooding woods and forests and of the profuse, silent growth of leaves, fruits and flowers that is always palpably about us. But there are moments when Keats makes us consciously aware of his delight in quietness. For instance, in *Endymion*, which is filled with this characteristic hush (how else when its creator's faith was that every 'thing of beauty' keeps 'a bower *quiet* for us'?) [99] we find him speaking of the 'silent workings of the dawn', [100] while in the sonnet 'At morn, at noon, at eve' he says of the poet:

> To his sight
> The hush of natural objects opens quite
> To the core. [101]

That arresting phrase 'the hush of natural objects' is a perfect definition of what we are trying to describe: little need be said further except perhaps to add that it illuminates that curious, though thoroughly characteristic, epithet in the *Ode to Psyche*— 'hush'd, cool-rooted flowers'.

Where sounds are described in Keats's poetry they are usually soft and delicate ones—the 'rustle of the reaped corn',* the whisper of leaves, the murmuring of breezes, fountains and streams, the humming of bees that wind their unobtrusive way in and out of so many of his poems. The following passage from *Endymion*—

> And as a willow keeps
> A patient watch over the stream that creeps
> Windingly by it, so the quiet maid
> Held her in peace: so that a whispering blade
> Of grass, a wailful gnat, a bee bustling

---

* *To Fancy*, l. 41. 'Rustle', 'murmur', 'hum', 'whisper' (and their derivatives) are significantly prominent in Keats's vocabulary. We may also note his ear for the rustling sound of dress: see 'the soft rustle of a maiden's gown' ('I stood tip-toe', l. 95); Madeline's attire 'rustling to her knees' (*The Eve of St Agnes*, l. 230); and 'rustle of those ample skirts' (*Hyperion*, III, 56).

> Down in the bluebells, or a wren light rustling
> Among sere leaves and twigs, might all be heard[102]

—is entirely typical of Keats's sensibility to the sounds of nature; and if we turn to the later and much more familiar sound picture in the last stanza of *To Autumn*, with its small gnats,* bleating lambs, crickets, redbreast, and 'twittering' swallows, our dominant impression is exactly the same. Characteristically his work contains a pleasant little sonnet on the songs of the grasshopper and cricket (true 'poetry of earth' to Keats's ear), and in the *Ode to a Nightingale* there is no description of the bird's song† half so memorable as the line,

> The murmurous haunt of flies on summer eves.

In this connexion it is interesting to note the synaesthetic effect of shadowy sound that Keats suggests in the poem 'Unfelt, unheard, unseen', with the lips that speak

> In ripest quiet, shadows of sweet sounds;[103]

and the sonnet *On the Sea* has a similar phrase in 'old, shadowy sound'. Indeed, such is his love of subdued, gentle sounds that sometimes they come close to silence itself and that he is conscious of a certain kind of music in silence:

> and then there crept
> A little noiseless noise among the leaves,
> Born of the very sigh that silence heaves.[104]

Such lines as these remind us that there was a characteristically individual sensation, as well perhaps as poetic fancy, behind the paradox that he states in a poem much concerned with the sensations of silence:

> Heard melodies are sweet, but those unheard
> Are sweeter.[105]

* Keats repeats the epithet 'wailful' from *Endymion*.
† Curiously there is very little description of bird-song in Keats's poetry.

We also understand why his sanctuary for Psyche should be set in a 'wide quietness'.[106]

Keats's pictures of the sea, though comparatively few in number, are also characterized by this love of soft, murmuring sound. Now and then there are hints of the sea in its more clamorous mood;* but the sea that is a background to the isle of Latmos in *Endymion* is a distant one of 'surgy murmurs', and a similar effect is created for the isle of Delos in Book III of *Hyperion:*

> Throughout all the isle
> There was no covert, no retired cave
> Unhaunted by the murmurous noise of waves,
> Though scarcely heard in many a green recess.[107]

Beside such characteristic passages as these we may also place those lines in his epistle *To J. H. Reynolds,* one of his loveliest pictures of the sea:

> 'Twas a quiet Eve;
> The rocks were silent—the wide sea did weave
> An untumultuous fringe of silver foam
> Along the flat brown sand.[108]

From these scattered impressions it is worth focusing our attention for a moment on a typical poem entirely concerned with the sea, the sonnet *On the Sea.* The feverish, compulsive inspiration behind this sonnet is well known: the escape from London and Keats's first walk in the Isle of Wight, the haunting of a line from *King Lear,* and the restless excitement of bringing himself to make a start on *Endymion.* 'For want of regular rest, I have been rather *narvus*—and the passage in Lear—"Do you not hear the sea?"—has haunted me intensely.'[109] What, in such circumstances as these, would Keats hear and behold in the sea of his own poem?

It is neither the continual agitation of the ocean nor its magnificent or terrifying surge and thunder that he attempts to express. His opening line, which establishes the impression

---

* For example *Hyperion*, II, 305–7.

of the whole sonnet, is just such another of those descriptions of murmuring sound as we have been quoting:

> It keeps eternal whisperings around
> Desolate shores . . .

From this his imagination turns for a moment to the 'mighty swell' (characteristic phrase) of the tide as it sweeps into innumerable caverns; but there is no sound-picture of this—of surging, roaring, booming water as the sea 'gluts' these caverns; and when he again describes sound the tide has receded, leaving the caves with 'their old shadowy sound'. For the rest of the sonnet it is the sea in 'gentle temper' that he pictures: we are invited—those of us 'whose ears are dinn'd with uproar rude'—to sit near some empty cavern's mouth, listening to the sound of hollow silence, its faint sea-echo, and —one may surely add—to the far-off whispering of the sea.

Occasionally, as with the 'silver snarling trumpets' in *The Eve of St Agnes*, a loud music obtrudes into the poetry; but Keats's marked preference is for the subdued sound of such instruments as lutes, lyres, pipes and flutes, or for the human voice in such gentle song as he describes in *Endymion*—

> snow-light cadences
> Melting to silence, when upon the breeze
> Some holy bark let forth an anthem sweet,
> To cheer itself to Delphi[110]

—lines that also illustrate one of the most individual and recurrent features of Keats's sensibility to sound—his love for an echoing, distant, or dying effect. In his early poems* nothing expresses this sensation more admirably than the close of his sonnet 'How many bards', where even the sound of the great bell is diminished by distance:

> So the unnumber'd sounds that evening store;
> The songs of birds—the whisp'ring of the leaves—
> The voice of waters—the great bell that heaves

* For further examples see 'I stood tip-toe', ll. 196–7: *To G. F. Mathew*, ll. 13–15: *Endymion*, I, 115–21; II, 358–60; II, 912–15; IV, 964–8.

> With solemn sound—and thousand others more,
> That distance of recognizance bereaves,
> Make pleasing music, and not wild uproar.[111]

However, the effect is just as common in the later poems: we experience it in the last stanza of the *Ode to a Nightingale*, where the fading-away of the bird's song is fully described; and a similar impression is created by the sound-picture that concludes *To Autumn*, with lambs bleating 'from hilly bourne' and swallows twittering 'in the skies'. Further, there is the effect that Keats creates in *The Eve of St Mark*—of the 'whispers hush, and shuffling feet'[112] of the church-goers that just penetrate into the silence of Bertha's room from the crowded streets outside; and all this is almost exactly paralleled by his description of Corinth in *Lamia:*

> And all her populous streets and temples lewd,
> Mutter'd, like tempest in the distance brew'd,
> To the wide-spreaded night above her towers.
> Men, women, rich and poor, in the cool hours,
> Shuffled their sandals o'er the pavement white . . .[113]

Lamia is notable for an outstanding example of a loud arresting sound used for imaginative or dramatic effect: this is the 'thrill of trumpets' that suddenly awakens Lycius from his long love-swoon into a realization of the outside world and its claims. Similar to this is the sound of the

> boisterous, midnight, festive clarion,
> The kettle-drum, and far-heard clarionet[114]

that suddenly bursts on Porphyro's ears as the doors of the distant banqueting-hall are momentarily flung open. But much more typical of Keats is the opposite—his use of silence for imaginative effect. On a small scale there is a good example of this in the sonnet *On first looking into Chapman's Homer*, where the wordless contemplation of Cortez and his soldiers,

> Silent, upon a peak in Darien,

epitomizes all their wonder at the sight of the Pacific and

rounds the poem off with a perfect conclusion*. Much of the deathliness and horror of the underworld in which Endymion first wanders is brought home to us by its silence; and again, in *The Eve of St Agnes*, an admirable imaginative effect is achieved by the contrast between the hushed atmosphere of Madeline's room and of those parts of the castle through which Porphyro moves and the distant but always menacing sounds from the banqueting-hall. There is also the *Ode on a Grecian Urn*, which, growing in some part from that germ in *Endymion*, 'silent as a consecrated urn', is filled with the mysterious sensation of silence in various forms.† Finally—and perhaps most impressive of all—there is that magical evocation of stillness and silence at the beginning of *Hyperion*, where the desolate Saturn sits

> quiet as a stone,
> Still as the silence round about his lair.[115]

This is the heavy silence of death, like that of Endymion's underworld; but it is also a soothing silence, and in time it is to be broken by sweet, gentle sounds—the 'murmurous noise of waves' around Apollo's isle of Delos and Apollo's own 'blissful golden melody'.[116]

These passages we have just been examining, and their numerous parallels, bear us—we may guess—fascinatingly close to the poet himself. More incontrovertible than any character-sketch left by friends and acquaintances, they bring us into contact with a man who, instinctively shunning loud noises, was agreeably soothed by gentle sounds and had an exceptionally appreciative ear for the minute sounds of nature—the stir of grass, the chirp of crickets, the wail of gnats; a man who was haunted by the sound of silence, that paradoxical fancy only to those who have never experienced it. Not for Keats, we may be sure, as for some other Romantics, the inspiration of clamorous winds or the roaring of some great

---

* There is a similar though less striking use of 'silently' to conclude the sonnet 'To one who has been long in city pent'.

† See Ch. IX, 'The *Ode on a Grecian Urn*', *passim*.

city. But we must go a little deeper than this if we are to understand this side of his nature. We must realize that his love of silence and soft sounds was intimately connected with a yearning for 'quietness' in the widest sense of the word,* for that serenity and calm poise of feelings that he cherished the more deeply for his long experience of feverish agitation. There is a poem that sets this aspiration in the context of his homely, everyday existence: this is the early sonnet *To My Brothers*, which, after its description of the faint cracklings of the fire, of the poet himself writing and Tom absorbedly reading, goes on:

> This is your birthday Tom, and I rejoice
> That thus it passes smoothly, quietly.
> Many such eves of gently whispering noise
> May we together pass, and calmly try
> What are this world's true joys.[117]

Hush and tranquillity of mind are felt everywhere in this sonnet, and we cannot doubt that Keats was expressing his ideal of ordinary domestic life. For this same aspiration at a higher level of feeling and imagination we may turn to his description of the Cave of Quietude, that profoundest passage of *Endymion*, or to the close of the sonnet 'After dark vapours', which creates a memorable combination of soft sounds and tranquil mood:

> The calmest thoughts come round us—as of leaves
>   Budding,—fruit ripening in stillness,—autumn suns
> Smiling at eve upon the quiet sheaves,—
> Sweet Sappho's cheek,—a sleeping infant's breath,—
>   The gradual sand that through an hour-glass runs,—
> A woodland rivulet,—a Poet's death.[118]

From this examination of the imagery and sensations of Keats's poetry we may see that they are predominantly of a pleasurable kind, what he himself would have called 'luxuries'. To adopt a phrase from one of his first sonnets,† our senses are continuously 'spell'd' with deliciousness; and it is significant

* These remarks should be read in conjunction with Ch. IX.
† *To a Friend who sent me some Roses*, l. 12.

that—at least in his early work—his favourite word 'soft' is sometimes applied by him to poetry itself.* The dangers of such a sensibility—exquisiteness, indulgence, voluptuousness, even touches of sloppiness and decadence—are clearly manifest in his writing, especially in the poetry written up till 1819, and even the works of that annus mirabilis, including the great odes, are not unmarred by these weaknesses. But in the main, for all its deliberate cultivation of beauty† and sensuous pleasure, his poetry communicates an admirable masculinity and vitality. What he enjoyed he usually experienced with a rare intensity and gusto; as well as a keen visual sense, particularly responsive to colour, he had what Wilson Knight, in an excellent phrase, calls a 'heavy, rounded perception' of things,‡ a firm, hand-feeling awareness of their texture, substance, and solidity; and (perhaps one of his final secrets) he was often able to render the objects of his sense-impressions with an altogether exceptional immediacy. In many of his finest passages we seem to pass, through some indefinable poetic magic, beyond the equivalences of mere description into the living actuality of his original experience.

From this cultivation of beauty and 'luxuries' it follows that the world of his poetry is a limited one, with some monotonies. On the other hand, because he was singularly endowed with acute perceptiveness in all his senses—perhaps more so than any other poet except Shakespeare—as we read his poetry we are inclined to forget its limitations. Intensity takes the place of range.

At any rate there can be no doubt that the images and sensations in his poetry do constitute a recognizable and distinctive 'world', and it is this achievement that establishes one of his strongest claims to be considered a major poet.

* See 'soft verse', Epistle *To My Brother George*, l. 108; 'soft numbers', 'I stood tip-toe', l. 237; and some of the implications of *Sleep and Poetry*—for example 'soft floatings from a faint-heard hymning', l. 34.

† Cf. Leavis, *Revaluations*, p. 255: 'His concern for beauty meant, at any rate in the first place, a concentration upon the purely delightful in experience.'

‡ *The Starlit Dome*, p. 265.

CHAPTER III

MELODY IN KEATS'S 'POESY'

By ear industrious, and attention meet . . .
Sonnet, 'If by dull rhymes'

WHEN Keats advised Shelley to be 'more of an artist, and "load every rift" of your subject with ore'[1] he was undoubtedly thinking chiefly of sensuous imagery in poetry; he had expressed the same fundamental belief nearly three years before in a letter to Taylor about poetry: 'Its touches of Beauty should never be half way, thereby making the reader breathless instead of content: the rise, the progress, the setting of imagery should like the Sun come natural to him—shine over him and set soberly although in magnificence, leaving him in the Luxury of twilight.'[2] But though there is no mention in all this of the music of poetry, the incomparable richness of Keats's own work does not arise solely from the abundance of imagery; his poetry lingers in the ear because of its resonance and beauty of word music: it is golden in sound as well as substance. Among our poets he is certainly one of the most musical.

Even his earliest poems, including many of the mediocre ones, are usually pleasant on the ear, and this is particularly true of *Endymion* where the writing, for all his fumbling and often clumsy handling of the heroic couplet form, is highly impressive for its sustained melodic beauty. How much of the richness and sweetness of his description of the sleeping Adonis, for instance, is communicated by the sound of the words as well as by the images they evoke:

> And coverlids gold-tinted like the peach,
> Or ripe October's faded marigolds,
> Fell sleek about him in a thousand folds—
> Not hiding up an Apollonian curve
> Of neck and shoulder . . .[3]

Besides this music that gives resonance to most of the main passages of the poem (and to the Pan and Bacchus odes), there are many wayside beauties of sound to delight and surprise us, like the description of the shout

> That lingered in the air like dying rolls
> Of abrupt thunder, when Ionian shoals
> Of dolphins bob their noses through the brine,[4]

or the description, so contrastingly different in sound quality, of the lions that draw Cybele's chariot, where the heavy but muffled vowels, the close and speed-slowing repetitions (m*a*ned h*a*le, s*u*rly—n*e*rvy, br*ow*—dr*ow*sily—c*ow*ering), and the weight of the consonants (especially the *r*'s combined with some other consonant) are so admirably suggestive of a ponderous, sleep- or spell-charmed strength:

> Four maned lions hale
> The sluggish wheels; solemn their toothed maws,
> Their surly eyes brow-hidden, heavy paws
> Uplifted drowsily, and nervy tails
> Cowering their tawny brushes.*

No doubt of course that this music, which comes to perfection in the great poems of 1818 and 1819, was to a large extent spontaneously and subconsciously achieved, an instinctive choice of words in which instinct had been deepened and assured by a close reading of poets like Spenser, Shakespeare, and Milton. Even the most musical-minded of poets do not deliberately set about creating some melodic pattern of

---

* II, 643–7. With all its individual beauty of sound, this passage, as De Selincourt has pointed out (*Poems of John Keats*, p. 434) owes much to Sandys's translation of Ovid. For example, compare 'Their tufted tails whisk up the dust' with Keats's original lines 'And nervy tails Cowering their tufted brushes to the dust'.

If any reader feels that the sound suggestions described above are purely subjective and imaginary (and our response to poetic melody can be that), he should also remember that Keats himself had a conscious appreciation of the meaningful associations of sound. Thus, in one of his annotations on Milton, we find him writing: 'there is a cool pleasure in the very sound of *vale*.'

alliterated consonants and chiming vowel sounds. But the poet who is particularly sensitive to the music of words will certainly have many moments when he consciously works for some melodic effect,* especially when it is to bring out and intensify something suggested by his initial inspiration, while improvement in sound will be a main consideration in his revision of what is either in his head or already down on paper. Such a poet is aptly distinguished by the term 'craftsman' or 'artist', and though it is often the mark of a small poet that he is simply an excellent craftsman (in other matters as well as word-music), neither of these terms necessarily impugns the depth or organic nature of the poetry that is finally produced.

Keats, as his advice to Shelley shows, certainly regarded himself as an 'artist',† and though he says very little about the music of poetry in his letters, his sonnet 'If by dull rhymes' furnishes the clearest possible evidence that an alert attention to sound effect constituted an important part of his artistry. 'Let us inspect the lyre,' he says,

> and see what may be gain'd
> By ear industrious, and attention meet;
> Misers of sound and syllable, no less
> Than Midas of his coinage . . .[5]

Admittedly he is concerned here chiefly with formal and rhythmical effect within the sonnet; but a poet who writes with such an 'industrious ear' (we note how the epithet implies a certain amount of hard work and deliberate contrivance) can hardly avoid paying attention to the melody of sound and syllable as well.

* I seem to remember reading somewhere of De la Mare's long search to find the word 'roves', which gave him a perfect alliteration and assonance for the line 'Roves back the rose' (*All that's past*, l. 8).

† It is true that Keats came to reject Miltonic verse because it 'can not be written but in an artful or rather artist's humour' (*Letters*, p. 384). But there is no real contradiction between this and his advice to Shelley. His rejection of Miltonic verse was the rejection of a poetry that (so he believed) was entirely of artistic 'making'. He wanted to devote himself to the sort of poetry that was *expression*—a working out through poetry of his individual experience.

83

It so happens that one of our two marginal quotations from *Endymion*—the description of Cybele's lions—affords an excellent example of what the music in Keats's poetry often owes to an artistry that must have been in some degree conscious. Beautiful and satisfying as these lines are in their melodic suggestiveness, they were certainly not native wood-notes wild, effortlessly and spontaneously produced. There is clear manuscript evidence that Keats had to work hard for his ultimate effect; and it is easy to see that his first draft is inferior to the final version largely because it is so much poorer in melodic quality:

> Four lions draw
> The wheels in sluggish time—each toothed **maw**
> Shut patiently—eyes hid in tawny veils—
> Drooping about their paws, and nervy tails
> Cowering their tufted brushes to the dust.[6]

All the melodic suggestions that we have already analysed in the final version are absent in these lines, while there is far too much of the light-weight *u* sound in 'sluggish', 'shut', 'tufted', 'brushes' and 'dust'. Merely from the difference of sound these nondescript lions of the first draft are altogether different from the lions of the final text, and though Keats may have rejected his first inspiration for various reasons, it is a reasonable guess that he was dissatisfied with the sound of what he had written and felt that something far more appropriate to his subject could be achieved. But if he did cancel his initial draft for its melodic weakness, the final perfection did not come at once, and it is interesting to note that the three near-rhymes (*maned-hale*, *surly-nervy*, *brow-drowsily*) that contribute so much to the passage as it now stands were all produced by late alterations.

Again, in the quoted description of the dolphins, there is also something that probably illustrates Keats's keen ear for the sound of his poetry. The fair copy of *Endymion* that went to the printer has opposite the line

Of dolphins bob their noses through the brine[7]

the words 'push', 'raise' in the hand of Taylor the publisher, and Woodhouse has left an explanatory note on this in one of his transcripts of Keats's poems: 'The words *raise push* were suggested to the author: but he insisted on retaining *bob*.'[8] No doubt Taylor (and possibly Woodhouse too) objected to 'bob' because it was, to his way of thinking, an unpoetic word of a colloquial or vulgar ring. But, to say nothing of the other arguments that Keats may have brought forward in its favour —the precedents in his beloved Shakespeare for such homely words, the sportive context in which 'bob' went with 'noses' in an appropriate phrase, and the flatness of the two suggested alternatives—he must have felt, as we do, the excellence of 'bob' in the melody of the line: its own sound was suitably abrupt and light, it formed a double alliteration with 'brine', and (depending on the way Keats pronounced the first vowel in 'dolphins') it may have furnished an assonance with that word.

Occasionally in his writing Keats produces the simple and more mechanical type of onomatopoeia: that is to say, he uses words whose sound directly imitates some sound that he is describing. A familiar instance of this is to be found in the *Ode to a Nightingale*, in a line that gives us the humming and murmuring of flies as they swarm about the musk-rose—

The *murmurous* haunt of flies on *summer* eves.

—However, as the few passages we have already quoted from his poetry plainly show, one of the most unmistakable signs of his mastery of poetic melody is his power over the more subtle sort of onomatopoeia, when, that is to say, the sound-texture of his verse matches or even suggests whatever he is trying to communicate—image, emotion or mood. Sometimes this power manifests itself in a single line like

Thy hair soft-lifted by the winnowing wind[9]

where the image is wonderfully suggested by the succession of light *i* sounds and the *f* and *w* consonants. Nothing in sound could be lighter and softer than that line: it is melodically perfect. Or again—to quote a less familiar illustration—how suggestively the full, fat sound of 'plump' contrasts with the shrivelled, flat vowels of the rest of the line in

> Ere a lean bat could plump its wintery skin.[10]

At other times this magic of suggestive sound is the effect of an entire passage, as in the description of Cybele's lions or the much admired beginning of the first *Hyperion*. For another impressive example of this sustained power we may turn to the opening stanza of the *Ode to a Nightingale*. This begins with four lines in which the monotonous, clogging, and half-rhyming combinations of *m* and *n* nasal sounds with some other consonant in 'numbness', 'sense', 'hemlock', 'drunk', 'emptied' and 'sunk' (along with the weighting monosyllabic words and the slow, laboured movement of the rhythm) create an exact musical equivalent of the poet's drugged, dull mood:

> My heart aches, and a drowsy numbness pains
> My sense, as though of hemlock I had drunk,
> Or emptied some dull opiate to the drains
> One minute past, and Lethe-wards had sunk . . .

The chief exception to the dominant melodic pattern here arises from those two sharp *a* sounds in 'aches' and 'pains' in the first line; but these words are perfectly in keeping with the poet's sensation: their sound expresses the momentary stabs of conscious pain into his drugged numbness and suspension of feeling. From this, through a short modulatory section of neutral sound—

> 'Tis not through envy of thy happy lot (*etc.*)

—we emerge into a passage of marked melodic contrast, where the clear, ringing, and sometimes richly intense sounds of the words perfectly correspond with the contrasting happiness of the nightingale:

86

> That thou, light-winged Dryad of the trees,
>   In some melodious plot
> Of beechen green, and shadows numberless,
>   Singest of summer in full-throated ease.

In 'numberless' and 'summer' we catch a reminiscence of the sound pattern of the opening lines, and 'numberless' in particular brings us back to 'numbness' in the opening line. This slight repetition—a quite instinctive touch no doubt—is good because it holds the two contrasting parts of the stanza in aural unity. But 'numberless' and 'summer' no longer have the effect they would have produced in the opening lines, for they are subdued in a very different sort of melodic texture in which, against a background alliteration of the *l* and *s* consonants, the *o* of 'melodious', 'shadows', and 'throated' is the dominant and recurring vowel sound, varied with the close repetitions of 'light'—'Dryad', 'beechen—green', and 'numberless'—'summer'.

At this point it is perhaps timely to mention two important reservations to what has so far been said. In the first place, the melodic suggestiveness is not always traceable to some fairly obvious phonetic cause and is perhaps best left as part of the 'magic' of poetic incantation. For instance, any inclination to yawn as we read

> Or on a half-reap'd furrow sound asleep,
>   Drows'd with the fume of poppies . . .[11]

is both appropriate to the image and a compliment to Keats's art. Yet though this hypnotic effect may be partly induced by the melody, especially by the phrase 'Drows'd with the fume', in which the lingering vowel 'drows'd' swiftly follows on 'sound', and by the half-rhyme of 'reap'd' and 'asleep', these explanations are not entirely satisfying.*

* As another example of Keats's attention to melodic effect in his revision it is interesting to note that the half-rhyme 'drows'd' was a second thought for 'dos'd' ('dozed'?) and 'dazed', and that the first draft had the hard-sounding 'field' in the place of the soft and sleep-inviting 'furrow'—'Or sound asleep in a half reaped field' . . .

In the second place, there are many passages in Keats's poetry where the verbal melody simply constitutes a pattern of pleasing sounds: it is appropriate as a sort of background accompaniment to the scene, mood, or sentiment that Keats is depicting, but not in itself particularly suggestive.

The substitution of 'furrow' for the original 'field' in line 16 of *To Autumn* leads us to another important feature of Keats's melody. Occasionally, especially in the first two books of *Hyperion*, in lines like—

> Instead of thrones, hard flint they sat upon,
> Couches of rugged stone, and slaty ridge
> Stubborn'd with iron[12]

—he successfully attempts a harsh, strong, or disturbing kind of music. Nevertheless, it would not be eccentric to observe of this quotation from *Hyperion* that the word that spoils the main sound effect—'couches'—is the most characteristically Keatsian word in it, for the general and predominant melody of Keats's verse is a rich, soft (but, as we shall see, weighted and measured) mellifluousness that is admirably described, and represented, by his own term 'poesy', which he almost always prefers to 'poetry'. Like that of the nightingale, his song, in the narrative poems as well as the shorter pieces, is usually one of 'full-throated ease'. In other words, his characteristic melody is the perfect counterpart of those typical images and sensations we examined in the last chapter, and though for convenience of description and analysis we may separate the melody and imagery of his poetry, in reality they are the reflections of the one and same sensibility expressing itself in language. Very roughly speaking, we may say that Keats moulded his poems out of words where the sound as well as the other sense-impressions satisfied his instincts for the rich, the soft, the smooth, the hushed, the easeful, and so on.* But if the melody of his poetry is in this way instinctive and highly

---

* See also Appendix I.

88

individual, there can be little doubt that it was stimulated and encouraged by the work of another great poet who had created a similar kind of music superlatively well. This poet was his first great love, Spenser; and when in his *Epistle to Charles Cowden Clarke* he writes of

> Spenserian vowels that elope with ease,
> And float along like birds o'er summer seas[13]

he is describing—and exemplifying—not only the essence of Spenserian melody, but of his own from *Endymion* to the Odes. Possibly, if he had lived longer, the characteristic sound-texture of his poetry would have changed; there was a departure of one kind, under a heavy influence of Milton, in *Hyperion*, and of another, probably more organic and individual, in *The Fall of Hyperion*. But as a description of the music in most of the poems he has left us that couplet from the *Epistle to Charles Cowden Clarke* would be hard to improve on. Its chief defect is that it suggests a fluidity and swiftness of rhythmical impulse that might be true of most of Spenser (and of Shelley) but is not true of Keats, for smooth and mellifluous as his melody is, in his best poetry it is crossed with a rhythm that is measured and slow-moving.* It is this gravid quality that most sharply distinguishes the rhythm of Keats from that of Shelley, of the ode *To Autumn* from that of the *Ode to the West Wind*, and, fully explored, this rhythmical difference would take us deep into the contrasting temperaments of the two poets.

It should also be added that Keats often reveals a keen ear for the effect of melodic texture on rhythmical movement. A small but capital instance of this sort of mastery of language (largely an instinctive matter, one guesses) occurs in the following lines from *Hyperion* (1, 39–41):

---

* Cf. Garrod, *Keats*, p. 89: 'A movement graver than lyric, harmonies of which the beauty, however richly sensuous, has yet a quality of earnestness —towards verse of this kind his temperament sets strongly almost from the beginning.'

As if the vanward clouds of evil days
Had spent their malice, and the sullen rear
Was with its stored thunder labouring up.

In the first line and a half, down to 'malice', the sounds, particularly of the vowels, are such that the rhythmical movement is rapid and comparatively light. This is in keeping with the sense, as the 'vanward clouds' are over and done with. Then, in the rest of the second line and the third line, the rhythm notably—and ominously—slows up, and one feels that the much more weighty vowel sounds have a good deal to do with this change and contrast in rhythmical movement. How admirably, for instance, 'stored thunder labouring up' matches the pace of massive, piled-up, heavily-moving thunder cloud.

There are many other passages in Keats's poetry where the ear will easily detect this kind of interplay between sound-texture and the rhythmic impulse. The odes, for instance, contain many examples. But analysis of them is a tricky business, and this is a 'mystery' of the art best left to the elucidation of a poet.*

Earlier we maintained that Keats is rightly considered as an 'artist' kind of poet since (to say nothing of other aspects of his craftsmanship) he possesses an exceptionally alert and subtle sense of the music of verse and often works for his effects with some degree of deliberation. But we must go further than this. In spite of the blankness of his letters in this matter, we must believe that he had thought deeply on the subject of poetic music and had indeed reached something as systematic as a 'principle of melody in verse'. Our evidence for this belief comes from his friend of the *Endymion* period, Bailey, who wrote in his memoranda for Monckton Milnes: 'One of his favourite topics of discourse was the principle of melody in Verse.'[14]

Unfortunately Bailey's attempt to describe this principle is

---

* Edith Sitwell would no doubt do the job admirably.

brief, fragmentary, and on one important point tantalizingly obscure. On the other hand, if we supplement Bailey's remarks with a close examination of Keats's actual practice, taking into account his revisionary work on some of his poems and paying special attention to passages that we know him to have thought well of, and if we utilize the clues to be found sometimes in his observations on other poets, it is not difficult to ascertain something of what this 'principle of melody' must have been.

For a start let us consider the sentence of Bailey that, from its phrasing, appears to give us the essence of Keats's speculation: 'Keats's theory was, that the vowels should be so managed as not to clash with one another so as to mar the melody,— and yet that they should be interchanged, like differing notes of music, to prevent monotony.' The meaning of this sentence, which is later repeated by the phrase, 'skilful variation of the vowel sounds', is fairly clear: verse is poor in melodic quality when the vowel sounds occur randomly, without any sort of pattern, and when, because of this randomness, they may clash discordantly. In verse that is melodically pleasing there is a combination of several dominant vowel sounds that are repeated and variously combined. There is a unifying and delightful *pattern* of sound that is more or less consciously perceived by the ear of the reader and to some extent at least deliberately contrived by the poet. At any rate there is sufficient poetic craftsmanship at a conscious level to justify such descriptive words as 'managed' and 'skilful'.

This interpretation is confirmed and clarified by what Bailey previously says in his memoranda about Keats's admiration for Chatterton:

The melody of the verses of the marvellous Boy who perished in his pride, enchanted the author of *Endymion*. Methinks I now hear him recite, or *chant*,* in his peculiar manner, the following stanza of the Roundelay sung by the minstrels of Ella:—

* An interesting record of Keats's manner of reading poetry.

Come with acorn cup and thorn
Drain my hertys blood away;
Life and all its good I scorn;
Dance by night or feast by day.
The first line to his ear possessed the great charm . . .*

Now if we read these lines from Chatterton attentively we shall perceive that they furnish a good example of what Bailey describes as Keats's theory of the management of vowel sounds. In this passage the *a* of 'acorn', repeated in 'drain', 'away' and 'day', is the chief sound in the melodic pattern, and it is combined ith the recurring *i* of 'life', 'I', and 'night'. (There is also a good deal of consonant repetition, notably in the alliteration of 'drain', 'dance', and 'day'; but Bailey says nothing of consonant melody in his exposition of Keats's theory.) Of particular interest is the fact that it was the first line that possessed the great charm for Keats's ear, for this has a very emphatic pattern of melody, with its *c* alliteration and its pairs of vowels closely interwoven:

$$\overset{1}{\text{Come}} \text{ with } \overset{2}{\text{acorn}} \overset{1}{\text{cup}} \text{ and } \overset{2}{\text{thorn}}$$

In his own practice Keats certainly made a very considerable use of the melodic principle embodied in this admired line from Chatterton, and there are innumerable examples in his own poetry of a line or two in which pairs, and sometimes triplets, of vowel sounds are variously combined, sometimes simply, sometimes complexly. Here are some varied examples† drawn from a wide range of his poetry:

$$\text{And } \overset{1}{\text{Ne}}\overset{2}{\text{ptune}} \text{ made for thee a } \overset{2}{\text{spu}}\overset{1}{\text{my}} \text{ tent.}[15]$$

$$\text{Though } \overset{1}{\text{Di}}\overset{2}{\text{do}} \overset{1}{\text{si}}\overset{2}{\text{lent}} \text{ is in } \overset{1}{\text{under}}\text{-grove.}[16]$$

* For the light thrown on other matters discussed in this study, the rest of the paragraph may be added: 'Indeed his sense of melody was quite exquisite, as is apparent in his own verses; and in none more than in the numerous passages of his *Endymion*.'

† We cannot of course always be sure of Keats's pronunciation of a vowel. The obvious cases of doubt are indicated by brackets.

And on her silver cross soft amethyst.[17]

And diamonded with panes of quaint device.[18]

By nightshade, ruby grape of Proserpine.[19]

Or sinking as the light wind lives or dies.[20]

Deaf to his throbbing throat's long, long melodious moan.[21]

From high Olympus had he stolen light

On this side of Jove's clouds, to escape the sight . . .[22]

down they came,

Crown'd with green leaves, and faces all on flame.[23]

at the rising of the sun,

About the wilds they hunt with spear and horn,

On spleenful unicorn.[24]

Sometimes, as in the fifth quotation above (from the *Ode on Melancholy*), these vowel patterns concentrate sounds that have been running through the previous lines, sometimes not.

Before proceeding any further in our analysis of what was almost certainly a part of Keats's 'principle of melody' we must also point out that, numerous as these instances of the melodically patterned line are in his poetry, he also had an appreciative sense of the pleasurable richness of sound that can be produced by a line of varied vowels. A very familiar example of such richness is to be found in the line from *To Autumn*,

While barred clouds bloom the soft-dying day.

Here, though there are of course two strong alliterations, all eight of the principal vowel sounds are different, so that the line forms the antithesis of Chatterton's 'Come with acorn cup and thorn'. Further, Keats appreciated, instinctively at any rate, the melodic pleasure that can be produced by contrasts between these two types of line, and it is interesting to observe that the line just quoted from *To Autumn* is followed by

And touch the stubble-plains with rosy hue,

where we have the closely placed assonance of 'touch', and 'stubble', a near-assonance of 'hue' with 'bloom', and where 'plains' repeats the sound of 'day' in the preceding line.

But to return to our main point: when Bailey attempts to describe Keats's principle of melody he is thinking, not of the line or two, but of the melodic pattern of combined and inter-changed vowels that runs through a substantial passage of verse, as for instance the *a*'s and *i*'s in the stanza from Chatter-ton's *Roundelay*. This indeed is the most impressive form of this kind of melodic effect, and examples of it are so abundant in Keats's poetry that it must also have constituted part of his theory. As an illustration from his early poetry we may in-stance one of the stanzas in the ode to Bacchus in *Endymion*, where the melody is mainly produced by the interweaving of two dominant vowel sounds:

Within his car, aloft, young Bacchus stood,
Trifling his ivy-dart, in dancing mood,
With sidelong laughing;
And little rills of crimson wine imbrued
His plump white arms, and shoulders, enough white
For Venus' pearly bite:
And near him rode Silenus on his ass,
Pelted with flowers as he on did pass
Tipsily quaffing.[25]

Two details in the melody of this stanza deserve notice. First, the interchange of the vowels is concentrated at one point to produce a patterned line of the type we have already described—

   1   1   2   2

Trifling his ivy-dart, in dancing mood.

Secondly (the significance of this will be more appreciated when we come to consider another aspect of Keats's probable theory), we may observe how the varied first three lines are followed contrastingly by a line of one much repeated sound:

And little rills of crimson wine imbued

For a later example of this same sustained chiming of two or three combined vowels we may turn to a passage from *Lamia*. This passage is particularly apposite here, for the two principal vowel sounds* are the same as those in the stanza from the Bacchus ode just quoted: also, since the passage is part of a specimen of *Lamia* that Keats included in a letter to Taylor,[26] we may reasonably suppose that he thought well of it:

A haunting music, sole perhaps and lone

Supportress of the faery-roof, made moan

                                1   2

Throughout, as fearful the whole charm might fade.

        1

Fresh carved cedar, mimicking a glade

  1   2   2

Of palm and plantain, met from either side,

 2   2

High in the midst, in honour of the bride:

  1

Two palms and then two plantains, and so on,

 2   2   1

From either side their stems branch'd one to one

          2

All down the aisled place; and beneath all

There ran a stream of lamps straight on from wall to wall.[27]

---

* Keats appears to have been particularly fond of one of these sounds, the open *a* of 'carved' etc. For instance the sound appears prominently in Stanza v of the *Ode to a Nightingale* and in the opening lines of stanza xxiv of *The Eve of St Agnes*.

Two interesting points of detail to note are, first, the prominent *o* sound of 'sole', 'lone',* 'moan', 'whole', which strongly patterns the first three lines and then disappears from the melody, and, secondly, the further example in the last line and a half of a close melodic pattern on the 'Chatterton' model, though this time the two combined sounds are different from those in the main combination and interchange:

1

and beneath all

2   1   2

There ran a stream of lamps . . .

To these illustrations we may add two further ones from *The Eve of St Agnes*, their additional interest being that they carry a known, manuscript record of revision that clearly demonstrates Keats's close and (we may believe) conscious attention to melodic effect. The first is the 'casement' stanza (xxiv), which, incomparable in its pictorial richness, is also an outstanding passage of Keatsian music. Its general melodic pattern very much resembles that of the lines just quoted from *Lamia*: it begins with three lines that are dominated by one vowel sound ('arch'd', 'garlanded', 'carven', 'grass') and then combines and interchanges two *a* and *i* vowel sounds. The chief difference from the *Lamia* passage is that there is a greater abundance of detailed melodic effect, especially in the alliteration (internal as well as external) of the *m*, *d*, and *s* consonants, and in the number of single, vowel-patterned lines. For instance, in addition to the line already quoted—

1   2   2   1

And diamonded with panes of quaint device

—there is also:

1 1   2   2

And twilight saints and dim emblazonings.

---

* Was it the charm of the repeated sound that justified for Keats the pronounced tautology here?

A further difference is that there is another vowel, the short *i* that runs from 'triple' to 'dim', which perhaps furnishes a third sound in the general pattern. It is these differences that make this stanza so much richer in its music than the extract from *Lamia*.

> A casement high and triple-arch'd there was,
>
> All garlanded with carven imag'ries
>
> Of fruits, and flowers, and bunches of knot-grass,
>
> And diamonded with panes of quaint device,
>
> Innumerable of stains and splendid dyes,
>
> As are the tiger-moth's deep-damask'd wings;
>
> And in the midst, 'mong thousand heraldries,
>
> And twilight saints, and dim emblazonings,
>
> A shielded scutcheon blush'd with blood of kings and queens.[28]

This stanza also shows how close some of this chiming of vowel sounds comes to rhyme and near-rhyme ('pains', 'stains', and 'saints'), while the melody of the last line is of particular interest since, after so much varied interchange of vowels, it is strikingly limited and repetitive:

> A shielded scutcheon blush'd with blood of kings and queens.

The autograph manuscript shows that Keats had to work hard before he achieved these greatly admired lines. It is unlikely, of course, that melodic improvement was his sole concern as he experimented with the phrasing of this stanza, but when we read the first and longest of his two cancelled openings, we cannot fail to notice how inferior this is to the final version, or how the inferiority largely arises from a lack of combined and interchanged vowels:

A Casement ach'd tripple archd and diamonded

With many coloured glass fronted the moon
                    were of
In midst of which a shilded scutcheon shed

High blushing gules; upon she Kneeled saintly down

And inly prayed for grace and heavenly boon.

The blood-red gules fell on her silver cross

And her whitest hands devout[29]

On the other hand, deficient as this first draft is in melodic beauty when compared with the final text, it contains, along with other experimental lines and phrases for the stanza, the germ of the ultimate melody, so that it seems reasonable to think that Keats worked to bring out what he perceived, perhaps subconsciously, in his initial inspiration. Two facts in particular point to this conclusion. First, in both of the cancelled openings he sticks to a first line—

A Casement ach'd tripple archd and diamonded

and

A Casement trpple archd and high

—that closely resembles the first line of the final version and so, as it were, establishes the four chief vowel sounds of that version—'casement', 'arch'd',* 'triple', and 'high' or 'diamonded'—along with the *m* and *d* consonants that were to become

* In connexion with the vowel sound of 'arch'd' it is interesting to see that the first of the cancelled openings retains this sound in 'glass', which may in turn have ultimately suggested 'grass', while the other, shorter cancelled opening—

A Casement trpple archd and high
All garlanded with carven imageries
Of fruits and trailing flowers and sunny corn ears parch'd

—plays with the sound in another word, 'parch'd', as a possible rhyme.

Stanza XXIV, *The Eve of St Agnes* (photostat from autograph MS. in possession of the Harvard College Library).

so heavily alliterated. Secondly, though the words that iterate the *a* of 'casement' in the rough draft largely disappear, the sound itself is retained in fresh words, and intensified: thus 'c*a*sement', 's*ai*ntly', 'pr*a*yed', 'gr*a*ce' from the first version, along with 'tr*ai*ling' from the second, become in the final version of the stanza 'c*a*sement', 'quaint', 'st*a*ins', 's*ai*nts', and 'embl*a*zonings'.

It is also revealing to glance at the MS. history of that lovely line,

> As are the tiger-moth's deep-damask'd wings.

Once again perfection did not come without a good deal of experiment. The first version went:

> As is the wing of evening tiger-moths.

Over this Keats wrote a line of much alteration (and presumably hesitation):

> sunset
> As is the tiger moths ~~rich~~ deep ~~damasked~~ wings.

Later the verb was made plural and 'damask'd' restored.

One point of melodic significance here is how, after contemplating the epithet 'rich' for the moth's wings, Keats scored it out in favour of 'd*ee*p-damask'd', thus retaining the strongest vowel sound in his original epithet '*e*vening'. Again, grammar and rhyme apart, the change of the verb is of interest in showing how an apparently unimportant word may have a notable effect on sound-texture, for 'are' is much more in keeping with the velvety softness of the line than 'is'. But the most revealing point is Keats's marked hesitation between 'sunset' and 'damask'd'.* Though he definitely preferred 'sunset' at one stage, the word had little to commend it except

---

* Ridley in *Keats's Craftsmanship*, which contains an excellent chapter on the development of the poem from the original drafts to the final text, suggests that Keats was distracted by the preceding 'innumerable' and 'splendid' into a reminiscence of Mrs Radcliff's 'sunsets'. He quotes what is certainly a coincidental parallel from one of Mrs Radcliff's novels—'The sun, involved in clouds of splendid and unnumerable hues, was setting.'

an assonance with "'mong' and a remoter one with 'bunches' and 'blush'd', and an alliteration on a consonant already alliterated enough. How right his ear was to return finally to 'deep-damask'd': this compound, in conjunction with 'moth's', gives us a delightful double alliteration on *d* and *m*, and 'damask'd', especially with its *m,* is admirably suggestive of the softness of a moth's wings.

Our second illustration from *The Eve of St Agnes* is stanza xxx, which is particularly appropriate to our purpose since Leigh Hunt records in his *Autobiography* how Keats read this passage to him 'with great relish and particularity, conscious of what he had set forth.'[30] No doubt much of Keats's 'relish' must have been for the luscious imagery, for nothing he had read in the *Arabian Nights*, Wieland's *Oberon*, or anywhere else, had ever evoked such a delectable feast of dainties. But, like his readers, he must also have relished the melodic delight of this stanza, where once again, along with the plentiful minor patterns of sound (sm*oo*th, s*oo*ther, *lu*cent; b*la*nched, *a*rgosy, and possibly Sam*a*rcand; and the *s, l,* and *c* alliterations), the chief musical effect is produced by the sustained interweaving of two dominant vowels:

> And still[1] she slept an a[2]zure-lidded[1] sleep,
>
> In blanched linen[1], smooth, and lavender'd[2],
>
> While he from forth the closet brought a heap
>
> Of candied[2] apple[1], quince[2], and plum[1], and gourd
>
> With jellies soother[1] than the creamy curd,
>
> And lucent[1] syrops[1], tinct with cinnamon[1 (2)];
>
> Manna[2 (2)] and dates, in argosy[2] transferr'd
>
> From Fez; and spiced dainties[1], every one,
>
> From silken[1] Samarcand[2 2] to cedar'd Lebanon[(2)].[31]

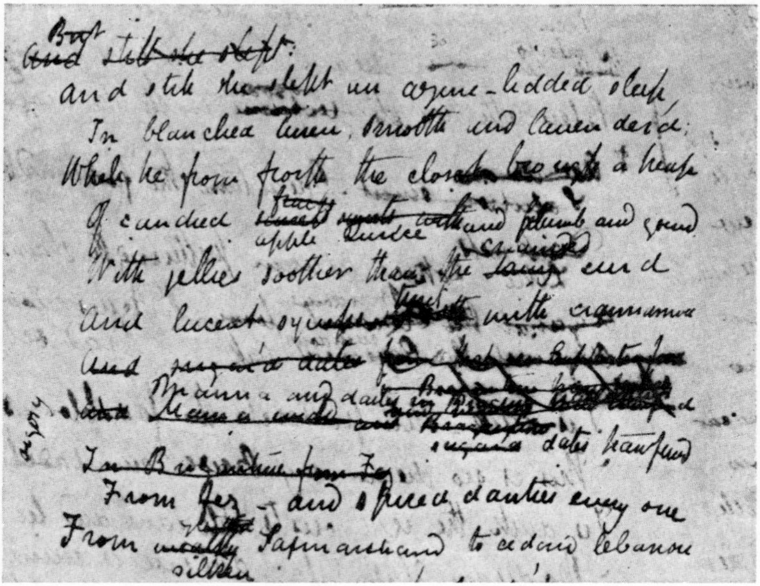

Stanza xxx, *The Eve of St Agnes* (photostat from autograph MS. in possession of the Harvard College Library).

The autograph MS. of this stanza shows it to have been even more heavily worked over than stanza xxiv, and it would therefore appear rather a jumble if transferred exactly to print.* From it we can however trace a process of composition much like the one that seems to have occured in stanza xxiv, though we cannot always be certain about the sequence of Keats's alterations. Down to 'candied' in line 4 there is only one trivial correction,† and we may reasonably think of the first four lines, like the more or less constant first line in the cancelled openings of stanza xxiv, as establishing the dominant melodic pattern of the stanza. In the numerous alterations that follow 'candied' the chief general effect is to sustain and intensify this pattern. Thus, in line 4, from the phrase 'Of candied sweets sweets with' (the last three words scored out), Keats went to 'candied fruits', and from that to the two specific fruits, 'apple' and 'quince',‡ that also gave him the two chiming sounds of his melody. In the next line but one 'tinct', carrying on the sound of 'quince' and 'syrops', was an afterthought for 'sooth' or 'smooth',§ while 'cinnamon' may have been clinched either by the sounds of the main melodic pattern or by 'tinct' if this correction was made before the rest of the line was written down.** Further, in the last line, 'silken', which carried the s and l alliteration along with the short i vowel, was a preference over 'wealthy', which had only the l to commend it in sound, and 'glutted', which had the l alliteration and possible a remote assonance with 'plum'.

Besides these alterations that so much improved the melodic pattern of the final version there are two other features of the

* Garrod's transcript of lines 268–9 (*Poetical works of Keats, app. crit.* p. 249) does not appear to be quite correct. For example, there is a 'new'(?) followed by some other word, that he does not record.

† 'But' for 'and' as the opening word of the stanza.

‡ Gittings (*John Keats: The Living Year*, p. 81) suggests an echo of Burton's *Anatomy* in Keats's choice of fruits.

§ Garrod reads 'sooth', Ridley 'smooth'. The fact that Keats had already used 'soother' in the preceding line adds some weight to the 'smooth' reading.

** Alternatively, 'tinct' may have been suggested by 'cinnamon'.

draft that indicate how much Keats's ear was possessed by the two vowel sounds that he had established in his opening lines. First, it will be noticed that these sounds are entirely absent from the third line. Perhaps on final consideration Keats approved of this as a desirable variation; but from the transcript of the poem made by George Keats and from a marginal entry in one of Woodhouse's transcripts we gather that at some time or other Keats was attracted to the alternative line, 'While he brought from the cabinet a heap'. Secondly, in the much corrected seventh line Keats twice tried to use 'Brigantine',* which contained both vowels of the melodic pattern; and how reluctant he was to lose the word is shown by his further attempt to crowd it into the following line—'In Brigantine from Fez'.

There are several other obvious instances in *The Eve of St Agnes* where revision has emphasized a melodic pattern. Thus, in the lines,

> Rose, like a mission'd spirit, unaware:
> With silver taper's light, and pious care,[32]

'mission'd spirit' was an alteration from 'spirit to her', and 'pious' a substitution for 'gentle'. Again, in two lines from stanza xxv—

> As down she knelt for heaven's grace and boon;
> Rose bloom fell on her hands, together prest[33]

—the marked assonance between 'boon' and 'bloom' came only by revision, for the second of these lines originally ran: 'Tinging her pious hands together prest'.

For one further example, outside *The Eve of St Agnes*, we may turn to lines 8 and 9 of the first book of *Hyperion*, which obviously gave Keats some trouble. The final version of line 8—

---

* There was also a third contracted 'Brigtine'.

Not so much life as on a summer's day

—was reached through

> Not so much life as what an eagles wing
> Would spread upon a field of green ear'd corn,

and

> Not so much life as a young vulture's wing
> Would spread upon a field of green ear'd corn,[34]

and the final version of line 9—

> Robs not one light seed from the feather'd grass

—from

> Robs not at all the dandelion's fleece.

There are several fascinating points of melodic composition in these drafts. For one thing, it is noticeable that there was never any intention of cancelling the emphatic opening phrase, 'Not so much life'—partly perhaps because 'life' carried on the previous pattern of 'fiery', 'quiet', 'silent', 'like'. Also, 'life' in turn may have suggested both 'dandelion' and the final 'light'. Again, the cancellation of 'Would spread upon a field of green ear'd corn' is interesting, since, to say nothing of the close repetition of sound (a matter to be discussed shortly), 'field', 'green', and 'ear'd' have a fresh, clean, and intense sound appropriate to the last lines in stanza 1 of the *Ode to a Nightingale* but unsuitable for this context of hush and deathly immobility. On the other hand, this emphatic *e* sound may very well have been carried over into 'fleece' and ultimately 'seed'. But for our immediate purpose perhaps the most significant point is Keats's final choice of a line that, with the word 'summer's', gave him one of the vowels that chimes prominently, through the words 'sunken', 'one' and 'hung', in the preceding lines; and it is interesting to see that he also had this sound in 'young' in one of his interim drafts.

However, this same opening of *Hyperion* also shows that Keats was not mechanically dominated by the sound patterns of his verse. One of his starts for line 7 reads:

Like clouds whose Thundrous bosoms . . .

In some ways 'thundrous' was an admirable word: it contained a good sound for stormy clouds, and it would have intensified the melodic line of 'sunken', 'one' and 'hung'. This pattern may indeed have suggested the word to Keats. But when he rejected it, and the phrase of which it formed part, he was not only preferring the visual image of massing clouds to an aural one: he was, as he probably sensed instinctively, cancelling a heavy, sonorous sound that would have been out of harmony with the quiet, muffled melody of his superb opening passage.

As will be seen from the passages we have quoted, these melodic patterns of combined and interchanged vowel sounds, whether concentrated in a line or two, or sustained through a stanza or passage of some length, are employed by Keats to achieve a great variety of musical effects. There may be two or three dominant vowels, and these sounds may be equally prominent or with one particularly obtrusive. Again, their combination and interchange may occur in an infinite number of ways. On the other hand, a poetry that depended entirely on this sort of melodic effect would be limited in its musical appeal, and there is evidence in Bailey's account of Keats's 'principle of melody in verse', supported by certain remarks of Leigh Hunt, that Keats fully realized this limitation.

But before examining this evidence we may notice one different kind of melodic effect that Keats certainly produces on numerous occasions, whether it formed part of his conscious theory or not.

As an illustration (and there are many of them to be found in the odes), we may take the opening stanza of *To Autumn:*

Season of mists and mellow fruitfulness,
   Close bosom-friend of the maturing sun;
Conspiring with him how to load and bless
   With fruit the vines that round the thatch-eves run;
To bend with apples the moss'd cottage-trees,
   And fill all fruit with ripeness to the core;
      To swell the gourd, and plump the hazel shells
With a sweet kernel; to set budding more,
   And still more, later flowers for the bees,
   Until they think warm days will never cease,
      For Summer has o'er-brimm'd their clammy cells.

These lines, we should all agree, are as beautiful in sound as anything Keats ever wrote. They have all his measured mellifluousness, and the melody, often highly suggestive in its effect as well as pleasing to the ear, is rich and subtly varied. But apart from the *s*, *m*, and *l* alliterations that run through the stanza from the opening to the final line, there is no pattern of interwoven and recurring vowel sounds of the kind we have lately been examining. On the contrary, the secret of the music here lies in a constant shift of melodic effect and in the complex organization of small, often contrasting, echoes of sound. There is, for instance, the *o* vowel (combined with the *l* consonant) of 'mellow', 'close', and 'load' in the three opening lines, very noticeable here but then disappearing from the melody. There are the marked but momentary alliterations like 'mists and mellow', 'fill all fruit'; the small chimes of sound like 'apples' with 'thatch', 'moss'd' with 'cottage', 'ripeness' with 'vines', and 'budding' with 'plump'; there is the internal half-rhyme of 'shells' with 'swell', and the prominent double *m* sound in the last line, that suggests the hum of the bees and perhaps a clogged or drowsy movement in a sticky sweetness. These are only some of the melodic effects of this stanza that happen to strike the ear of one reader, but they should be sufficient to establish our point.

It may be added that the melody in both of the other stanzas of *To Autumn* resembles that of the first in its nature, and as a matter of fact there are many stanzas in the odes where Keats achieves this sort of melody rather than a pattern of combined and interchanged vowel sounds. We might, for example, have taken the 'little town' stanza (IV) in the *Ode on a Grecian Urn* as an alternative illustration to the first stanza of *To Autumn*. However, there is no reason to suppose that the musical variety to be produced by this other kind of melodic effect came to Keats only from a considerable experience of verse-writing; and since we have in mind the theoretical matters that he may have discussed with Bailey in 1817, we should realize that passages of verse depending on a combination of small, varied, and often fugitive effects for their melodic appeal are common enough in his early work. We may instance part of the second stanza of the hymn to Pan in *Endymion* (an apt illustration here, first, because the substance and general manner of writing so clearly prelude *To Autumn*, and secondly, because Keats thought well enough of this hymn to read it to Wordsworth as a specimen of his work):

> O thou, to whom
> Broad leaved fig trees even now foredoom
> Their ripen'd fruitage; yellow girted bees
> Their golden honeycombs; our village leas
> Their fairest blossom'd beans and poppied corn;
> The chuckling linnet its five young unborn,
> To sing for thee; low creeping strawberries
> Their summer coolness; pent up butterflies
> Their freckled wings; yea, the fresh budding year
> All its completions—be quickly near,
> By every wind that nods the mountain pine,
> O forester divine![35]

Another detailed examination of melodic effects would perhaps be a little tedious at this point, and any reader with a good ear will readily appreciate that the musical appeal of these lines arises from the succession of small, shifting effects— the passing alliterations like 'fig trees', 'foredoom' and 'fruit-age', the repetitions of vowel sounds like 'pent', 'freckled', 'fresh', and 'summer', 'butterflies' and 'budding', and the occasional line or two of the kind that Keats relished in Chatterton:

our village leas

Their fairest blossom'd beans and poppied corn.

To come now to the other kind of melodic effect that Bailey hints at in his account of Keats's 'theory'. Following a quotation of the first six and a half lines of *Hyperion*, Bailey adds the comment: 'These lines . . . are beautifully varied in their vowel sounds, *save when the exception proves the rule, and monotony is a beauty.*' That such deliberate monotones were most probably a part of Keats's theory is confirmed by what Leigh Hunt says after his description of the relish with which Keats read stanza xxx in *The Eve of St Agnes*. Hunt quotes the line,

And lucent syrups tinct with cinnamon,

which of course contains four very close repetitions of the same vowel sound in 'syrups', 'tinct', 'with', and 'cinnamon'. He continues: 'Mr Wordsworth would have said the vowels were not varied enough; but Keats knew where his vowels were *not* to be varied. On the occasion above alluded to, Wordsworth found fault with the repetition of the concluding sound of the participles in Shakespeare's line about bees—

The *singing* masons *building* roofs of gold.

—This, he said, was a line which Milton would never have written. Keats, thought, on the other hand, that the repetition was in harmony with the continued note of the singers, and that Shakespeare's negligence, if negligence it was, had instinctively felt the thing in the best manner.'*

* *Autobiography*, p. 270. It is interesting that the dispute should have been over a line from Shakespeare, for had Keats ever been forced to defend his theory it is almost certain that he would have turned to Shakespeare for support. Thus one of the lines he had marked in his copy of the Sonnets,

The teeming Autumn big with rich increase—

would have furnished almost an exact precedent for his own,

And lucent syrups tinct with cinnamon.

Before examining Keats's practice in this matter of a close repetition of a vowel sound we should perhaps glance at one obvious type of sound repetition about which neither Bailey nor Hunt say anything at all, and which so far we have only touched incidentally. That is alliteration.

Not that there is very much to be said. It is obvious enough that, like all highly musical poets, Keats was fond of alliteration, that he was especially prompted to it by his delight in compound formations (we recall phrases like 'deep-damask'd wings' and 'deep-delved earth'), and that many of his most memorable phrases and lines, like

> While barred clouds bloom the soft-dying day,

owe much to the chiming and recurrence of consonantal sounds. Further, besides the external type of alliteration that occurs in this line from *To Autumn*, there are numerous examples to be found of the more subtle internal alliteration, like the *n* sound in

> *N*ot i*n* lo*n*e sple*n*dour hu*n*g aloft the *n*ight,[36]

while sometimes a pleasing melodic effect is created by a combination of the two kinds of alliteration, as with the *l* and *b* consonants in

> And full-grown lambs loud bleat from hilly bourne.

In general the alliteration in Keats's poetry makes more for smoothness and sweetness than for emphasis, and in all probability most of it arose spontaneously from his own individual and instinctive feeling for poetic language. On the other hand, there are times—especially when the alliteration produces some onomatopoeic or suggestive effect—when we

Of course Keats did not mark his Shakespeare for this purpose, but it is perhaps worth noting that a quarter of the marked sonnet lines contain clear examples of close repetition of a vowel sound, while there are half a dozen in the eleven marked *Merchant of Venice* lines. (For further details see Miss Spurgeon's *Keats's Shakespeare*.)

have the impression of the deliberately contrived art. Thus in the line from the *Ode to a Nightingale*,

> With beaded bubbles winking at the brim,

the 'b' alliteration is so marked and so suggestive of bursting bubbles that we suspect Keats to have employed it for a thoroughly conscious effect; and this suspicion becomes almost a certainty when we notice that 'beaded' was a substitution for 'cluster'd', which, while it makes an agreeable assonance with 'blushful' and 'bubbles', fails to produce the onomatopoeia of the final version of the line. This last point, of manuscript correction and revision, also reminds us that, if most of the alliteration in Keats's verse was spontaneously and instinctively produced, alliterative effect was certainly one of the considerations that he had in mind, subconsciously at any rate, when he was turning over alternatives and second thoughts.

To these fairly obvious general remarks two or three qualifications may perhaps be usefully added. First, while alliteration certainly comes pat with compound epithets, it is not in any way a marked or characteristic feature of Keats's recurrent compound words. Again, it should perhaps be pointed out that the more elaborate kinds of alliteration that occur in the second and third quotations (triple alliterations and alliterations in close pairs for instance) are not outstanding in Keats's verse. And this leads to a rather more important observation. That is that most of us probably tend to think of Keats's writing as more highly alliterative (in the obvious external way) than it really is. This mistaken impression, which a careful reading of the admired opening of *Lamia* will help to correct, arises from two chief causes: first, from the fact that some of Keats's poems, like the sonnet *To Sleep* and 'Bright star', are indeed alliterated to an exceptional degree, and secondly, because many external alliterations, barely noticeable in themselves, are powerfully sustained by the internal alliterations of the context. An excellent illustration of the last effect is provided by a line from the *Ode on a Grecian Urn*—

Lead'st thou that heifer lowing at the skies.

—If we listen to that line in isolation the *l* alliteration of 'Lead'st' and 'lowing' is not particularly obtrusive. But when we hear the line in its context we probably have the vague impression of a pronounced alliteration hereabouts, for it is followed by a more subtle internal alliteration of which we are probably not consciously aware:

And all her silken flanks with garlands drest.*

Finally, it is probably true to say that in general there is rather less alliteration (particularly of the elaborate kind) in Keats's later poetry than in his early writing, and an analytical comparison of specimen passages of *Endymion* and *Hyperion* shows that while the amount of alliteration in the rhetorical sections remains constant, in the descriptive and narrative sections it declines very slightly. But even without the help of prosaic analysis this is rather what we should expect, for the melodic effects of triple or paired alliterations are fairly easily achieved in English, and they commonly make an excessive appeal to poets in their first apprentice work. In addition the youthful Keats would have found ample warrant for almost anything he wrote in this way in the highly alliterated poetry of Spenser and Milton.

To return to the more important matter of vowel repetition: the instances that Bailey quotes from the opening of *Hyperion* of vowel sounds 'touching by their sameness and monotony'— 'hēalthy brēath of morn', 'Sāt grey haired Sāturn', 'fōrest on fōrest', 'like clōud on clōud'—are mild and not particularly striking illustrations of this melodic effect. Hunt's example—

And lucent syrups tinct with cinnamon

—is much more remarkable, and innumerable instances of

* This 'l' sound is immediately and strongly maintained in 'little', 'built', 'peaceful', 'citadel', 'folk'.

such close and frequent iteration of a vowel sound in a line of two can be found in Keats's poetry. The following is a brief but varied and widely ranging sample of this melodic effect:

> Look'd at each other with a wild surmise—
> Silent, upon a peak in Darien.[37]

> O Thou, whose mighty palace roof doth hang
> From jagged trunks, and overshadoweth . . .[38]

> How long is't since the mighty Power bid
> Thee heave to airy sleep from fathom dreams?[39]

> Tall oaks, branch-charmed by the earnest stars.[40]

> In the retired quiet of the night.[41]

> And feed deep, deep, upon her peerless eyes.[42]

> Thou still unravish'd bride of quietness,
> Thou foster-child of silence and slow time.[43]

> A pillar'd porch, with lofty portal door.[44]

> Bright star! would I were steadfast as thou art.[45]

These examples will serve well enough to illustrate the kind of vowel repetition we are discussing. However, fuller quotations, giving the melodic context, would be necessary to show the variety of effects that these lines may produce. Sometimes such a line will please the ear because it suddenly concentrates some vowel sound of which we have been vaguely conscious in the preceding lines; sometimes, when the iterated sound is a new one, it will afford a pleasurable contrast. Or again there may be a melodic contrast when the monotone concludes, or temporarily breaks, a passage that is rich in chiming combinations of vowels and consonants. This is the effect of the already quoted line—'In the retired quiet of the night'—in *The Eve of St Agnes:*

> These delicates he heap'd with glowing hand
> On golden dishes and in baskets bright
> Of wreathed silver: sumptuous they stand
> In the retired quiet of the night,
> Filling the chilly room with perfume light.[46]

Here (among other effects) the monotone of the fourth line agreeably checks what might have become an excess of melodic sweetness and richness.

There are two particular and characteristic forms of this repetition of a single vowel sound that deserve special mention. First, Keats was singularly fond, especially in his compounds and his combinations of epithet and noun, of using the same sound twice in close proximity, either in succeeding syllables or with an interval of one syllable. From the odes alone, with phrases like 'soft-conched', 'cool-rooted', 'sunburnt mirth', 'embalmed darkness' and 'mossed cottage', we could assemble a sizeable group of such repetitions. But this sort of melodic effect is common through all Keats's poems, and since there are many occasions when it is produced by a manuscript alteration or revision, we may reasonably think that he consciously approved of it in general. No doubt most readers will accept, and usually delight in, the examples we have just quoted from the odes. On the other hand, this melodic effect is one that the ears of readers will respond to in various ways, and there have always been those who have objected to what is sometimes described as the 'caw-caw' of two like vowels or syllables following hard upon each other. There may very well be some readers whose ears are offended by such repetitions as 'branch-charmed' and 'forlorn moor'—to confine ourselves to two examples from *Hyperion*.⁷ However, setting these possible objections on one side, there can be little doubt that this common feature of the melody of Keats's poetry often contributes to the characteristically weighted and measured quality of his rhythm, though this of course arises chiefly from his habit of bringing several *speaking* stresses close together, especially at the end of lines, as in

> Thou fóster-chíld of sílence and slów tíme,

or

> Máke nót your rósary of yéw-bérries,
> Nór let the béetle, nor the déath-móth bé
> Your mournful Psyche

The other special form of repetition to be noticed is the internal rhyme and near-rhyme. This again is common all through Keats's poetry, and once more we need look no further than the odes for examples. It is a somewhat remarkable fact that all the odes, including the *Ode on Indolence*, contain at least two instances of full internal rhyme, while most of them have more. Sometimes, as in the line

> To toll me back from thee to my sole self,

or in

> And be among her cloudy trophies hung,

the rhyme is so unobtrusive that we may fail to notice it, and this is particularly likely to happen where both the rhymes are internal or where one rhyme is concealed because it is part of a word of more than one syllable. Two lines from *To Autumn* will illustrate both of these ways in which the internal rhyme may be masked:

> Thee sitting *care*less on a granary floor,
> Thy *hair* soft-lifted by the winnowing wind.

But sometimes the internal rhyme and assonantal rhyme is very clearly marked, notably in:

> Nor let the b*ee*tle nor the death-moth *be*
> Your mournful Psy*che*, nor the *dow*ny *owl*
> A partner in your sorrow's mysteries;
> For shade to shade will come too *drow*sily,
> And *drow*n the wakeful anguish of the soul.

Admittedly this is an exceptional example so far as the odes are concerned, but it could be paralleled by a few passages elsewhere in Keats's poetry—by these lines in *Endymion*, for instance:

> O Harkener to the *loud* clapping shears,
> While ever and anon to his *shorn* peers
> A ram goes bleating: Winder of the *horn*,
> When *snouted* wild-*boars rout*ing tender *corn*
> Anger our huntsmen.[48]

The manuscript evidence of Keats's process of composition is particularly revealing on this matter of sound iteration in the various forms we have described. We have already pointed out that a number of instances may be discovered where such repetitions were intensified, or even produced for the first time, by revision. Thus, in that line that Leigh Hunt singled out—

> And lucent syrups tinct with cinnamon

—'tinct' was an afterthought for 'sooth' or 'smooth'. In the same poem the marked sound repetition at the beginning of stanza x—

> He ventures in: let no *buzz*'d whisper tell:
> All hearts be *mu*ffled, or a *hu*ndred swords . . .

—is chiefly an effect of revision, for originally 'damn'd' stood in the place of 'buzz'd', while the assonance in the first line of stanza XIII—

> He follo*w*'d throughly a lo*w*ly arched way

—only came when Keats cancelled his first draft:

> He follow'd her along a passage dark.

So with the slight assonance in the lines,

> Through many a *dusky* gallery, they gain
> The maiden's chamber, silken, *hush*'d, and chaste;

originally Keats had '*oaken* Galleries' in the first line.

Hyperion, too, furnishes several examples of revisions that produce this sort of effect. For instance, in the line,

> With backward footing through the shade a space,[49]

'shade' was an alteration from 'gloom'. It is just possible, of course, that the correction was an instantaneous one made before Keats had settled the conclusion of the line; but whichever came first, 'shade' or 'space', Keats finally composed a line that concludes with a marked repetition of sound; and from the evidence of the correction it is likely that this ending was a carefully considered one. Somewhat later there is a clear internal rhyme in:

> the porches wide
> Open'd upon the dusk demesnes of night
> And the bright Titan, phrenzied with new woes . . .[50]

Keats's ear could hardly have missed this rhyme, and it was produced by the substitution of 'bright' for 'enraged'.

On the other hand, there are just as many instances (perhaps rather more) where the effect of Keats's revision is to weaken or remove some repetition of sound. Naturally we cannot always be certain that this was his deliberate or chief intention. Among the *membra disjecta* of *Hyperion* we find:

> Thus the old Eagle drowsy with great grief
> Sat moulting his weak Plumage never more
> To be restored or soar against the Sun,
> While his three Sons upon Olympus stood.[51]

Possibly Keats rejected this because (among other reasons) his ear reacted against the close and rhyming repetitions of 'more', 'restored' and 'soar' and the awkward proximity of 'Sun' and 'Sons'. Certainly the tripping effect of the internal rhyme is most inappropriate to the context. But we cannot be sure that this was the chief reason—or indeed a reason at all—for his cancellation of the passage. However, when we compare

> Upon the sodden ground
> His old right hand lay nerveless, listless, dead,
> Unsceptred; and his realmless eyes were closed;
> While his bow'd head seem'd list'ning to the Earth,[52]

with the earlier draft, which appears at one stage to have read in part,

> on the ground
> Unscepter'd; and his whitebrowd eyes were closed;
> While his bow'd head seem'd list'ning to the Earth,

we may be fairly certain that in this instance Keats was troubled by the close repetition of like sounds in 'ground' 'whitebrowd' and 'bow'd'. In his final version 'realmless' replaces 'whitebrowd', and 'ground' goes back a line. Sometime in the drafting of this passage he also put his pen through 'bow'd', but he changed his mind and restored the word. Nevertheless, if we are right in believing that he was dissatisfied with his draft here because of a displeasing sound repetition, we should notice that only two lines before he had let pass the pronounced iteration of

Along the margin-sand large foot-marks went.

Possibly the drawn-out quality of this repeated sound, and the rhyming of 'marks' with 'margin', appealed to him for its appropriate suggestion of a slow, dragging, ponderous footfall.*

Similar examples of revision that have the effect of diminishing a repetition of sound may be discovered elsewhere in Keats's poetry. For instance, in the line

Her rich attire creeps rustling to her knees,[53]

'rich' appears to have been a last minute alteration; Keats's epithet for 'attire' had been 'sweet', which had furnished a triple iteration of sound with 'creeps' and 'knees'. By substituting *'beaded* bubbles' for *'cluster'd* bubbles' in line 17 of of the *Ode to a Nightingale* Keats certainly, as we have already pointed out, improved the onomatopoeic effect of the line; but, willingly or not, he lost the triple repetition of

. . . the *blush*ful Hippocrene
With *clus*ter'd *bub*bles winking at the brim.

* There are some smaller revisions in *Hyperion* where a sound repetition disappears because it is plainly cacophonous or pointless. Thus in i, 87–8 the substitution of 'earth' for 'sand' avoids the jar with the immediately following 'and', while in i, 115–16 'spot' is an obvious improvement on the original 'bit', which produced an insipid internal rhyme. Again, 'no stir of *air* was *there*' (l. 7) disappears in *The Fall of Hyperion*.

Again—to cite some very familiar lines—there appears to be an instance of a rejected internal rhyme in the fourth stanza of *La Belle Dame Sans Merci*—

> I met a lady in the meads,
>   Full beautiful—a faery's child;

the draft of this in his letter to his brother and sister-in-law reads:

> I met a Lady in the ~~Wilds~~ Meads

From the evidence of these contrasting revisions and re-draftings it appears that the principle of the closely repeated vowel sound was the least settled part of Keats's 'theory'; and—whether theory is to be blamed or not—it must be added that repetitions of sound, like the notorious 'O Attic shape! Fair attitude!', do occasionally spoil Keats's music. Once at least we appear to catch him in the middle of his doubts and uncertainties, for line 243 of *The Eve of St Agnes* has the fascinating manuscript reading:

> shut
> ~~close~~
> As though a rose should ~~shut,~~ and be a bud again.

Here Keats's found himself faced with two choices of melodic effect: either the full internal rhyme of 'rose' and 'close', or the assonance of 'shut' with 'bud' and with 'sun-shine' in the previous line. It is easy to approve of the final choice of the more delicate assonantal effect, and it is quite likely that our approval was Keats's own. Yet his choice cannot have been an easy one, for at one stage he did reject 'shut' and entertain the emphatic rhyme seriously enough to put it down on paper.

Further, in support of what Bailey and Leigh Hunt say about Keats's ideas on poetic melody, we must not overlook the obvious fact that he never considered a different-sounding verb or any alteration of 'rose' or 'bud': one way or the other, he seems to have been determined to have a sound-correspondence in this line.

The melodic pattern of combined and interchanged vowel sounds occurs, as we have seen, in both short and sustained passages. The closely repeated single sound, on the other hand, is usually confined to a line or two, the reason for this being that a prolonged monotone is rarely pleasing to the ear. Nevertheless, there are some striking instances in Keats's poetry where a similar sound is prominently repeated through many lines of verse, though usually such repetitions are accompanied by a certain amount of minor melodic play with other sounds. A good example of this sort of effect is to be found in the opening of *Hyperion*, and it is rather curious that Bailey, with his ear for the smaller monotones, should have missed the marked recurrence here of certain long vowels and diphthongs:

> Deep in the shady sadness of a vale
> *Far* sunken from the healthy breath of *morn*,
> *Far* from the f*ie*ry noon, and eve's one *star*,
> Sat gray-*haired* Sat*urn*, quiet as a stone,
> Still as the silence round about his *lair;*
> *For*est on *for*est hung above his head
> Like cloud on cloud. No *stir* of *air* was *there* . . .

It is these italicised syllables,* with their resemblances of sound, that largely account for the muffled effect of this opening. Possibly Bailey's ear missed this because he was concerned with exact repetitions of sound; even so, it is odd that he should have ignored the internal rhyme of 'far' (twice) with 'star', and the closeness of this to 'haired', 'lair', 'air', and 'there'.

An almost identical muting effect, with a considerable use

---

* The concluding 'r' consonant in these syllables, though it is often only a spelling symbol and sometimes of doubtful pronunciation, contributes to their similarity. So, too, in the extract from the *Ode to Psyche* below.

of the same vowels and diphthongs, is created in the first eight lines of the second stanza of the *Ode to Psyche:*

> O latest *bor*n and loveliest vision *far*
> Of all Olympus' faded h*ier*archy!
> *Fair*er than Phoebe's sapp*hire*-region'd st*ar* ,
> *Or* Vesper, am*or*ous glow-w*or*m of the sky;
> *Fair*er than these, though temple thou hast none,
> *Nor* altar heap'd with flowers;
> *Nor virgin-choir* to make delicious moan
> Upon the midnight hours . . .

Incidentally, it is some proof of the way in which Keats's ear must have been dominated by this sound to find him, in an early draft of the third line, toying with the phrase '*or*bed Phoebe'.

Sometimes in such passages the dominant sound is exactly repeated, as in the sonnet *On first looking into Chapman's Homer:*

> Oft of one wide expanse had I *been* told
> That *deep*-brow'd Homer ruled as his d*emesne;*
> Yet did I never *breathe* its pure ser*ene*
> Till I heard Chapman *speak* out loud and bold.

For another such example we may instance part of stanza v in the *Ode to a Nightingale*, where Keats repeats a sound that always seems to have pleased his ear:

> But, in emb*al*med d*ar*kness, guess each sweet
> Wherewith the seasonable month endows
> The *grass*, the thicket, and the fruit-tree wild;
> White hawthorn, and the p*as*toral eglantine;
> F*as*t fading violets cover'd up in leaves . . .

Finally, we may observe how these repetitions sometimes stand out through being set in a surround that is rich in melodic play of the varied sort. Such is the effect of an *o* sound that occurs in the middle of one of the stanzas of the *Ode on Melancholy:* it is not heard once in the first four lines, highly melodic as they are; then it is repeated five times in four lines, only to disappear completely in the last two lines:

> But when the melancholy fit shall fall
>   Sudden from heaven like a weeping cloud,
> That fosters the droop-headed flowers all,
>   And hides the green hill in an April shroud;
> Then glut thy sorrow on a morning rose,
>   Or on the rainbow of the salt sand-wave,
>   Or on the wealth of globed peonies;
> Or if thy mistress some rich anger shows,
>   Emprison her soft hand, and let her rave,
>   And feed deep, deep upon her peerless eyes.

In examining some of Keats's revisions and corrections of his work, we have used them chiefly to substantiate certain probable conclusions about his 'principle of melody'. But there is another feature of them, so far only glanced at incidentally, that clearly shows us how important sound was in the composition of Keats's poetry. This is his habit, discernible all through his work, of transferring a sound, or sound pattern, into his alteration—and this sometimes when a considerable change of phrasing was involved.

Two clear examples of this habit are to be found in *To Autumn*. First, in the final version of the lines,

> And fill all fruit with ripeness to the core;
>   To swell the gourd, and plump the hazel shells
> With a sweet kernel,

'ripeness' has replaced 'sweetness' in the autograph version and 'sweet' has replaced 'white'. But the two chief vowel sounds have been retained, 'white' going into 'ripeness' and 'sweetness' into 'sweet'. The second example concerns his final preference of 'twined flowers' (l. 18) to 'honied flowers'. Here one guesses that he cancelled 'honied' only after considerable hesitation or when the passing of time had weakened certain original compulsions, for there is clear evidence that the sound of the first syllable was an insistent one in the early stages of composition. In his drafts for the previous line he had used 'slumbrous' and 'slumbers', and when neither of these words found a place in the line that finally satisfied him, he attempted to bring 'slumbrous' over into the next line:

> Spares for some slumbrous minutes the next swath.

It is a fair guess that something of the sound of this repeated 'slumbrous' was retained in 'honied'. In the same way the rhyme-word 'store' in line 12 significantly keeps much of the sound of the cancelled 'haunts'.

Similar instances are to be found in *The Eve of St Agnes*. Thus when Keats changed the line,

> He follow'd her along a passage dark,

to

> He follow'd through a lowly arched way,[54]

the vowel sound of 'dark' survived in 'arched'. But the most revealing group of such changes occurs in the drafting of *Hyperion*. For instance, the phrase

> $\overset{1}{\text{stay'd}}$ $\overset{2}{\text{Ixion's wheel}}$[55]

emerged from

> $\overset{2}{\text{eased}}$ $\overset{1}{\text{Ixion's}}$ pain;

and there is another such double transference of sounds in

> $\overset{1\,1}{\text{twilight}}$ in the $\overset{2}{\text{rear}}$[56]

which replaced

> $\overset{1}{\text{just lighted}}$ from the $\overset{2}{\text{air.}}$*

Though any value that this chapter possesses must lie chiefly in its examination of Keats's practice as a poet, we

---

* Much more numerous are examples of the retention of a single sound, usually in one-word alterations: for example, I, 199, 'panting' for 'mad'; I, 263, 'might' for 'gripe' and a cancelled opening 'with spite'; II, 60, 'sacred' for 'shaded'; II, 217, 'strife' (not used in final version) for 'lifeless' (?); II, 330, 'singe' for 'lick'; II, 365, 'darkness' probably for 'clear *spar*'; III, 16, 'morn' probably for 'corn' in the cancelled opening.

have also attempted to reconstruct something of what Bailey records as Keats's 'principle of melody in verse'. From this latter point of view our analysis has one serious limitation. We have said nothing about the 'management of open and close vowels', which, from Bailey's account, constituted a most important part of Keats's theory.

One or two very general observations may be safely made on this subject. For one thing, lines where open and close vowels alternate closely and with considerable regularity are quite common in Keats's poetry. A good sustained example of such patterning will be found in stanza xxx of *The Eve of St Agnes*—'And still she slept an azure-lidded sleep', etc.* Again—though this is rarer—there are occasions when Keats, probably with deliberate intention, writes a line that is composed entirely of open or close vowels. But of course neither of these types of line is as common as the one in which open and close vowels occur without close alternation; and in these perhaps the most striking feature is the flowing smoothness (often in a kind of graded sequence of vowels) with which Keats so frequently manages his transitions. The line, 'While barred clouds bloom the soft-dying day', with its satisfying sound-shifts between 'barred' (open), 'bloom' (close), and 'dying' (open), is an excellent example of this very characteristic effect in his melody; and it is quite possible that Bailey was referring particularly to this when he wrote: 'Keats's theory was, that the vowels should be so managed as not to clash with one another so as to mar the melody.'

However, a detailed examination of Keats's melodic practice along these lines might be a little perilous for the amateur phonetician. The problem is one that would well repay the investigation of some expert in phonetics.

---

* The line that Keats so much admired in Chatterton, 'Come with acorn cup and thorn', is another clear example.

CHAPTER IV

'ENDYMION' I: SOME PRELIMINARY CONSIDERATIONS

Who is more happy, when, with heart's content,
Fatigued he sinks into some pleasant lair
Of wavy grass, and reads a debonair
And gentle tale of love and languishment?
To one who has been long in city pent.

MODERN readers would probably not differ much in their estimate of the poetic value of *Endymion*. Most of its conspicuous, and often distasteful, faults—sandy foundations, mawkishness, and 'slip-shod' writing—* have been pointed out clearly enough by Keats himself. It is most fairly judged as an ambitious, perhaps over-ambitious, apprentice task-piece that is on the whole more impressive for its promise than its achievement.† On the other hand, to say nothing of innumerable odd lines of great beauty, it contains a number of sustained passages, notably varied in kind—the odes to Pan and Bacchus, the descriptions of the sleeping Adonis and of the Cave of Quietude—that strike us with a force only surpassed by that of Keats's finest achievements.

Where readers will divide sharply is over the meaning of the poem. Is it merely what it seems at first, an amalgam of visual and other sense impressions, fancies and dream-like fantasies, erotic sentiment, and reminiscence and re-creation of Keats's reading (with one or two reflective passages); or

* See the Preface to *Endymion* (*Poetical Works of Keats*, ed. Garrod, p. 64).

† As Shelley said in his letter to *The Quarterly Review* (Pisa, 1820, but never sent): 'Surely the poem with all its faults is a very remarkable production for a man of Keats's age, and the promise of ultimate excellence is such as has rarely been afforded by such as have afterwards attained high literary eminence.' See also Shelley to Keats, printed in the *Letters*, p. 506.

had Keats some deeper intention—philosophic, visionary, we may leave the exact word for the moment—beyond the artistic and narrative one of re-telling an ancient myth? And if the poem has some profound general meaning, how do we elicit or interpret this through our immediate and overwhelming impression of sensuousness, fantasy, and eroticism?

To be honest with those who have read little twentieth century writing on Keats it must be admitted that if we follow the majority of modern critics and commentators—including the best of them—these questions have been emphatically answered. *Endymion*, we are told, certainly has a general intention and meaning, and this meaning is to be apprehended by an allegorical reading of the poem. The allegorized ideas and intuitions that constitute the meaning, even if they are not fully neo-platonic, since there is no suggestion of divine love or communion with God, may nevertheless be interpreted in neo-platonic terms. Endymion represents the Poet and the soul of man, and Cynthia ideal or essential Beauty. Endymion moves through the poem in quest of this ideal Beauty, and though he is granted moments of ecstatic, mystical union with Cynthia, it is not before he has undergone a spiritual development and regeneration that a lasting and complete communion is possible. In particular, he has to learn that the approach to ideal Beauty is through its particular and material manifestations, the highest form of which is woman and human love. This is the allegorical significance of the Indian Maid; and at the end of the poem the poet or the soul of man has discovered that all the highest aspirations, for terrestrial beauty and absolute Beauty, for love of woman and love of humanity, are one. This final harmony of the soul's aspirations may be expressed in another way: that love creates beauty and beauty creates love.

On the other hand, while we may fairly summarize the general neo-platonic interpretation in this way, we must also recognize that there have been notable variations among its exponents*— variations that may in themselves raise doubts about the validity of this reading. For instance, critics and commentators differ widely in their elucidations of the various spiritual stages and experiences through which Endymion is supposed to pass, particularly if they try to relate these specifically to the book-divisions of the poem. For Bridges† Book II signifies an initiation into the mysteries of earth; for Colvin,‡ whose general commentary on *Endymion* gave perhaps the most influential impetus to the allegorical, neo-platonic interpretation, this book appears to be largely the outcome of fancy and day-dreaming, with very little symbolical purpose; for Thorpe§ the book represents a deeper experience of sensuality; and for Finney,** another American Keats scholar of deserved repute, Endymion is passing through the imaginative world of art, in particular the world of poetry. Possibly some of these readings may be reconciled with one another; but there also appears to be a good deal of serious discrepancy. Again, while some critics, like Middleton Murry, keep their interpretations in general terms and base them on what they consider to be particularly significant parts of the poem, others are prepared to extend their allegorical reading to most detailed items;†† and where this occurs further divergencies of inter-

* In his most recent study of *Endymion* in *The Mystery of Keats* Middleton Murry sometimes dismisses certain points in the usual neo-platonic reading. But Murry undoubtedly discovers in *Endymion* a substantial metaphysical attitude that has much in common with the neo-platonic interpretation and is often barely distinguishable from it. Also Murry has moved much nearer to the neo-platonic view than he was in his earlier *Keats and Shakespeare*, where he wrote (p. 27): 'I do not believe that Keats meant anything in particular by a good deal of it.'

† *Collected Essays*, vol. IV, p. 89.
‡ *Life of John Keats*, p. 188.
§ *The Mind of John Keats*, pp. 57–8.
** *The Evolution of Keats's Poetry*, pp. 306–7.

†† Thus to Finney (*op. cit.* p. 305) 'the bud, which became in turn the rose, the butterfly, and the nymph (II, 55–130) symbolizes the fleeting beauty of this ever-changing world of matter, which, despite its imperfect and evanescent nature, is the only guide by which man can be led into the region of ideal beauty.' See also (p. 317) Finney's explanation of the two winged horses provided by Mercury for Endymion and the Indian Maid.

pretation arise. Nevertheless, through all these variations and discrepancies most of the influential writers on Keats in this century have held firmly to two central assumptions: first, that *Endymion* is to be read allegorically for the discovery of an ulterior meaning, and secondly, that Keats's intention was to show the Poetic soul in quest of a transcendental reality that is perhaps best described as essential Beauty.* So well established are these assumptions to-day that they have acquired all the authority and respectability of text-book platitude.

At the same time it should be noticed that there has always been a small minority of opposition to this way of reading *Endymion*. In 1921, following Colvin's great study of Keats and before the influence of Murry, Thorpe, and Finney had made itself felt, Saintsbury raised a vigorous voice of protest: 'I have been told that it is not quite the thing to admire *Endymion* now; at least to admire it *simpliciter*. You must busy yourself with its problems; present the Latmian with a complete set of allegorical, symbolical, and all sorts of other -ical explanations of himself and his adventures, and so forth. Thank goodness nobody suggested anything of that kind to me in the Boilers sixty years since.'† Amy Lowell also remained unconverted to the fashionable view of the poem, and recently—of particular interest since so much of the fully elaborated allegorical interpretation of *Endymion* has been American—another American, Newell Ford,‡ has forcefully contested the allegorical and neo-platonic reading.

---

* Colvin (*op. cit.*, p. 205) furnishes a good summary of what has become the standard interpretation: 'a vital, subtly involved and passionately tentative spiritual parable, the parable of the poetic soul in man seeking communion with the spirit of essential Beauty in the world.' E. de Selincourt (*Poems of John Keats*, p. xl.) has a slightly different phrase for Endymion's quest—'the development of the poet's soul towards a complete realisation of itself'. But elsewhere (p. 445) he talks of the 'search for ideal beauty and truth'.

† 'A Reminiscence of *Endymion*', *John Keats Memorial Volume*, pp. 162–3.

‡ *The Prefigurative Imagination of John Keats*; and two earlier articles '*Endymion*—A Neo-Platonic Allegory?' (*E.L.H.*, March 1947) and 'The Meaning of 'Fellowship with Essence' in *Endymion*' (*P.M.L.A.*, December 1947).

The most conclusive answers to these problems about the meaning of *Endymion* must of course be based on the text of the poem itself. But before examining this we should certainly consider some highly relevant circumstantial evidence.

Of this evidence the most important is that provided by Keats himself, in the poems written immediately before and concurrently with *Endymion*, in his letters (particularly those of 1817), and in his two Prefaces to *Endymion*, the suppressed and the published.

Among the poems the most revealing ones are unquestionably 'I stood tip-toe' and *Sleep and Poetry*.* The first of these, which originally bore the title of *Endymion*,[1] is relevant for two reasons—the long apostrophe to the Moon that is included in it, and its substantial commentary on the Endymion-Cynthia story. In the apostrophe there is nothing to suggest that Keats at this time attached any important symbolical significance to the moon: it is merely what it had always been from his earliest poems, a central image of luxurious delight, a supreme example of earthly beauty:

> Queen of the wide air; thou most lovely queen
> Of all the brightness that my eyes have seen![2]

Admittedly, he does address the moon as 'Maker of sweet poets', but, as the following lines show, this invocation simply means that the moon is regarded as an outstanding instance of the inspiration of nature that is behind myth and genuine poetry. What he is expounding is not any sort of neo-platonism but a primary article of Romantic faith that he had probably learnt from Wordsworth, particularly, as Leigh Hunt stated in his review of the 1817 *Poems*, from Book IV of *The Excursion*. Nor, when Keats goes on to give us his observations on the Endymion story, is there any hint that he regarded it allegorically. At least in December 1816, some four months before

* Finney believes that there is a neo-platonic attitude in the December 1816 sonnet, 'At morn, at noon, at eve'. For a discussion of Finney's argument see Appendix III.

the commencement of *Endymion*, the legend is still simply 'that sweetest of all songs', a tale of 'pure deliciousness'. In order to re-tell the story himself he prays, not for any kind of imaginative, visionary or speculative experience, but for artistic power, a command over honeyed words to match the sweetness of the tale; while, from a moon-image that repeats itself compulsively from the August sonnet *To My Brother George*—

> Cynthia is from her silken curtains peeping
> So scantly, that it seems her bridal night[3]

—it appears that the erotic quality of the legend is still exercising a powerful attraction:

> O for three words of honey, that I might
> Tell but one wonder of thy bridal night![4]

Further, the creative impulse that Keats ascribes to the poet who first related the story is one of humanity, of pity for the loneliness of Diana-Cynthia:

> The poet wept at her so piteous fate,
> Wept that such beauty should be desolate:
> So in fine wrath some golden sounds he won,
> And gave meek Cynthia her Endymion.[5]

Sleep and Poetry, which also belongs to the last part of 1816, is apposite here chiefly for the programme of poetry-writing that Keats set out for himself in it. In this part of the poem (ll. 96–154) he first of all dreams of a long, leisurely period of time in which he may overwhelm himself in 'poesy'—by which term, as the imagery indicates, he meant a kind of poetry that expresses, and in poet and reader stimulates, sensuous and erotic pleasure. In other words, he hopes that for some considerable time yet he may continue writing poetry of the sort that he had been steadily composing for a year or more, that poetry of 'luxuries' of which 'I stood tip-toe' is perhaps the best example. If he does hint at any important immediate development it is in the line

> A lovely tale of human life we'll read,[6]

where he appears to be suggesting some venture into narrative poetry. But if the line is read in this way, the reference must surely be to narrative poems like the *Calidore* fragment or the Endymion story of 'pure deliciousness' in ' I stood tip-toe', not to anything of psychological or metaphysical complexity.

No one would wish to pin Keats down to a literal meaning in his *ten years* of 'poesy'. But he obviously had in mind some considerable period of time, and it is not easy to believe that, having indulged in this aspiration during the later part of 1816, he would embark, only four or five months later, on the elaborate metaphysical allegory with which he is now commonly credited. Had he undergone some profoundly transforming experience during the early months of 1817, we could conceive of such a rapid and drastic change in his poetic intentions: his later history as a poet reveals just this phenomenon. But while, as Thorpe pertinently reminds us,* we must recognize the imaginative and intellectual stimulus of his brooding over the Elgin marbles, his re-reading of Shakespeare, and the solitary, exhausting thought in the Isle of Wight immediately preceding his start on *Endymion*, none of these experiences—on the evidence of the poems and letters of early 1817—appears to be of such intensity and profundity that he would abruptly turn from one kind of poetry to another. Moreover, until the shattering experiences of late 1818 and 1819 and the feverish speculations these experiences generated, most of the poetry he wrote after *Sleep and Poetry* is indeed 'poesy', and the *Isabella* of 1818 is still, for all its romantic morbidities, a 'lovely tale of human life'. Why then are we to believe that in *Endymion* he departed suddenly and most emphatically from the type of poetry he had been writing, planned to go on writing for some time, and did in fact continue to write for at least eighteen months after *Sleep and Poetry*?

Again, it is important to note carefully what Keats says

* *The Mind of John Keats*, p. 53.

about the poetry that is to follow the ten years of 'poesy' and
luxuriating in the realm of 'Flora and old Pan':

> And can I ever bid these joys farewell?
> Yes, I must pass them for a nobler life,
> Where I may find the agonies, the strife
> Of human hearts.[7]

Here he appears to envisage a poetic evolution something
like that described by Wordsworth in *Tintern Abbey*, a passing
from poetry that reflects sensuous pleasure in Nature to a
poetry of the 'still, sad music of humanity'. This programmatic
statement is powerfully and beautifully elaborated by the
image, comparable with a passage[8] in Shelley's later *Triumph
of Life*, that follows, where we have the heavenly charioteer
(poetic imagination) most awfully intent upon the complex
and unceasing pageant of human life. All this, visionary as it
is, is vivid and explicit enough, and it has no reference whatever to that subjective, idealistic sort of poetry to which
Endymion would belong if it were indeed the neo-platonic allegory that most twentieth-century critics have made of it. But
the first *Hyperion*, while to some extent allegorical, or at least
to be understood at two different levels, fits exactly into Keats's
vision of his poetic development, for it is an imaginative
brooding over the agonies, the strifes, of hearts that are human
rather than Olympian. Once again it is the commentators'
Endymion, with its sustained allegory and its platonic and neo-
platonic idealisms and abstractions, that stands out as an
immense, unaccountable oddity in what would otherwise be
a pattern of consistent and organic poetic growth.

About the letters that Keats wrote in 1817 and the first two
or three months of 1818 the first thing to be said is that although
they are rich in information of an artistic and psychological
sort about the composition of *Endymion*, only three of them can
be taken to refer to its meaning and intention. Negative as this
fact is, it is not without some significance for our problem, for

had Keats indeed been engaged on a long philosophical poem in 1817 we should expect that a good deal of this preoccupation would have overflowed into his letters to his various friends. Further, it is not merely that there is relatively little in these letters that can be regarded as speculation of a neoplatonic kind; the truth is that it is not till 1818 that philosophical speculation of any sort becomes at all marked in them.

Of the three letters* that may be taken to concern the meaning of *Endymion* the most illuminating appears to be the letter of 22 November to Bailey, where, in the middle of one of the acutest and best known speculative passages in all his correspondence, Keats lets slip the aside: 'In a Word, you may know my favourite Speculation by my first Book and the little song I sent in my last.'⁹ By 'my first book' Keats must be referring to Book 1 of *Endymion*, in which, apart possibly from the opening section, the only passage that bears any discernible relation to the ideas he is discussing in the letter is Endymion's long speech on happiness (II, 769–842). Since the third letter touching on the meaning of *Endymion*, that to his publisher Taylor (30 January 1818),¹⁰ also alludes to this speech, these two letters should obviously be considered together.

No doubt some of the finer implications of Keats's thoughts in the November letter to Bailey lend themselves to subtle and infinite discussion.† But the broad drift of his argument is clear enough. Bailey, who, for all his Wordsworthian fervour,

* Another of these three letters is the one to Bailey in October (*Letters*, pp. 55–6). This letter—as well as some parts of the letter 22 November to Bailey—affords clear evidence of Bailey's zealous attempts to convert Keats to the doctrine of benevolence and humanitarianism in *The Excursion*, and it certainly has a bearing on Book III of *Endymion*. But since the humanitarian implications of Book Three are generally accepted by most commentators, the letter throws little light on our problem.

Middleton Murry's attempt (*The Mystery of Keats*, pp. 125–6) to relate some of the remarks in this October letter, especially the phrase, 'self-spiritualised into a kind of sublime Misery', to the Cave of Quietude passage is not at all convincing.

† For an intelligent and detailed analysis of this letter see N. Ford's *The Prefigurative Imagination of John Keats* (pp. 20–38) where the writer examines Keats's argument sentence by sentence.

131

was apparently much of a rationalist, 'a consequitive man' like Taylor, had apparently confessed some 'momentary start about the authenticity of the Imagination'. Just what form Bailey's doubts had taken we can only guess, for there is no record of his observations; but from the context of Keats's letter of reply 'authenticity' must mean primarily 'truth', while we may probably assume that the value of imagination had been called into question. Attempting to meet Bailey half way, Keats forces himself to admit—it is obviously a hard wrench for him, against the grain—that there is a sort of significant 'truth' to be discovered by the exercise of consecutive reason: 'I have never yet been able to perceive how any thing can be known for truth by consequitive reasoning— and yet it must be.' Later he agrees, and less reluctantly, that the sort of 'philosophic Mind' to which he aspires must be, in part at least, a process of 'thought'. But the 'truth' of pure reason is not the only kind of truth, and for Keats himself it is not the most valuable. There is also the truth that is directly and immediately apprehended in whatever the imagination perceives as beautiful, the truth that is therefore synonymous with beauty: 'What the imagination seizes as Beauty must be truth.' It is when the imagination is stimulated by intense feelings* (which include love but are not limited to love) that

---

* This is the significance of that much debated sentence in the letter, 'O for a life of Sensations rather than of Thoughts!' Here 'sensations' is not, as commonly glossed, another word for 'intuitions' but a synonym for the earlier 'Passions' and 'Heart's affections', and it is used in the same way when Keats attempts to define the truly philosophic mind: 'I am continually running away from the subject—sure this cannot be exactly the case with a complex Mind—one that is imaginative and at the same time careful of its fruits—who would exist partly on Sensation partly on Thought—to whom it is necessary that years should bring the philosophic mind.' From his close investigation of Keats's use of 'sensation' N. Ford concludes that it 'almost invariably refers to a state of bodily feeling or emotion produced by direct sensory or imaginative experience' (*op. cit.* p. 26 n.). In his comment on the 'life of Sensations' sentence Ford writes: 'By "a life of sensations" Keats seems frankly to have meant a comparatively unreflective, predominantly sensuous and feelingful kind of aesthetic experience' (p. 25).

it perceives the beauty that is also truth, and in this way the 'truth of Imagination' is inseparable from 'the holiness of the Heart's affections'.

Up to this point Keats's argument is tolerably easy to follow. But in endeavouring to convert Bailey to his point of view he is not content with the claim that the imagination apprehends a valuable kind of truth. He maintains that the imagination can also *create* this truth-beauty, and the simple affirmation 'What the imagination seizes as Beauty must be truth' is immediately followed by 'whether it existed before or not—for I have the same Idea of all our Passions as of Love: they are all in their sublime, creative of essential Beauty.'

These are more perplexing words; but some light is thrown on this idea of an imaginative creation of beauty and truth if we remember, first, that Keats is confessedly talking of 'speculations', of notions, that is to say, that he would like to believe but cannot conclusively prove, even to himself, and, secondly, that these speculations themselves are primarily attempts to vindicate dreams, imaginings, and wishful feelings. Something (the face of a girl seen in Vauxhall Gardens, an elysium for dead poets, the thought of immortal fame) works us up to a state of intense emotional and imaginative excitement, or, alternatively, is revealed to us in such a state. We call that something 'beautiful' because it so stirs us and because it is admirable and desirable. But in the full optimism of youth, and with all the encouragement of the Romantic attitude about him, Keats feels that this beauty must be realized (that is to say, given its 'truth'), even if such realization is postponed to some after-life. Whatever is beautiful cannot just remain an imagining; it *must* come true, and its revelation to the imagination, is, like Adam's dream, a guarantee that it will come true.*

Yet while much of Keats's notion is a wishful optimism, it

---

* This is the attitude that Newell Ford in his book on Keats describes as the poet's 'prefigurative imagination'—a 'feelingful faith in the prefigurative veracity of blissful imaginings' (*op. cit.* 88).

is not entirely that, and we cannot overlook the fact that most of his stress falls on the imaginative creation of *beauty*: truth comes into the argument chiefly by implication. This being so, we can hardly doubt that he was also entertaining the familiar notion that in a state of intense feeling we perceive beauties in the world around us not noticed before, these perceptions being in a certain sense the creation of beauty. There is also in all probability some expression of a central Romantic doctrine—the tacit rejection of the old 'truth to Nature' dogma and the assertion that poetry is a re-creation of Nature. We know how closely Keats had read *Tintern Abbey*, and he would certainly have been in full agreement with the Wordsworth who wrote

> of all the mighty world
> Of eye, and ear,—*both what they half create*,
> And what perceive.[11]

Granted that poetry is some sort of re-creation of Nature, then it cannot be judged entirely by 'truth to Nature', which is much the same as the objective truth of 'consecutive reasoning'; it must be allowed its own intrinsic 'truth'. As Keats puts it in his letter, 'What the imagination seizes as Beauty must be truth—*whether it existed before or not.*'

So much—if at some necessary length—for the nature of Keats's 'favourite Speculation' as expressed in the letter to Bailey. How far does it provide us with a clue to his intentions in *Endymion*?

One thing at least should be clear. In spite of his phrase 'essential Beauty'* Keats is not really expounding any neo-platonic doctrine, for this idea of the creation of essential beauty is by no means the same as belief in a communion with the spirit of ideal beauty. Yet even if Keats's ideas in this letter were considered neo-platonic, it would certainly not follow

---

* '"Essential beauty" can be translated as the beauty of "essences", provided it is understood that "essences" in this usage is merely a loose synonym for "things of beauty" or "shapes of beauty"—mundane and concrete' (Ford, *op. cit.* p. 23).

that *Endymion* is a neo-platonic or metaphysical poem. What we must never forget in relating the letter to *Endymion* is that Keats was referring Bailey not to the whole of the poem for an illustration of his favourite speculation but merely to Book I and to a single lyric from Book IV.* Moreover, it is highly probable that when he was alluding to Book I he was thinking of only one or two passages in it.

Nowhere in the letter is there a suggestion either of a broad and substantial metaphysical meaning in *Endymion* or of a key to such meaning in his 'favourite Speculation'.

A thorough examination of those passages in *Endymion* that the Bailey and Taylor letters point to—especially of Endymion's speech on happiness—must be deferred to the next chapter, where we shall be directly concerned with the poem itself. But there are one or two points concerning these references that may be considered here.

In the letter to Taylor, who by Keats's account is a 'consequitive Man', Keats states that Endymion's speech about happiness 'was a regular stepping of the Imagination towards a Truth'[12]—in other words, it was an imaginative apprehension of reality such as he had earlier described in his letter to Bailey. The comment is plain enough, and there is no reason to question Keats's word. But it should be thoroughly understood that Keats is talking about an imaginative process in himself of which Endymion's speech is the fruit; he is not saying that the creation of essential beauty and the perception of truth is the subject of that speech. This simple distinction

---

* This simple point cannot, apparently, be overstressed. For instance, Middleton Murry's essay on *Endymion* in *The Mystery of Keats* (pp. 118–50), though illuminating in parts, goes badly astray for the reason that Murry uses this letter of 22 November to Bailey to elaborate a substantial metaphysical meaning for the whole poem. Even Ford (*op. cit.*), after a penetrating and in the main acceptable analysis of the letter, proceeds to interpret *Endymion* as a large-scale poetic enactment of Keats's 'favourite Speculation', though by the time his commentary reaches Books III and IV the interpretation is wearing thin and he shifts his emphasis to what he considers to be the theme of infidelity in these two books.

must be emphasized because Murry in his latest essay on *Endymion* patently confuses the two things, and, determined to make Keats's favourite speculation the general key to the meaning of the poem, wills himself to believe that it also supplies the primary meaning to Endymion's argument. 'If we want to understand what, in 1817, Keats meant by saying "What the Imagination seizes as Beauty must be truth", we must look for the answer here.'* However, critical honesty compels Murry to add immediately: 'We confess it is not easy to find.' That at least is truly said, for Endymion's speech is in fact chiefly about happiness—'a kind of Pleasure Thermometer' as Keats describes it in the Taylor letter—and happiness is defined as a sense of oneness and self-destroying that is possible through a range of human experience. To read the speech as primarily an elaboration of Keats's favourite speculation is to distort it beyond recognition.†

All the same Keats did say that this speculation was to be found in Book I, and since he stresses the significance of the 'Pleasure Thermometer' passage in his letter to Taylor, we cannot but assume that he was referring to this passage. Where then is the speculation? Surely it is in those lines where Endymion tells us how the influence of love

> Thrown in our eyes, genders a novel sense,
> At which we start and fret;[13]

or again where Endymion doubts whether the lute would have its tones,

> Tones ravishment, or ravishment its sweet,
> If human souls did never kiss and greet.[14]

In these lines we have a poetic expression of what Keats later wrote in his letter to Bailey—'I have the same Idea of all our

---

* *The Mystery of Keats*, p. 144.

† Ford, who also analyses this speech mainly against the Bailey Letter, completely misinterprets it. For him it is chiefly a defence of 'the prefigurative veracity of erotic dreams' (*op. cit.* p. 18).

Passions as of Love: they are all in their sublime, creative of essential Beauty'. Further, if, as seems most probable, Keats was writing Endymion's speech with Berowne's great paean on love in *Love's Labour's Lost* echoing in his ear, it is reasonable to think that he was trying to say what Shakespeare had said so much more eloquently, and that this reminiscence gave the speech a certain overtone of meaning—for himself at least:

> But love, first learned in a lady's eyes,
> Lives not alone immured in the brain;
> But, with the motion of all elements,
> Courses as swift as thought in every power,
> And gives to every power a double power,
> Above their functions and their offices.
> It adds a precious seeing to the eye . . .[15]

This is of course to find in Book I only a fragmentary, incidental, and passing expression of Keats's favourite speculation. But Keats himself seems to be sensible of this, and in order to illustrate his contention that other passions beside love may create beauty he is compelled to refer Bailey to another small and unconnected fragment of the poem, the 'sorrow' song in Book IV. The 'meaning' of this lyric, which is, as he himself admits, a fanciful representation of what he is trying to say, appears to be that in a state of pure and intense sorrow we perceive new beauties in the world: our sensibilities are heightened through grief. That is true, as many besides great poets have discovered, for sorrow does not invariably benumb us.

Before leaving the letters we may glance at one other point in the Taylor note that, while it does not seem to have been raised by the commentators, may throw some light on Keats's intentions in *Endymion*. Keats concludes his letter with this sentence about the 'happiness' passage: 'It set before me at once the gradations of happiness even like a kind of Pleasure Thermometer—*and is my first Step towards the chief attempt in the Drama—the playing of different Natures with Joy and Sorrow.*' Without any notable objections to the interpretation, many critics—including Murry—have taken the last part of the sentence as another confession of Keats's undoubted ambition to become a great dramatist. Possibly that is what Keats meant; but the curious turn of phrase, especially the two definite articles in '*the* chief attempt in *the* Drama', should make us a little hesitant about plunging from possibility to certainty. And may not Keats have meant something else that is more closely connected with his immediate subject, *Endymion*? Is he perhaps saying that the speech has not only set out for him the gradations of happiness, but is the first important comment on what he has chiefly attempted to do in his poem, namely to reveal the various reactions of different natures towards joy and sorrow? There are some obvious and perhaps insuperable difficulties in this interpretation: 'Drama' would perhaps be an odd word for *Endymion*, though it might explain the preceding definite article; so too would 'playing', unless this word was suggested by 'drama'. But there is at least this much to be said for the conjecture: that there is in the poem, as we shall see, a great deal about joy and grief (some of it very direct writing), about the juxtaposition of joy and sorrow, and about the way characters respond to joyful and sorrowful experience. Is it entirely fanciful to detect a theme-note of all this in the very opening line of the poem?

A thing of beauty is a joy for ever.

Finally among the writings of Keats that may be expected to yield some elucidatory clue to his meaning and intention in *Endymion* there is his Preface, in both the suppressed and published version. The evidence of this is negative but still of some importance. In the first place, for all Keats's indifference to the popular reception of his poem, he is, in both drafts of the preface, apologetic and on the defensive. Now if, in addition to the purely artistic strain of composing his first long poem and filling four thousand lines with one bare circumstance,[16] he had also been striving for the first time to give poetic utterance to certain abstruse metaphysical ideas, we should expect him to mention this in his defence, especially since he is so readily apologetic when trying to explain his speculations in his letters. But nowhere is there a hint of such a defence or a phrase that would help his reader to grasp some important, esoteric meaning in his poem; on the contrary, we find him in his suppressed version of the Preface writing about his subject-matter in a straightforward aesthetic manner that is entirely consistent with his comments on the Endymion tale in 'I stood tip-toe': then it had been a story of 'pure deliciousness', and now he writes, 'I have to apologise to the lovers of simplicity for touching the spell of loveliness that hung about Endymion.'[17] Of course this deference to the 'lovers of simplicity' might, just conceivably, imply that his treatment of the story had been complex and allegorical; but it is much more likely that he is thinking of the highly decorative and thinly spun nature of his version. From the sermonizing of Haydon, and from his own, much more valuable, knowledge of the Elgin Marbles, he must have been completely aware that, whatever he had achieved in his retelling of the Greek legend, he had certainly not achieved a Greek simplicity.

In the second place, the most striking self-accusation that emerges from both drafts is that of uncertainty in thought and imagination: 'as I proceeded my steps were all uncertain';[18] 'the imagination of a boy is healthy; but there is a space of life between, in which the soul is in a ferment, the character undecided, the way of life uncertain.'[19] And all this was repeated three years later in his letter to Shelley when he referred to 'the writer of Endymion! whose mind was like a pack of scattered cards.'[20]

Now if we take any of the chief commentaries that have been written on *Endymion* during this century, by writers like Colvin, Thorpe, Murry and Finney, we find that these provide us with a body of meaning to the poem that is fairly elaborate, generally consistent in itself, extensively patterned to the narrative in a line of steady development, and tolerably complete within its own metaphysical frame of reference. This is all very satisfactory no doubt for the reader who has been taught to believe that there are obscure profundities beneath the surface enchantment of *Endymion*. Yet if the poem really embodies this sort of meaning, is it conceivable that Keats would have condemned himself so strongly for uncertainty of imagination and for having written it at a time when his mind was like a pack of scattered cards? Candour and self-knowledge were qualities that Keats possessed to an exceptionally high degree, and if there is an evident discrepancy between what he says about his poem and what his commentators say, it is safest to look for misunderstanding and misrepresentation among the commentators, however authoritative.

Before closing this survey of those writings of Keats that appear to have any bearing on his intentions in *Endymion*, we should say something about the man himself. Keats was in his twenty-first year when he wrote the poem, and though such a youthful poet might have taken readily enough to the familiar, neo-platonic attitude in the late sixteenth and early seventeenth century, this attitude is not ordinarily one that would make much appeal to a very young writer when it is no longer part of a living literary tradition.

To this objection the neo-platonic exponents of *Endymion* reply that Keats was trying to revive Elizabethan modes of writing and that his fairly extensive reading of Elizabethan literature had familiarized him with allegory in general, and, through Spenser's *Faerie Queene* and *Four Hymnes*, with neo-platonism in particular. It is also suggested—by Finney, for instance—that he was influenced in the same direction by Drayton's two versions of the Endymion story, *Endimion and Phoebe* and the *Man in the Moone*, while some critics refer us to Shelley's *Alastor* and *Hymn to Intellectual Beauty*.

However, so far as the meaning of *Endymion* and Keats's treatment of his material are concerned these alleged influences cannot weigh very much as evidence. The two Drayton poems can be ruled out for a start: first, because it is very improbable that Keats ever read the earlier *Endimion and Phoebe*, which existed in only two copies, and secondly, because the *Man in the Moone*, which he probably did read, is not particularly allegorical in nature. We may also dismiss Shelley's *Hymn to Intellectual Beauty*, since, as Colvin says,* the ideal that Shelley was celebrating in this poem was not one that was at all likely to attract Keats. *Alastor* does perhaps deserve some consideration, for as Leonard Brown† has demonstrated, following some hints in Colvin's study, there are parallels in design and phrasing between *Alastor* and *Endymion* that can hardly be accidental. Keats had certainly read *Alastor* intently, and he was in some respect influenced by it. But Brown's principal thesis is that Keats 'took *Alastor* as a kind of anti-model, and, using the Drayton story and Huntian and Wordsworthian thought, wrote *Endymion* as a philosophical rebuttal of Shelleyan thought.'‡ Whether this reaction from Shelley's *Alastor* is to be taken as a reaction from neo-platonism (or, perhaps it would be truer to say, platonic elements) in the poem, Brown does not explicitly state, and there is some apparent confusion in the implications of his argument; but in the main he appears to suggest that Keats' rebuttal of Shelley involved a less platonic or spiritual attitude.§ Finally, though Keats had an intense love for Spenser, there is no compelling

* *Life of John Keats*, p. 237.

† 'The Genesis, Growth and Meaning of *Endymion*', *Studies in Philology*, Vol. xxx (1933), pp. 618–53. Among the parallels to which Brown draws attention are (1) The Poet's passionate embrace of the 'veiled maid' in dream and Endymion's first embrace of Cynthia in dream as described to Peona; (2) The harp-playing and singing of the veiled maid and Peona's singing and lute-playing; (3) The sense of a desolated earth when the Poet awakens from his vision and *Endymion* 1, 691 ff.; (4) The little shallop floating near the shore that the Poet finds before he sets out on his sea-journey and Peona's 'little shallop, floating there hard by' (1, 423). Some of the imagery in Book ii of *Endymion* is very reminiscent of parts of *Alastor*.

‡ *Art. cit.* pp. 627–8.

§ As when he writes (*op. cit.* p. 628): 'It would seem that the possibility of success in this earthly quest is the rock upon which Keats split from Shelley'; or again, when he interprets Endymion's descent into the earth (Book ii) instead of away from it as a sign that the hero is going to conduct himself like a mortal, not a would-be immortal.

reason to think that his admiration went beyond those Spenserian qualities that he manifestly aspired to in his own poetry before *Endymion* and was to aspire to afterwards, notably in in *The Eve of St Agnes*—the dream world of medieval pageantry, the sensuous and pictorial opulence of ornament, and mellifluousness of language. And if he had read *The Faerie Queene* closely—or *Alastor* and the *Man in the Moone* for that matter—he had read much else besides. For one thing he had certainly read, and relished, Shakespeare's straightforwardly sensuous, erotic, and sometimes lovely *Venus and Adonis*.

Which brings us, through the antithesis of Spenser and Shakespeare, Shelley and Keats, to Keats's temperament. Spenser and Shakespeare both lived in an age when allegorical writing was still a vigorously live tradition and when neo-platonism was widely current. Spenser wrote poetry in the allegorical, neo-platonic mode, Shakespeare did not;* and the fundamental reason for this difference between the two poets is probably that, underneath a common Elizabethan conditioning, they belong to different, and possibly antithetical, psychological types. In the same way all those elements in Shelley's poetry that we may define as neo-platonic or platonic are entirely consistent with everything we know of Shelley's personality, behaviour, and characteristic, general way of looking at things. But Keats was very nearly the psychological anti-type to Shelley. It was his nature to live intensely through his senses; his instinctive tendency, in speculation as in language, was always towards the material, concrete, and sensuously apprehensible; and his highest aspiration as a poet was drama, the direct presentation of human life and of the joys and suffering of flesh and blood men and women. That is why he reminds us of Shakespeare, just as Shelly—though the kinship is much less close—reminds us of Spencer. And if we accept this picture of Keats's psychological make-up and fundamental attitude to life, it is hardly

* The measure here is of course Shakespeare's non-dramatic poetry.

possible to believe that he would have written such a poem of abstruse spirituality and tenuous idealisms as his chief twentieth-century commentators have made out of *Endymion*.

While the representation of *Endymion* as a sustained neo-platonic or generally metaphysical allegory is mainly a product of this century, this interpretation goes back a little further than that—not quite to the boyhood days of Saintsbury's untroubled and unsophisticated reading in the 1860's, but to Mrs F. W. Owen's *John Keats*, which, published in 1880, is properly acknowledged by Colvin to have laid 'the foundations of a true understanding of *Endymion* as a parable of the experiences of a poet's soul in its quest after Beauty'.*

But before that, over a period of sixty odd years, no one among the contemporary or Victorian readers of *Endymion* appears to have believed that the poem was really a 'parable' of this sort. For instance, we find such an acute critic and admirer of Keats as Matthew Arnold writing: '*Endymion* . . . although undoubtedly there blows through it the breath of genius, is yet as a whole so utterly incoherent, as not strictly to merit the name of a poem at all.'† This response of the overwhelming majority of nineteenth-century readers is a significant fact that renders the modern account of the poem suspect, for while each generation may be legitimately expected to re-interpret literary works of the past in the sense of finding new points of significance and relevance and of shifting the focus of critical attention, that is a very different matter from changing a universally accepted work of one kind into another and completely opposing kind. We cannot transform *Venus and Adonis* into the shape of a book from *The Faerie Queene*.

Nor, as it happens, is this consideration simply a negative one. On the contrary, we have some very positive evidence from one of Keats's earliest readers, his friend Bailey. In 1818

* *Op. cit.* p. 544.
† Preface to *Poems* (1853) (Oxford ed. 1930), p. 10.

Bailey and John Taylor, the publisher of *Endymion*, exchanged a series of letters on a matter that bothered them both a good deal—the tone of the poem and especially Keats's treatment of love in it. Now Bailey, who was clearly anxious to do all in his power to help and defend Keats, is likely to have known better than anyone else at this time what Keats had in mind in writing *Endymion*, for there had been long and intimate discussions between the two when, engaged on Book Three, Keats had stayed with Bailey for a fortnight at Oxford.* If Keats had intended his love story to bear the allegorical significance that modern critics have found for it, here was a crying occasion for Bailey to declare what must almost certainly have been his knowledge of Keats's intention. Eroticism would be obscured in the respectable veils of allegory and Spenserian neo-platonism, and all would be well. But, anxious and unhappy as he is about the poem, Bailey never thinks of this interpretation. In fact, in his last and most important letter (29 August 1818) he can only regret Keats's stress on 'sensual love':

> The quarter I *fear* and cannot defend, is the moral part of it. There are two great blotches in it in this respect. The first must offend every one of proper feelings; and indelicacy is not to be borne . . . The second Book, however, was concluded before I knew Keats. The second fault I allude to I think we have noticed. The approaching inclination it has to that abominable principle of Shelley! —*that sensual love is the principle of things.* Of this I believe him to be unconscious, and can see how by process of imagination he might arrive at so false, delusive and dangerous conclusion . . . If he be attacked on these points, and on the first he assuredly will, *he is not defensible.*†

* Keats gives us at least one testimony to Bailey's privileged position at this time as his confidant: 'I wish you knew all that I think about Genius and the Heart,' he wrote in some comment on Haydon, 'and yet I think you are thoroughly acquainted with my innermost breast in that respect' (*Letters*, p. 67).

† Quoted by Finney, *The Evolution of Keats's Poetry*, p. 319. The italics are Bailey's.

These sentences are not, admittedly, conclusive evidence for the solution of our problem. Bailey does allow something to a 'process of imagination', while once we correct the misinterpretations of Shelley, this link that Bailey establishes between the two poets might suggest that there was, after all, some ideality in the belief 'that sensual love is the principle of things'. All the same, we may believe that Bailey in his eagerness to defend Keats from attack would have given a great deal for one clairvoyant glimpse of Colvin or Finney writing their parable interpretations a century later!

When we survey this body of mainly circumstantial evidence bearing on Keats's intentions in *Endymion*, we must admit that no completely convincing conclusion emerges about the manner in which we should read it. Yet, as we weigh the evidence, the scales fall emphatically enough on one side. Apart from one or two passages in the letters—and these can be interpreted in other ways—there is nothing that would lead us to suppose that Keats was writing an allegory full of metaphysical or neo-platonic significance. On the other side, the bulk of the evidence—of Keats's other poetry of the period (especially 'I stood tip-toe' and *Sleep and Poetry*), of his Preface, his temperament, and the response of the first three generations of his readers—points to the belief that he intended *Endymion* simply as a tale of 'pure deliciousness', more like *Venus and Adonis* than the *Man in the Moone* or a book of *The Faerie Queene*, though including here and there a passage of a thoughtful and speculative kind.

CHAPTER V

ENDYMION II

When I was a Schoolboy I thought a fair Woman
a pure Goddess.
Letter to Bailey, 22 July 1818

As one who sits ashore and longs perchance
To visit dolphin-coral in deep seas . . .
To Homer

A very pretty piece of Paganism.*
Wordsworth

I T is just possible that when Keats wrote to Bailey that his 'favourite Speculation' might be known by his 'first Book' he was referring to the two opening paragraphs of *Endymion*, as well as to the later speech on happiness. Whether he was or not, these two paragraphs, speculative in kind and occupying a significant position, deserve our closest attention.

The poem opens with a gnomic line that, quotation-worn as it is, certainly epitomizes the whole of the Introduction and may also provide a key to much else in the work:

A thing of beauty is a joy for ever.

In particular, we should notice that prosaic '*thing* of beauty', which is repeated ten lines later as 'some shape of beauty', for plainly it is not beauty in any ideal or general and abstract sense that Keats is considering here but the beauty of real and concrete things—a quality of them that is directly apprehended by the senses and the imagination. First among these 'thing(s) of beauty' are all those delightful objects of Nature that had already furnished so much of the imagery of his poetry; and Keats lists them in a way that reminds us of

---

* It was the hymn to Pan, not *Endymion* as a whole, that prompted this remark.

the 'poesy of luxuries' that he had wreathed together in 'I stood tip-toe'. Next there is the beauty attached to the memory of dead poets and noble spirits of the past, 'the grandeur of the dooms We have imagined for the mighty dead'—an unusual form of beauty perhaps but one that always moved Keats most profoundly.* Finally there is literature, 'all lovely tales that we have heard or read', and, coupled with this, the exhilaration, so intensely and almost intolerably real to Keats at this time, of discovering oneself to be a poet and dreaming of what could be done with those miraculous powers never to be fully comprehended even by the poet himself—

The passion poesy, glories infinite.

Such 'things of beauty' as these are not of course material in the crudest and simplest sense of that word. They owe something to subjective emotion and imagination, while the poet responds to them not merely with his senses but with what—to use another vague but indispensable word—we may call his whole spirit. In these respects Keats's conception of beauty here may, if we please, be described as a spiritual one. But at the same time we must clearly realize that the beauty he is writing about is in no way transcendental. His speculations are on *things* of beauty, which, however entangled with 'the passion poesy, glories infinite', and perhaps in some measure created by these subjective feelings, are concrete realities of this human life, whether musk-rose blooms, lovely tales, or a poet's thrilling sense of ecstasy. These things of beauty are not intimations or symbols of some ideal or abstract Beauty beyond; and in his first conclusion Keats emphasizes beyond any doubt his quite unplatonic conception:

* Beside these lines we may place a phrase from one of his later letters —'the overpowering idea of our dead poets' (*Letters*, p. 347). Rightly Newell Ford also stresses here Keats's familiar, delighted fancy of the elysium existence enjoyed by dead poets (*The Prefigurative Imagination of John Keats*, p. 42 and pp. 51–2).

> Therefore, on every morrow, are we wreathing
> A flowery band *to bind us to the earth.**

As there is nothing transcendental about the nature of beauty as Keats describes it, so (he implies) there is nothing mystical in our response to it. Nowhere does he so much as hint at an experience that is spiritualizing, purifying, or visionary. The chief effect of beauty on us, he declares, is the stimulation of joy: the joy of perceiving that not everything passes into nothingness, the joy of healthfulness, especially in our sleep and dreams, and, above all else, the joy of solace for our inevitable miseries and depressions of spirit:

> Spite of despondence, of the inhuman dearth
> Of noble natures, of the gloomy days,
> Of all the unhealthy and o'er-darkened ways
> Made for our searching: yes, in spite of all,
> Some shape of beauty moves away the pall
> From our dark spirits.†

It is because all things of beauty, including 'lovely tales', stir us to such joy that Keats is prepared to devote most of the year to the arduous task of writing a long poem on the story of Endymion; he is not, apparently, inspired or fortified by any spiritual vision:

> Therefore, *'tis with full happiness* that I
> Will trace the story of Endymion.[1]

Following a third introductory paragraph, in which he pleasantly outlines his programme of work against the leafy calendar of the seasons, he begins his story, which opens with a description of the Festival of Pan in a forest clearing on the

* 1, 6–7. Yet in spite of these lines an exponent of the neo-platonic interpretation like Finney can write of Keats: 'The material world, he believed, is an unreal, imperfect, ever-changing reproduction of the ideal world, which is real, perfect, and unchanging' (*The Evolution of Keats's Poetry*, p. 301).

† 1, 8–13. This passage is also interesting for Keats's rejection of part of the Romantic attitude. (See also *Sleep and Poetry*, ll. 242–7.)

isle of Latmos. Though this account takes up no less than a third of the book, most of the metaphysical commentators skip rapidly over it—* for the reason that no one has yet been ingenious enough to give it an allegorical interpretation. But if, taking our direction from the clear signpost of the Introduction, we are reading *Endymion* simply as a narrative poem, we shall find several interesting points of significance in the episode, apart from the beauty of odd lines. We shall also discover that, despite the diffuseness of the writing, the Festival is no mere fill-up in the thousand lines that Keats had to compose before Book I was completed to plan.

In the first place, the whole of the description is contrived, somewhat like the peasant gathering in Beethoven's Pastoral Symphony, to produce an overwhelming impression of joyfulness. The occasion itself is of course a supremely joyful one: the folk of Latmos are gathered to render thanks and homage to Pan, their protector and the God of fertility, laughter and merriment. The seasons have been propitious, and it is heady spring-time again:

> Are not our lowing heifers sleeker than
> Night-swollen mushrooms? Are not our wide plains
> Speckled with countless fleeces? Have not rains
> Green'd over April's lap? No howling sad
> Sickens our fearful ewes; and we have had
> Great bounty from Endymion our lord.
> The earth is glad: the merry lark has pour'd
> His early song against yon breezy sky,
> That spreads so clear o'er our solemnity.[2]

But, besides the general occasion of rejoicing, we are constantly reminded of the happiness of the assembled Latmians,

> of this goodly company,
> Of their old piety, and of their glee.[3]

---

* Finney (*op. cit.*) pretty well ignores this episode in his long commentary on Book I, though elsewhere he fully discusses the literary reminiscences in it.

The troop of little children, the first arrivals on the scene, enter 'with joyful cries'; when the folk are all gathered round him, the venerable Priest, for all his solemnity, 'eyed them with joy'; there is continuous music, song, and dancing; and even when the older men join the Priest in serious discussion their speculations turn to Elysium,

> vieing to rehearse
> Each one his own anticipated bliss.[4]

Just how consciously Keats created this impression of universal joy we do not know; nor do we need to. But the effect is certainly there, and it forms a pleasurable part of the pattern of the poem. For one thing, the grief-stricken Endymion, who is present at the Festival, stands out in sharp contrast, though he neither says nor does much. Again, this predominant tone of happiness in the first part of Book I gives variety to it since it is balanced by the contrasting tone of the second part, where Endymion is pouring out his wretchedness to Peona. Further, it is possible to regard this Pan Festival as a theme that is directly developed out of the opening, for in presenting this picture (touched on in other poems)* of a primitive Greek community full of piety and simple delight Keats appears to be giving us a thing of joy that is also a thing of beauty. Admittedly, the beauty of this unsophisticated, joyful way of life is mainly implied; but on one occasion at least it does seem to be explicitly stated and also to link this part of the poem with Keats's recent discovery of Greek art and sculpture. After the hymn to Pan has been sung Keats stands aside for a moment contemplating these happy people of a golden age in the remoteness of history:

> Fair creatures! whose young children's children bred
> Thermopylae its heroes—not yet dead,
> But in old marbles ever beautiful.
> High genitors, unconscious did they cull
> Time's sweet first-fruits.[5]

* See Ch. IX, pp. 334-9.

Joy and beauty: reading those lines, are we altogether fanciful if we hear an echo of those opening phrases of the poem?—

> A thing of beauty is a joy for ever:
> Its loveliness increases; it will never
> Pass into nothingness.

There is one further significance to be noticed in this first part of Book I: though the predominant effect is one of beauty and joy, there is also—and it recurs again and again in the poem—that haunting, characteristically Keatsian, juxtaposition of joy and melancholy. The effect of Endymion's woeful presence is obvious enough. But we should also notice the intertwining of joy and grief in the hymn to Pan, for while Pan is the merry satyr king, laughing at the antics of the fauns and satyrs, he is also the disconsolate lover who

> through whole solemn hours dost sit, and harken
> The dreary melody of bedded reeds—
> In desolate places, where dank moisture breeds
> The pipy hemlock to strange overgrowth;
> Bethinking thee, how melancholy loth
> Thou wast to lose fair Syrinx.*

Some, too, of the dancing and singing Latmian folk, amid their holiday mood, listen with pity to the 'sad death Of Hyacinthus' and the even sadder tale of Niobe, while all of them in their different ways feel an intense and sympathetic grief for the unguessed misery of their lord Endymion.†

Perhaps it is safest to regard this note simply as characteristic of the Keats who was one day to write:

---

* I, 238–43. In 'I stood tip-toe' (ll. 159–62) this joy and grief of Pan is compacted into a more striking paradox.

† We should also notice a passage towards the end of Book I that, in its emphatic intensity, reads very much like an intrusion of Keats himself into the narrative:

> Pleasure is oft a visitant; but pain
> Clings cruelly to us, like the gnawing sloth
> On the deer's tender haunches: late, and loth,
> 'Tis scar'd away by slow returning pleasure. (ll. 906–9)

> Ay, in the very temple of Delight
> Veil'd Melancholy has her sovran shrine.[6]

On the other hand, it may indicate that those last words in his letter of January 1818 to Taylor—'the chief attempt in the Drama—the playing of different Natures with Joy and Sorrow'—re-interpreted, offer something of a guide to his intentions in the poem.

The pity that the Latmians feel for their lord Endymion should be noticed for another reason: that is, the way the theme of sympathetic grief emerges time and again in the course of the poem.* The theme is very prominent, for instance, in the second half of the first book. Not only is Peona unhappy: she is unhappy because her brother Endymion is unhappy; she sympathizes with him in his sorrow; and she is determined to do everything she can to help him. Since an actively sympathetic sister to Endymion was no inevitable part of the story, Keats must have meant this attitude of Peona to be a significant part of his effect.

The narrative in the second half of Book 1 is simple and easily summarized. Peona takes Endymion away from the Pan festivities to her island bower, where he falls asleep. Refreshed by his slumbers, he promises, on awakening, to be more his old active and carefree self. For a while Peona plays to him on her lute; but then she abruptly throws it aside to ask him what it is that has so completely transformed him, and at last Endymion confesses that he is in love. But his beloved is a mysterious figure, a goddess seemingly, who has appeared first to him in a dream. Not that she is entirely a remote vision, for in that dream they had passionately embraced. Peona rallies her brother with a Mercutio-like attack on the absurdity of dreams and on the shame of the pining lover's death; and in reply to this Endymion tries to defend himself with a

---

* The poet whom Keats imagines in 'I stood tip-toe' as first telling the story had been chiefly moved by the pity of it.

long speech in which he defines the supreme happiness of the lover and unrepentantly joins himself with all those who have sacrificed their worldly ambitions for the sake of love. Nevertheless, in spite of this speech, and though, as he confesses, the unknown goddess had appeared to him on two further occasions, he promises Peona to bear up patiently and subdue his grief.

As we read all this we can have no doubt about the sort of poem that Keats is writing. It is a straightforward love poem that, we suspect strongly, owes a good deal to the young poet's own secret dreams and unsatisfied erotic impulses. The unknown goddess is the heroine of all true love tales, supremely beautiful and physically desirable, and Endymion, who plunges characteristically from intolerable ecstasy to 'deadly yellow spleen' and then soars back again into delirium, defends himself explicitly as a lover, ready to sacrifice all for love. There are some less familiar features, to be sure, such as the meeting of Endymion and his beloved in a dream and her unsubstantial elusiveness. But all these features—the dreams, the fleeting appearances, the flights through the air—are understandable enough; there is no need for us to make a mystery of them, for after all we know that we are reading a special sort of love story, common enough in Greek legend, where a mortal falls in love with an immortal. With one possible exception* there is nothing to suggest that this part of the poem bears anything other than its obvious surface meaning.

But if we follow the commentators and their allegory of the imagination (or poetic soul) in quest of ideal Beauty, difficulties—and absurdities—begin to pile up—notably in the account of Endymion's first and third encounter with Cynthia. To begin with, there is Keats's detailed picture of the physical attractions of the goddess.[7] As a description of the heroine of a love-story this passage, including its mawkish touches, is straightforward enough. But, even allowing that in a neo-

---

* Endymion's speech on happiness—to be discussed later.

platonic allegory Keats would have been compelled to represent his ideal in some sort of human form,* can we possibly believe that this full and sensuously luxuriating description of physical charms—and charms that, as the revealing phrase 'paradise of lips and eyes' indicates, are to be physically enjoyed—symbolizes transcendental Beauty?

Even more perplexing, if we follow the commentators, is the notorious passage that describes the dalliance of Endymion with Cynthia:

> I sigh'd
> To faint once more by looking on my bliss—
> I was distracted; madly did I kiss
> The wooing arms which held me, and did give
> My eyes at once to death . . .
> Ah, desperate mortal! I ev'n dar'd to press
> Her very cheek against my crowned lip,
> And, at that moment, felt my body dip
> Into a warmer air.[8]

This, we have to believe, is Keats's allegorical way of expressing the neo-platonic ecstasy in which the soul or poetic imagination finds itself for the first time in mystical union with ideal Beauty!

Of course poets do sometimes communicate a spiritual, even specifically religious, meaning through imagery of a highly erotic sort. But this explanation will not serve here, for the descriptions of the love-making between Endymion and Cynthia are entirely sensuous and erotic. Moreover, at the one point where Keats allows his thought to play over what he is writing his comment comes close to a positive rejection of the neo-platonic attitude:

> 'twas to live,
> To take in draughts of life from *the gold fount*
> *Of kind and passionate looks.*[9]

---

* The description of Moneta in *The Fall of Hyperion* (1, 264–71) shows how Keats could inform physical features with symbolical suggestion—when he wished. And the Cave of Quietude passage indicates that symbolical writing of this kind was not beyond Keats in 1817.

Nor is it possible for the neo-platonic commentators to side-step the absurdity that their allegorical reading of Book 1 creates by arguing that Endymion represents the soul or poetic imagination that is still at this stage in the trammels of physical love. Cynthia, the alleged ideal Beauty, speaks exactly the same language as Endymion:

> Echo hence shall stir
> No sighs but sigh-warm kisses, or light noise
> Of thy combing hand, the while it travelling cloys
> And trembles through my labyrinthine hair.[10]

Some of the commentators* have tried to conceal the gap between their allegorical reading and Keats's words by stressing the artistic failure of this part of the poem: Keats, they say, had not yet learnt how to treat love except in a mawkish fashion. But 'treatment' can never be regarded as a merely superficial matter of style; however distasteful we may find Keats's treatment of Endymion and Cynthia, we must recognize that it expresses a real and substantial part of his attitude to sexual love at this time. Further, it is extremely doubtful whether a poet who wrote like this about love could ever have seriously entertained the neo-platonic attitude.†

In discussing the second part of Book 1 we have reserved for special attention Endymion's speech on happiness (ll. 769–842), since this passage is commonly used as a main founda-tion-stone for the neo-platonic, allegorical interpretation. Here

---

* Thus Colvin (*Life of John Keats*, p. 213) remarks on 'Keats's treat-ment of love as an actuality, which in this poem is in unfortunate and distasteful contrast with his high conception of love in the abstract as the inspiring and ennobling power of the world and all things in it.'

† A smaller difficulty created by the neo-platonic interpretation arises from Endymion's sense of a world transformed into loathsomeness when he awakens from his first dream of Cynthia. (ll. 691–8). This passage is easily acceptable so long as we are thinking of Endymion as the con-ventional romantic lover; but if he has just been afforded his first vision of essential beauty, we should rather expect him to return to the beauties of the material world with a renewed sense of delight.

we are told, Keats is asserting that the highest form of happiness is the mystical communion with ideal or essential Beauty.

To appreciate the fallaciousness of this reading and to understand what Keats is really saying we must keep the speech firmly in its context. One of the means Peona had adopted to rally her brother had been to appeal to his old heroic aspirations, and in his first words Endymion takes up the matter of his ambition. He never allows it to become the main theme of his argument, but by the end of his speech he explicitly renounces his earlier ambitions to identify himself with those who

> Have been content to let occasion die,
> Whilst they did sleep in love's elysium.[11]

This familiar antithesis between ambition and love of the Mark Antony kind makes plain, straightforward sense—especially when we remember that it probably sprang from a conflict in Keats himself at the time.* But if we take Endymion as the poetic soul in quest of essential Beauty we are faced with an obvious difficulty. Why did he not defend himself against Peona's charge with some intimation that, so far from abandoning lofty endeavour, he was merely substituting a more spiritual for a lower and wordly aim?†

The love for which Endymion is prepared to sacrifice everything is certainly no mere 'commingling of passionate breath'. It is an elevating experience that stimulates our senses and imagination and so is creative of beauty;[12] it prompts us to humanitarian good;[13] it is part of the whole generative process of nature[14] and indeed the vital sustenance of human life itself:

> when we combine therewith,
> Life's self is nourish'd by its proper pith,
> And we are nurtured like a pelican brood.[15]

But, notwithstanding all these lofty claims, it is unmistakably

---

* See the later comment on Book IV and also Ch. VI, 'La Belle Dame Sans Merci'.

† And why Endymion's sense of shame (I, 761–2)?

human sexual love that Endymion is choosing and defending, the love of those who 'kiss and greet', even—we must admit—love of an enervating, deliquescent sort; for the sentiment that had informed the earlier description of the love-making between Endymion and Cynthia—

> madly did I kiss
> . The wooing arms which held me, and did give
> My eyes at once to death[16]

—is here consciously celebrated as the 'ardent listlessness' of those who 'sleep in love's elysium'.[17] There is nothing at all in Endymion's speculations of the spiritualized, transcendental love of neo-platonism, nothing even to suggest that the love he is defending is an intermediate stage, since it is itself an 'unsating food'.

However, what gives Endymion's speech its main pattern and impetus is a claim for human sexual love that we have so far not discussed. Not unnaturally in the circumstances, Peona has, with gentle mockery, made much of her brother's love-sickness and misery. Endymion does not deny his present wretchedness, but he maintains, as his 'higher hope', that love, paradoxically, is also the source of the supreme kind of happiness. Happiness, he contends—at least the only sort of happiness worth seeking—is the state in which the self, with all its barriers and limitations, is destroyed and we are conscious of a union, a sense of 'oneness', with the world outside us.* To some extent the higher pleasures of the senses and imagination in natural beauty and music† may afford this sensation:

> Feel we these things?—that moment have we stept
> Into a sort of oneness, and our state
> Is like a floating spirit's.[18]

But the richest and intensest experience of this 'oneness' lies in love and friendship:

* There has already been a prelude hint of this conception in ll. 97–100.
† This part of the speech is, admittedly, a little obscure.

> there are
> Richer entanglements, enthralments far
> More self-destroying, leading, by degrees,
> To the chief intensity: the crown of these
> Is made of love and friendship.[19]

Above all, there is the oneness, and therefore happiness, of love:

> Nor with aught else can our souls interknit
> So wingedly.[20]

Because this self-destroying that, according to Keats here, constitutes true happiness is a refined, subtle, and comparatively rare psychological state, he is compelled to use language that is highly metaphorical and sometimes reminiscent of neo-platonic and other mystical descriptions of 'ecstasy'. That is why the commentators who have utilized this speech as a basis for their allegorical reading of the poem have thrown such immense stress on the lines,

> Wherein lies happiness? In that which becks
> Our ready minds to fellowship divine,
> A fellowship with essence; till we shine,
> Full alchemiz'd, and free of space. Behold
> The clear religion of heaven![21]

But, as Newell Ford has convincingly shown, the key-word 'essence' has no metaphysical reference for Keats: its primary meaning for him is *existence* or *entity*, inanimate or objective for the most part, and here it is equivalent to 'a thing of beauty'.* Further, to say nothing of the fact that Keats is, after all, relating a tale of a mortal and a goddess, we must remember his persistent fondness for religious turns of ex-

---

* 'When he wrote "Feel we these things?" at l. 795 he assumed that his readers would understand the equivalence of "things" (of beauty) with "essences". Had he written "fellowship with essences" or had the first line of the poem read: "An *essence* of beauty is a joy for ever", philosophic-minded critics might not have been misled.' ('The Meaning of "Fellowship with Essence" in *Endymion*', *P.M.L.A.*, December 1947, p. 1072: later incorporated in *The Prefigurative Imagination of John Keats*.)

pression when we consider such words and phrases as 'divine'*
and 'clear religion of heaven'. What he really had in mind
was clearly and simply brought out by his first version of
these lines:

> Wherein lies happiness? In that which becks
> Our ready minds to blending pleasurable:
> And that delight is the most treasureable
> That makes the richest Alchymy.[22]

'Blending pleasurable' is entirely consistent with the later
'sort of oneness', 'enthralments', and 'self-destroying', and we
may be certain that he revised his first draft not because he
had a new idea to express but because he realized that it was
poor stuff poetically.

To sum up: what Endymion is defending, in direct answer
to Peona's attack, is human and sensuous love, and his chief
argument is that from love arises supreme happiness—
happiness being defined as a state of 'self-destroying' and
sense of 'oneness' with the outside world, including other
human beings. All this has nothing to do with neo-platonic
vision or ecstasy, for there is nothing beyond this self-destroying, no transcendental communion with ideal Beauty. If we
should require any outside key to Endymion's speech this is
to be found not in Spenser's *Hymnes* or that part of the letter
to Bailey where Keats is expounding his 'favourite Speculation' but in a more casual sentence from the same letter: 'The
setting Sun will always set me to rights—or if a Sparrow come
before my Window I take part in its Existence and pick about
the Gravel'.† Here, more prosaically and succinctly expressed,
is the same 'fellowship with essence' that Endymion attempts
to describe to Peona, for when Keats used the word 'existence'

---

* 'Divine' probably came in as a forceful antithesis to the previous
'earthly wrecks'.

† *Letters*, p. 69. This sentence from the letter to Bailey is particularly
relevant since its immediate context is a denial of 'worldly happiness' in
the conventional sense of the phrase.

he might just as well have substituted his own particular synonym 'essence'.

It must certainly be granted that while Endymion's speech is thoroughly appropriate to him as the hero of a love-story involving a goddess, it goes beyond the strict needs of the narrative and must be considered primarily as an expression of some of Keats's own speculations at the time. Yet the speech is not a digression. For one thing, it can be regarded as an elaboration to the Introduction to the poem: things of beauty, the 'essences', are again lovingly listed; but this time they are arranged in an hierarchy of values, while, more important still, Keats endeavours to show why, fundamentally, 'a thing of beauty is a joy for ever'. Again, as we shall see, one part at least of the speech points forward to a main development in the poem.* Finally, because Endymion throws so much emphasis on happiness and because happiness is a 'higher hope' contrasting sharply with his present wretchedness, this speech once more confronts us with that juxtaposition of joy and sorrow that is recurrent through the poem. Here we might well believe that Keats is revealing for us 'the playing of different Natures with Joy and Sorrow'.

The reflective passage that opens Book II presents the clearest of pointers to the kind of poem that Keats is writing. Eulogizing the 'sovereign power of love'† and dismissing 'pageant history', he asserts that all the heroic and martial deeds of the past have little imaginative effect on us as they recede into the mists of time, and that it is only the famous love-stories—of Troilus and Cressida, Juliet, Hero, Imogen, and Pastorella—that remain alive and moving in our memory. Even in most summary catalogue these tales spell passionate human love,‡ nothing at all of the spiritualized, neo-platonic

* Ll. 826–7, to Book III.
† The complete line should be noted as another pointer to one of Keats's intentions—'O sovereign power of love! O grief! O balm!'
‡ When reading l. 13, 'The close of Troilus and Cressid sweet', we

attitude; but Keats establishes our associations beyond any possible doubt. From these living records of love

> One sigh doth echo, one poor sob doth pine,
> One kiss brings honey-dew from buried days;[23]

while the Juliet he pictures for us is leaning

> Amid her window-flowers,—sighing,—weaning
> Tenderly her fancy from its maiden snow.[24]

What we are treading is the 'path of love', like that of *Troilus and Cressida* and *Romeo and Juliet*, and—revealing word—of 'poesy',[25] that is to say, of sensuous enchantment and tales of 'pure deliciousness'. The poet's intention is simply

> to uprear
> Love's standard on the battlements of song.*

The narrative of Book II, which undoubtedly served to expel from Keats's imaginative system intoxicants that he had taken from *Vathek*, the *Arabian Nights*, Mrs Radcliff's novels, and other sources,† begins with an account of Endymion's descent‡ into 'the silent mysteries of the earth'. This episode is clearly to be understood as a descent into the realms of death, and we have been admirably prepared for this by a prelude passage in Book I, where the innocent bird in front of Endymion's footsteps was seen by him as

should perhaps recall that 'close' in *Troilus and Cressida* (3. 2. 51) signifies sexual relations.

* Ll. 40–1. A critic, like Colvin, so wedded to the idea of *Endymion* as a poem of deep spiritual and allegorical significance that he will write of this introductory passage, 'must one not believe that all poor flawed and fragmentary human loves . . . are far off symbols and shadowings of that Love which, unless the universe is quite other than we have trusted, "moves the sun and the other stars" ' (*Life of John Keats*, p. 183) will believe anything; and he is philosophizing far from the text of the poem.

† Keats may also have been striving to outdo the phantasmagoria of *Alastor*.

‡ Endymion's pursuit of the butterfly nymph is obviously a piece of narrative embroidery, though we should certainly notice the re-emergence of the pity theme (ll. 121–2).

> A disguised demon, missioned to knit
> My soul with under darkness; to entice
> My stumblings down some monstrous precipice.[26]

So now, Keats says, Endymion has been cheated

> Into the bosom of a hated thing;[27]

and the 'rapacious deep' of 'dismal elements'[28] that Keats's imagination conjures up for us is a region of 'silence dead',[29] a hard, bright, sterile world of stone, minerals and jewels, totally bare of vegetation.*

As well as this impression there are other powerful and corresponding suggestions, as in the lines:

> he sat down before the maw
> Of a wide outlet, fathomless and dim,
> To wild uncertainty and shadows grim;[30]

while much of the architecture—the 'mimic temple', the 'long pillard'd vista,' the 'fair shrine' and the 'sidelong aisles'— is almost identical with the setting of Book 1 of *The Fall of Hyperion*, which is generally accepted as a poetic description of 'dying into life'. Also, Endymion's own sensations are just those experienced by the Poet in *The Fall of Hyperion*—a feeling of deathly cold that comes especially from the marble floor:

> Chilly and numb
> His bosom grew . . .

> And when, more near against the marble cold
> He had touch'd his forehead . . .

---

* We are reminded of Baudelaire, *Rêve parisien*, 10–16, cv, *Les Fleurs du Mal*. Baudelaire goes on, reinforcing this idea of unnaturalness, to present us with an image of water arrested, metallic or mineral-like, 'comme des rideaux de cristal'. So close is the correspondence between the sensibilities of the two poets that Keats also, in his long description of the thousand fountains (600–26), represents them as petrified into various shapes and substances.

lowly bow'd his face
Desponding, o'er the marble floor's cold thrill.*

And what, if not the approach of death, is suggested by the
lines:

Upon my ear a noisy nothing rings . . .
Before mine eyes thick films and shadows float.[31]

Has this unmistakable poetic effect any significant meaning
that is consistent with a tale of a mortal hopelessly in love
with a goddess and consistent with the internal logic of the
poem?

To this question there are at least two possible answers,
neither of which necessarily excludes the other. First, we recall,
from the speech on happiness in Book I, that the chief joy of
love as Endymion conceives it is fellowship, oneness, self-
destroying. Here in this underworld experience of Endymion
we have beyond reasonable doubt a poetic statement of the
obverse of this attitude: that solitude, self-isolation, is spiritual
death, and death is solitude. Continually through this episode,
with an epithet or a phrase, Keats emphasizes the loneliness
and isolation of his hero, and the climax to this part of the
poem, just before Endymion makes his first bid for renewed
life, occurs in the lines:

What misery *most drowningly* doth sing
In lone Endymion's ear, now he has raught
The goal of consciousness? Ah, *'tis the thought,
The deadly feel of solitude.*†

* II, 243–4; II 265–6; II, 337–8. Cf. *The Fall of Hyperion*, I, 122 ff.:
suddenly a palsied chill
Struck from the paved level up my limbs,
And was ascending quick to put cold grasp
Upon those streams that pulse beside the throat, etc.
† II, 281–4. Possibly there is a close identity here between Keats and
his hero. One is reminded of his own experiences in the Isle of Wight
when he was trying to make a start on *Endymion:* 'Another thing. I was too
much in Solitude, and consequently was obliged to be in continual burning of thought as an only resource' (*Letters*, p. 25). There may also have
been some recollection of *Alastor*.

At the same time Endymion's first wanderings in the under-world do not merely constitute a poetic statement, an elaboration, principally through imaginative effect, of ideas implicit in the speech on happiness. The episode is part of the narrative movement of the poem. In the lines just quoted Endymion is represented as coming back to full self-consciousness, and immediately before them we read:

> When new wonders ceas'd to float before,
> And thoughts of self came on, how crude and sore
> The journey homeward to habitual self![32]

From what is Endymion returning? The answer to that question appears to be, from a mood of escapism that has taken the form of a secret death-wish.* In his misery of apparently hopeless love Endymion has been 'half in love with easeful death'.

Certainly when Endymion first plunges into the underworld at the bidding of the airy voices, Keats is teasingly niggard of illuminating clues. But at least it is transparently clear that Endymion is impelled by an irresistible mood of escape, and since this 'fearful deep' into which he plunges is soon and overwhelmingly established as the realm of death, it is reasonable to believe that Keats's intention in this episode was to represent an impulse of Endymion towards death and self-extinction—not perhaps as a calculated narrative stroke but because, momentarily identified with his hero, he was projecting into him a characteristic impulse of his own. That there is some connexion between this part of Book II and the movement towards 'easeful death' in the *Ode to a Nightingale* seems to be borne out by the similarity between the lines,

---

* There is a hint of this in Book I. Though Endymion realized that the bird in his path might be some demon enticing him into 'under darkness', he nevertheless
> *eager* followed, and did curse
> The disappointment.
> (l. 704–5)

When new wonders ceas'd to float before,
And thoughts of self came on, how crude and sore
The journey homeward to habitual self![33]

and the last stanza of the ode:

Forlorn! the very word is like a bell
To toll me back from thee so my sole self!
Adieu! the fancy cannot cheat so well
As she is fam'd to do, deceiving elf.*

This verbal similarity between the two poems is probably
not fortuitous or merely incidental. The *Ode to a Nightingale* is
an attempt through fancy to escape from the pressing reality
of misery and pain; and this escapism reaches its climax in a
momentary longing for the 'intensity' of death. But at the
very moment of near surrender to the death-instinct, there is
an abrupt and decisive reversal in the movement of the poem:
Keats recognizes this culmination of the escapist mood for the
deception it is and simply and poignantly admits the reality
of this last 'luxury':

Still wouldst thou sing, and I have ears in vain—
To thy high requiem become a sod.[34]

So Endymion, fleeing from his misery of a seemingly hopeless
love and also tempted to plunge into the oblivion of death,
suddenly, just before it is too late, realizes that he has been
cheated 'Into the bosom of a hated thing'. For him, as we
have already suggested, part of the discovered horror is that
death is only another name for his excruciating loneliness—
'the *deadly* feel of solitude'. But like Keats himself in the *Nightingale* ode, and in spite of his earlier, all too facile belief that
the earth was robbed of its beauty because Cynthia had gone
away, he also realizes that death is the deprivation of these

* Ll. 71–4. Ford draws attention to this parallel (*The Prefigurative
Imagination of John Keats*, p. 53, n.). But Ford interprets the *Endymion* lines
as one of the moods of scepticism in the hero about the veracity of prefigurative imagination. 'Endymion's disillusioned confession constitutes the
very obverse of that staunch faith in the letter to Bailey and in the first book
of *Endymion*' (p. 52).

beauties—and not only of their sensuous pleasure but of that 'fellowship with essence'* that constitutes supreme happiness. A sudden prayer breaks from him that he may once more see the beauties of the green earth and be delivered from the 'rapacious deep'; and with this entreaty there is a turn in the poem as decisive as the reversal in the sixth stanza of the *Ode to a Nightingale.*†

The return to life is symbolized in a most arresting way: vegetation suddenly springs up through the marble floor, and all the dead, mineral and metallic world is obliterated in flowers and vegetation:

> lowly bow'd his face
> Desponding, o'er the marble floor's cold thrill.
> But 'twas not long; for, sweeter than the rill
> To its cold channel, or a swollen tide
> To margin sallows, were the leaves he spied,
> And flowers, and wreaths, and ready myrtle crowns
> Up heaving through the slab: refreshment drowns
> Itself, and strives its own delights to hide—
> Nor in one spot alone; the floral pride
> In a long whispering birth enchanted grew
> Before his footsteps.[35]

Through this description we are transported to the world of Book I again, with all its imagery of prolific vegetal life; and in a minute or two,‡ after another passage that repeats the

---

* It is highly significant that the word 'companionship' (with no reference to Cynthia) occurs at this point (l. 291).

† This parallel with the *Nightingale* ode suggests another possible way in which we may take the first part of this underworld journey. What Keats particularly renounces as a cheat in the ode is 'fancy', and it may be that in depicting this underworld of extravagant fantasy that is also an image of death Keats was implying that an escape from painful reality on the wings of fantasy is a similar sort of deceit. At least it is when 'new wonders ceas'd to float before' that Endymion's 'journey homeward to habitual self' begins.

‡ This interlude includes a description of mysterious sleepy music that Endymion hears (II, 355–75). Endymion's thoughts—of the intolerable power of music, of love that destroys all other joys—are understandable if we take him as a typical romantic consumed with 'elemental passion'. Orsino in *Twelfth Night*, which Keats may have had in mind, expresses

impression of growth and vegetation,[36] we come upon Adonis, who is slumbering, not on a chill marble floor, but 'upon soft verdure'.[37]

The description of the awakening of Adonis that follows is richly effective in the pattern of poetic impressions.* To begin with, the Venus-Adonis story is a vegetation myth, of the renewed life of leaves and flowers rising in spring-time out of the barrenness and death of winter; and from this merely general association of the story we receive a satisfying sense of elaboration of what has just gone before in the poem. But there is much more in Keats's treatment of the story than this: in his description of the sleeping Adonis, he suggestively and powerfully accentuates† all the vegetative associations of the myth, as well perhaps as recalling the thought in the speech on happiness that sexual love is part of the process of re-birth in nature. The chamber in which Adonis lies is walled with myrtles, his coverlids are tinted like a peach or 'ripe October's faded marigolds', his mouth is like 'a dew-lipp'd rose', and one of the attendant Cupids shakes perfumes from a willow bough over him and rains violets on his eyes. Most striking of all, there is the very full description of the bower in which Adonis reclines smothered with flowers and green growth.[38] Again, when Endymion, invited by one of the attendant Cupids to recline on living flowers, is offered wine, pears, and 'a bunch of blooming palms', there is another passage that is luxuriously suggestive of all the bounty of nature, while to signalize the approach of Venus Keats evokes a world of summer breezes, leaves, finches, and clover-sward.‡

just such sentiments. But would the neo-platonic lover experience this feverish 'pest' of love or feel himself incapable of enjoying music and the other arts that may be initiation into ideal beauty?

* It is a pity that the main narrative is not substantial enough to bear the episode, which, when we are judging *Endymion* as a story poem, must strike us as over-elaborated.

† It is odd to find Ford writing (*op. cit.* p. 54): 'Keats is not interested in the naturalistic symbolism of the myth.'

‡ The imagery also creates a certain sense of a transition from darkness to light: the chamber in which Adonis lies is filled with 'panting light' (II,

However, it is not only—or chiefly—because it is a vegetation myth that the Venus-Adonis story falls so appropriately into place at this point in the poem. It powerfully and poetically sustains the idea of Endymion's returning life because it is one of the great archetypal legends of resurrection, and in particular of love that triumphs over death.

About the nature of that love it would not be necessary to waste many words were it not that our response to *Endymion* has been distorted by so many attempts to turn it into a work of spiritual significance. But plainly for Keats—as for Shakespeare—this Greek myth was an affirmation of pagan, sensuous love; and indeed no one has ever dreamt of turning it into a symbol of the neo-platonic attitude. The Venus of this story is a goddess who

> scuds with summer breezes, to pant through
> The first long kiss, warm firstling, to renew
> Embower'd sports in Cytherea's isle.[39]

Moreover, there is more than a general prompting to this sort of love in the scorn that the 'feathered lyrist' pours out for the passionless creature that Adonis was in his earthly life:

> Who would not be so imprison'd? but, fond elf,
> He was content to let her amorous plea
> Faint through his careless arms; content to see
> An unseiz'd heaven dying at his feet.[40]

All the time we are reading the poem we are conscious that, with a change of the sex-roles, this story of 'how the seaborn goddess pin'd for a mortal youth' is parallel with the story of Cynthia and Endymion.* So there is a lesson for Endymion —and Cynthia—in this to some extent unhappy fate of Venus

383), and the coming of Venus's chariot gives us a glimpse of the 'blue heaven' (II, 518). However, the underworld, illumined by the various jewelled substances, has never been a region of complete gloom—'nor bright, nor sombre wholly' (II, 222)—and the contrast is not so striking as that between the stones and metals and the vegetation.

* This is of course a further reason for the relevance of the story.

and Adonis; and when the Cupid reproves the old frigidity of Adonis he is also, and pointedly, reminding Endymion and Cynthia not to despise the love of 'embracements warm'. The Endymion and Cynthia of the neo-platonic fable would have nothing to learn from this episode. Keats's Endymion, on the other hand, drinking wine and feasting on luscious fruits as the story of Venus and Adonis is unfolded, is certainly identified with the passionate, sensuous love whose triumph he witnesses.

This impression of a lover-hero who belongs to the company of Venus and Adonis is confirmed by what follows. To Venus Endymion is a gentle youth whose

> days are wild
> With love. [41]

She has always felt a sympathetic bond with him in his pining after 'some fair immortal', and now—with a return, be it noted, of the theme of sympathy and active pity—she entreats the god Cupid to assist Endymion towards the consummation of his desire. Before she passes out of sight she sustains Endymion with the promise of ultimate bliss in his love. Both her entreaty and promise mark a further stage in Endymion's recovery from his deathly dejection. He is still in the underworld, still in loneliness; but now

> he felt assur'd
> Of happy times, when all he had endur'd
> Would seem a feather to his mighty prize. [42]

After this encounter with Venus and Adonis Endymion wanders further through the underworld. Probably a good deal of the narrative here is written in the spirit that, with humorous exaggeration, Keats describes in a letter to Jane Reynolds, [43] and much of it reads like more fantasy-spinning to fill up the book. But though the description momentarily takes us back to a world of

> caves, and palaces of mottled ore,
> Gold dome, and crystal wall, and turquoise floor, [44]

there is no very serious repetition, nor does Keats destroy the imaginative impression of life and efflorescence that he has just created. A delicate and probably instinctive sense of poetic fitness saves him, and this time we are not overwhelmed by images of sterile stone and minerals. The dominant image, of the thousand fountains, is one of activity, and it is elaborated in such a way that our chief impression is still one of life and vegetation. The columns of the fountains rise a 'poplar's height'; their sound is like 'dolphin tumults'; and sometimes they are

> weeping trees,
> Moving about as in a gentle wind,
> Which, in a wink, to watery gauze refin'd,
> Pour'd into shapes of curtain'd canopies,
> Spangled, and rich with liquid broideries
> Of flowers, peacocks, swans, and naiads fair.[45]

Further, not long after this description* there is an outstanding instance of a characteristic Keatsian 'sensation', when Endymion (and the readers of the poem) are smothered in rich and teeming vegetation.[46]

All this richly sensuous evocation of flowers and vegetation creates a most effective prelude to the next important episode

---

* Something perhaps should be said about the encounter with Cybele (II, 639–49). De Selincourt (*Poems of John Keats*, p. 433) is probably right in suggesting that much of Keats's description of the goddess came from Sandys's translation of Ovid's *Metamorphoses*. It also looks very much as though Keats was familiar with representations of Cybele in art. An *Encyclopaedia Britannica* article, in reference to Cybele's manifestation in art, states: 'she appears usually with mural crown and veil, well draped, seated on a throne, and accompanied by two lions.' This is very close indeed to Keats's description.

Was this episode merely ornamental or—since it follows the Venus and Adonis episode—had Keats picked up somewhere in his reading the knowledge that Cybele was a goddess of fertility connected by the Romans with a cycle of spring festivals and in some forms with a belief in immortality, that she had a youthful lover Attis, a god of vegetation, who in a Lydian version of the legend was killed like Adonis by a boar? The strong association with the Venus-Adonis episode is certainly a remarkable coincidence if Keats was unaware of it.

of Book II—Endymion's meeting with Cynthia in the underworld. But of course it is not simply the imagery that brings
us with a feeling of inevitability to this climax. The whole
course of the story of Book II has led us expectantly to this
culmination of an actual (as opposed to dream-like) meeting
between the lovers. Endymion has struggled out of life into
death; he has seen the resurrection of Adonis, a mortal, and
his happy reunion with the goddess Venus; he has been given
a promise of bliss and has come to feel an assurance of happy
times. We have some while ago heard the key-note of this
book, 'Once more sweet life begin'; [47] and we know that
Endymion must have his Cynthia, as Venus has had her
Adonis.

The climax is, notoriously, a disappointment, and probably
the worst passage in the poem; it is a piece of unabashed
eroticism, vulgar and sickly-sentimental by turns. But if we
rightly choose to skip it,* we must at the same time recognize
that in its essential spirit it entirely harmonizes with the preceding Venus and Adonis story and indeed with all that has
gone before in a love tale of sensuous human passion. The
Endymion who embraces Cynthia is one whose

> every sense had grown
> Ethereal for pleasure; [48]

and it is utterly impossible to believe that lines like,

> just into the air
> Stretching his indolent arms, he took, O bliss!
> A naked waist, [49]

or Cynthia's passionate protest that she will

> press at least
> My lips to thine, that they may richly feast
> Until we taste the life of love again, [50]

* However, Ford (*The Prefigurative Imagination of John Keats*, p. 56) notes
an interesting parallel between II, 739–45 and the 'Bright star' sonnet.

represent the neo-platonic union of the soul with ideal beauty.*
Moreover, Keats himself offers us the clearest possible indication how this episode is to be taken:

> *Ye who have yearn'd*
> *With too much passion*, will here stay and pity
> For the mere sake of truth.[51]

It is true that this account of the most physical kind of love-
making is followed by the lines:

> Now I have tasted her sweet soul to the core
> All other depths are shallow: essences,
> Once spiritual, are like muddy lees,
> Meant but to fertilize my earthly root,
> And make my branches lift a golden fruit
> Into the bloom of heaven.[52]

But so long as we keep these sentiments in their context there
is no call to read anything spiritual or neo-platonic† into them.
They are uttered by a youth who, we have just been told,

> swoon'd
> Drunken from Pleasure's nipple;[53]

and whatever he may say in the idealizations of after-reflection,
we know that there has been singularly little of the soul in his
ecstasies. What he has discovered beyond any doubt now is
that it is a goddess he is in love with, and he has been promised
'an immortality of passion'.‡ In such circumstances as these it
is only natural that he should be dismissing earthly things and
dreaming of heaven.§

---

    * The 'nympholeptic dream', as Finney chooses to call this episode,
does not merely 'distort' the neo-platonic theme of the romance (*The
Evolution of Keats's Poetry*, p. 450); it completely explodes it.
    † As Finney and Thorpe do, for example.
    ‡ II, 808. Ford takes this as the key phrase of the poem, laying great
stress on 'immortality'.
    § The 'essences' (things of beauty) had been in a sense 'spiritual' since
they had offered that experience of oneness and self-destroying that
constitutes true happiness. But Endymion's most recent meeting with
Cynthia has convinced him now of the truth of what had always been his
'higher hope': that love is the most intense form of oneness and therefore
the supreme form of happiness.

It is also relevant at this point to glance back at an impressive piece of descriptive writing that immediately precedes Endymion's elevated reflections on his love-making with Cynthia:

> It was a sounding grotto, vaulted vast
> O'er studded with a thousand, thousand pearls,
> And crimson mouthed shells with stubborn curls,
> Of every shape and size, even to the bulk
> In which whales arbour close, to brood and sulk
> Against an endless storm. Moreover too,
> Fish-semblances, of green and azure hue,
> Ready to snort their streams.*

Probably there was some calculated contrivance in this passage, for the poem was moving towards the interlude of Alpheus and Arethusa, and towards the third book, which was to be set under the sea. But it is no less probable that there was some free fantasy-writing too; and the chief images of the cave, shells, fish, and spouted water are all familiar sexual symbols. Caves, shells, along with pebbles and fountains (also sexual symbols), are recurrent and key-images throughout the poem, and they point unmistakably to a fundamental erotic impulse behind it.† Such a subconscious inspirational urge does not of course necessarily rule out the possibility of some

---

* II, 878–85. This reference to the 'sounding grotto' reminds us how all the main imagery in Book II is announced—summary-wise— in the apostrophe to Sleep in Book I (ll. 456–60):

> Great key
> To golden palaces, strange minstrelsy,
> Fountains grotesque, new trees, bespangled caves,
> Echoing grottos, full of tumbling waves
> And moonlight!

† Another passage comparable with the one quoted above for the sexual significance of its images is II, 918–26, with its references to outgushing springs, shells, rocks and lofty grottos. Again, much of the imagery in the first description of the underworld—of the vast antre, winding passage, silver grots, columns, floods and waterfalls—has an obvious sexual association that is fused with the other main association of death. Notable, too, in the poem are the fairly numerous descriptions of soaring flights through the air.

neo-platonic or spiritual intention in Keats's conscious mind when he was writing the poem; and those who argue for such an intention might retort with the psycho-analytical doctrine of sublimation. But there is nothing automatic about sublimation; it demands strong determinant conditions, and a realization of this underlying impulse in *Endymion* should at least make us hesitate before we accept the neo-platonic interpretation. If, on the other hand, we regard the poem as primarily a tale of sensuous, passionate love, then the conscious and subconscious levels of the poem perfectly correspond.

The last of the principal episodes of Book II is Endymion's encounter with the river spirits, Alpheus and Arethusa, and so long as we are not expecting a continuous and substantial narrative this episode falls in the main satisfyingly into place. To begin with, it forms another parallel with the main story: like Endymion, Alpheus is pursuing one who appears reluctant to return his love; he experiences all Endymion's anguish of frustration, and his opening words express what must at this time be Endymion's own feelings towards Cynthia, even if, after his recent meeting with her, he is no longer a prey to Alpheus' (and his own past) despair. As poetry these opening words of Alpheus are poor stuff, but they deserve notice because, like most of the Venus-Adonis passage, they emphasize that physical kind of love that forms so much of the substance of the poem:

> O that her shining hair was in the sun,
> And I distilling from it thence to run
> In amorous rillets down her shrinking form!
> To linger on her lily shoulders, warm
> Between her kissing breasts, and every charm
> Touch raptur'd![54]

However, the episode has a little more relevance to the poem than this. Both lovers—Arethusa no less than Alpheus—express the pain and unhappiness of love, those notes that surely constitute one of the principal themes of *Endymion*. In their way they serve to carry over Cynthia's departing question—

> woe! woe! is grief contain'd
> In the very deeps of pleasure?[55]

—into the unhappy love story of Glaucus in the next book. Again, all the impulse and direction of Alpheus' thought, which is to

> fly
> These dreary caverns for the open sky,[56]

suggestively corresponds with the mood and situation of Endymion, while Endymion's pitiful entreaty to Cynthia to bring Arethusa and Alpheus to happiness introduces what is to be one of the main themes of Book III. Further, at the level of simple narrative linkage we have Arethusa represented as being under the sway of Cynthia—a piece of dove-tailing that produces some ironical effect, as when Alpheus remarks:

> Dian's self must feel
> Sometimes these very pangs.[57]

Finally, the episode has an imaginative effect that is satisfying. Just as the Venus-Adonis story concentrates the random vegetation imagery of the poem into a point of central significance and integrates it into the pattern of the poem, so this Alpheus-Arethusa myth concentrates and integrates the recurrent imagery of fountains and outbursting water. It furnishes a fitting close to a book that is full of imagery of this kind and from which—if we recall nothing else—we shall certainly remember the description of the thousand fountains.

Nearly a fifth of Book III is taken up by two long and somewhat repetitive apostrophes to the moon—the first directly uttered by Keats himself, the second by Endymion.

There can be no mistaking the main effect of the first passage. In this Keats lovingly pictures the moon shining and pouring her benediction on the earth and its creatures below, and through this impression he clearly introduces the pre-

dominantly humanitarian themes of the book.* When he turns
to the moon herself his description of her physical features
emphatically suggests the heroine of a love-story,[58] and she is
represented entirely as a woman in love, a figure with no
implication at all of ideal significance:

> Alas, thou dost pine
> For one as sorrowful: thy cheek is pale
> For one whose cheek is pale: thou dost bewail
> His tears, who weeps for thee. Where dost thou sigh?[59]

Before we consider the second apostrophe something should
be said about the short passage that follows the first:

> O Love! how potent hast thou been to teach
> Strange journeyings! Wherever beauty dwells,
> In gulf or aerie, mountains or deep dells,
> In light, in gloom, in star or blazing sun,
> Thou pointest out the way, and straight 'tis won.[60]

Taken from their context, these lines are often pressed into
service of the allegorical and metaphysical interpretation of
the poem. Thus we find Middleton Murry writing: 'Nothing
could show more clearly how completely in the poem the
moon Goddess has lost her particularity, and become simply
the symbol of that "Principle of Beauty" to which alone, along
with the Eternal Being and the Memory of Great Men, Keats
at this time said he paid reverence.'† But, set in the context
of the following lines, which Murry ignores, the passage
shows no such thing. By his reference to various love stories—
Leander crossing the Hellespont to Hero, Orpheus searching
for Eurydice through the underworld—Keats makes it plain
that he is writing about lovers, not about metaphysical matters; and the 'beauty' that dwells in gulf and aerie is not some
philosophical abstraction, 'the Idea of Beauty' or the 'Principle of Beauty', but the beloved whose beauty impels the
lover to the most hazardous journeys and to the remotest

* Keats's use of 'benevolence' (l. 37) is to be noted.
† *The Mystery of Keats*, p. 144.

places. So Cynthia, through her love for the beauty of Endymion, has been drawn down irresistibly, if surprisingly, to the 'deep, deep water-world' where Endymion now is.

The second apostrophe, which occurs after Endymion's memorable vision of the wreckage and ruins on the ocean floor, is admittedly more open to misunderstanding. As we read it and are carried to its emphatic crescendo—

> And as I grew in years, still didst thou blend
> With all my ardours: thou wast the deep glen;
> Thou wast the mountain-top—the sage's pen—
> The poet's harp—the voice of friends—the sun;
> Thou wast the river—thou wast glory won[61]

—we certainly have the feeling that the moon is something more than itself, that from Endymion's childhood it has been a focusing symbol of all his aspirations. Nevertheless, there is no reason to regard the moon here as an intimation of ideal, transcendental Beauty. Quite apart from Keats's own passionate delight in the moon, which almost certainly accounts for some of the rhapsodic hyperbole of the passage, we must remember the implications of the story. Endymion has found a love that he supposes to be the highest and most intense form of happiness. His beloved is the moon goddess; but at this time he does not know, as the reader knows, that the moon and Cynthia are one. Thus to resolve some of this mystery in Endymion's love and also to suggest that it is the goal to which all his life has moved, Keats quite naturally represents Endymion here as feeling more strongly about the moon than if it were simply a 'thing of beauty' and also as tracing this complex of feeling right back to childhood. Though Endymion does not realize the truth yet, it was really awakening love that had blended with all his ardours; and it is most significant that the crescendo (incompletely quoted above) strikes its climax not with any suggestion of spiritual or mystical insight but with

> Thou wast the charm of women, lovely Moon!

The passage, a brief recapitulation of the speech on happiness, that immediately follows this line appears to confirm such a reading of the first part of the apostrophe. In the past Endymion had experienced a harmony or sense of oneness with things of beauty;* and because of this harmony with Nature and the escape from isolated self he had known a feeling almost of immortality:

> O what a wild and harmonized tune
> My spirit struck from all the beautiful!
> On some bright essence could I lean, and lull
> Myself to immortality: I prest
> Nature's soft pillow in a wakeful rest.†

But, Endymion continues, he has found a 'nearer bliss', his 'higher hope' of love, which is the supreme felicity:

> But, gentle Orb! there came a nearer bliss—
> My strange love came—Felicity's abyss!
> She came, and thou didst fade, and fade away.[62]

This contrast of two phases of development certainly implies, if it does not directly state, that for all Endymion has just said about his feelings towards the moon, in actuality the moon of his childhood and youthful delight had been simply one particular 'bright essence', a part of 'all the beautiful', but not a symbol of ideal and ultimate beauty. However, Keats is no longer, as in the speech on happiness, expressing predominantly subjective ideas; he is now deeply involved in

---

* There can be little doubt about the meaning of 'essence' in this context.

† III, 170–4. This is virtually a re-statement of I, 777–80.

As I read this passage I feel (1) that a transitional pause must be understood before the first two lines, and (2) that their reference is much more explicitly to what follows than to what has gone before. If these two propositions are rejected, it is of course possible to argue that it was because the moon was really ideal beauty that Endymion's spirit had struck a harmonized tune from all the beautiful. But this would mean that ideal beauty was the harmonizing agent. In the first two lines (taken with the context of what follows) Keats surely envisages this harmony as something created by Endymion himself.

a story of a mortal in love with a goddess who, according to myth, is personified by the moon, itself a 'thing of beauty'. The fable is not entirely apt for the conception; hence there is, inevitably, some confusion. So, just after the lines quoted above, Endymion goes on to say of the moon:

> Now I begin to feel thine orby power
> Is coming fresh upon me.[63]

And this is immediately followed by another sharp distinction between his 'dearest love' and that 'airy planet' whose delight can only be a matter of 'argent *luxuries*'!

In short this second apostrophe is to be regarded not as a key to some neo-platonic allegory* but as a dramatic statement, the words of a mortal in love with a goddess who was mythically supposed to be a personification of the moon.

In spite of these introductory apostrophes Cynthia does not enter at all into the following story of Glaucus. Instead Endymion is concerned—and actively now—with the welfare of others. After a first instinctive start of terror his hostility towards the old man of the sea suddenly changes into pity,† and this commiseration deepens as Glaucus unfolds his story. There is thus a link with the last narrative incident, where Endymion had been moved to utter his prayer for the happiness of Alpheus and Arethusa. But now he is no longer a passive spectator. He is eager and active to free Glaucus from the curse upon him, and it is he who plays the leading part in the resurrection of the drowned lovers.

All the commentators are agreed in thinking that what Keats was trying to express in this episode was the idea that active humanity is a part, and perhaps an effect, of genuine

---

* One further point: the superstitious lore about the moon that is woven into this apostrophe is appropriate to the musings of a primitive chief like Endymion but hardly to a neo-platonic hero.

† See especially III, 282–4.

love.* It is true there has been some disagreement among the exponents of the neo-platonic allegory about the relation of this book to the rest of the poem. The majority treat the humanitarian theme as something of an excursus prompted by a strong Wordsworthian influence.† Others, like Thorpe,‡ insist that Endymion's active love for his fellows is an essential part of his initiation into the neo-platonic mystery. But there is no pressing need to take sides over this conflict of views. Even if humanitarianism can be regarded as an essential part of the neo-platonic attitude—and this is very much open to doubt—we can still accept the humanitarian theme in Book III without committing ourselves in any way to the general neo-platonic and allegorical interpretation of the poem.

On the other hand, while the commentators' interpretation is generally acceptable, their judgment on the book is often seriously at fault. For obvious reasons they tend not only to treat the narrative part very sketchily but also to suggest that it is more of a digression, more a matter of space-filling than it actually is.

---

* Ford (*The Prefigurative Imagination of John Keats*) advances an interpretation that differs from the generally accepted one. For him the central theme in Book III is fidelity and infidelity in love. Glaucus has suffered because he has committed the cardinal sin of love, infidelity. Circe's other victims are unfaithful lovers. Endymion is able to do good to Glaucus and the drowned lovers because of his fidelity, while the drowned lovers are resurrected to immortality because they have been faithful.

We cannot rule out such a theme entirely. But there are good reasons for not taking it as dominant. (1) Ford completely ignores the prelude note of the moon's 'benevolence'. (2) We are not particularly conscious at this stage of Endymion standing for fidelity, for he has not been really tested. (Ford himself admits *op. cit.* p. 64, that the impression of Endymion's positive faithfulness is not strong.) (3) Though Keats may not 'dwell on the sensuality of Circe', his description of her as the 'arbitrary queen of sense' makes it clear that he was using her in the traditional way as the personification of sensual love.

† So Finney, though he tries to soften this criticism by the unsubstantiated claim that before Keats was diverted by Bailey he intended to embody in Book III the neo-platonic ideal of friendship.

‡ Thorpe regards Book III as 'all an act of human love and sympathy that prepares the poet's spirit for the next higher experience, a complete union of the soul with the heart of humanity, which is the final key to the Penetralium of Mystery' (*The Mind of John Keats*, p. 60).

But (to exclude for a moment the story of Glaucus's enchantment) Endymion's active humanity can be regarded in at least two important ways as integral to the pattern of the poem. In the first place, while no one would deny that Bailey's Wordsworthianism probably influenced Keats a great deal at this time, it is possible that we are inclined to exaggerate this influence; and there is reason for believing that Book III might have been substantially what it is even if Keats had never spent that Oxford long vacation with a young man in the first flush of an enthusiasm for Wordsworth. We should again recall the speech on happiness in Book I where Endymion, having identified himself with those great men who have abandoned some progressive cause for love's elysium, hastens to qualify this apparently selfish view of love with the remark:

> I have ever thought that it might bless
> The world with benefits unknowingly.[64]

Endymion's conduct in Book III—a book that opens with that picture of the moon blessing the world—may be satisfactorily considered as a narrative development of this idea; and if his actions are not performed 'unknowingly', at least they are without any deliberate intention to do good. They arise naturally from his conquest of a deathly self-isolation, his assurance of Cynthia's love, and his new-found pity for the misery of others.

In the second place, too much use of terms applicable to the Wordsworthian doctrine—'humanitarianism', 'benevolence', and the like—may cause us to overlook the fact that Endymion's attitude in Book III, one of pity and active sympathy for the unhappiness of others, is after all only a particularly sustained elaboration of a note that, as we have observed, has been recurrent from the beginning of the poem. Moreover, this attitude of Endymion is to be further stressed in Book IV when he encounters the disconsolate Indian Maid. Hence, regarded as a part of this continuous pattern, Endymion's adventures in Book III are to be seen not as a digression produced by the exceptional Wordsworthian influence on Keats at this time, but, on the contrary, as a central and organic part of the poem.

Further, also contributing to the unity of the work, there is the fact that Endymion's chief action in Book III is his bringing back to life of the legions of drowned *lovers*,—and lovers, it should be noted, who, when they are re-united the one to the other, resume a kind of love that is certainly not spiritual:

> Then dance, and song,
> And garlanding grew wild; and pleasure reigned. [65]

Thus we have a linking repetition of the resurrection theme in Book II, while the incident of Scylla restored to Glaucus essentially repeats the awakening of Venus to Adonis. It may of course be questioned whether the recurrence of this theme adds very much of positive value to the poem; but at least, since Endymion is directly involved in this second resurrection*, it does immensely strengthen our feeling that his love is richly associated with life and life-giving. As a lover, he is utterly removed from the stricken, death-longing figure at the beginning of Book II, and the predominant note of the poem now is all joy and life.

Inset in this main narrative of Book III we have the retrospective story of the early life of Glaucus and his enchantment by Circe, and though one or two of the commentators† have tried to press some of this into their allegory, in general it has

---

* Whether or not Keats intended this theme to be more than an imaginative and symbolizing representation of the development of Endymion's love it is hard to say. Ford (*op. cit.* p. 47) maintains that Keats was expressing a quite literal belief in the immortal existence of true lovers. What is at least fairly clear is that there was some curious connexion in Keats's mind between the Cynthia—Endymion myth and restoration to health and life, for his description of the sea-drowned lovers coming to life is extremely reminiscent of the recovery of the 'languid sick' that follows Cynthia's bridal-night in 'I stood tip-toe' (ll. 225–30). Ford draws attention to this parallel.

† Finney, for example.

been regarded as even more of a digression from the main business of the poem than Endymion's restoration of Scylla to Glaucus and his resurrection of the drowned lovers.

Certainly, if we are judging *Endymion* strictly by the criteria of narrative poetry, this life-history of Glaucus should have been treated much more compactly. Yet it is by no means irrelevant, nor is it lacking in imaginative impressions that contribute to the total effect of the poem. To begin with, like the stories of Venus and Adonis, and Arethusa and Alpheus, it clearly parallels the situation of Endymion and Cynthia. There is again a mortal and an immortal lover, and again one of the lovers fails to respond to the passion of the other. Once more, too, the outcome of this frustration is wretchedness and suffering, so that Glaucus can sum up his sad history in words that are perfectly appropriate for the listening hero:

> Woe, alas!
> That love should be my bane![66]

But, if with less hope than Endymion for an ultimate fruition of his love, Glaucus too has learnt humanity from his experience—an humanity that, in this love poem, is fittingly directed towards the welfare of lovers:

> I am a friend to love, to loves of yore.[67]

Partly because of this theme of the love that is a bane—though only partly—there re-emerges in delicate, easily missed notes that basic antithesis in *Endymion* of joy and grief. Glaucus opens his story with the words:

> My soul stands
> Now past the midway from mortality,
> And so I can prepare without a sigh
> To tell thee briefly all my joy and pain;[68]

he gives us a curiously paradoxical description, which is typically Keatsian, of the bird-song of Circe's island:

> And birds from coverts innermost and drear
> Warbling for very joy mellifluous sorrow—
> To me new born delights;[69]

the scroll that he recovers from the sea informs him:

> *He must pursue this task of joy and grief;*[70]

and when Endymion enters the undersea sepulchre that Glaucus has tended we read:

> So in that crystal place, in silent rows,
> Poor lovers lay at rest from joys and woes.[71]

However, the Glaucus story is not simply one of repetitive parallels.* Essentially it underlines for Endymion that ever-present and most serious hazard that attends such a quest as his, the temptation to turn aside from a high and difficult love to a cheaper one that is more easily attained. In this way we are prepared for the final climax of the poem where, although the issue is by no means the same, Endymion is torn between love for his goddess and the Indian Maid.

But when Glaucus faithlessly turns from Scylla to Circe he is not simply giving himself up to someone who is in a general way inferior to Scylla. Keats's Circe is the traditional 'arbitrary queen of sense', and surrendering to her, Glaucus is surrendering to that base and destructive kind of love that is wholly sensual. It is true that we can hardly distinguish between the description of Glaucus's dalliance with Circe† and the earlier passage in the poem where Endymion encounters his divine goddess, and this must be set down as a fault in the poem arising from confusion and contradiction in Keats's own attitude to love. On the other hand, we may be fairly certain that Keats's intention at least was to affirm—for him-

---

* We may perhaps see in that incident in Glaucus's early history when he had dived into the oblivion of the sea another manifestation of that love for 'easeful death' that had sent Endymion into the underworld. In particular, compare III, 378–80 with I, 637–40.

† See, for instance, III, 440–3.

self no less than for his hero—that love is no 'mere comming-ling of passionate breath'.

There may also be something vaguer and less fully con-scious behind the episode—Keats's sense of destruction and death in love, and an embodiment of this intuition in the romantic symbol of the *femme fatale*.* Certainly from the time of *Endymion* this theme of death-in-love is persistent in Keats's poetry, and there are at least two passages in the Circe episode where the phrasing and imagery appear to establish an imaginative association between Circe on the one hand and Lamia and La Belle Dame Sans Merci† on the other.

However, in 1817 the theme was not yet a dominant one. The Endymion who releases Glaucus from Circe's spell and resurrects the drowned lovers is abundantly associated with life and a love that is supremely life-giving; and Book III closes with an outburst of immense joy and happiness that takes us back to the spirit of the Festival of Pan. Rejoicing, making its way through scenes of resplendent beauty, the vast 'Paphian army' moves towards the palace of Neptune, where on each hand the sea god is attended by winged Love and Venus, 'smiling Beauty's paragon'. Endymion hears a promise from Venus that his love is soon to be fulfilled,‡ and the com-pany fall to a pagan revelry of song, dance, garlanding, feast-ing and drinking. Amid the festivity a choral hymn is sung celebrating Neptune in his more auspicious mood, Venus 'the white Queen of Beauty', and the young god of love as

> sweetest essence! sweetest of all minions!
> God of warm pulses, and dishevell'd hair,
> And panting bosoms bare.[72]

Nothing here of the spiritualities of neo-platonic love; and the

* This theme had already emerged in Keats's best love poem of the pre-*Endymion* period, the sonnet *On a Leander Gem*. Finney dates this March 1817, and it may have been written in 1816.

† See p. 230 and p. 216.

‡ If Endymion really is the poetic soul who is to be wedded to ideal beauty, he is promised a curious sort of honeymoon by Venus in her Cytherean isle.

Endymion who swoons at Venus's feet from the intolerable
pleasure of it all is almost transformed before our eyes into
another sleeping Adonis tended by Nereids in some remote
bower:

> A sudden ring
> Of Nereids were about him, in kind strife
> To usher back his spirit into life:
> But still he slept. At last they interwove
> Their cradling arms, and purpos'd to convey
> Towards a crystal bower far away.[73]

However, in the star-written words above him Endymion is
able to read another promise of love and immortal bliss, and
it seems that all that remains now in the poem is for Endymion
to be finally united with his Cynthia.

This impression of joyfulness and exuberant life is admirably
reinforced by the imagery. It is true that a world is once more
evoked of stone and precious jewels—'portal columns',
'jasper pillars', 'rich opal domes', 'marble steps', and 'rocks of
glittering spar'. But the effect of all these images is nothing like
those of the deathly underworld of Book II. The cold diamond
gleams are now mixed with the warm golden glow of amber
and the blush of coral; there is the splendour of gold everywhere, and everywhere a brilliance of light—in the brightening
east, and above all in the

> light as of four sunsets, blazing forth
> A gold-green zenith 'bove the Sea-God's head.[74]

Further, the vegetal type of imagery becomes boldly prominent again, introduced by a startlingly synaesthetic metaphor
that Keats uses to describe the music in the resurrection scene:

> Delicious symphonies, like airy flowers,
> Budded, and swell'd, and, full-blown, shed full showers
> Of light, soft, unseen leaves of sounds divine.[75]

The most extensive example of this imagery occurs in the
description of the revelry in Neptune's palace, where the
writing is very reminiscent of the awakening of Adonis:

And plunder'd vines, teeming exhaustless, pleach'd
New growth about each shell and pendent lyre;
The which, in disentangling for their fire,
Pull'd down fresh foliage and coverture
For dainty toying . . .

In harmless tendril they each other chain'd,
And strove who should be smother'd deepest in
Fresh crush of leaves.[76]

It is with this kind of imaginative impression that Book III
closes—of the dove hatching her eggs, of the 'forest green',
and of the 'grassy nest' in which Endymion happily discovers
himself again.

There is always something of a surprise as we turn from
Book III to Book IV. Only twenty lines from the beginning we
come upon a passage that in its dejection contrasts most
sharply with the joyous tone of the preceding book:

Great Muse, thou know'st what prison
Of flesh and bone curbs, and confines, and frets
Our spirit's wings: despondency besets
Our pillows; and the fresh tomorrow-morn
Seems to give forth its light in very scorn
Of our dull, uninspired, snail-paced lives.[77]

Nor—as we soon find—is this a passing strain of melancholy;
on the contrary, it preludes a good deal of what is to follow,
and as the story itself reopens the first thing we hear is a voice
of wretched lament:

'Ah, woe is me! that I should fondly part
From my dear native land! Ah, foolish maid! . . .
To one so friendless the clean freshet yields
A bitter coolness; the ripe grape is sour.'[78]

For the moment we are as startled as Endymion himself,
not only from the sudden inrush of grief but from the intrusion
of such a character into the poem at this point. But as the
Maid renews her lament she at once becomes a less alien

figure: much of her grief obviously arises from her unsatisfied hunger for love, and the love she yearns for is the sort that has been celebrated throughout the poem—sensuous and passionate, idealized with the romantic conventions.* She makes the same high claim for love that Endymion had made in his speech on happiness:

> There is no lightning, no authentic dew
> But in the eye of love: there's not a sound,
> Melodious howsoever, can confound
> The heavens and earth in one to such a death
> As doth the voice of love: there's not a breath
> Will mingle kindly with the meadow air,
> Till it has panted round, and stolen a share
> Of passion from the heart!†

Indeed, as she sings her roundelay 'O Sorrow', she becomes for a moment Endymion's very counterpart—at least as he was at the beginning:

> Beneath my palm trees, by the river side,
> I sat aweeping: what enamour'd bride,
> Cheated by shadowy wooer from the clouds,
> But hides and shrouds
> Beneath dark palm trees by a river side. [79]

Besides such sentiments as these there is much else that renders the opening of Book IV readily accessible once we have recovered from our initial bewilderment. Whatever else the Indian Maid may represent she evidently embodies the poem's familiar theme of sorrow-in-love; and she perhaps expresses—if at a much fainter remove—the old juxtaposition of joy and grief. It is also in keeping with another of the chief strains of the poem that Endymion should respond to her grief in a mood of deep pity. All the same, in spite of these familiar themes and in spite of the barely resistible enticement for Endymion, we are a little surprised that the compassion he

---

* For example, ll. 47–51.

† IV, 78–85. Like Endymion's speech on happiness too, this passage is reminiscent of Berowne's great apostrophe to love in *Love's Labour's Lost*.

feels for the Maid so rapidly changes—and without much conflict—into a declaration of entire love for her.*

On two black steeds conjured up by Mercury Endymion and the Indian Maid soar into the sky. They fall asleep, Endymion dreaming that he is in heaven. Towards the end of his dream he beholds Cynthia, and, suddenly awakening, continues to see her. He is torn excruciatingly† between her beauty and that of the sleeping Maid at his side, but when she fades away he renews his love to the awakened Indian Maid as passionately as ever. There is, however, something curiously paradoxical—if thoroughly Keatsian—in their mood:

> Whether they wept, or laugh'd, or griev'd, or toy'd—
> Most like with joy gone mad, with sorrow cloy'd.[80]

Again Cynthia appears, and this time, to his horror, Endymion sees the Indian Maid disappear before his very eyes. Abruptly, in his solitude, he finds himself in the Cave of Quietude, the wonder of which is the tranquillity of mind that lies behind all grief and sorrow. He next hears a sort of epithalamion to Cynthia, but when the heavenly voices die away he discovers himself back on earth. Though his first feeling is one of profound anguish—

> His first touch of the earth went nigh to kill[81]

—he encounters the Indian Maid again, and ecstasy flares up in him once more for her warm, flesh-and-blood reality. Renouncing his dream-goddess, he decides for the earth and an earthly love, and he paints a picture of the idyllic pastoral life that he and the Maid will live together. But, at this moment of decision, the Maid declares that it is forbidden for her to be Endymion's lover; she also (for those reading the poem for the first time) drops a strong hint that she is not what she seems, when she declares that if she surrenders to the human

---

* To some extent of course the long, rhapsodic ode to Bacchus momentarily blurs for us what is happening.

† See especially IV, 447–55.

love of Endymion she will also be surrendering herself to the doom of mortality.

Endymion is once more plunged into misery. Peona suddenly re-appears on the scene and attempts to revive the spirits of her brother, who, with another turn-about, again dedicates himself to the 'higher' pleasures.* He announces his decision to live as a hermit for the rest of his days and dismisses the Maid and Peona, only—as an afterthought he cannot repress —imploring that he may meet the Maid for one last time. The three meet again when the day has passed, and this time, revealing herself as Cynthia, the Indian Maid accepts Endymion, who, we understand, is to become a sort of god and so immortalized.†

Such in bare outline is the curious narrative, so different in its dramatic and psychological interest from that of the other three books, that completes the poem. What are we to make of it? Why did Keats introduce this figure of the Indian Maid‡ into the original myth, and why did he present Endymion as torn between love for the Maid and for Cynthia? What significance, if any, is there in the discovery that Cynthia and the Indian Maid are in reality one?

Those who interpret the poem as a neo-platonic allegory have never had much doubt over these questions. Book IV, they say, represents the final stage in the spiritual growth of the poetic soul: through human and earthly love for the Indian Maid this soul at last achieves communion with ideal Beauty (Cynthia), and at last realizes the truth that this human and this spiritual love are ultimately one.§

* See IV, 851–4.
† This meaning of 'spiritualiz'd' (IV, 993) is all we need for the word, though naturally the neo-platonic commentators have read other implications into it.
‡ Possibly suggested by the Arab Maid in *Alastor*.
§ Colvin's summary of Book IV—'Endymion's earthly passion, born of human pity and desire, was one all the while, had he but known it, with his heavenly passion born of poetic aspiration and the soul's thirst for Beauty' (*Life of John Keats*, pp. 203–4)—is virtually repeated by Finney—

Were all the books of *Endymion* like the fourth,* we should no doubt be much more willing to entertain the neo-platonic interpretation, for beneath its surface narrative there certainly appears to be some level of significant meaning. Nevertheless, even when we consider Book IV in isolation, a cluster of strong objections to the usual allegorical reading emerges. For one thing, there is not a single phrase in the Introduction that points to a neo-platonic parable. Moreover, the sadness and dejection of the opening preludes the tone of the whole book, which is subdued and markedly joyless even to the end, when Endymion at last wins his Cynthia. Surely if Keats had really intended the book to represent the final ecstasy of union with ideal Beauty he would have felt, and communicated, some of the joy and triumph that is so significantly lacking?†

Again, while conflict between earthly love and beauty and ideal Love and Beauty may be accepted as an inevitable stage in progress towards the final vision and union, we should expect the emphasis in this last book to be on harmony and reconciliation. But from beginning to end—almost to the point of monotony—the Endymion Keats presents to us is a figure torn and divided by seemingly irresoluble conflict, whose union with Cynthia must always strike us as a purely mechanical narrative contrivance for bringing the poem to

'The beauty of a particular woman is a manifestation of ideal or essential Beauty, Keats meant, and the love of the beauty of a particular woman the highest means by which a man can attain a fellowship with essence' (*The Evolution of Keats's Poetry*, p. 319).

Thorpe's conclusion is different: 'The union with the Indian Maid is the marriage of the soul of the poet with the spirit of sorrow and suffering in the world, with the "Misery and Heartbreak, Pain, Sickness, and Oppression" of mankind' (*The Mind of John Keats*, p. 60). But Keats had to go through the excruciating fires of late 1818 and 1819 before he perceived the necessity of this marriage.

* It is significant that most of De Selincourt's interpretation is concentrated (*Poems of John Keats*, pp. 443–5) on Book IV. This is the only detailed exposition of the allegory that he offers.

† Colvin himself was forced to admit (*op. cit.* p. 204) that 'the poem ends on no such note of joy and triumph over the attained consummation as we might have expected'.

some sort of conclusion. Nor is this the only weakness of Endymion regarded as the hero of a neo-platonic allegory. He also singularly fails to suggest anything in the way of spiritual growth. His own final free choice is for the Indian Maid and an idyllic sort of earthly love, and when at last he dedicates himself to the 'higher' pleasures and a hermit's life, he is only in that state—desperately, feverishly, and somewhat rebelliously—because the Indian Maid has refused his offer. It is quite impossible for us to believe that he has, by his own voluntary choice, risen from earthly to ideal Beauty.

We are likely to come much closer to the underlying meaning of Book iv if we proceed from that powerful eroticism, often idealized of course, that constitutes so much of the first three books, and remember that what we are reading is the work of a young man, barely out of late adolescence and unusually sensuous and warm-hearted, who must in the nature of things have been thinking and feeling about sexual love with all that cloudy tumultuous urgency that young men of this age universally experience. What we chiefly need in order to understand those thoughts and feelings is not a knowledge of neo-platonic ideas (with which Keats may or may not have been acquainted) but a steady recollection of our own attitudes and emotional experiences at twenty. And if anyone considers that this is too subjective a mode of criticism, that a great poet's sexual feelings are somehow, and essentially, different from those of common human nature, he should remind himself of the experience of other poets at this age—of the 'austere' Milton, for instance, as he reveals himself in the fifth and seventh of his Latin *Elegies*. 'Lacking all prescience, I sent my glances to meet their glances, nor could I withhold my eyes. One by chance I marked, towering [in beauty] over others: that radiance was the beginning of all my woe . . . Straightway unwonted frenzies entered my heart: I burned within with love, aye, all my being was afire.' [82] But, alas, Milton's fortune when he encountered this company of girls was the common one of young men—and of Keats, too, as we shall see in a moment: 'Meanwhile, the lass who, alone of lasses, pleased now my tortured soul, was withdrawn from my gaze, ne'er again to return to my eyes.'[83]

Even more illuminating as a clue to the heart of *Endymion* (and of Book iv in particular) is Proust's account of the young Marcel's experience at Balbec[84]—his dream of an ideal lover, his encounters with girls in the lanes around and on the sea-shore, and the discovery of his Indian Maid in Albertine. What an admirable commentary, packed and to the point, we may find in the following passage for instance:

> I was passing through one of those periods of our youth, un-provided with any one definite love, vacant, in which at all times and in all places—as a lover the woman by whose charms he is smitten—we desire, we seek, we see Beauty. Let but a single real feature—the little that one distinguishes of a woman seen from afar or from behind—enable us to project the form of beauty before our eyes, we imagine that we have seen her before, our heart beats, we hasten in pursuit, and will always remain half-persuaded that it was she, provided that the woman has vanished: it is only if we manage to overtake her that we realise our mistake.[85]

Or again, what light is thrown on Endymion's vacillations between the Indian Maid and Cynthia by such a remark as: 'Confronted with the commonplace though appealing Alber-tine to whom I had spoken that afternoon, I still saw the other, mysterious Albertine outlined against the sea.'[86]

We cannot of course hope for the fine subtlety of Proust's recollections; but at least we can remember a time when, as older and cooler heads will have it, we were madly in love with love, obsessed with a rapturous dream of some perfect lover, who, shaped out of many faces and continually chang-ing her countenance, was always supremely beautiful, who would bring us unimaginable felicity, would magically fuse into coherence all our tangled impulses and aspirations, and who, if we had poetic ambitions, would fire us with the in-spiration that would immortalize our name. It is out of this absurd, extravagant, irresistible dream that Keats, employing

a delightful Greek myth of love for his purpose, has created
the vague, elusive goddess-figure of Cynthia; and it is because
Cynthia springs from this sort of dream, not from any known
lover, that she is invested with an aura of significance that has
deceived so many of the scholarly commentators into thinking
that she symbolizes neo-platonic love and beauty. No question
that she represents the young man's 'ideal' in the loosest sense
of that word; but this is far removed from the 'ideal' of any
identifiable platonic or neo-platonic philosophy.*

There is another feature of Keats's Cynthia that a recollection of ourselves at twenty will help us to appreciate.
Frequently the passionate gallantry of our private fantasies is
all too distressingly contradicted by our shyness and constraint
in the presence of the girls and young women we actually
meet. This was Keats's experience, too.† But we usually find
a fantasy-compensation: the lover of our intoxicating dream
is always obligingly accessible and forthcoming. It is she who
will make the first overtures; and she surrenders easily to our
embraces. This fantasy is a recurrent and fundamental part
of Keats's images of both Cynthia and the Indian Maid, and
lines like

> madly did I kiss
> The *wooing* arms which held me,[87]

could be quoted from a dozen places in the poem.

At first this ideal lover (for she is born of obscure feelings
and instincts, of hearsay, and the books we read) is entirely a
goddess of the imagination, attached to no living face or form.
But as time goes on, like the young Milton, the young Proust
at Balbec, we begin to glimpse her—now here, now there, in
the real world that presses inexorably on us; and we pursue

---

* The moon of the second apostrophe in Book III is without doubt the
young and amorous poet's 'ideal' in the first sense; but she is not the
'ideal' of the more particular denotation.

† See the sonnet 'Had I a man's fair form' and various references in
the *Letters*.

her through many agonizing, tantalizing disappointments. The enchanting girl who for a few cruelly swift minutes sat opposite us in the bus or train—if only she had not alighted at a different stop from ours, to be lost hopelessly and for ever, if only by some rare chance we could meet her again—might be the destined one; there was a moment when we felt certain of it. Or—for we are usually fortunate enough to forget our last disappointment—it might be this one, seen for a whole week on a seaside holiday, though we never summoned up the courage to speak to her. So she continually comes and goes; and we are continually repeating those bitter words of the young Milton: 'ne'er again to return to my eyes'.

All this common experience, too, is reflected in the elusive lover, coming and going, a dream-visitant, that Keats creates for Endymion in the goddess Cynthia. Moreover, we know that he had himself suffered the exquisite pangs we have been describing. His Cynthia—in one of her manifestations*—he had glimpsed at Vauxhall Gardens in the summer of 1814, and as was proper, she had inspired him to one of his earliest poems.† So far as we know, he never saw her again, but 'the beaminess of those bright eyes', like Cynthia's for Endymion, must have returned on many occasions to haunt him with a bitter-sweet sense of hopelessness, for three and a half years later, not long after the completion of *Endymion*, we find him still recalling her. He sees her in the midnight sky much as Endymion sees Cynthia:

> And yet I never look on midnight sky,
> But I behold thine eyes' well memoried light.‡

---

* Perhaps Mrs Isabella Jones, whom Keats met at Hastings in the summer of 1817, was another. Finney (*The Evolution of Keats's Poetry*, p. 450) blames her for the distorting 'nympholeptic dream' of Book II.
† 'Fill for me a brimming bowl.'
‡ 'Time's sea', ll. 5–6. Colvin follows the testimony of Woodhouse in connecting this sonnet with 'Fill for me a brimming bowl' and also with the sestet of another sonnet written in early 1818, 'When I have fears'. Finney, too, accepts this connexion.

But if this familiar experience of youth gives us all the clue we need to Cynthia, what of the Indian Maid, and what in particular of Book IV?

Recollection will again help us. Our disappointments and frustrations do not last for ever. Sooner or later—unbelievably at first—more propitious circumstances occur. Somehow we manage to meet a girl who this time does not disappear as soon as we have glimpsed her; she gives us some encouragement (crude word for something inexpressible), and, if we are constrained or nervous, perhaps makes at least some slight movement towards us. For once it does not seem to matter that we are shorter, less handsome, or less eloquent than we should like to be, while—another wonder—this girl appears prepared to accept us in all our trailing, fantastic dream-world —perhaps, though we rarely imagine it at the time, because she is moving in the clouds of one herself. Cynthia has been transformed into the Indian Maid, who stands steadily and palpably in front of us; with an upsurge of courage and resolution we may perhaps become her accepted lover. But, though intoxicated, we are just a little less deliriously drunken than of old: sometimes quite early, and usually without the knowledge seriously diminishing our rapture, we realize in the deepest, most secret place of our heart—the more certainly the more imaginative we are—that this girl is not identical with the dream-goddess who haunted us for so long, though she may resemble her very closely. She is—we know it with the faintest suspicion of cheat and disenchantment—the Indian Maid, not Cynthia; she is the eternal Fanny Brawne or Albertine, who can never be more than a compromise, never, since she is human, more than half or a quarter of our dream:

> 'Thwart my wistful way did a damsel saunter,
> Fair, albeit unformed to be all-eclipsing;
> 'Maiden meet,' held I, 'till arise my forefelt
> Wonder of women.'[88]

At times this suspicion flares up into certainty; we have moments when, in protest, we turn back to the old unsubstantial, unrealized dream-goddess and when we try to re-create her ineffable wonder. Sensing some surrender, we rebel against the idea of it, especially if our love-affair is prospering and necessary material considerations begin to press on us. But in the end, still of course abnormally happy and still not entirely out of dream, we do usually surrender, for we cannot pursue phantoms of dream and imagination for ever:

> I have clung
> To nothing, lov'd a nothing, nothing seen
> Or felt but a great dream![89]

Here, in this remembrance of ourselves at twenty, is all the key we require to the superficially puzzling narrative of Book IV—the creating for Endymion of a new and second lover, seemingly human and distinct from his dream-goddess, the representing of him in a state of intense conflict, and the suggestion that while in the inevitable order of things he must and will surrender himself to the Indian Maid, at the same time he is still somehow faithful to the memory of Cynthia. Further, we can hardly help recalling those vulgarly phrased but quite explicit later lines from *Lamia*:

> Let the mad poets say whate'er they please
> Of the sweets of Fairies, Peris, Goddesses,
> There is not such a treat among them all,
> Haunters of cavern, lake, and waterfall,
> As a real woman, lineal indeed
> From Pyrrha's pebbles or old Adam's seed;[90]

and it is no wild guess to believe that some of this feeling, along with the chivalric dream, went into Keats's treatment of Endymion in Book IV.

Whether this knowledge of how the dream-goddess comes to take shape in some living woman was still largely intuitional, or whether it had become rapidly and vividly real through his summer meeting with Mrs Isabella Jones at Hastings, we cannot finally decide. But with Fanny Brawne still to enter his life and an unwritten poem, *Lamia*, that turns to a large extent on the same conflict as that embodied in Book IV of *Endymion*, our guess must be that in 1817 his real-life experience of love was as yet superficial. Hence when he finished off his poem he was still free to indulge in the fancy that the dream-goddess and the human maid are actually one—which is of course what we should all like to believe at one stage.

However, though remembrance of ourselves at twenty will take us far and sympathetically into the meaning of Book IV, some features of the story can only be understood if we appreciate certain special peculiarities of Keats. In the first place he was a poet. And not merely that: he was a poet who had dedicated himself with a singularly religious fervour and a whole-heartedness to his vocation. Further, he was, on his own confession, intensely ambitious. No doubt, since this too is familiar experience, all these passionate aspirations, general and poetic, were entangled and confused in his dream of love. But when actual love does come, in the form of a living woman, it often seems to demand that we shall be lovers and nothing else. We are too absorbed, too distracted, for other interests and purposes. So, while the common human nature in Keats and his Endymion welcomed the release from unsubstantial, unsatisfying dreams, could say truly to the human lover,

> Here will I kneel, for thou redeemed hast
> My life from too thin breathing,[91]

the poet in him, by intuition or initial experience, felt uneasy lest such a love might entail some surrender in his ambitions* and high poetic aspirations. That is probably why Endymion, for all his lyrical painting of a life of love in an earthly paradise, so often seems strangely sad with the Indian Maid and sometimes not a little morose and querulous, as if in surrendering to her he is helplessly in the grip of some inevitability:

* We should of course recall the conflict between love and ambition in Endymion's speech on happiness in Book I.

I've no choice;
I must be thy sad servant evermore. [92]

Nor was it simply Keats's poetic genius and ambition that made love an exceptionally complicated experience for him. There is no doubt at all that he suffered acutely from an unusually divided attitude towards women—a conflict between his romantic idealizations and what he seemed to find in everyday life. Perhaps his confessional outpouring in a letter to Bailey, written six months after the completion of *Endymion*, is the clearest and frankest statement we have on this matter: 'I am certain I have not a right feeling towards Women—at this moment I am striving to be just to them but I cannot—Is it because they fall so far beneath my Boyish imagination? When I was a Schoolboy I thought a fair Woman a pure Goddess, my mind was a soft nest in which some one of them slept, though she knew it not—I have no right to expect more than their reality. I thought them etherial above Men—I find them perhaps equal—great by comparison is very small.'*

It cannot of course be maintained that this personal dilemma is directly translated into Book IV, for there the living reality, the Indian Maid, is entirely desirable, and Endymion is prepared to surrender his boyish imagination of a pure goddess for her love. Nor is there any strong suggestion of disappointment or disenchantment. But though it is impossible to regard Cynthia and the Indian Maid as symbols of Keats's ambivalent attitude to women, it may well be that his own personal conflict was a deep inspirational force behind his picture of the conflict-torn Endymion. Certainly he put a great deal of himself into his hero, and it would be surprising if, in such a long and (for him) absorbing poem about love, he did not communicate something of that contradictory, distressing attitude to women that we know to have been his

---

* *Letters*, p. 192. The sentences that follow are also relevant here. Something of the same conflict is to be traced in some of Keats's early poems, notably in the sonnet, 'Woman! when I behold'.

at this time. Here was experience felt on his pulses as a few neo-platonic ideas picked up from Spenser and elsewhere could never be.

There is one section of Book IV, the description of the Cave of Quietude, that calls for some special comment,* since as well as being the finest and most mature passage in the poem it is also the most complex.

Though introduced—and terminated—with a singular abruptness, its application to the hero is tolerably clear. In his depth of despair now that the Indian Maid has just faded from his sight, Endymion is saved by a certain resource of the human soul—

> O wondrous soul!
> Pregnant with such a den to save the whole
> In thine own depth[93]

—and this resource brings him, paradoxically, from the worst of misery to a 'content,' a 'quietude', on the other side of it:

> never since thy griefs and woes began,
> Hast thou felt so content: a grievous feud
> Hath led thee to this Cave of Quietude.
> Aye, his lull'd soul was there, although upborne
> With dangerous speed: and so he did not mourn
> Because he knew not whither he was going.
> So happy was he . . .[94]

Further, he has attained this peace of soul in the only possible way, through an extremity of suffering, since it cannot be reached by an effort of will:

> Enter none
> Who strive therefore: on the sudden it is won.
> Just when the sufferer begins to burn,
> Then it is free to him.[95]

---

* Consideration of three other passages in Book IV that present some difficulty is left to Appendix IV.

What complicates the passage, giving it an exceptional intensity and range of reference beyond the possible experience of Endymion, is the serious engagement of Keats himself.* For one thing the vision of the Cave is almost certainly infused with his yearning for tranquillity of spirit, that state that his more habitual 'fever' made so desirable. In this connexion it is significant that the Cave, though it is only to be attained through suffering, does not simply represent a release from 'anguish' and 'woe-hurricanes'; it is also a release from the pleasure that inevitably palls.†

Again, the vision probably owes something to those moods of insensibility to which Keats several times refers in his letters of the period,‡ while it almost certainly expresses something of his characteristic attitude of 'half in love with easeful death'.§ Admittedly, most of this latter impression is created by tenuous associations and implications—the reference to sleep, the 'draught' that is usually in his poetry the means to oblivion, and a line like

> lids shut longest in a dreamless sleep.[96]

But once at least, in an unintended confession as it were, he reveals fairly explicitly where some of his deepest thoughts lie. This occurs through that unexpected simile he employs to suggest the silence of the Cave:

> No sound so loud as when on curtain'd bier
> The death-watch tick is stifled.**

* As De Selincourt remarks (*Poems of John Keats*, p. 449): 'the whole description of the den of the soul's quiet seems made out of the stuff of real experience, and stands out with a strange vividness from its vague and somewhat fantastic surroundings.'

† It is to be noticed that suffering is described as a feverish burning, relieved by the coolness of ice.

‡ For example, *Letters*, pp. 55, 69, 176.

§ In this way the passage is linked with II, 154–9.

** 530–1. The suggestion of this latent death-wish might explain why De Selincourt (*op. cit.* p. 444) does not regard Keats's insight here as wholly admirable. And (p. 449) De Selincourt quotes Mrs Owen: 'There could be no truer description of apathy.'

Nor does this by any means exhaust the significance of the passage. For instance, the phrasing of the opening lines—

> There lies a den
> Beyond the seeming confines of the space
> Made for the soul to wander in and *trace*
> *Its own existence*, of remotest glooms

—sounds very much like a prelude to some of the speculations in the great journal-letter of February–May 1819: '. . . the *World* or *Elemental space* suited for the proper action of *Mind and Heart* on each other for the purpose of forming the *Soul* or *Intelligence destined to possess the sense of Identity.*'[97] Again, there is something of that typical Romantic perversity (rare in Keats) of confusing or inverting accepted values:

> Happy gloom!
> Dark Paradise! where pale becomes the bloom
> Of health by due; where silence dreariest
> Is most articulate; where hopes infest;
> Where those eyes are the brightest far that keep
> Their lids shut longest in a dreamless sleep.[98]

Finally, we notice that he uses the word 'happy' (l. 552) to describe Endymion's state in the Cave. Possibly it is wrong to attach much importance to a word that may have slipped out without any premeditation. But if he really did believe Endymion to be happy, he was entertaining a conception of happiness very different from the one expounded in the early speech to Peona, for while it might be argued that death is the ultimate end of the quest for 'oneness' and 'self-destroying', in that previous intimation of happiness his mind had been entirely on living, immediate realities—natural beauty, art, friendship, and love.

This conflict, as the *Ode to a Nightingale* shows, is an important and persistent one in Keats's poetry.

CHAPTER VI

'LA BELLE DAME SANS MERCI'*

A thousand more he show'd, and by name
Pointed them out, whom love bereaved of life.
> Carey's translation of the *Divine Comedy: Hell*, Canto v

. . . Love which has so long been my pleasure and torment.
> Letter to Fanny Brawne, February 1820

IN discussing *Endymion* we have already examined in some detail what Keats himself described as his 'gordian complication of feelings'[1] about women and love. There is, however, one further skein in the complication that we have so far had no cause to mention—his exceptionally close and affectionate tie with his brothers: 'the thought of them has always stifled the impression that any woman might otherwise have made upon me.'[2]

For the year following *Endymion* this relationship with his brothers is the chief key to his personal life. There was the loss of George, who married and emigrated to America; there was also—and of greater consequence—the long illness of Tom, to whose welfare and nursing he sacrificed himself with entire devotion. On the other hand, whatever his doubts and fears about love, he was no ascetic; he was still haunted by the dream of Cynthia, and in the inevitable course of things he met women who might be the goddess. Hence, his experience in 1818 was one of much repression, and his situation was epitomized in a sentence that occurs in one of his Scotch letters to Tom: 'With respect to Women I think I shall be able to conquer my passions hereafter better than I have yet done.'[3]

---

* Though the main theme of this chapter emerges in that impressive sonnet *On a Leander Gem* of 1817 or 1816, I am ignoring Keats's treatment of love in the pre-*Endymion* period—partly because love is not a prominent subject in his earliest poetry and partly because *Endymion* subsumes all that had gone before.

203

Who these women were who aroused his passions is to a large extent guesswork. There was certainly Isabella Jones,* probably Marian Jeffrey,† and possibly George's bride, Georgiana Wylie. Nor have we any evidence, except in the episode of Isabella Jones, with whom he contemplated—and perhaps achieved—a platonic relation of 'mind and friendship alone',‡ how his impressions were 'stifled'. However, we are unlikely to go far wrong if we take as typical the one acquaintanceship that is fully described in his letters. This was with Jane Cox ('Charmian' as he called her) whom he met in the Reynoldses' family circle.

His first mention of her is dramatic in its cryptic intensity: 'I never was in love—yet the voice and the shape of a Woman has haunted me these two days—at such a time when the relief, the feverous relief of Poetry seems a much less crime.' A few lines later he adds: 'Poor Tom—that woman—and Poetry were ringing changes in my senses.'⁴

In these few agonizing words is compressed much of the complication of his attitude to love at this time. There is the conflict between the natural emotions roused by 'the voice and the shape of a Woman' and the desperate, mainly wishful belief, 'I never was in love'. There is the stringent judgment on himself that to surrender to such emotions when he was nursing his dying brother would be a 'crime', and the anguish of yet another repression. There is also perhaps a pessimistic premonition that love for him holds nothing but misery: 'I feel escaped from a new strange and threatening sorrow.'⁵

For further insight into this episode we may turn to his

---

* See Gittings, *John Keats: The Living Year, passim.*

† Keats became friendly with Marian Jeffrey of Teignmouth during the Devonshire holiday with Tom in the spring of 1818. Mr M. Buxton Forman in the *Letters* (p. lvi) reminds us of a local tradition that Keats was in love with Marian.

‡ *Letters*, p. 240. But Gittings (*op. cit.* pp. 62–3) believes that on one occasion at least Keats had physical relations with Isabella Jones. However, even if Gittings's deductions hold, this episode belongs to January 1819.

journal letter to George and Georgiana (14–31 October). One of the most interesting things in this is his confession of what it was that had so strongly attracted him to Charmian. She was a handsome creature certainly;* but much more captivating was her air and manner, which had somehow swept away all his usual diffidence in the company of women. Her vivacious spontaneity had also enchanted him; and in describing this aspect of her he almost certainly hits at the young-ladyish self-consciousness, artifice, and sentimentality that repelled him from so many of the girls of his acquaintance: 'I like her and her like because one has no *sensations*—what we both are is taken for granted.'†

Having painted the fascination of Charmian, he insists that he is not in love; and he manages to strike a note of man-of-the-world nonchalance that entirely conceals the pangs he had confessed to Reynolds. However, guessing that George and Georgiana might not be completely satisfied with the bare assertion, he throws out a reason or two to justify it. For one thing, Charmian is a little too magnificent and impressive for his taste—or for a possible conquest; for another, 'there are the Miss Reynoldses on the look out.'⁶ It is not till the end of his account that, through a quotation, he hints at a deeper reason; 'Do not think my dear Brother from this that my Passions are headlong or likely to be ever of any pain to you —no

'I am free from Men of Pleasure's cares,
By dint of feelings far more deep than theirs'.'

This journal letter is of great interest for the sentiments‡

* When Keats comments on her 'rich eastern look' (*Letters*, p. 233) one recalls the turn in the sestet of his early sonnet, 'Happy is England'.

† *Letters*, p. 233 (Keats's italics). One guesses that 'her like' would have included Marian Jeffrey since the tone of Keats's letters to her suggests a sensible, independent sort of girl, Isabella Jones whom Gittings (*op. cit.* p. 31) describes as a 'very decided and lively character', and later Fanny Brawne who had an independent and unconventional side to her personality.

‡ See especially the passage beginning, 'I have a tenderness for you' (*Letters*, p. 230).

that Keats addresses to Georgiana. It would be out of place here to discuss the whole problem of his attitude to her—whether he had himself been secretly in love with her; but at least it is clear that the schoolboy who had 'thought a fair Woman a pure Goddess'⁸ was still far from dead in him, and that in 1818 this inclination that he had to idealize and romanticize woman was focused on Georgiana. Further, there is candid confession of a dichotomy in his attitude to women, with the Charmians on one side and the Georgianas on the other; 'As a Man in the world I love the rich talk of a Charmian; as an eternal Being I love the thought of you.'⁹ In isolation that phrase 'rich talk' might deceive us; but from the sentence that follows it is evident that Charmian represents sensuous, physical woman (and love), as Georgiana represents the romantic vision. Again, in view of what we know is shortly to come in Keats's life, there is something ominous in his thought of a self-immolation to love: 'I should like her [Charmian] to ruin me, and I should like you to save me'.¹⁰

Yet while he felt these opposed attractions of a Charmian and a Georgiana, he could at the same time write with deep and sincere feeling of the joy of an independent and solitary life. No doubt he was to some extent trying to make a virtue out of present necessity; no doubt either that, for the peace of mind of George and Georgiana, he was pretending to be happier than he truly was. Yet reading what he wrote on his disinclination to marry—a passage* that paradoxically brings out the voluptuousness of his love-fancies—we feel that at the heart of his sentiments there was the intense, celibate spirit of a devotee, vowed to 'poesy', beauty, and the boundless worlds of imagination.

To sum up, this journal letter brings us as close as we can ever come to a heart that two or three months later, caught up in a familiar paradox of human existence, was to fall

* *Letters*, pp. 240–1. Gittings (*op. cit.* p. 33) believes that the early part of this passage was suggested by the furnishings in Isabella Jones's apartments in Gloucester Street.

irresistibly and desperately in love. What it reveals is a young poet prone to idealize women in a romantic dream, yet holding a poor opinion of most of those he met, regarding them as at best children to be satisfied with sugar-plums; a man torn between imaginations of luxuriously sensuous love and love of a more elevated and spiritual kind; a man who believed that love was one of the most profound of human experiences and at its best the height of human happiness, and who yet, because he was a dedicated poet, felt uncertain of its inexorable demands; a man of intense erotic feelings that he was prepared to repress partly because of an immediate sense of duty to his brother and partly because of his devotion to poetry. An awareness of this complex psychological background is at least as important as that of the havoc of disease in Keats and the difficulties of his material circumstances when we try to follow the difficult and distressing story of his love for Fanny Brawne. It will not do to simplify that story to one of painful misunderstandings between a sick, impecunious poet of a rather jealous disposition and a young woman, fond of the gaieties of life, who at first did not love him as he loved her; and while the first wave of our sympathy goes out instinctively to Keats, we must at the same time remember the immense task of understanding that was imposed on a girl of ordinary sympathies and intelligence* when fate transformed her into the idol of a genius deeply entangled in a 'gordian complication of feelings' about love and women.

It is not surprising that Keats's chief poem of 1818, the first *Hyperion*, written most of it while he was nursing Tom, has nothing to do with love, though Middleton Murry is probably right in his suggestion that the inflowing warmth and rapture

* I feel that Edgcumbe exaggerated a little when he described Fanny Brawne as 'a young woman of remarkable perception and imagination, keen in the observance of character and events, possessing an unusual critical faculty, and intellectually fitted to become the wife of Keats' (*Letters of Fanny Brawne to Fanny Keats*, p. xvii).

of the opening[11] of Book III owes something to the awakening of his love for Fanny Brawne. *Isabella*,[12] on the other hand, is certainly a sort of love poem; and there is much in its early part—in the Lorenzo dying with love but too timid to declare himself until the obliging Isabella makes the first overture, and in the tender-swooning luxury of their courtship, tartly described by Bridges as an 'aegritude of passion'*—that reminds us of *Endymion*. However, Keats does not dwell on the courtship of his lovers, and the love-interest as a whole, often reminiscent of the Romeo-Juliet prototype, is without urgency or significance. In this respect at least the poem warrants Keats's own later strictures: 'There is too much inexperience of life, and simplicity of knowledge in it . . . Isabella is what I should call were I a reviewer "A weak-sided Poem" with an amusing sober-sadness about it.'[13] It was a true critical instinct that drew Lamb in his commendation to the description of the disinterment of Lorenzo (particularly to stanzas XLVI–LIII): true not only because this passage contains the finest poetry of the piece but because it without doubt embodies the inspirational core.† As we read the lines immediately preceding Lamb's quotation—

> Who hath not loiter'd in a green church-yard,
>   And let his spirit, like a demon mole,
> Work through the clayey soil and gravel hard,
>   To see scull, coffin'd bones, and funeral stole;
> Pitying each form that hungry Death hath marr'd,
>   And filling it once more with human soul?‡

—we surely come closer to the Keats who created this particular poem than we do through any of the stanzas where he is describing the love of Isabella and Lorenzo. In this account of the disinterment of Lorenzo, with its juxtaposition of tender

---

* *Collected Essays*, Vol. IV, p. 121.

† Wilson Knight (*The Starlit Dome*, p. 280) describes the poem as one 'focused mainly on death'.

‡ Ll. 353–8. This stanza, from which I have omitted the atrocious concluding couplet, is almost certainly an echo from *Romeo and Juliet*.

passion, violence, and physical horror—this horror the more impressive for its delicacy and restraint—Keats is for once indulging in a characteristically Romantic *frisson*. He is absorbed in the centre of a poem that belongs, more entirely than any other work of his, to Romanticism—Romanticism on its side of abnormal 'agony'.*

Perhaps from our present standpoint, when we are considering Keats as a love-poet, the most interesting feature of *Isabella* is that it is an unhappy tale of love's destruction. One makes that simple observation with some hesitancy. Keats's choice of subject may have been fortuitous—if subjects for poems ever are that—or at least without any very serious premeditation. Also he is himself at some pains to minimize the wretchedness of Lorenzo and Isabella.† Nevertheless, considered as a whole, *Isabella* is a sad poem; and in retrospect Keats himself called it a work of 'sober-sadness'—admittedly at the same time qualifying that phrase with the epithet 'amusing'. Further, while it is possible to dismiss such matters as mere chance, it is a little surprising, even when we allow for that peculiarly romantic quality in the tale already indicated, that Keats should have chosen this of all Boccaccio's stories to turn into English verse. But if we may believe that he had some sense, however faint, of what he was doing when he selected this tale of unhappy, destroyed and destructive love,‡ then *Isabella* has some continuity with one of the themes of *Endymion* and is related to what we have seen to be part of his attitude to love in 1818.

Apart from *Isabella* the garner of Keats's love-poetry between *Endymion* and the end of 1818 is of the slightest. There

---

* I am of course thinking of the title of Mario Praz's well-known study of Romanticism. Wilson Knight (*op. cit.* p. 281) comments: 'Isabella's keeping and caressing of Lorenzo's head mixes love and horror in a most questionable fashion.'

† See especially ll. 89–94.

‡ Was this the point of Keats's cryptic aside (*Letters*, p. 391), 'there are very few would look to the reality'?

is one section in *To Fancy* that, with its mood of disenchantment, may be linked with 'Hither, hither, love' of late 1817
and parts of the odes of 1819:

> O, sweet Fancy! let her loose;
> Everything is spoilt by use:
> Where's the cheek that doth not fade,
> Too much gaz'd at? Where's the maid
> Whose lip mature is ever new?
> Where's the eye, however blue,
> Doth not weary? Where's the face
> One would meet in every place?
> Where's the voice, however soft,
> One would hear so very oft?*

On the other hand, even if this mood was heart-felt rather
than a matter of conventional literary sentiment, passion and
emotion were not entirely 'stifled' in Keats's poetry as we may
see from the sonnets, 'Time's Sea' and 'When I have fears', both
inspired by memory of the young lady he had seen in Vauxhall
Gardens in 1814.†

To these sonnets we may add 'Hither, hither, love', 'You
say you love', and 'Hush, hush, tread softly'. Most of the
writing in these love lyrics suggests mere literary exercise,‡
though the second, which has a charming metrical movement,
might have been an effective little piece in a derivative, Wyatt-
esque manner. Unfortunately it is marred grossly by touches
of the *Endymion* sort of love-making:

> You say you love; but then your hand
>   No soft squeeze for squeeze returneth,
> It is like a statue's, dead,—
>   While music to passion burneth—
>   O love me truly![14]

Finally, and in its way just as closely related to Keats's
attitude to love and women in 1818, there is a handful of

---

* Ll. 67–76. See 'Hither, hither, love', ll. 13–16.
† See p. 195.
‡ Gittings (*op. cit.* pp. 57–60) plausibly argues that there was much
more to 'Hush, hush, tread softly' than literary exercise.

mildly cynical, or earthy, love-poems—'O blush not so', 'Oh, I am frightened', *Modern Love*, 'Over the hill, over the dale'. The last, a light-hearted and casually written memento of Keats's spring visit to Devonshire, is worth a glance if only for its amusing sidelight on the poet who is commonly supposed to have written the Spenserian neo-platonic allegory of *Endymion:*

> Rantipole Betty she ran down a hill
> And kick'd up her petticoats fairly;
> Says I, I'll be Jack if you will be Gill.
> So she sat on the Grass debonnairely.
>
> Here's somebody coming, here's somebody coming!
>   Says I, 'tis the Wind at a parley;
> So without any fuss, any hawing and humming,
>   She lay on the grass debonnairely.
>
> Here's somebody here, and here's somebody there!
>   Says I, hold your tongue, you young Gipsey.
> So she held her tongue and lay plump and fair
>   And dead as a Venus tipsy. [15]

No harm is done to Keats to recall such a trifle as this, which in its kind has something to tell us about his attitude to love and about the stuff of common (or Regency) human nature that was mixed with his divine imagination. Sometimes, too, such unpremeditated verses may illuminate more important works, or the way in which we should approach them. What, for example, is the picture of Endymion's first approach to the Indian Maid—

> He sprang from his green covert; there she lay,
> Sweet as a muskrose upon new-made hay;
> With all her limbs on tremble, and her eyes
> Shut softly up alive [16]

—but a sublimated vision of Rantipole Betty in a Devonshire meadow? What even Psyche and Cupid, 'couched side by side In deepest grass', but essentially that, a flower magically conjured from an earth that is not to be entirely forgotten?

Whoever inspired *The Eve of St Agnes*, Fanny Brawne or Isabella Jones,* there can be no other way of reading the poem than as a great affirmation of love—of an intense, happy, achieved love that makes it the antithesis of *Isabella*.† Porphyro passing from the bleak winter world outside through the dark castle of danger and emblemed mortality to discover at the heart of it Madeline, all colour, warmth, music and passionate love, Porphyro triumphant, bearing that warmth and colour away over the southern moors, is the Keats who has escaped from the death of Tom's bedside, with all its anguish and starvation of natural feelings, into life and love. All this has been truly and most excellently said by Middleton Murry:

It is the poem of awakened sensuous love, not quite confident— was not Keats at the very moment he wrote it kept indoors by his sore throat?—for it is a dream that vanishes. Yet we may fairly call it a poem of opulent and triumphant love. It has the rapture and enchantment, the rich and deep and right sensuousness, of complete surrender to the god; it is the brief dayspring of Keats's passion translated into terms of poetic imagination. If the crude equation be taken with enough imaginative margin, we may say that Madeline is Fanny and Keats Porphyro.‡

* In *John Keats: The Living Year* (pp. 57–63) Gittings presents quite a strong case for considering Isabella Jones, not Fanny Brawne, as the inspiration of *The Eve of St Agnes*. But though he speaks of 'an attachment both passionate and intellectual which lasted through the first six months of this year' (this estimate of the duration of the attachment is contradicted by the statement that in April 'Isabella has been pushed back into the shades'—p. 130), there is no real evidence that Keats's undoubted relations with Mrs Jones were more than a passing affair. Most of us will probably continue to feel that *The Eve of St Agnes* was written by a poet who had fallen truly and deeply in love for the first time.

† In *The Finer Tone* (pp. 97–137) E. R. Wasserman offers a highly elaborate metaphysical interpretation of the poem, which is seen, among other things, as an expression of the 'pleasure thermometer' and the 'mansion of life'. Personally, I cannot accept this interpretation, nor can I see why Wasserman so stresses Madeline's dream or why he is so confident that her dream was a 'divine vision'. However, I agree that Keats is celebrating a love that is both warmly sensuous and at the same time pure, and Wasserman is excellent in demonstrating how this is suggested by the contrasting (and interpenetrating) imagery of red colours on the one hand and silver and moonlight on the other.

‡ *Keats and Shakespeare*, p. 109.

Like Murry we may feel that the work is not, after all, the complete antithesis of *Isabella;* that there is some uneasiness, uncertainty (a premonition perhaps?) lurking at the back of the mind of the poet, preventing him from giving us a picture of entire and overwhelming joy. Somehow in our response we have to recognize the shadows as well as the glowingly colourful lights of the poem; and it is not easy to dismiss the Beadsman, the icy chapel of the tombs, and the reminders of death and mortality as merely conventional 'gothic' accessories. Yet if there is this sort of doubt intruding into *The Eve of St Agnes*, there is for the moment no uncertainty about love itself. As Murry says, there is 'complete surrender to the god'. We might almost believe that everything Keats had thought and written about love before is to be discounted as the usual extravagant bachelor's nonsense of a Longaville and Dumain, with this poem as the decisive recantation, like Berowne's great apostrophe to love. Do we not find Keats himself confessing, just at this time, in his journal-letter to George and Georgiana: 'the man who ridicules romance is the most romantic of Men . . . he who abuses women and slights them— loves them the most'?[17] And so it indeed seems—as simple as that—if we turn back from the love-rhapsody of *St Agnes* to what Keats had written in his letters of the previous year.

Yet if we form any such impressions as this we are in error, as we realize when we come to his next notable poem of 1819, that strange lovely ballad *La Belle Dame Sans Merci*, which he wrote only two months after *The Eve of St Agnes*.

No doubt there are several possible ways of reading* *La*

---

* Thus—to give a recent example—Wasserman (*The Finer Tone*, pp. 65–83) concludes that the ballad is an intermixture of 'the three coexistent themes that dominate Keats's deepest meditations and profoundest system of values: the oxymoronic heaven's bourne towards which his spirit yearned; the pleasure thermometer which he conceived of as the spiritual path to that goal; and the self-annihilation that he understood to be the condition necessary for the journey' (p. 83). This interpretation, which seems to me entirely astray, cannot be contested in a footnote. In brief, Wasserman fails to appreciate the significance of love in the poem,

Belle Dame, for the situation it presents—enchantment, dream, awakened disillusion—as well as much of the imagery, is archetypal. On the other hand, whatever the marginal symbolism, it seems as clear as such things ever can be that the Lady stands for love in some form or other. The sad lonely figure who speaks most of the poem is that traditional literary embodiment of romantic love, the Knight, while the love-making between the Knight and the Lady, described with what we might be tempted to call Keats's clichés were it not for the beauty of the phrasing, must be literal, not a symbolical representation of something else:

> She look'd at me as she did love,
>   And made sweet moan . . .

> She took me to her elfin grot,
>   And there she wept, and sigh'd full sore,
> And there I shut her wild wild eyes
>   With kisses four.

Once again there is the familiar Keatsian association of love with sleep, the sleep that from *Endymion* onwards is represented as a sort of consummation of love—'And there she lulled me asleep'. But this sleep is not the erotic luxury (and possibly, as the psychologists might have it, the latent death-wish) that he expresses in another poem of this period,* the first draft of 'Bright star'—

> To hear, to feel her tender-taken breath,
> Half passionless, and so swoon on to death. [18]

It is, on the contrary, a sleep of terrifying dream revelation, of love as a cruel destroyer, of the love that is death:

and he is wrong to relate it to the *Ode on a Grecian Urn*. Its revealing kinship is with the Paolo and Francesca sonnet.

* Gittings (*op. cit.* pp. 25–36) advances arguments for dating the first version of the 'Bright star' sonnet as October 1818—that is to say, five or six months earlier than the usually accepted date. Personally, I am by no means convinced by the case that Gittings makes for this revised composition date. But the precise date to the month does not matter very much for the comment I am making here.

I saw pale kings and princes too,
  Pale warriors, death-pale were they all;
They cried—'La Belle Dame Sans Merci
  Hath thee in thrall!'

I saw their starved lips in the gloam
  With horrid warning gaped wide . . .

Nor is there merely a premonitory vision; the Knight knows himself to be a victim: he is alone and dying in a world of death and winter desolation, his countenance an image of all the ravaged and feverish torment of love:

I see a lilly on thy brow,
  With anguish moist and fever dew,
And on thy cheeks a fading rose
  Fast withereth too.

In short, *La Belle Dame Sans Merci*, which is well described by Colvin as a 'masterpiece of romantic and tragic symbolism on the wasting power of Love',* signals the re-emergence, from the Circe episode of *Endymion* and perhaps the sonnet on Leander, of that romantic theme of the Fatal Woman† that was to haunt so much of his remaining poetry. When we read the poem we cannot help recalling those words he later wrote to Fanny Brawne: 'I never knew before, what such a love as

* *Life of John Keats*, p. 350. See also Kenneth Muir (*Essays in Criticism*, Vol. IV, 4, p. 435): 'On the surface Keats's poem is concerned with a knight's seduction by a witch or fairy; but it clearly symbolizes the destructive effects of sexual passion.'

† In *The Romantic Agony* Mario Praz uses 'La Belle Dame Sans Merci' as the title of his chapter on the theme of the Fatal Woman. Considering this theme in Keats's poetry, one is tempted to Rossetti's surmise that *The Eve of St Mark* (started in February 1819) was intended to show the remorse of a young girl for the suffering of mind, leading to death, that she had inflicted on her lover.

Wilson Knight (*The Starlit Dome*, p. 275) has a good comment on this aspect of Keats's love poetry: 'Keats's pagan sensuousness does not forget that there is something subtly wrong with human love: that it is subject to tragic necessity, and that ugliness . . . may be at the core of its luscious bloom.'

you have made me feel, was; I did not believe in it; my Fancy was afraid of it, *lest it should burn me up.*'[19] In this letter he is admittedly writing, at the level of conscious intention, as love's devotee. But *La Belle Dame Sans Merci* is an abiding reminder that what he himself admits to be an old fear, a fear that was certainly behind his attitude in the previous year, still lurked in some part of him after he had fallen in love with Fanny Brawne. This emotion, and its poetic crystallization in the ballad, in no way invalidates his love for Fanny, for of course he was deeply in love with her; it merely expresses those warring contradictions we have already traced in his attitude. The truth is that he was infinitely more complex than a Dumain, Longaville, or even a Berowne, who had suddenly and completely surrendered to love.

It is just possible that the destructive and fatal love represented in *La Belle Dame Sans Merci* is love that is entirely sensuous, with the Lady, like Circe, an 'arbitrary queen of sense'. Indeed, the description of the Knight's appearance and the emphasis on the word 'pale', so reminiscent of those lines in the Circe episode—

> O Dis, even now,
> A *clammy dew* is beading on my *brow*,
> At mere remembering her *pale* laugh, and *curse*,[20]

seem to point to some common association in Keats's mind; and we have elsewhere* referred to Finney's suggestion that the Lady of the ballad is to some extent a re-creation of Spenser's Phaedria. Further, this interpretation of *La Belle Dame Sans Merci* as a poem of baneful sensuous love might be supported by one of the possible ways of reading *Lamia*. Yet when we recall Keats's own nature and his attitude to physical love, so plainly and passionately re-affirmed in *The Eve of St Agnes*, we can hardly believe that he would have pressed the antithesis between sensuous love and the love that we call 'spiritual', especially now he was himself devoted to a woman.

---

* See p. 35.

Another poem very close to the ballad* in its date of composition (April), its dream-suggestion, its tone, and—as some of us may believe—in its latent intention, is his sonnet to Paolo and Francesca, notably the sestet:

> But to that second circle of sad hell,
>   Where in the gust, the whirlwind, and the flaw
> Of rain and hail-stones, lovers need not tell
>   Their sorrows,—pale were the sweet lips I saw,
> Pale were the lips I kiss'd, and fair the form
> I floated with, about that melancholy storm.[21]

For these lines to make their maximum impact we should come to them immediately from their prose-matrix in one of the letters, a revealing account of the dream-genesis of the poem, with some curious discrepancies† between dream-symbolism and the resultant sonnet, that should fascinate the psychologist.—'The dream was one of the most delightful enjoyments I ever had in my life ... O that I could dream it every night.'[22]

Some resemblances between this sonnet and *La Belle Dame* are obvious enough: the iterated 'pale' of the lips, the wintry-world setting (this 'storm' and 'flaw Of rain and hail-stones' also reminiscent of the bleak outside world in *St Agnes*), and the intimation of the normal misery of lovers from which this particular dream was a momentary release:

> lovers need not tell
> Their sorrows.

But what are we to make of Keats's remark in the letter that 'the fifth canto of Dante pleases me more and more'?[23]—this canto of the second circle in Hell where, in the words of the Carey translation that Keats read,

---

* Murry (*Keats and Shakespeare*, p. 124) notes the 'manifest' connexion between these two poems.

† For example, the 'flowery tree tops' and the sensation of warmth are suppressed in the poem.

The carnal sinners are condemn'd, in whom
Reason by lust is sway'd.[24]

What are we to make of Keats's imaginative self-identifica-
tion, not with the living and mainly happy Paolo and Francesca of Leigh Hunt's poem, but with two doomed spirits
whom love had destroyed? What of the confusion that con-
verts the agonizing, perpetual restlessness of Dante's vision—

So bears the tyrannous gust those evil souls . . .
It drives them: hope of rest to solace them
Is none[25]

—into a sensation of joy, a joy admittedly more strongly
impressed by the description in the letter? What, in particular,
are we to make of these questions if Paolo and Francesca are,
as seems most probable, Keats and Fanny Brawne, and if
Finney is right when he describes the sonnet as 'a dream consummation of [Keats's] love for Miss Brawne'.*

These are hard and tantalizing questions arising from an
extremely elusive poem, and maybe they are the proper business of a psychologist rather than of a literary critic. But possibly
the basic answer to them is a fairly simple one so long as it
includes the confusion and does not attempt to rationalize this
away in some neat reconciliation. Perhaps (as with *La Belle
Dame*) we may believe that, conscious of the doom and destruction in love, in his own love for Fanny Brawne, dimly aware,
from his early attitude to love (his high dedication to poetry,
and so on), of some wrong-doing in his abandonment to an
experience so largely physical, Keats identified himself and
Fanny Brawne with Paolo and Francesca in their retributive
fate, and yet by the accident of a real dream was able on this
occasion to wring a desperate, precarious joy out of the vision,
as he certainly was able to find joy in his everyday life with
Fanny. If this answer is anywhere near the truth, it follows

* *The Evolution of Keats's Poetry*, p. 587.

that *La Belle Dame Sans Merci* is Keats's equivalent, without the religious significance, of what Dante had really written in Canto v of *Hell* and that the ballad expresses what satisfied Keats most deeply in this canto. The sonnet, on the other hand, probably written shortly before *La Belle Dame*, is an interim poem, a struggling confusion before the pure crystallization of the ballad, though at the same time it is a work that must have given Keats a momentary comfort and satisfaction, like the dream that produced it—even if some of the joy has visibly evaporated between the two experiences.

Both *La Belle Dame Sans Merci* and the sonnet to Paolo and Francesca (the second of course more remotely than the first) contain implications of death. But what is particularly strange in the poetry of early 1819, composed when Keats had at last fallen in love, is the re-emergence of that close association of love and death that had been so strikingly evident in the purely imaginative *Endymion*. It is not simply that, as a poet and a lover, he is haunted by a premonition and fear of death: that, in his circumstances, would be understandable and not strange. What we have to accept is the passionate lover of Fanny Brawne who is at the same time half in love with death as a consummation devoutly to be wished and who feels some mysterious connexion between love and death. What he later writes in the *Ode to a Nightingale*—

> Darkling I listen; and, for many a time
> I have been half in love with easeful Death,
> Call'd him soft names in many a mused rhyme,
> To take into the air my quiet breath

—is the exact truth. His sonnet 'Why did I laugh', written in March, concludes with the lines

> Verse, Fame, and Beauty are intense indeed,
> But Death intenser—Death is Life's high meed.

Here the 'Beauty' that he renounces for the intenser consummation of death must have included Fanny Brawne, and some part of him must have realized this, for he was always insistent that it was her beauty that had drawn him to her: 'I cannot conceive any beginning of such love as I have for you but Beauty.' And what is the 'Bright star' sonnet in its first version but a sense of love and death as one common, confused consummation, with 'swoon', that chiming, characteristic word in his love-poetry, as the link?—

> yet still steadfast, still unchangeable,
> Cheek-pillow'd on my Love's white ripening breast,
> To touch, for ever, its warm sink and swell,
> Awake, for ever, in a sweet unrest;
> To hear, to feel her tender-taken breath,
> Half-passionless, and so swoon on to death.

'Half-passionless'—it is bewildering to find this desire of escape from some of the exhausting urgency of passion. But we may recall again that later confession: 'my Fancy was afraid of it, lest it should burn me up.'

We have described such lines as those just quoted from 'Bright star' and 'Why did I laugh?' as strange. Yet is there anything in them quite so startling or baffling as those mysterious words—certainly related to the feeling of the two sonnets —that he wrote to Fanny on 25 July?—'I have two luxuries to brood over in my walks, your Loveliness and the hour of my death. O that I could have possession of them both in the same minute.'[26]

The troubled, ominous mood of the poems we have been considering appears to be totally obliterated by the first of the odes, *To Psyche*, which once more, in the words of the last line, lets 'the warm Love in'. For the moment at any rate we are back in the mood of *The Eve of St Agnes*, and perhaps—in the first strophe at least—to *Endymion*. There is all the old sensuousness, and once again love is richly and suggestively associated with the luxuriance, fertility, and beauty of vegetative nature. As so often in *Endymion*, that characteristically

Keatsian image of the arbour is used to blend the two sensations:

> I wander'd in a forest thoughtlessly,
>   And, on the sudden, fainting with surprise,
> Saw two fair creatures, couched side by side
>   In deepest grass, beneath the whisp'ring roof
>   Of leaves and trembled blossoms, where there ran
>   A brooklet, scarce espied.[27]

But this imagery of blossoms, flowers, foliage and trees is not confined to the first strophe; it is abundantly prominent all through the rest of the ode, from the 'altar heap'd with flowers' to the 'gardener Fancy' at the close, giving the poem a memorable and most satisfying unity. In particular, the strophes are closely bound together by the master-image of the forest: it is in a forest that the poet beholds the god and goddess of love; he evokes the 'haunted forest boughs' in conjuring up the ancient world of happy pieties; and the imaginary temple to Psyche is built where

> dark-cluster'd trees
> Fledge the wild-ridged mountains steep by steep.*

Another outstanding feature of *To Psyche*—and this in spite of the fact that it was composed with a leisurely deliberation that was new to Keats—[28]is its fervently rhapsodic note, which individualizes it from all the other odes. This effect is produced by the prominent repetitions in rhythm, movement, and phrasing, and by the frequent recurrence of lines like 'No voice, no lute, no pipe, no incense sweet' that create an impression of mounting, insistent urgency. Yet it would be a superficial response to the ode to regard this note simply as a matter of style. Rhapsody is the essence and intention of the poem, which rises to its climax when Keats, with the same intensity and the same kind of hieratic language that had once

---

* Ll. 54–5. This image, for all that it owes to a recollection of the Scottish tour the previous year (see *Letters*, p. 161), is also a compact reminiscence of his description of the isle of Latmos in *Endymion*.

marked his self-dedications to poesy, vows himself to love. For the moment he is literally the priest of Psyche, intoxicated with her inspiration:

> So let me be thy choir, and make a moan
>   Upon the midnight hours;
> Thy voice, thy lute, thy pipe, thy incense sweet
>   From swinged censer teeming;
> Thy shrine, thy grove, thy oracle, thy heat
>   Of pale-mouth'd prophet dreaming.[29]

On this account, and because there is not the slightest trace of those shadows of doubt and uncertainty that had marginally intruded into *The Eve of St Agnes*, we must surely regard *To Psyche* as Keats's epithalamion to Fanny Brawne.*

However, while this first ode harmonizes perfectly with the idyllic picture that some writers have painted of the relations between Keats and Fanny during the period from April to June, when they were living in different parts of the same house,† and is exactly the kind of poem we should normally expect, the four odes immediately following show that Keats still suffered from that 'gordian complication of feelings', which, as he had acutely foreseen, would take 'time to unravell and care to keep unravelled'.‡

In the first place, whatever ultimate view we take of the odes, whether we regard them mainly as beautiful compensatory dreams for painful reality and tentative explorations

---

* I find it quite impossible to follow John Holloway when he writes: 'Keats's mood here is much like that of *On Indolence*', and 'the genesis of the poem . . . lies in "soft-handed slumber"' ('The Odes of Keats', *Cambridge Journal*, April 1952, pp. 418 and 419).

† See, for example, *The Mystery of Keats*, p. 30.

‡ *Letters*, p. 193. Commenting on Keats at this period Gittings writes (*John Keats: The Living Year*, p. 140): 'His uneasy and ambivalent feelings about women and about sex in general still haunted his inward being.' He then draws attention to Keats's annotation on Burton: 'Here is the old plague spot: the pestilence, the raw scrofula. I mean there is nothing disgraces me in my own eyes so much as being one of the race of eyes, nose and mouth beings in a planet called the earth who all from Plato to Wesley have always mingled goatish, winnyish, lustful love with the abstract adoration of the deity.'

of ways of escape from it, or whether, like Middleton Murry,
as profound spiritual exercises in 'soul-making', we must all
agree that they were written by a poet deeply tormented by

> The weariness, the fever, and the fret
> Here, where men sit and hear each other groan.[30]

It may well be that this poet was not necessarily and in all
respects the Keats who walked with Fanny in the springtime
garden of Wentworth Place. On the other hand, this sense of
human misery behind the odes makes it impossible for us to
believe that Keats was at the same time living through a
spring idyll of that intoxicated, self-absorbing emotion that is
the usual and fairly simple state of most of us when we first fall
seriously in love.

Secondly, it is a remarkable fact about these odes that while
they are much concerned with the quest for solace and escape,
nowhere in them is the love that we know on earth contemplated as a recompense or alleviation of our misery. Keats is half
prepared to accept death as an anodyne, but never love.
Indeed, the odes have singularly little to say about love at all,
and what they do say is spoken with a voice of disillusionment.
The *Nightingale* ode carries the burden of fading physical
beauty and love's impermanence—

> Where Beauty cannot keep her lustrous eyes,
> Or new Love pine at them beyond to-morrow[31]

—and the *Grecian Urn* contrasts a dream of a perpetually
youthful, uncloying love with the actuality of 'breathing
human passion',

> That leaves a heart high-sorrowful and cloy'd,
> A burning forehead, and a parching tongue.[32]

In the *Ode on Indolence* love is dismissed as one of the three
delusive phantoms that continually work the poet into a
'fever fit'—

> O folly! What is Love! and where is it?[33]

—and in the *Ode on Melancholy* love is tortured into a neurotic luxury:

> if thy mistress some rich anger shows,
> Emprison her soft hand, and let her rave,
> And feed deep, deep upon her peerless eyes. [34]

Any one of these notes, in isolation, might be discounted as fugitive, dramatic, or conventional. But together, and along with the more general points we have mentioned, they show quite clearly that even in its happiest season Keats's love for Fanny remained clouded by those doubts and uncertainties that all his previous history would lead us to expect. That is why Murry is quite wrong when he writes: 'It was when he had to part from Fanny at the end of June 1819 that "the hateful siege of contraries" *began* in Keats's being.'*

Though the possibility that Keats found Fanny's physical presence too distracting for sustained poetic work cannot be entirely dismissed,† his separation from her, which lasted from the end of June till the second week of October, was mainly forced upon him by unavoidable circumstances.‡ During this parting there were certainly times when he seems to have felt that she did not love him as he loved her. It is probable, too, that in the last weeks of the separation, while he was staying at Winchester, something of the fever of his passion was allayed. But if his letters of this period leave one clear impression it is that neither his removal of himself from Fanny nor his absorption in a fury of creative work did any-

---

* *The Mystery of Keats*, p. 17. (My italics.)

† Besides the considerable number of references in his letters to the 'indolence' of the Wentworth Place idyll we should notice the following remark in a letter to Fanny Keats: 'I propose to retire into the Country and set my Mind at work once more' (*Letters*, p. 348).

‡ As usual Brown was letting his half of Wentworth Place for the summer. Also Keats was hard pressed financially and realized it would be cheaper living in the country. The chief prospect of making money seemed to be the joint tragedy that Brown proposed, and to some extent Keats was committed to this project by the loan he had accepted from Brown.

thing of consequence to weaken his love;* and when he returned to her his passion flared up with all its most hectic intensity: 'Love is my religion—I could die for that. I could die for you. My Creed is Love and you are its only tenet. You have ravish'd me away by a Power I cannot resist . . . I cannot breathe without you.'[35]

At the same time it is equally plain that throughout their separation his love was still beset by a profound unease and still complicated by moods of rebellion. If at the end he confessed, 'You have absorb'd me',[36] there had been a stage when he had written, 'You absorb me *in spite of myself*';[37] and there are recurrent complaints in the letters of lost freedom and independence. Thus, in his very first letter to Fanny, he wrote: 'Ask yourself my love whether you are not very cruel to have so entrammelled me, so destroyed my freedom.'[38] For a later example of this feeling there is his letter to Taylor of 23 August, which contains the most striking of all his remarks on love and independence: 'I equally dislike the favour of the public with the love of a woman—they are both a cloying treacle to the wings of independence.'[39] His metaphor here may serve to remind us that he was not expressing a new sentiment, for a year previously he had written: 'These things combined with the opinion I have of the generality of women—who appear to me as children to whom I would rather give a Sugar Plum than my time, form a barrier against Matrimony which I rejoice in.'[40]

The complement of all this, to be traced in the letters written when he was staying at Winchester, was his expression of the pleasure he enjoyed in his solitude. To Reynolds he wrote (24 August): 'I think if I had a free and healthy and lasting organisation of heart, and lungs as strong as an ox's so as to be able [to bear] unhurt the shock of extreme thought and sensation without weariness, I could pass my life very nearly alone though it should last eighty years';[41] to George and Georgiana

* See, for instance, the 'ungallant' letter of 16 August (*Letters*, pp. 369-71).

a month later: 'You would scarcely imagine I could live alone so comfortably "kepen in solitarinesse".'* Further, it is evident from this letter to his brother and sister-in-law that he did not value an independent solitude solely for its pleasure: he also conceived it as a defence against the troubles that were pressing on him: 'I feel I can bear anything,—any misery, even imprisonment—so long as I have neither wife nor child.'†

No doubt there was a certain amount of defensive simulation in this praise of the joy of 'kepen in solitarinesse'; but, as the journal letter of October, 1818, to George and Georgiana shows—'my Solitude is sublime'—[42] it was a joy that he had cherished before he had known Fanny Brawne, while the ode *To Autumn* remains as an impressive reminder that it was in such undistracted solitude, away from Fanny, that he found for a moment a serenity of spirit he had never experienced before and was never to experience again. In the same way his fear of absorption in Fanny sprang, as we have seen, from old, deep, and complex causes. Hence, it is impossible to accept Murry's conclusion that everything in Keats that ran counter to his love for Fanny was temporary and superficial— a kind of psychological defence that he had to set up if he were to resist the pain of separation and the temptation to return to Hampstead before he had exerted his full endeavour for fame and fortune.‡

As we have so far described it, Keats's attitude during this period of separation—including its fundamental contradictions—is not difficult to understand, for it falls within the range of normal experience. But there was another subtle strand in it that runs into obscurity. This was his deep and

---

* *Letters*, p. 422. On the same day he wrote to Reynolds. 'I "kepen in solitarinesse" . . . I am surprised myself at the pleasure I live alone in.' (*Ibid.* p. 383).

† *Ibid.* p. 399. This letter is also notable for its mocks at love—the lengthy quotation from Burton, and the long passage (complete with illustrative poem) in which Keats makes fun at the absurdity of lovers.

‡ See *The Mystery of Keats*, pp. 11–75. This essay on the love of Keats and Fanny Brawne is often extremely illuminating in its detail.

instinctive association of love with death—a complex of feelings that both drew him irresistibly towards Fanny and at other times led him to fight against her fascination.

Some of the expressions of this subconscious impulse to 'swoon to death' through the dissolution and extinction of love, like 'a few more moments thought of you would uncrystallize and dissolve me',[43] or 'You have absorb'd me. I have a sensation at the present moment as though I was dissolving',[44] may possibly be interpreted in more simple and superficial ways. But for proof of the death that was always at the heart of his erotic feelings—so much at the heart of them that one is tempted to conclude it was his destiny to be destroyed in love—there can be no questioning the passage in the letter he wrote to Fanny on 25 July. We have already quoted two of its arresting, enigmatic sentences—'I have two luxuries to brood over in my walks, your Loveliness, and the hour of my death. O that I could have possession of them both in the same minute.' But what follows is even more baffling in tangled contradiction: so closely does he confuse love and death that he can play with the fancy of death coming to him from the hand of his beloved—and voluptuously desire it: 'I hate the world . . . would I could take a sweet poison from your lips to send me out of it'.[45]

There is one further point to be made before we turn to the poetry of this period. This is that Keats probably suffered more, and more continuously, during the separation than his letters of the time would lead us to suppose. Agonizing as these letters often are, as a whole they do not convey what he wrote to James Rice in February 1820: 'I may say that for 6 Months before I was taken ill I had not passed a tranquil day.'[46]

Probably most of us are inclined to Keats's own preference for *Lamia** among his narrative poems. The work has almost

* It is rather curious to find Graham Hough writing of this intense and complex poem, so close to some of Keats's deepest experience, 'it

227

as much sensuous richness as *The Eve of St Agnes*, though this quality is more diffused than it is in the earlier poem; it presents a dramatic, substantial story that has psychological interest and some lively touches of characterization; its narrative is compact and swiftly moving; and its heroic couplet form, revealing an enormous advance from *Endymion*, is admirably manipulated. Of all Keats's poems it is the one that augurs most favourably for his ambitions in poetic drama, and it certainly comes near to the fulfilment of what he modestly set down as an aspiration three months later: 'The little dramatic skill I may as yet have however badly it might show in a Drama would I think be sufficient for a Poem. I wish to diffuse the colouring of St Agnes eve throughout a Poem in which Character and Sentiment would be the figures to such drapery.'[47]

However, for all this achievement, *Lamia* is a puzzling poem, the more puzzling as our acquaintance with it grows. There is the disturbing reappearance of early crudities of taste and expression*—not all to be dismissed as moments of Byronic inspiration. There is the problem of how far we are to read the poem as veiled autobiography,† with Lycius, Lamia, and Apollonius standing for Keats, Fanny Brawne, and Charles Brown; and, most baffling of all, there is our uncertainty of direction in imaginative response to the work. Colvin long ago underlined this last difficulty of *Lamia* when he wrote of 'the bewilderment in which it leaves us as to the effect intended to be made on our imaginative sympathies',‡ and it is a legitimate criticism of the poem to say that its chief strength is also the source of its chief weakness. It is the most truly dramatic

---

remains . . . a rather purposeless poem, and it looks rather like an exercise in verse-narrative' (*The Romantic Poets*, p. 167).

* See, for instance, 1, 197–99.

† It is interesting to note that Gittings, who heavily stresses the effect of personal experience on Keats's poetry, writes that *Lamia* 'is the most consciously artistic of all his productions, and he was not likely to allow unconscious autobiography to stray in' (*John Keats: The Living Year*, p. 150).

‡ *Life of John Keats*, p. 408.

of the narrative poems because of its conflict and human interest; but having engaged us in this way, as none of the other narrative poems does, it leaves us unsettled and fluctuating.

Nothing can alter this uncertainty, for it is demonstrably an effect of the poem itself, not of our inadequate reading. On the other hand, there can be little doubt that the work is a poetic reflection of Keats's turmoil of feelings about love and Fanny during the period of separation from her. Once we appreciate the nature of this personal conflict behind *Lamia* —and especially if we realize that the conflict derived from an deeply rooted ambivalence in Keats's attitude to love—we can understand this uncertainty of the poem and accept it without that sense of 'bewilderment' that so obviously bothered Colvin.

One thing at least is clear enough in the poem: that is the re-emergence from *La Belle Dame Sans Merci* of the theme of love's fatality. Lycius is destroyed, spiritually and physically, by his unfortunate love for Lamia, and the significance of this conclusion of the story is heightened when we remember that it was Keats's own invention, owing nothing to the anecdote from Burton on which he based his narrative. Moreover, this theme is thrown into sharp relief by our inevitable recollection of *Endymion*, whether or not Keats himself was conscious of the comparison that he forces us to make. In Part I, against a background of the island of Crete, which, with its forests, hills and mountains, is highly reminiscent of the isle of Latmos in *Endymion*, we have once more the tale of a mortal youth who falls in love with a maiden of non-human kind.* But whereas, after much anguish and some doubt, Endymion had found

---

* Besides this general parallel there is some considerable correspondence of detail. Thus when when Lamia tries to drive Lycius into desperation with the pretence that she is an immortal goddess who cannot surrender herself to a gross mortal existence, she is voicing the same sentiments that the Indian Maid truthfully utters in *Endymion*. Again, for correspondence of imaginative effect, the unfolding of the love of Lycius and Lamia is once more strikingly associated with a rich impression of vegetal imagery (see especially I, 316–20 and II, 215–20). It is interesting that the first of these passages was at one time followed by the cancelled lines,

fulfilment and immortal happiness in one who was truly a goddess, the love of Lycius brings him from assurance and rapture to disillusionment and death. Yet *Lamia* is the poem of Keats's experience in love, *Endymion* in the main of imaginative innocence. It is a strange contrast.

From this theme of baneful love it follows that Lamia is to some extent another incarnation of the Fatal Woman. At first indeed, in her snake form, that immemorial and primary symbol of evil, she appears wholly a personification of lurking, menacing ill:

> She seem'd, at once, some penanced lady elf,
> Some demon's mistress, *or the demon's self*.[48]

Later this suggestion of 'penanced' is caught up again in the implication that Lamia had once been a woman, for since there is nowhere a hint that she is suffering under a malicious enchantment, we can only imagine that her transformation is the punishment for some evil-doing. We also find Keats talking of her 'Circean hand', and though this allusion is sufficiently explicit as it stands, it is interesting to recall two lines from the Circe episode in *Endymion*. These lines, admittedly, refer to Circe's fire, not to the goddess herself; but they strongly suggest the existence in Keats's mind of some curious associative complex of Circe, gordian snake, fascination, and evil:

> This fire, like the eye of gordian snake,
> Bewitch'd me towards.[49]

If we do happen to recall these lines in reading the first part of *Lamia*, we can hardly doubt that this other 'gordian shape' is also an enchantress of malevolent fascination.*

> Ah! never heard of, delight never known
> Save of one happy mortal! only one.

Who else can Keats be referring to here, at a crucial point of his story, but Endymion?

* One of the chief weaknesses in Wasserman's discussion of the poem (*The Finer Tone*, pp. 158–74) is that in describing Lamia as 'a vision of

As we have already noticed, her first address to Lycius is entirely made up of a lie about her ethereal, goddess-like nature, and when, with song and kisses, this cruel lady of the bright eyes casts Lycius *'pale* with pain', into a trance, we are reminded very much of *La Belle Dame Sans Merci:*

> The cruel lady, without any show
> Of sorrow for her tender favourite's woe,
> But rather, if her eyes could brighter be,
> With brighter eyes and slow amenity,
> Put her new lips to his, and gave afresh
> The life she had so tangled in her mesh:
> And as he from one trance was wakening
> Into another, she began to sing . . .[50]

Further, in one of the most convincing parts* of his book, *Keats and the Daemon King*, W. W. Beyer has shown that Lamia derives much of her nature and significance from the snake-like enchantress queen in Wieland's *Oberon*, who, under the will of the demon-king, tempts Hüon and endeavours to reduce him to a lustful sensuality.

Yet plainly Lamia is not a simple embodiment of the Fatal Woman and destructive evil, and right from the outset we have to reconcile ourselves to contradictions in her significance. This penanced lady elf, whom we are later to take, among other things, as a personification of sensual love, is first introduced to us as the kindly protectress of a woodland nymph whose beauty she had kept concealed from

ideal beauty to Lycius' and Lycius as 'caught up in the essence of the ideal' (p. 167) he fails to realize the evil and destructive side of Lamia or the deception in her love. 'Tangled in her mesh' (1, 296) is a curious expression for Keats to have used of Lycius if his love in Part I is indeed 'an intensity that leads to essence' (p. 171); while it is quite impossible to equate Keats's line 'That purple-lined palace of sweet sin' with Wasserman's description—'the bourne of heaven that the magic palace symbolizes' (p. 168).

Wasserman ignores the key lines (II, 11-15) in which the god of love is represented as a destroyer and makes no attempt to relate this love poem to Keats's own intense experience in love at this time.

* Pp. 196–238, *passim.*

> the love-glances of unlovely eyes,
> Of Satyrs, Fauns, and blear'd Silenus' sighs?[51]

and while it is true that she helps Hermes to this nymph chiefly for the reward of release from her serpent body, there is no suggestion of pandering to a lustful god—in spite of Keats's early reference to 'ever-smitten Hermes'.

Again, we may be surprised to read of a Lycius who is 'happy' because he is fated to meet the transformed serpent woman. But when we go on to read how this Lamia was

> of sciental brain
> To unperplex bliss from its neighbour pain;
> Define their pettish limits, and estrange
> Their points of contact, and swift counterchange,[52]

we realize, from the evidence of other poems like the first canto of *The Fall of Hyperion*, that Keats is projecting something entirely admirable into his serpent-enchantress.

This fundamental ambiguity of Lamia, manifest in the beginning of the poem, persists to the end. We cannot forget that she is a cheat and that all her power and awakening of Lycius' love is based on illusion; ultimately she is the cause of his death and disenchantment. But she is never evil in the sense of deliberately willing Lycius' destruction. Just as the poet himself admits that he would like to forget the disastrous climax of his story,[53] so Lamia would prefer to live on in the love of deception; and, realizing the danger involved for Lycius no less than for herself, she strives her utmost to deter him from his plan for a public wedding. Indeed, in the second part of the poem (which was added to the first after an interval of six weeks) the 'tender-personed' Lamia strikes us as being almost as much a victim as Lycius himself, or at least, if that is a distorted interpretation, as a helpless instrument of fate. A strict sense of truth compelled Keats to bestow on her the symbolical wreath of 'adder's tongue'; for she was serpent and baneful. But sympathy also entwined the adder's tongue with leaves of willow, the traditional (and here contradictory) symbol of the unhappy, abandoned lover.

Again, we cannot attach any responsibility to the Lamia that Keats has created for us in his poem, and hence we cannot pass any moral judgment on her. She simply *is* destruction for anyone fated to fall in love with her, and neither the good in her nor the fact that she is truly in love with Lycius makes any difference to the doom she carries with her. In this (and it matters very little whether we take Lamia as Fanny Brawne in particular or the woman of sexual love in general) she reflects part of Keats's attitude to love in the tortured weeks when he was writing the poem. As we have seen, he certainly had moments when he regarded Fanny as his doom and destruction.* But he would not really blame her for that: no more responsibility could be attached to her than to Lamia for the fate of Lycius.

This sense of the ravage, destruction, and ultimate un-happiness of sexual love is here and there underlined by details of the poem. For instance, there is that odd line, sad and ominous, that rounds off the introductory episode of Hermes and his nymph: at the very moment when these spirits achieve their felicity we are abruptly reminded of the very different lot of human lovers—

> Nor grew they pale, as mortal lovers do [54]

—words that recall some of the poignant lines in the *Ode to a Nightingale* and the *Ode on a Grecian Urn*. Again, whether, as is generally supposed, the proem to Part II owes something to a

---

* Murry appears to have been much nearer to the truth of Keats's attitude in his earlier book, *Keats and Shakespeare*. Thus we find him writing of a Keats who 'must have wondered many times whether Fanny Brawne had not entangled him to his own perdition' (p. 157). It appears to be Murry's determination in his later study to vindicate the character of Fanny Brawne that has led him away from these earlier perceptions. But, admirable young woman as we now know Fanny Brawne to have been, she was still Keats's 'perdition'—as anyone would have been with whom he had fallen passionately in love.

passing impulse of Byronic inspiration, or whether, as Beyer plausibly argues, it is one of the most evident recollections of Wieland's *Oberon*, the passage certainly smacks of a deep disillusionment about love:

> Love in a hut, with water and a crust,
> Is—Love, forgive us!—cinders, ashes, dust;
> Love in a palace is perhaps at last
> More grievous torment than a hermit's fast.[55]

A moment or two later Keats enlarges a little on the 'grievous torment', and it is an amplification we should hardly expect from a young love poet: short as the happiness of Lamia and Lycius was, at least, he declares, they were saved from the love that turns into distrust and hatred:

> too short was their bliss
> To breed distrust and hate, that make the soft voice hiss.[56]

So charged with snake-associations is that emphatic 'hiss' that we are half inclined to take it as a cynical aside on woman's common, Lamia-reversion to serpent form after marriage!

This proem to Part II ends with another curious passage in which the god of Love himself is represented, in the image of a hawk, as the destroyer of his devotees—not, we observe, because Lamia and Lycius are indulging in the wrong sort of love, but simply because he is jealous of their felicity:

> Besides, there, nightly, with terrific glare,
> Love, jealous grown of so complete a pair,
> Hover'd and buzz'd his wings, with fearful roar,
> Above the lintel of their chamber door,
> And down the passage cast a glow upon the floor.
> For all this came a ruin.[57]

Apart from his representation of Lamia there is much else in the poem that expresses Keats's tortured turmoil of feelings about love when he was writing it. We may notice, for instance, the desperate and unhealthy contradiction in his description of Lamia's house as

That purple-lined palace of *sweet sin;*[58]

and the confusion of this line is even more forcibly brought home to us when we discover from a working draft of this passage that he had also been meditating the phrase 'happy palace'. Again, into his description of Lycius as he is trying to persuade Lamia to a public marriage Keats gratuitously intrudes that note of sexual sadism that mars his *Ode to Melancholy:*

> Besides, for all his love, in self despite
> Against his better self, he took delight
> Luxurious in her sorrows, soft and new.
> His passion, cruel grown, took on a hue
> Fierce and sanguineous as 'twas possible
> In one whose brow had no dark veins to swell.[59]

As if these lines were not pathological enough, Lamia is shown as masochistically relishing Lycius's cruelty, and the line 'She burnt, she lov'd the tyranny' had at one time in composition been more fully elaborated as

>   she
> Became herself a flame—*'twas worth an age*
> *Of minor joys to revel in such rage.*[60]

This same rough draft of a passage between lines 81 and 82 in Part II of the published version also has another section that most strikingly reveals both Keats's obsession with the theme of destruction and his mental confusion:

>   Which lov'd most,
> Which had the weakest, strongest, heart so lost,
> So ruin'd, wreck'd, destroy'd: [for certes they
> Scarcely could tell] they could not guess
> Whether 'twas misery or happiness.[61]

However, more notable than any of these points of detail in producing an impression of confusion and uncertainty, is Keats's treatment of the character who finally exposes Lamia for the serpent she really is, the philosopher Apollonius. Whatever we take Apollonius to represent—reason against passion, reality against illusion, moderation against excess, age against youth, Charles Brown against Keats (and he probably represents all of these things)—he must be inherently more good than bad, however unattractive the purely rational attitude may seem in some respects; and Keats in his saner, more balanced moments would have appreciated this as much as anyone. Yet in the poem, apart from Lycius's retrospective tribute to a 'trusty guide and good instructor', Apollonius appears entirely repellent. So far as we see him through the eyes of the hero that impression is acceptable. Abandoning himself to pleasure and a love of delirious infatuation, Lycius has renounced the philosophic attitude, the 'calm'd twilight of Platonic shades', so that inevitably his old master becomes the voice of a guilty conscience that has to be opposed so long as he persists in his rebellion. This Lycius realizes from the outset, for when he and Lamia pass the philosopher on their return to Corinth he immediately recognizes in him

The ghost of folly haunting my sweet dreams.[62]

Nor is it merely rebellion and a troubled conscience that turns him bitterly against his old master; he is also impelled in the same direction by Lamia's deep and openly confessed dread of the man.

What really disturbs us is Keats's own attitude to Apollonius. Having imposed on Apollonius the necessary and (as he himself would have to admit) morally desirable task of releasing Lycius from the spell in which he is ensnared, he does nothing at all to qualify for us the impression of Lycius's prejudiced view-point. Cold as steel, even at one point dryly laughing at the poor joke of the situation, Apollonius never reveals the slightest trace of pity or human sympathy for his ill-fated pupil, and we have no image except of the mere 'sophist', full of spleen. When Keats comments on him, he dismisses him with an emblematic wreath of 'spear-grass' and 'spiteful thistle'. Yet this is the same philosopher who had once been described as a 'trusty guide and good instructor'. We wonder where that goodness and trustiness have disappeared to—unless Lycius (and the Keats who is here so closely identified with him) is blinded with sexual infatuation.

We have still to consider the most characteristic feature of *Lamia*, for even if we are right in stressing its theme of destructive and fatal love, it is impossible to believe that Keats would have written another poem—and a lengthy one at that—to repeat what he had already expressed in his work, notably in *La Belle Dame Sans Merci*. The fact is that, in advance from the poems he had written earlier in the year, he was moving from simple statement of an intuition to understanding and explanation; and in *Lamia*, above everything else, he is expressing the idea that love is an ultimately destructive force because its world is one of illusion and unreality. In a quite literal sense love is an enchantment, and this is the truth that he felt to be perfectly symbolized in the tale from old Burton. We cannot possibly mistake the main line of his intention, for out of this simple story of a young man who is cheated into loving a witch he has elaborated a poem which is filled from beginning to end with false appearances, deceptions, and hallucinations, where everything seems what it is not. It begins, prologue-fashion, with a god who is vainly pursuing an invisible nymph; it comes to a climax in an unsubstantial palace of double-seeming and false impression, of mirrors and carven wood and stone confused into a semblance of living vegetation. We read of

> Fresh carved cedar, *mimicking* a glade
> Of palm and plantain, [63]

and of the wreaths of smoke from fifty censers

> still *mimick'd* as they rose
> Along the mirror'd walls by twin-clouds odorous. [64]

The guests are intoxicated, with 'bright eyes double bright', and when, immediately following this description of the drinking, Keats distributes the emblematic garlands to his three main characters, it is the thyrsus that he presents to Lycius. We can hardly doubt Keats's awareness in this crucial and summarizing paragraph that the thyrsus was a symbol of Bacchus and his devotees. All through the poem Lycius has been in a state of intoxication. He is about to be shocked into an unbearable sobriety.

Two years previously, in *Endymion*, Keats had played with the fancy of this dream and enchantment of love becoming actuality or at least persisting indefinitely. But though he is still prepared to believe that the dream-spell of love may persist for the gods—

> It was no dream; or say a dream it was,
> Real are the dreams of Gods, and smoothly pass
> Their pleasures in a long immortal dream—[65]

he now realizes that for mortals the beguiling illusion of love is inevitably, and perilously, transient. Love is the chief of those charms that fly—and must fly—at the mere touch of cold philosophy; 'philosophy' being the rational faculty that (as always for Keats) binds us to reality:

> but a moment's thought is passion's passing bell.[66]

It is worth examining in some detail the paragraph in which this key line occurs, for the passage is the turning point of the poem. The two lovers are on a couch in that luxurious swoon that Keats so often appears to regard as the consummation of love:

> there they reposed,
> Where use had made it sweet, with eyelids closed,
> Saving a tythe which love still open kept,
> That they might see each other while they almost slept.[67]

It is hushed twilight, no louder sound than the swallow's twitter, no reminder of the outside world other than the remote blue sky seen between marble pillars. Suddenly, through the challenging clamorous urgency of a trumpet call, the outside world of everyday reality crashes into the swooning enchantment, and both of the lovers are at once fully and restlessly awake. For the first time since he had met Lamia, Lycius is a rational creature again, his thinking revived by the impact of the real world:

> the sounds fled,
> But left a thought a-buzzing in his head.
> For the first time, since first he harbour'd in
> That purple-lined palace of sweet sin,
> His spirit pass'd beyond its golden bourn
> Into the noisy world almost forsworn. [68]

His particular thought, though it is the ultimate cause of his disillusionment and destruction, is a trivial one, nothing more than the idea of a formal and public marriage ceremony. But at least he *is* thinking, no longer drugged and tranced in a spell, and Lamia knows that her dominion is at an end:

> The lady, ever watchful, penetrant,
> Saw this with pain, so arguing a want
> Of something more, more than her empery
> Of joys; and she began to moan and sigh
> Because he mused beyond her, knowing well
> That but a moment's thought is passion's passing bell. [69]

Lycius inquires why Lamia sighs, and her first words strike significantly at the heart of the situation—'Why do you *think*?' She is not exaggerating when she complains that Lycius has deserted her, for now that he is again a creature of restless thoughts that bring him into relation with the actual world, he is no longer entirely absorbed in her. Passion's passing bell has indeed struck, and the conclusion of the poem is now ordained.

Yet while Keats knows that reason and the claims of the real world cannot be permanently suppressed, while he is entertaining the belief that the ravage and hurt of sexual passion is brought about by our inevitable awakening from a dream and a world of illusion, while he has the courage and candour to work out this belief fully through the story he has borrowed from Burton, he cannot achieve a mood of calm acceptance. He, the poet, is himself a young man of passionate feelings desperately entangled in love, and he cannot but feel bitterly regretful, even resentful, that the charm must indeed fly. This is the explanation of his vehement and distorted attack on 'philosophy' in a passage that might at first appear of superficial relevance* and also of his harsh, unsympathetic attitude to the philosopher, Apollonius.

Reading *Lamia* we must always remember the personal conflict that was being fought out inside the poet who wrote it—'You absorb me *in spite of myself*'.

In a letter to Fanny Brawne of 5–6 August. Keats wrote: 'I am not idle enough for proper downright love-letters— I leave this minute a scene in our Tragedy and see you (think it not blasphemy) through the mist of Plots, speeches, counterplots and counter speeches—The Lover is madder than I am—I am nothing to him—he has a figure like the Statue of Meleager and double distilled fire in his heart.'[70] Here of course he is simply confessing—and humorously— that he is so absorbed in *Otho the Great* that he finds it hard to switch to the very different key of a love-letter. But there is every reason to believe that the reverse of this confession holds true: that he also saw the plots and speeches of the tragedy that he was writing with Brown through the mist of his own love for Fanny, and that much of what *Otho* has in common with *Lamia* springs from the same personal experi-

---

* Haydon's account of the 'immortal dinner' almost certainly gives us the origin of this passage. Haydon writes how Lamb 'in a strain of humour beyond description, abused me for putting Newton's head in my picture; "a fellow," said he, "who believed nothing unless it was as clear as the three sides of a triangle." And then he and Keats agreed he had destroyed all the poetry of the rainbow by reducing it to the prismatic colours. It was impossible to resist him, and we all drank "Newton's health, and confusion to mathematics"' (*Autobiography and Journals*, ed. Elwin, p. 317).

ence.* Even in this letter there are some faint hints that point
to this conclusion: for instance, the description of Ludolph as
'madder than I' suggests at least some degree of identification
between Keats and his hero.

We can hardly doubt that the sheer infatuation in Ludolph's
love for Auranthe owes its existence to the poet's own feelings
at the time. Particularly in the wedding scene (III, ii) do we
seem to catch Keats's own voice through the lips of his
character. The lines,

> O, my bride, my love!
> Not all the gaze upon us can restrain
> My eyes, too long poor exiles from thy face,
> From adoration,[71]

sound very much as though they were prompted by Keats's
own exile from his beloved, while Ludolph's following
speech,

> Soft beauty! by to-morrow I should die,
> Wert thou not mine,[72]

rings with the accent of Keats's letters and personal poems.
'Soft beauty' (as we can see from the sonnets 'The day is gone'
and 'Bright star', and the *Ode to Fanny*) is a recurrent sentiment in his own poems to Fanny, and there are several familiar parallels to the general tone of Ludolph's speech, notably

> Yourself—your soul—in pity give me all,
> Withhold no atom's atom or I die.[73]

If these two identifications of Ludolph with his creator are
open to any doubt, at least there can be little question of the
identification to be traced in the hero's most lyrical outburst:

> Though heaven's choir
> Should in a vast circumference descend,
> And sing for my delight, I'd stop my ears!
> Though bright Apollo's car stood burning here,

---

* See the footnote on p. 366 of the Forman edition of the *Letters*: 'Probably a good deal of the torture which that wretched prince [Ludolph] is
depicted as undergoing was painfully studied from experience.'

> And he put out an arm to bid me mount,
> His touch an immortality, not I!
> This earth, this palace, this room, Auranthe!*

Here the idea of Ludolph renouncing an immortality offered by Apollo, the god of poetry, is entirely unconvincing; but if we read Fanny for Auranthe, the speech is deeply and authentically Keats, giving us one of his responses to that conflict between love and poetic ambition that so long troubled him.

Again—reaction to this initial infatuation—there is that hysterical temper in Ludolph that most critics† have commented upon. No doubt much of this quality was a deliberate contrivance, for the part of Ludolph was written specially for Edmund Kean, whose highly emotional style of acting in Shakespeare was thoroughly familiar to Keats. At the same time the frantic mood of Ludolph in his tortured love bears a definite resemblance to some of Keats's own feverish outpourings in his letters to Fanny.

Admittedly, this parallel, as we have so far described it, is of a vague general sort. But it can be pressed very much closer. In the play's last act, which is entirely Keats's own work, all the dramatic emphasis is on the anguish of Ludolph, leading to insanity and death, when he learns beyond doubt that Auranthe has played him false with Albert. Remembering how deeply Keats's love for Fanny was cankered by jealousy and suspicion—'My greatest torment since I have known you has been the fear of you being a little inclined to the Cressid' [74] —can we possibly doubt that the last part of *Otho* is a dramatic expression of that nightmare that had drawn him so often to

---

* III, ii, 38–44. It is interesting to notice Otho's remark immediately following this speech:
> Conrad, if he flames longer in this wise,
> I shall believe in wizard-women loves
> And old romances; but I'll break the spell.
This sounds very much like a significant subconscious association between Ludolph and the no less infatuated Lycius.

† For example Finney, *The Evolution of Keats's Poetry*, p. 665: 'His [Ludolph's] tragic trait is an excessive emotional instability which makes him oscillate between extremes of feeling.'

Shakespeare's play, or that into Ludolph he has not poured all the agony of spirit that would be his if one day he were to discover that Fanny had deceived him?*

However, significant as this aspect of *Otho* is, it has no cross-bearing on *Lamia*, for the theme of infidelity is entirely absent in the poem, where, as we have seen, Keats was preoccupied with a very different sort of disillusionment. All the torture in his own love that arose from his doubts and suspicions appears to have been concentrated into the play. What brings *Otho* closest to *Lamia* is its general expression of destruction in love and, more particularly, its concern with the figure of the Fatal Woman.

There can be no doubt that Auranthe represents Keats's fullest sketch of this symbolic Romantic type.† Not merely is she a Cressid who destroys her lover, Ludolph, through her infidelity. She is wholly evil, completely deserving of the terms 'demon', 'she-devil', and 'witch' that fix our impression of her. Her very appearance, so far as we rely on the text, has the right sort of Romantic paradox, for though we are naturally

---

* Gittings (*John Keats: The Living Year*, p. 162) writes: 'It is likely that Ludolph's picture of his unfaithful bride in the last scene of the play is a picture of Fanny Brawne, drawn in exact physical detail; he also echoes the tone and words of Keats's letter to her on 16 August.'

† It is necessary at this point to say something about Keats's collaboration with Brown, for since Brown provided the plot it may be objected that this re-appearance of the Fatal Woman was mere coincidence. But Keats must have had some voice in the selection of a subject, and other stories may have been considered. It seems reasonable to think of him accepting the *Otho* suggestion, as he had used a similar ready-made story in *Lamia*, because it offered scope for themes that particularly attracted him.

Again, the main impression of any play is created by what the characters say; and what they say in three hours' life can never be reduced to the comparatively simple statements of situation and plot. This part of *Otho*, the words, was entirely Keats's business; there was no other *writer* at work in this collaboration. That is why the play is Keats as it could never be Brown.

Finney is one of the few critics who have appreciated this, as when he writes (*op. cit.* p. 656): 'Keats's creative faculties were more vitally engaged in the composition than Brown in his vanity was willing to admit.'

243

carried away by Ludolph's lyrical apostrophes to her beauty
—that 'blushing fair-eyed purity' that so deceitfully conceals
her essential nature—we should not altogether forget her
brother's earlier description of her 'sin-worn cheek'. She has so
manipulated things (the narrative is obscure and incredible
on this point, but our main impression is clear) that the virtuous and innocent Erminia bears the blame for her own
midnight amours, and she is entirely without compunction
for the degradation and suffering of the scapegoat. Her single
admirable feature is that in the early part of the play she
protects her other lover Albert from her brother, who would
be glad to have Albert out of the way. But in the end, when
Albert is threatening to expose the treacheries of Conrad and
herself, she is won over without much hesitation to the plan of
Albert's murder. There is even a slight hint—though no more
than that—of incestuous relations with her brother. Albert at
one point remarks:

> The duke is out of temper; if he knows
> More than a brother of a sister ought,
> I should not quarrel with his peevishness.[75]

Perhaps nothing in the play more sharply impresses us with
a sense of the destructive evil that works through and from
Auranthe than her influence on Albert. Though he has been a
secret lover of hers, we are to understand that he is inherently
a knight of the noblest character. Erminia reports that he

> was ever known to be a man
> Frank, open, generous;[76]

and this impression is later re-inforced by the tribute that
Otho pays to him:

> Albert, I speak to you as to a man
> Whose words once utter'd pass like current gold.[77]

But 'fast-limed in a cursed snare, The limbo of a wanton',[78] the
noble Albert is corrupted by his love for Auranthe and morally

destroyed; and when Erminia puts in his hands the proof of her innocence and Auranthe's illicit armours for communication to Otho, he betrays her trust, torn by a certain sense of loyalty to Auranthe and dreading his own exposure in dishonour. It even seems in the last part of the play—though the motivation of Albert is huddled and obscure—that in spite of his knowledge of Auranthe he will still take her if she will flee away with him.

All this is far removed from that older romantic doctrine of the moral good of love that Keats had seriously entertained only two years previously:

> For I have ever thought that it might bless
> The world with benefits unknowingly.[79]

In yet another respect we are surely witnessing his transition from innocence to experience.

The return to Fanny in early October was decisive, and had it not been for his illness Keats would certainly have married her sometime in the following year. Apart from the three ecstatic letters to Fanny immediately following their reunion, there is nothing in his surviving correspondence for the rest of the year that throws much light on his attitude. But the 1820 letters, especially those written at the time of his illness in the spring, show us that he had at last convinced himself that Fanny's love was as deep and genuine as his own. Whatever the consequences to his poetry, as a man he could not live without her, and though the 1820 letters are filled with an anguish that makes them almost unbearable to read, this agony is the prospect of another parting and of the death that will take Fanny away for ever. He is no longer harrowed by doubts about love itself.

On the other hand, if the sonnet 'The day is gone' revives that unquestioning rapture that he had last expressed in *The Eve of St Agnes* and the *Ode to Psyche*, the other love-lyrics belonging to 1819 reveal plainly a troubled aftermath to the conflict that had so torn him during the months of separation. Never before, either in his letters or his poetry, had he so nakedly or emphatically confessed his 'torturing jealousy' as he did in the *Ode to Fanny*;* and it is the entire indulgence in this unlovely, deliquescent emotion, without pride, rebellion, anger, cynicism, or other bracing attitude, that makes this poem so distastefully mawkish.† We are forced to admit its biographical interest, but it is certainly one of Keats's poems that we wish he had seen fit to destroy in the cool light of some morning's afterthought. Were all his personal poems so embarrassing to read, we should have no grounds for protesting against the exaggeration of Garrod's comment that 'upon whatever page of Keats's poetry there falls the shadow of a living woman, it falls calamitously like an eclipse.'‡

Much more interesting and readable is the poem *To* [*Fanny*], which certainly belongs to this period of Keats's life. The poem begins with some lines that, though easily skipped, are a little surprising if we give them a moment's reflection:

> What can I do to drive away
> Remembrance from my eyes? for they have seen,
> Aye, an hour ago, my brilliant Queen![30]

To this we are inclined to respond with another question: what sort of lover is this who prays to be freed from the memory of his beloved? And how are we to reconcile these lines with that slightly earlier poem of enchanted memories of Fanny, 'The day is gone'?

In the light of what we know of Keats's past attitude there is only one answer to these questions. In spite of his return to Fanny, his surrender and ecstasy, there is still a part of him that rebels because Fanny so entirely absorbs him, when he is

---

* The date of this poem is still not finally settled. Most writers have accepted Colvin's date of February 1819. Like Murry and Gittings I fancy that the ode belongs to late 1819—October–November.

† Murry, however, speaks of 'this lovely and touching poem' (*The Mystery of Keats*, p. 46).

‡ *Keats*, p. 57.

away from her as much as when he is with her. That this is the underlying meaning of the opening lines is made quite clear by what follows, for, reviving the old complaint of a lost independence, he looks back with some envy to the days of casual flirtations:

> What can I do to kill it and be free
> In my old liberty?
> When every fair one that I saw was fair,
> Enough to catch me in but half a snare,
> Not keep me there.[81]

Further, this poem explicitly states why there is this hankering in him after the old days of his freedom. In the sonnet 'I cry your mercy', which was written about the same time, he begged for the entirety of Fanny's love lest he should

> Forget, in the mist of idle misery,
> Life's purposes,—the palate of my mind
> Losing its gust, and my ambition blind![82]

Here, in *To Fanny* he describes this poetic sterility not as a fear but an actuality; and to conquer it he feels that he must somehow escape from his absorption in love:

> How shall I do
> To get anew
> Those moulted feathers, and so mount once more
> Above, above
> The reach of fluttering Love,
> And make him cower lowly while I soar?[83]

We must not overstress these lines, since the wish they express is contradicted by another part of the poem. At the same time they are extremely significant. They show that Keats himself was thoroughly aware of that decline of poetic power* that we can now clearly see to have set in after the *Ode to Autumn* and *The Fall of Hyperion;* and while there had been

---

* A decline more perhaps in quality than quantity. We are inclined to overlook the extensive composition of *Cap and Bells* (probably from November 1819 to February 1820).

periods of barrenness before, while we must certainly take into account his state of health, his money worries, and his anxious concern for George and his wife in America, we cannot ignore his own confession that this sterility is connected with his too-absorbing love for Fanny. What he had always feared in those earlier intuitions of his had seemingly come to pass: love was not the inspiration that the poets whom he had read had represented it to be; it was an exhausting distraction, a compelled renunciation of his self-dedication to 'poesy'. Apollo and Eros could not be worshipped at one and the same time.

After these lines on his own 'moulted feathers' Keats's thoughts turn to his brother and sister-in-law, who, so it rather seemed at the time, had come to ruin in the harsh land of colonial America. He goes on to give a full picture—in imaginative impress the most memorable part of the poem—of the untamed and hostile north American landscape:

> whose dull rivers pour,
> Ever from their sordid urns unto the shore,
> Unown'd of any weedy-haired gods;
> Whose winds, all zephyrless, hold scourging rods,
> Iced in great lakes, to afflict mankind;
> Whose rank-grown forests, frosted, black and blind,
> Would fright a Dryad; whose harsh herbag'd meads
> Make lean and lank the starv'd ox while he feeds;
> There bad flowers have no scent, birds no sweet song,
> And great unerring Nature once seems wrong. [34]

The predominant and immediate reference of these lines is of course to those 'dismal cares' that afflict Keats whenever he thinks of George and Georgiana. But, divorced from this context, the passage is an arresting one, for it conflicts in the sharpest possible way with our impression of his poetry as a whole, with his usual fanciful delight in dryads and weedy-haired gods, his continuous pleasure in zephyr-soft breezes, his fascination for rivers and streams (nearly always associated with flowers and the bathing of the roots of plants and grass), and with his primary and most characteristic feeling for a Nature of fruitful, luxuriously teeming vegetation. Remembering how intimately this sort of imagery, especially the vegetal, has always been associated with his dream of love's fulfilment, we may very well wonder whether this descriptive passage in *To Fanny*, besides expressing his imagination of the land where his brother had apparently come to ruin, is not also closely connected with the rest of the poem, and an expression, from some subconscious level of his mind, of disillusionment and poetic sterility in love.

Such an interpretation, if it is valid, brings us back again to the problem of his fundamental attitude to love, which appeared to have been settled by his return to Fanny and his declaration that 'Love is my religion—I could die for that', and which, so far as we can judge by the surviving letters, was truly settled by 1820. But in this poem at least the paradox and the contradiction of his love is still there, inescapable. In the last paragraph he not only pretends that all would be well if fortune took a more favourable turn for George and his wife; he completely forgets what he has earlier written about love's snare and his loss of freedom in a delighted vision of sexual pleasure:

> O, let me once more rest
> My soul upon that dazzling breast!
> Let once again those aching arms be plac'd
> The tender gaolers of thy waist!
> And let me feel that warm breath here and there
> To spread a rapture in my very hair.[85]

He hates his captivity and yet he yearns for it, and he is still vainly hoping for that same impossible miracle of contradictions that he had dreamed of in the first letter to Fanny at the time of their separation: 'Ask yourself my love whether you are not very cruel to have so entrammelled me, so destroyed my freedom. Will you confess this in the Letter you must write immediately and do all you can to console me in it—make it as rich as a draught of poppies to intoxicate me—write the softest words and kiss them that I may at least touch my lips where yours have been.'[86]

All through his short life—it was one of his chief and most characteristic feelings—Keats was obsessed by the close juxtaposition of joy and grief, delight and pain. Nothing can have done more to intensify this obsession than his experience of love, and here in one of his last poems no sooner has he confessed his dream of sensuous delight than the old paradox bursts from him—

O, the sweetness of the pain![87]

Three months or so later, during his illness in February 1820, we find him writing to Fanny of 'the Love which has so long been my pleasure and torment'.[88]

Into that sentence is compressed the true nature of the love that he had experienced. Probably in his day-to-day life as the lover of Fanny Brawne—that life that had a crucial bearing on his love-poetry but was not identical with it—the pleasure and torment approximately balanced. But in his poetry, after the day-dream of *Endymion*, it was the torment that predominated.

CHAPTER VII

THE 'ODE TO A NIGHTINGALE'

It is a flaw
In happiness, to see beyond our bourn—
It forces us in Summer skies to mourn,
It spoils the singing of the Nightingale.

Epistle to Reynolds

Oftentimes I pray'd
Intense, that Death would take me from the vale
And all its burthens.

The Fall of Hyperion

THE *Ode to a Nightingale* has a special interest in that most of us would probably regard it as the most richly representative of all Keats's poems. Two reasons for this quality are immediately apparent: there is its matchless evocation of that late spring and early summer season which, as we have shown elsewhere, constitutes such a large part of the Keatsian world, and there is its exceptional degree of 'distillation',* of concentrated recollection, that is to say, of images and turns of expression, sensations, sentiments, ideas and moods that are common, though scattered, in the rest of Keats's poetry. Further, while all the odes together may be considered as the climax and crucial turning-point of the poetry that he has left us, the *Ode to a Nightingale* is his most intense *cri de coeur*—the one that vibrates most directly and plaintively with that personal anguish that had so much to do with the creation of this part of his work. It is also, for all its links with actuality, the ode in which his yearning dreams of release from the misery of the human lot is the most

---

* This term is used by Ridley in his *Keats's Craftsmanship*, though he does not seem to appreciate that there is much more of this distillation in the *Nightingale* ode than in the others. The main distillations are considered in this chapter; some of the others are noted in Appendix v.

generalized and the closest to what had always been a dominant impulse in his writing—of easy, soaring flight into remote, lovely worlds of 'poesy' and 'fancy'.

There are several lines of approach to the ode that are always likely to afford a fresh and stimulating insight into it. One of the most important of these starts from that speech of Endymion[1] in which he describes happiness as an effect of 'self-destroying' and of oneness with 'things of beauty' and other forms of life. Admittedly, Keats never again expressed the ideas of this speech at such length in his poems and letters. But there is nothing to contradict them in his subsequent writings and much to suggest that he not only maintained this faith of *Endymion* but also personally experienced this kind of rapture in which self is lost in identification with something outside it. There can be no doubt that the *Ode to a Nightingale* records such moments of rapture as he listened to the nightingale that sang in some Hampstead grove or garden in the spring of 1819. To go no further than the first stanza there is the line,

> But being too happy in thine happiness,

which, indicating a state of happiness that arises from absorption in the bird's song, points straight back to Endymion's speech.

On the other hand, Keats's oneness with the nightingale cannot have been the effortless, fully achieved experience that he envisages in Endymion's speech or that he indicates when he writes of a more prosaic bird: 'if a Sparrow comes before my Window I take part in its existence and pick about the Gravel.'[2] In spite of his iterated wish to 'fade away' with the nightingale, the first part of the ode leaves an unmistakable impression of a deliberate, desperate, and as it were screwed-up, striving to achieve rapture and a sense of identity with the bird; and when the rapture comes it is broken and momentary. There is no need to stress the return to 'sole self' in the last stanza: even when, 'on the viewless wings of Poesy', he can for an instant cry,

> Already with thee! tender is the night,
>   And haply the Queen-Moon is on her throne,
>   Cluster'd around by all her starry Fays,

there is, with the lapse into an artificial, markedly 'poetic' diction, a suspicion of the merely fanciful and a hint that he is still in a sense earth-bound, not entirely one with the nightingale. Again, in the sixth stanza, where there is a very strong implication that he is indeed sharing the 'ecstasy' of the nightingale, this transport is suddenly—and decisively—broken by a realization of what death may mean in actuality. Finally, we must never forget his confession in the last stanza that what he has been experiencing is chiefly an effect of 'fancy'.* There is no suggestion of the operations of fancy in Endymion's speech, where the 'fellowship divine' is represented as something spontaneous and intuitive.

Those vitally important lines in the last stanza that are so frequently lost sight of in some of the more metaphysical interpretations of the ode—

> Adieu! the fancy cannot cheat so well
>   As she is fam'd to do, deceiving elf

—remind us of another significant approach to the ode, the poem *To Fancy*. This charming, superficial piece would be entirely spoilt if, when we read it for its own sake, we insisted on reducing it to a prosaic definition of 'fancy'. But if we may treat it for once in this way in order to illuminate the ode, we see that 'fancy', here regarded as largely a voluntary power, is a means of delightful release from unpleasant experience (the pleasure that 'cloys with tasting') into a world totally removed from the one we are actually experiencing. The pleasures that

---

* One of the central weaknesses of Wasserman's study of the ode (*The Finer Tone*, pp. 178–223) is, I think, that he ignores this word and all its implications.

fancy brings are entirely sensuous, and they differ from those
of reality only in that they are uncloying (or so the poet affects
to believe), and untied to times and place. Here at least there
is no hint that 'winged Fancy' transports us into vision,
mystical ecstasy, or a mystical awareness of timelessness and
the 'Eternal Moment'.*

Besides these two avenues of approach to the meaning and
significance of the ode (and we might also add the passage
in the *Epistle to Reynolds* quoted at the beginning of this
chapter), there are many lines from earlier poems that bear
revealingly on its imagery and sensations. Most of these
will be considered as we discuss the ode in detail. But there is
one that is of quite exceptional importance. This is the conclusion to *Calidore*, written three years before, in which occurs
a complex of images that surely constitutes a recognizable, if
crude, embryo of the ode. Already in close association we
find a forest and a forest breeze, a nightingale, a bower, the
'incense' of a blossoming tree, and the moon:

> Softly the breezes from the forest came,
> Softly they blew aside the taper's flame;
> Clear was the song from Philomel's far bower;
> Grateful the incense from the lime-tree flower;
> Mysterious, wild, the far-heard trumpet's tone;
> Lovely the moon in ether, all alone.†

The *Ode to a Nightingale* begins with a description, admirably
suggestive in its sound effect, of a certain 'sensation':

---

* I take this last phrase from Miss Janet Spens's article (*Review of
English Studies*, Vol. III, No. II, pp. 234–43): 'Unless we really believe the
poet has captured that Eternal Moment and to some extent share it, the
poem has failed' (p. 236).

† *Calidore*, ll. 152–7. Ridley (*op. cit.*) notes this passage. The reference
here to 'Philomel' underlines one rather surprising feature about the
inspiration of the ode. This is that there are few references to the nightingale
or its song in Keats's previous work, and that all of these are brief and
undistinguished. There are none of those enraptured first sketches and
rich accretions that we may observe in his treatment of the moon-image.

My heart aches, and a drowsy numbness pains
    My sense, as though of hemlock I had drunk,
Or emptied some dull opiate to the drains
    One minute past, and Lethe-wards had sunk.

The main part of this sensation, the drugged intoxicated
'numbness' that is like some Lethean existence, is easy enough
to understand, particularly since Keats gives us several other
descriptions of it. In one of the first two or three poems he
ever wrote, 'Fill for me a brimming bowl', composed in
August 1814, we find him invoking some 'draught' from
'Lethe's wave' in which to drown his unhappiness.³ Here of
course the reference is purely conventional, but in the Cave
of Quietude passage in Endymion the 'draught' and the state
of 'drowsy numbness' take on a deeper significance:

> Just when the sufferer begins to burn,
> Then it is free to him; and from an urn,
> Still fed by melting ice, *he takes a draught* . . .
>   *Happy gloom!*
> *Dark Paradise!* where pale becomes the bloom
> Of health by due: where silence dreariest
> Is most articulate; where hopes infest;
> *Where those eyes are the brightest far that keep*
> *Their lids shut longest in a dreamless sleep.**

It is in 1819, at the time of the odes, that this mood of
'drowsy numbness' or 'indolence' becomes most marked. There
is a full description of it in his long journal letter to his brother
and sister-in-law: 'This morning I am in a sort of temper
indolent and supremely careless . . . My passions are all asleep
from my having slumbered till nearly eleven and weakened
the animal fibre all over me to a delightful sensation about
three degrees on this side of faintness . . . In this state of

---

* IV, 533–42. There is another fugitive reference to this sensation in the
conclusion of 'In a drear-nighted December' (late 1817):
> To know the change and feel it,
> When there is none to heal it,
> *Nor numbed sense to steal it,*
> Was never said in rhyme.

effeminacy the fibres of the brain are relaxed in common with the rest of the body, and to such a happy degree that pleasure has no show of enticement and pain no unbearable frown . . . This is the only happiness; and is a rare instance of advantage in the body overpowering the Mind.'[4] From the mood (and the day-dreams) of this March morning came a little later the *Ode on Indolence:*

> Ripe was the drowsy hour;
> The blissful cloud of summer-indolence
>   Benumb'd my eyes; my pulse grew less and less;
>   Pain had no sting, and pleasure's wreath no flower.[5]

'Drowsy', with its suggestion of a state midway between waking and sleep ('Do I wake or sleep?') is a recurrent word in these descriptions; and in the first stanza of the *Ode on Melancholy*, which is another description of the Lethean mood and of 'poisonous wines', we have the line

> For shade to shade will come too drowsily . . .

However, there is a difficulty in the opening of the *Ode to a Nightingale* that familiarity with the lines may easily lead us to overlook and that the passages we have so far quoted rather intensify than diminish. The sensation that Keats is expressing is not simply one of Lethean 'drowsy numbness': contradictorily as it may seem, there is feeling in it too—and painful feeling; 'My heart aches'. What he describes as separate, mutually exclusive states in the *Ode on Melancholy*—the shades that come too drowsily and the 'wakeful anguish of the soul'—are here, apparently, fused together.

It might just possibly be considered that the comma after 'My heart aches' has a logical as well as a rhythmical significance, and that the heart-ache is a state before the 'drowsy numbness' supervenes, not co-existent with it. But this cannot be the right way to read the lines, for the opening phrase is surely taken up again in the later line,

> But being too happy in thy happiness,

while Keats immediately goes on to say that the drowsy numbness '*pains* My sense'. Further, this 'pains' cannot be dismissed as a casual rhyme, since as well as echoing something he had written about a year before—

More warm than those heroic tints that pain a painter's sense*

—it replaces a first draft version, 'and a painful numbness falls'.

Other references in Keats's writing to this sensation of 'numbness' should convince us that we must simply accept the contradictions in his initial mood and not attempt to explain them away. No doubt for a full apprehension of these opening lines we must at some time have actually experienced what Keats is describing. But an acceptance of them is undoubtedly made easier if we appreciate that, for him at any rate, this 'drowsy numbness' sometimes arose from a pressing burden of pain and grief, and that it could be painful as well as pleasurable in effect. Thus, in one of his letters to Bailey, he writes: 'I am now so depressed that I have not an Idea to put to paper—my hand feels like lead—and yet it is an unpleasant numbness: it does not take away the pain of existence.'⁶ This remark appears to have a very close bearing on the opening of the *Ode to a Nightingale* and on why the drowsy numbness '*pains*', for the 'unpleasant numbness' is related to the 'pain of existence', just as the opening phrase in the ode, 'My heart aches', is certainly related—if more remotely—to the 'weariness, the fever, and the fret' of life in the third stanza. Another

* *Lines Written in the Highlands*, l. 36. The draft of the poem to Bailey (22 July 1818) reads 'that fill a Painter's sense'. The alteration may have been prompted by a wish to avoid a repetition from 'filling' in the previous line. But the fact that Keats has fallen into the ugly jingle of 'pain' and 'painter's' suggests that he was trying to say something of importance. The revised line is not easy to interpret, but it is probable that 'pain' implies a pleasurable sort of pain, and that Keats's notion was of a painter who, as he contemplates one of his pictures, experiences a pleasure that is excruciating in its intensity. At all events this interesting prelude note should remind us that 'pains' in the ode is conditioned by the pleasure-pain contradiction at the heart of what Keats is trying to express.

revealing parallel occurs in some lines from *Hyperion*, which were probably composed some two or three months before the ode:

> For me, dark, dark,
> And painful vile oblivion seals my eyes:
> I strive to search wherefore I am so sad,
> Until a melancholy numbs my limbs.[7]

This description of the poet's sensation at the beginning of the ode is followed by an attempt to account for it, in the particular circumstances of listening to a nightingale's song. He begins with a negative—

> 'Tis not through envy of thy happy lot . . . .

Once we have become thoroughly acquainted with the poem we cannot quite accept this line as literal truth, for whether by implication, or overtly in lines like

> What thou among the leaves hast never known,
> The weariness, the fever, and the fret . . .

he does indeed envy the lot of the nightingale. However, a poet's truth is not witness-box truth, and we may accept the denial for a relative truth at this particular moment in the poem, or for what Keats imagines to be true at this point. In any case there is enough to concern us in his words of positive emphasis—

> But being too happy in thine happiness.

What, we may ask, is implied by this belief that his mood of heart-ache and 'drowsy numbness' arises from the condition of being 'too happy' in the nightingale's imagined happiness, which he goes on to describe for the rest of the stanza?

As we have already said, this line certainly suggests some degree of identification with the bird. For the rest there are several possibilities of interpretation. The thought may be that which Keats had given to Peona towards the close of *Endymion:* that joy at its pitch, because barely endurable, passes beyond pleasurable feeling. Peona is puzzled that Endymion, hand in hand with his beautiful lady, should be weeping:

> Now, is it not a shame,
> To see ye thus,—not very, very sad?
> Perhaps ye are too happy to be glad.[8]

Or again Keats may be expressing the full paradox of the *Ode on Melancholy:* that joy in its intensity is transformed into its opposite. However, in spite of these possibilities, it appears much more likely that the line is to be interpreted against what immediately follows and against the poem's central point of reference in the third stanza. The happiness of the nightingale (here standing as a symbol of a poet) is that, embowered in a world of beauty, it is able to sing of beauty and sensuous joy effortlessly and whole-heartedly—in 'full-throated ease'. But the more this happiness is shared by Keats the more pain it ultimately brings, for he knows that such smothering beauty and serene singing is not—and never can be—his own reality. For him, in an ineluctable existence of weariness, fever, and fret, there is no singing 'of summer in full-throated ease'.* He cannot remain absorbed in the imagined happiness of the nightingale because, as he had realized in his *Epistle to Reynolds* a year before, thought always compels him out of it:

> It is a flaw
> In happiness, to see beyond our bourn—

---

* For Wasserman (*The Finer Tone*) this pain arises because Keats's 'enthralment by essence is more intense than his senses can bear' (p. 201). The poet seeks 'ease' from this pain by striving for the wrong kinds of empathic experience, and much of the ode consists of 'proposals for empathic union' (p. 197).

On the contrary, I think that the pain is the thought of mortal woe and that Keats *is* yearning after 'self-forgetfulness', not 'self-involvement' (p. 209). Wasserman appears to me greatly to overstress the relationship between the poet and the nightingale as a dynamic force in the poem, and I cannot agree that 'the nightingale appears to take on additional degrees of symbolic value' (p. 197)—for example, that in stanza IV the nightingale 'is perhaps ("haply") partaking of ultimate truth' (p. 199).

> It forces us in Summer skies to mourn,
> It spoils the singing of the Nightingale.*

Passing from the first to the second stanza, we are conscious of one clear link in the development of the ode. The hemlock and 'dull opiate' of the opening lines, with their deathly, Lethean associations, are paralleled by the invocation to a 'draught of vintage', which stands for vitality and fresh joyfulness—

> Tasting of Flora and the country green,
> Dance, and Provençal song, and sunburnt mirth!

But the continuity is probably more formal than organic, and it would be wrong to take the two stanzas together as the expression of a single wish of which the double-sided pattern is, *not* hemlock or some dull opiate, *but* rather a draught of vintage, 'a beaker full of the warm South'. There are two reasons for saying this: first, these various draughts referred to in the second stanza also lead up to the desire for identity with the nightingale; and secondly, the beaker full of the warm South carries a suggestion of drugged intoxication that is not so far removed from what is described in the opening of the poem—

---

* *Epistle to Reynolds*, ll. 82–5. In her interpretation of the ode Miss Janet Spens writes (*art. cit.* p. 239): 'Keats compares his more real grief with the ecstasy of the nightingale's song.' Bowra, too, speaks of 'the contrast between the lethargy of the poet and the rapturous song of the bird' (*The Romantic Imagination*, p. 136). But, strictly speaking, there is no comparison or contrast: first, because Keats's mood here is too closely identified with the imagined state of the nightingale, and secondly, because his mood is a contradictory blend of pain and happiness. There is no joyful bird on the one hand and wretched poet on the other.

Graham Hough, on the contrary, seems to me to have a firm grasp of what Keats is saying: 'The poem is not, as is sometimes said, a contrast between [Keats's] own despondency and the happiness of the bird. It is about the contrast between his own immediately experienced happiness in the bird's song, his imaginative participation in an untroubled natural life, and a less immediate but more enduring knowledge of sorrow' (*The Romantic Poets*, p. 174).

That I might drink, *and leave the world unseen,*
And with thee fade away into the forest dim.

So far as the organic pattern of the ode is concerned it is perhaps best to take the first stanza as a somewhat detached prelude to which Keats returns at the end of the poem. In this prelude he describes what was for him a familiar state of sensibility and explains how this arose through listening to the song of a nightingale. Then comes the second stanza, which, chiefly expressing a desire to escape the miseries of human life (this desire not to be understood as following strictly in time upon the mood described in the first stanza), communicates the impulse that is to give the poem its main line of continuity.

To some readers all this may seem a laboured, and unnecessarily obscure, explanation of beautiful lines of poetry that they have always regarded as clear and self-explanatory raising no problems of interpretation. But, as we shall see later, an appreciation of some sort of break between the first two stanzas helps us to avoid the difficulty of those readers who feel that there is some contradiction between the general ecstatic mood of the poem and the 'plaintive anthem' of the last stanza. To keep the first prelude note of 'My heart aches' and the static, almost inert, quality of much of the opening stanza separate from the 'luxury' and enraptured soaring flight that are already strongly apparent in the second stanza is to have established a point of reference to which we can return when we come to the word 'forlorn' and to the 'plaintive anthem'. Further, unless—excusably—we are entirely engaged by the rich sensuous appeal of the second stanza, we cannot regard it as entirely straightforward. There is a palpable contradiction here—one of several that complicate the ode;* for the 'draught of vintage' that Keats is invoking in

---

* Cf. Wasserman (*op. cit.* p. 178): 'Forces contend wildly within the poem, not only without resolution, but without possibility of resolution.' But I think Wasserman goes too far when he describes the ode as 'the poet's chaos' (p. 179).

order that he may fade away with the nightingale from the world is at the same time powerfully associated with the intense joys of that world, with nature, dance, song, and merriment. It is the note, always leading to contradictions, that occurs in some of the other odes. No ascetic, but full of sensuous appetites, Keats would have the 'world' if he could have it on his own terms, if it could be re-shaped to his heart's desire.

However, this contradiction is soon forgotten in the third stanza, which is straightforward, and indeed, in comparison with the rest of the ode, almost prosaic. Here Keats sets out plainly what it is that he wishes to forget and flee from in the world, all the unhappiness that is pressing so hard upon himself at the time—physical decay and the disease that had carried off his brother in youth and might strike down himself, the brief transience of sexual love and things of beauty: in a word, mortality, and the 'fever' of trying to speculate upon it and account for it.

This sombre passage, which in some of its lines—

> Fade far away, dissolve, and quite forget,

and

> Where but to think is to be full of sorrow
> And *leaden-eyed* despairs,

brings back a recollection of the opening mood of dull, 'drowsy numbness', is both an explanation of the desire in the second stanza and a renewed impetus to it. It is followed by Keats's renewed yearning to be identified with the nightingale, to be caught up in an oblivious rapture that will bear him away from the 'weariness, the fever, and the fret'. But now there is a new note of willed, desperate determination: if he cannot escape by means of Bacchus he will escape by his own power of 'poesy', by which, as the last stanza of the ode explicitly tells us, he means 'fancy', delightful make-believe that is unrestricted by thought and painful knowledge:

> Away! away! for I will fly to thee,
>   Not charioted by Bacchus and his pards,
> But on the viewless wings of Poesy,
>   Though the dull brain perplexes and retards.

Poesy responds instantly—if only for an instant—to the summons:

> Already with thee! tender is the night,
>   And haply the Queen-Moon is on her throne,
>   Cluster'd around by all her starry Fays . . . .

There is nothing here of vision or mystical ecstasy: Poesy with her 'viewless wings' is the 'winged Fancy' of Keat's lyric of six months previously, and the impulse in this part of the ode is identical with that of the lyric:

> send abroad,
> With a mind self-overaw'd,
> Fancy, high-commission'd:—send her!
> She has vassals to attend her:
> She will bring, in spite of frost,
> Beauties that the earth hath lost.⁹

Of course there is the difference that in the ode Fancy is only bringing Keats the early summer beauties that are around him all the time—'the grass, the thicket, and the fruit-tree wild'. But this difference is not an important one, for Fancy is releasing him, momentarily, from the 'frost' of a spiritual winter.

Around this part of the ode there are some interesting echoes of *Endymion*, an awareness of which can be extremely helpful as we try to follow, as closely and sensitively as we can, what Keats is saying. First, the total impression of the fourth stanza, with its passing allusion to 'Bacchus and his pards', its centre image of the Queen-Moon, its wings and soaring, unrestrained flight into the air, and its sudden return to a world of woodland verdure and 'winding mossy ways', is very much that of *Endymion* in miniature.* But much more striking

* The similitude of the stars as attendants on the Queen-Moon had also been established in *Endymion* (II, 184–5 and III, 50–1).

than this general resemblance is the particular connexion of
the last three lines of the stanza,

> But here there is no light,
> Save what from heaven is with the breezes blown
> Through verdurous glooms and winding mossy ways,

with

> So saw he panting *light,* and toward it went
> Through *winding alleys;* and lo! wonderment!
> Upon soft *verdure* saw, one here, one there,
> Cupids a-slumbering on their pinions fair.[10]

Not only does the *Ode to a Nightingale* repeat, in a quite remarkable way, this already associated cluster of images, but
just as these *Endymion* lines are immediately followed by a
description of Adonis smothered in flowers and vegetation (including woodbine and violets) in a chamber filled with incense,
so stanza IV of the ode is followed by the picture of the poet in
a bower of 'soft incense', violets, and eglantine. This parallel,
as we shall see in a moment, is vitally important for a true
interpretation of the ode.

Again, the allusion to 'Bacchus and his pards' carries more
than a vague and fugitive reminiscence of *Endymion.* If we
allow this phrase to transport us to the Indian Maid and the
pageant of Bacchus in Book IV, we may recall some movements
of Keats's imagination that are very relevant to the ode. To
the Maid, in her grief,* Bacchus and his crew had appeared—

> All madly dancing through the pleasant valley,
> To scare thee, Melancholy![11]

—and she had allowed herself to be borne away by the joyous,
tumultuous throng whose life would be perfectly described
by the line from the ode, 'Dance, and Provençal song, and

---

* It should be noticed that her song of sorrow includes one of Keats's
fullest references to the nightingale prior to the ode (IV, 158–63). Another
link between this part of *Endymion* and the ode may be, as Ridley suggests,
that 'lustrous eyes' in stanza III is a recollection from this song:
> Why dost borrow
> The lustrous passion from a falcon's eye.

sunburnt mirth'. This Bacchic rapture had been a transient one, and though she had not quite faded 'away into the forest dim', *'sick-hearted, weary'* she had broken from the rout

> To stray away into these *forests drear.*[12]

In the light of these correspondences there can be little doubt that the transitions between stanzas II and IV in the ode approximately follow those of the imaginary Indian Maid in a poem of two years earlier and that Keats was to some extent repeating in these two stanzas an old complex of ideas, sentiments, and images. Further, the recapitulation points to a criticism of this part of the ode: it looks as though Keats in his desperate attempt to flee from the 'weariness, the fever, and the fret' is regressing into an earlier, immature attitude that he had mainly abandoned.

The last three lines of the fourth stanza, with their evocation of 'verdurous glooms', lead directly into the fifth stanza, which is the outstanding example of Keats's characteristic 'bower'-image and sensation of smothering in leaves and flowers.* As we have said earlier in this chapter, he does communicate some sense of self-oblivious rapture and 'fellowship with essence', since the triumphant 'Already with thee!' in the fourth stanza is followed by

> I cannot see what flowers are at my feet.

Yet the ecstasy he experienced cannot have been as complete as the one he records in *Lines written in the Highlands* when he had, apparently, become completely blind to his physical surroundings, since, in spite of its opening line, the fifth stanza is at the same time an expression of very vivid seeing and sensuous impression. On the other hand, while in his ecstasy he is still to some extent bound to earth, he is not simply describing an actual environment in a Hampstead garden or on the Heath, in which he had heard the nightingale singing.

* Ch. II, pp. 50–3.

The 'Poesy' that he had invoked in the fourth stanza is still at work, and it is certainly 'winged Fancy' that brings him much of this rich picture of May-time's flowers and vegetation. That is why he talks of 'guessing' at the sweets of the month.

No doubt most readers of the ode take this fifth stanza simply as a piece of enraptured descriptive writing. Yet it is extremely likely that there is much more to it than this: that it is the expression of a luxurious death-wish and so intimately related to the following stanza.

There are several grounds for advancing this interpretation. To take the most general one first, the prominence of this peculiar sensation of being buried in flowers and vegetation strongly suggests that it came to bear some deep and special significance for Keats. Next, the lines in *Endymion* that contain the same complex of images that we find at the end of the fourth stanza of the ode are immediately followed by the description of Adonis smothered in leaves and flowers and enjoying a luxurious sleep-in-death. Not only is the fifth stanza of the ode, in a loose sort of way, a description of what might have been the sensations of the imaginary Adonis; as we have already indicated, there is some striking correspondence of detail between the ode and the picture of the sleeping god. Again, as a significant pointer to our interpretation of the ode, there is the sonnet *To Sleep*, which Keats had written a week or two earlier. There can be no doubt that this sonnet has a particularly intimate connexion with the ode, especially in its opening lines, which show that both poems must have emerged from the same stream of ideas and sensations, words and images:

> O *soft embalmer* of the *still midnight*,
>   Shutting, with careful fingers and benign,
> Our *gloom-pleas'd eyes, embower'd from the light*,
>   Enshaded in *forgetfulness divine*.[13]

These lines, through 'embalmer' ('embalmed darkness'), 'gloom-pleased eyes', and 'embowered from the light,' have a special bearing on the fifth stanza of the ode, and though in the sonnet Keats makes no deliberate play on the immemorial association of sleep and death, that association is certainly felt, both in the particular suggestions of words like 'embalmer' and in the general tone of the writing, which resembles that in

> many a time
> I have been half in love with easeful Death,
> Call'd him soft names in many a mused rhyme,
> To take into the air my quiet breath.

There are two other features of the sonnet that show, fairly clearly, how Keats's subconscious mind was concerned with death. First, the Woodhouse transcript has 'enshrouded' pencilled against 'enshaded' at the beginning of line 4; secondly—and even more significantly—the original eighth line in the autograph reads:

> Its sweet-dath [*sic*] dews o'er every pulse and limb.

None of these clues clinches our interpretation of the fifth stanza of the ode beyond doubt. But for those who are rightly hesitant about reading a poem too much by some external illumination it should be stressed that the stanza itself suggests the underlying meaning we are giving to it. There is its position, midway between the mortality theme of stanza III and the explicit death-preoccupations of stanzas VI and VII, and there is the very obvious association of that striking phrase 'embalmed darkness'—'embalmed' being a very rare word in Keats's vocabulary* and here supported in the previous line by his favourite 'incense', which he generally uses with some sort of liturgical signification. With all these pointers, internal and external, it seems likely that the fifth stanza represents a moment in which Keats, driven by his desire to escape the miseries of human existence, conceives of himself enjoying the kind of fate he had imagined for his embowered Adonis in

---

* Besides the phrase 'soft embalmer' in the sonnet *Sleep* there is also a use of the word in *Isabella* (101–2):
> Though young Lorenzo in warm Indian clove
> Was not embalm'd.

Endymion—a death that is not the doubtful blessing and release of blank extinction but a 'luxury' full of pleasant sensation. Particularly close to the mood of the ode are those lines describing how Venus

> with a balmy power,
> Medicined death to a lengthened drowsiness:
> The which she fills with visions, and doth dress
> In all this quiet luxury.[14]

What we have in the fifth stanza—if this interpretation holds—is something that is common enough in most of the odes: it is a dream of enjoying the best of two worlds, of the pain-ending 'ease' of death combined with the exquisite sensuous joys of living. There is no need to stress the naïvety and immaturity of this attitude. But if Keats is indulging in 'fancy' that deep down in him he knows to be a 'cheat', the stanza is not 'fanciful' in the shallowest sense of the word. Behind it there is, most probably, some deep and authentic feeling; and as we read it we should recall those poignant words he was to utter when death did come upon him: 'I shall soon be laid in the quiet grave—O! I can feel the cold earth upon me— The daisies growing over me—O for this quiet—it will be my first.'[15]

The ode reaches its climax (and, as we shall see, its crucial turning-point) in the sixth stanza. Keats is fully conscious now that he is 'half in love with easeful Death'; his desire to escape the pain of human existence and his moments of oblivious identification with the nightingale tempt him into an openly-expressed longing for death;* and, from his use of the highly

---

* Miss Janet Spens (*art. cit.* p. 241) talks about 'a change from ecstasy to the thought of death at the beginning of stanza VI' and ingeniously tries to account for this change by way of some of Hazlitt's lectures. But the problem is unreal, for there is no important change. The ecstasy in the poem is never pure; it is closely involved with the thought of death, and the Keatsian ecstasy of swooning intoxication always has a certain death-like quality. But Miss Spens may be right in suggesting (p. 252) that there are echoes of Hazlitt's lecture on Spenser in the ode. She draws particular

characteristic word 'rich', he is contemplating death as an intense and supreme luxury:

> Darkling I listen; and, for many a time
> I have been half in love with easeful Death,
> Call'd him soft names in many a mused rhyme,
> To take into the air my quiet breath;
> Now more than ever seems it rich to die,
> To cease upon the midnight with no pain,
> While thou art pouring forth thy soul abroad
> In such an ecstasy!

Some remarks on the 'distillation' of this passage seem particularly called for: partly because a number of readers will certainly question an interpretation of the ode that regards death as its principal theme, and partly because we are concerned with something that is both profound and profoundly Romantic.

The most obvious immediate reference of these lines, as many critics have pointed out, is to the sonnet 'Why did I laugh to-night'; and it is probable, from the re-echoing phrase 'cease upon the midnight', that Keats was consciously aware of the reminiscence. Cryptic as this sonnet is in some respects, there can be no mistaking the main drift. As in the odes, Keats is endeavouring to resign himself to the possible loss of 'Verse, Fame, and Beauty'; and on this occasion he is persuading himself into the belief that none of the happinesses of human life, which he has fully savoured in imagination at least, compares in intensity of experience with death. Death is the supreme ecstasy, the crown of a 'Life of Sensations';

> I know this Being's lease,
> My fancy to its utmost blisses spreads;
> Yet would I on this very midnight cease,

attention to: 'The Cave of Despair is described with equal gloominess and power of fancy; and the fine moral declamation of the owner of it, on the evils of life, almost makes one *in love with death;*' and also to the passage: 'Spenser was the poet of our *waking dreams* . . . from which we have no wish ever to be recalled.'

And the world's gaudy ensigns see in shreds;
Verse, Fame, and Beauty are intense indeed,
But Death intenser—Death is Life's high meed.[16]

This sestet of the sonnet is almost an epitome of the first six stanzas of the *Ode to a Nightingale:* stimulated by the song of the nightingale, Keats's fancy* has been spreading to the utmost blisses of being, and once more, on another imagined midnight, he half cheats himself into the belief that death is the luxurious, desirable consummation of sensuous ecstasy—

Now more than ever seems it *rich* to die.

The sixth stanza of the ode also immediately points—though less directly—to *La Belle Dame Sans Merci* and to the 'Bright star' and Paolo and Francesca sonnets,† which we have discussed elsewhere as marking the re-emergence in Keats's poetry of the association of love and death. However, it would be a mistake to regard the note of 'half in love with easeful death' as arising entirely or primarily from his experience in 1819, when a certain longing for the ease of death might seem to some extent a common or natural human reaction. The truth is that this note is to be heard in less clouded days, and right from the beginning. *Sleep and Poetry*, of late 1816, includes as part of an invocation to Poesy the lines

yet, to my ardent prayer,
Yield from thy sanctuary some clear air,
Smoothed for intoxication by the breath
Of flowering bays, that I may die a death
Of luxury;[17]

---

* In view of the obvious importance of the word in the ode it should be noted that in 'Why did I laugh to-night?' 'fancy' is the power that brings to Keats the 'utmost *blisses*' of his being. This is entirely consistent with his poem *To Fancy*.

† See also the lines in the *Ode on Indolence*, though we cannot be sure whether they preceded the *Nightingale* or not:

O, why did ye not melt, and leave my sense
Unhaunted quite of all but—nothingness?

while in the sonnet 'After dark vapours', composed a few weeks later, the catalogue in the sestet of those sensations that induce 'calmest thoughts' leads up to the climax:

> The gradual sand that through an hour glass runs,—
> A woodland rivulet,—a Poet's death.*

Endymion, too, for all its exuberant sensuousness, is, as G. Wilson Knight well puts it, a poem in which 'love becomes almost synonymous with swooning, if not death',† and though we have fully discussed elsewhere the general significance of the death theme in this work, especially in Book II, it is worth recalling one or two particular passages that have a clear bearing on stanza VI of the ode, like Endymion's description of his first encounter with Cynthia—

> Madly did I kiss
> The wooing arms which held me, and did give
> My eyes at once to death[18]

—or Cynthia's delirious fancy:

> we might die;
> We might embrace and die: voluptuous thought!
> Enlarge not to my hunger, or I'm caught
> In trammels of perverse deliciousness.‡

Further, there is the interesting reflective passage in Book II in which Keats justifies the pains and frustrations of restless human activity:

---

* Was it, among other reasons, this fascinated thought of a 'Poet's death', that drew Keats so strongly to Chatterton?

† *The Starlit Dome*, p. 273.

‡ IV, 758–61. It is perhaps significant that Keats underlined the main images in Shakespeare like
> If I must die,
> I will encounter darkness as a bride
> And hug it in mine arms, (*M. for M.*, III, i, 83–5)
in which death is erotically regarded. Miss Spurgeon (*Keats's Shakespeare*) also records the underlining of *A. and C.* IV, xiv, 99–101 and V, ii, 288–9.

To make us feel existence, and to show
How quiet death is.*

Admittedly, this kind of death-wish is not apparent in the poems of 1818, though, as we have shown,† *Isabella* is much preoccupied with death. But it clearly emerges on two occasions in his letters of that year: first, in his confession to Bailey, 'now I am never alone without rejoicing that there is such a thing as death',[19] and secondly, in a letter to Reynolds, where he writes: ' I have spoken to you against Marriage, but it was general. The Prospect in those matters has been to me so blank, that I have not been unwilling to die.'[20] Also, though these words of Keats take us a few weeks beyond the *Ode to a Nightingale*, we·should recall that strange revealing utterance to Fanny Brawne: 'I have two luxuries to brood over in my walks, your Loveliness and the hour of my death.'[21]

These various quotations, from the letters and the poems, not only show that there was a part of Keats that had always been romantically 'half in love with easeful death'; they also bring out that abiding conception of death as a 'luxury' from which emerges the chief and most characteristic distillation in the sixth stanza of the ode. 'Luxury' is of course a complex and highly individual word in Keats's vocabulary. From our quotations it is evident that death is a 'luxury' because it is desirable and because—to use two other unavoidable words of the poet himself—it is imagined as the most 'intense' of all 'sensations'. Yet Keats's 'death of luxury' meant much more than this, and it certainly had complex and obscure ramifications into many of the most important parts of his sensibility—his death-tending sexual instincts, his peculiar obsession with swooning and sleep, his impulses to a 'self-destroying' oneness with things, and his experience of 'drowsy numbness'.‡

* II, 158–9. See the whole passage, 142–60.
† Pp. 208–9.
‡ Also Haydon may have been giving the truth when he wrote: 'He used sometimes to say to his brother he feared he should never be a poet, and if he was not he would destroy himself. He used to suffer such agonies

Abruptly, at the moment of deepest temptation and indulgence, the ode takes its most decisive turn. There is a sudden revulsion from what has been caressed, and Keats's ecstatic fancy of the 'luxury' of death is shattered by the thought that its reality may be blank extinction:

> Still wouldst thou sing, and I have ears in vain—
> To thy high requiem become a sod.

This sudden recoil—almost identical with that of Endymion two years before:

> Upon my ear a noisy nothing rings—
> O let me hear once more the linnet's note!—*

is not unexpected in the ode, nor is it detrimental to its organic structure. Nowhere has Keats written as one wholly possessed by some irresistible death-wish. He has never been more than '*half* in love with easeful Death', and there is that crucial, uncommitted 'seems' at the very point of climax:

> Now more than ever seems it rich to die.

But more than this the last two lines of stanza vi bring out explicitly, in Keats's own conscious awareness, the basic contradiction, the loving and loathing of death, that underlies the central part of the ode. The pain of human existence, described in the third stanza, that he had desired to forget had been largely that of mortality. Yet, hoping to win a release from this in flights of fancy and an oblivious rapture, he has come to find himself half in love with the very thing he believed himself to be escaping from. In the formal development of the ode there is an entirely satisfying line of continuity between the third and sixth stanzas. But if we isolate these stanzas, they represent attitudes to death that are quite irreconcilable. Small wonder that in the confused, perplexed last stanza of the ode

at this apprehension that his brother said they really feared he would execute his threat' (*Autobiography and Journals*, ed. Elwin, p. 297).

* ii, 321–2. See pp. 164–6.

Keats should describe fancy as a 'cheat'. Like his own hero in *Endymion* he has been cheated

> Into the bosom of a hated thing.[22]

After this intense revulsion from 'easeful Death' the significance of the nightingale suddenly and emphatically changes. The bird has been associated with death.* Now, as all Keats's hunger for the sensuous joys of living burst through his indulgent contradictory fancy of the luxury of death, he denies this association. Somehow the bird is—or, in the implicit idiom of the odes, *must be*—an emblem of something that is deathless—

> Thou wast not born for death, immortal Bird!†

Much critical ink has been spent over this line. Some writers have condemned it for obscurity, others have exercised considerable ingenuity in defending its sense. But most of the argument—whether Keats is talking about the individual or species or 'Dryad of the trees'—is beside the point. He is not writing a nature poem of Hardy or Edward Thomas; nor, it must be emphasized, is the nightingale that he had heard singing his main theme. The nightingale's song—and it might have been that of some other bird—has started him thinking of the 'weariness, the fever and the fret' of human life and of release from it; and the nightingale is entirely a creature of fancy, standing for whatever he chooses to feign. For most of the poem the bird is the embodiment of his desire to fade away and forget, to lose himself in rapture and in death; and, outside the language of poetry, this 'meaning' is as illogical as the 'immortal bird' that has so much bothered critics. In the seventh stanza, as the main direction of the ode changes, so inevitably does the poetic nature of the nightingale. Recoiling

---

* On a point of detail, the word 'darkling' has, almost certainly, associations that extend beyond the colour of the bird.

† For speaking, this line raises a problem. Does the emphatic stress fall on 'Thou' or 'death', or on both equally?

from death (and therefore returning to the thought of the third stanza, though on a different level, spiral-wise) Keats is filled with a longing for something that is not transient and mortal, and this longing he pours into the transformed nightingale of his fancy. He feels that there must be something within human experience that is deathless, and it is because of this latent 'must' that the nightingale becomes an 'immortal Bird', not because it stands for the species or the dryad of mythology.

What this deathless 'something' is it is hard to say; and perhaps Keats was expressing nothing more than a general aspiration. But the representation of the nightingale's song as a source of profound and unfailing solace (at least this main impression is clear in a stanza filled with allusive detail),* and the strong hint of Spenser and *The Faerie Queene* in the concluding lines suggest that the bird may have become the voice of one immortal thing that Keats always believed in unreservedly —'poesy'.† Though it is impossible to confirm this interpretation of the stanza, it is not easy to think of anything apart from poetry‡ that would embrace the emperor and clown of ancient days, Ruth, and magic casements; and we may recall that in a deeply considered poem soon to be written the true

* Most puzzling, of course, are the beautiful lines on Ruth. One suspects that this reference, particularly when the other two are extremely general, must have had some particular cause; but so far no one has been able to discover this. Garrod's suggestion of an echo from Wordsworth's 'Highland Reaper' is not convincing, and in any case Garrod does not explain what it was that brought Wordsworth's poem into Keats's mind. Could it be that 'hungry generations' reminded Keats of the Bible story that begins: 'There was a famine in the land'? Did his preoccupation with death remind him of this story in which death presses so hard on the generations, with Naomi losing first her husband and then her sons? Yet, if Keats was thinking of the Bible story, it is odd that he should have stressed Ruth's homesickness, which is not mentioned in the Old Testament tale.

† Hough has also made this suggestion: 'by a startling transformation in the seventh stanza the nightingale becomes a symbol of the artist and its song a symbol of art' (*The Romantic Poets*, p. 175).

‡ Possibly Keats is thinking of the nightingale's song here as a thing of beauty that is a joy for ever.

poet was for Keats one who 'pours out a balm upon the world'.[23] Possibly there is even a hint of the distinction that he makes in this later poem between the dreamer-poet and the mere dreamer: that, having written most of the ode as a feverish dreamer vexing the world, cheating himself with fancies, he is granted—for a moment—an insight into the nature of true poetry.

Recently two critics, Sir Maurice Bowra and Miss Janet Spens, in sharp reaction to Bridges's opinion that the penultimate stanza is 'fanciful and superficial', have given us an interpretation of it that may appear more intellectually satisfying, because more explicit, than the one just offered. For both of these writers this stanza, not the sixth, constitutes the climax of the poem, and it is that because Keats at last achieves a vision of the timeless and transcendental, the 'Eternal Moment' as Miss Spens calls it. Sir Maurice Bowra writes: 'He sees that the bird's song belongs to a timeless order of things, and the climax comes at the end of the seventh stanza with its recognition that song like this is beyond the grasp of death.'* Miss Spens, in a much more detailed exposition of the ode, and relating the stanza to the speech on happiness in *Endymion*, says: 'It is surely clear that in this penultimate stanza . . . the poet did feel himself to have "stept" for a moment "into a sort of oneness", to have become like a "floating spirit" independent of space and time.'†

One naturally hesitates a good deal before disagreeing with the unanimous conclusion of two such excellent critics. Yet when we give proper consideration to those key words of the poem—

> Adieu! the fancy cannot cheat so well
> As she is fam'd to do, deceiving elf

—we cannot believe that 'vision' in the penultimate line of the ode refers to some spiritual or mystical insight that is

---

* *The Romantic Imagination*, p. 136.
† *R.E.S.*, Vol. III, No. II, p. 236. A little later Miss Spens adds: 'The penultimate stanza of the *Nightingale* ode . . . holds the key of its mystery' (p. 237).

expressed in the seventh stanza, or that the final stanza is primarily a comment on the transitoriness of such visionary experience and on the pain of return to mundane reality. In the two quoted lines Keats is stating, quite explicitly, that the ode is chiefly a product of 'fancy', and though this word has a wide range of reference in Romantic writing, it is inconceivable that the operations of fancy could ever have led to a vision of the timeless and transcendental, especially when the poet describes it as a 'deceiving elf'.* The reasons for his pejoratives lie partly in his realization that the release fancy affords from the 'sole self' and the world of human suffering is only momentary, and partly in his knowledge that—for himself at least—it involves a swooning intoxication that comes close to death. On the other hand, as the last two lines of the ode imply, he is still reluctant to dismiss fancy altogether, still uncertain of himself, and perhaps dimly conscious of the several unresolved contradictions he has been expressing. While he has come to doubt the luxurious indulgence of fancy, there has been no decisive experience or discovery, and the ode is not immediately followed by the Induction to the revised *Hyperion*.†

One or two other parts of the concluding stanza also call for some comment. For instance, the opening word 'Forlorn!' raises something of a problem. Is this repetition of the last word of the previous stanza simply a rhetorical trick to secure

* Two other objections to Miss Spens's interesting analysis of this part of the ode may be noted. (1) One can hardly think of Keats stepping 'into a sort of oneness' when the opening lines of the stanza speak of an agonising awareness of division between himself and the nightingale. (2) When Miss Spens (*art. cit.* p. 242) describes this oneness as being 'of the world of pure emotion', and adds 'that emotion is of infinite sadness', she ignores the fact that the main stress of the stanza is on the solace of the bird's song. What sadness there is arises from the sorrows of life (these most evident in the Ruth allusion) that need such solace and from the implied difference between Keats's death-doomed fate and the one that, as a kind of compensation, he fancies for the nightingale.

† This is a good point to quote Leavis's comment, which, if it underrates the consequence of the ode, deserves to be deeply pondered: 'the pang in it has little to do with moral or spiritual stress, but is, like the swooning relapse upon death, itself a luxury' (*Revaluations*, p. 244).

an effect of continuity, or is there indeed something about the 'faery lands forlorn' that brings Keats back to his 'sole self'?

This question, which rapidly proliferates into others, is extremely difficult to answer, and furnishes a classic example of the obscurities and ambiguities that often lurk beneath the deceptively simple surface of Romantic poetry. 'Forlorn', often contracted to 'lorn', is a common word with Keats* and with the Romantics generally, and has at least two distinct (though frequently confused) denotations, with a wide and varied range of imaginative and emotional connotations. Further, Keats's context-use of the word, in stanza VII, occurs in some lines of singular Romantic vagueness. But it seems most likely that when Keats described the faery lands as 'forlorn' he intended the word in the sense of *unfrequented* or *desolate*, with little or none of the emotional significance (*wretched*, *pitiful*) that the word usually had when applied to persons. The closest parallel usage in his own poetry is probably to be found in his description of Sleep in *Endymion:*

his cave forlorn
Had he left more forlorn.[24]

However, even if the word in the seventh stanza is to be taken with the minimum of emotional tone, it is certainly a strange one to be attached to a dream and a sort of poetry that Keats had always regarded with such unqualified imaginative delight. Possibly—for even in 1819 rhyme sometimes ran away with him—the word slipped in without much consideration as an easy, sound-pleasing, alliterative rhyme to finish the stanza.†

* See *Endymion*, I, 885 and II, 859; *Isabella*, ll. 279, 492, 497: *Eve of St Agnes*, l. 333: *Hyperion* I, 118: *Lamia*, II, 282.

† There is also a strong possibility that the word may have come by a subconscious recollection of some lines in a poem that Keats probably knew (Shakespeare, *Sonnets to Sundry Notes of Music*, xxi):
> Every thing did banish moan,
> Save the nightingale alone:
> She, poor bird, as all forlorn,
> Lean'd her breast up—till a thorn.

It is certain that there is some shift in the meaning of 'forlorn' as he repeats it at the beginning of the last stanza. The degree of the shift must be left to the interpretation of the reader. It may be that Keats is taking his preceding use of the word (as *unfrequented*) to imply loneliness, isolation, and therefore to indicate a parallel state to that of his 'sole self'; or the shift may be a more marked one in that he has taken up the word again in its other main sense of personally wretched or pitiful. In either case, it is difficult to see that the return to sole self has anything to do with the 'forlorn' nature of the faery lands, or indeed with the seventh stanza as a whole; and the emphasis on 'the very word' seems to suggest that it is purely 'forlorn' as a word that reminds him of his own state. This is not to suggest, as some critics have maintained, that he is superficially playing with words in order to effect, by a rhetorical trick, an important transition in the ode. The fact is that he has already returned from ecstasy and flights of fancy to his 'sole self'—at the end of the sixth stanza and the beginning of the seventh. That sudden realization of what death may mean in actuality—

> Still wouldst thou sing, and I have ears in vain—
> To thy high requiem become a sod—

is the end of those intoxicated swoonings away from self that have tempted him into the belief that it is 'rich to die'.

Another phrase in the last stanza that has bothered some critics is the description of the nightingale's song as a 'plaintive anthem', and it has been alleged* that this expression introduces an inconsistent note into the poem. But there is no reason why we should object to it. For one thing, the nightingale is always an embodiment of whatever Keats chooses to project into it, and we have earlier described one important

---

* For example Bridges complained that Keats 'loses hold of his main idea in the words "plaintive anthem" which, in expressing the dying away of the sound, changes its character' (*Collected Essays*, vol. IV, p. 130). Garrod also describes the phrase as 'the only false note which the ode discovers'.

change of its significance in the middle of the poem. For another, the bird was associated with heart-ache, as well as with
joyousness and escape, in the very opening words of the poem.
Further, it is probable that 'plaintive' is not to be understood
in the simple sense of sad or melancholy but as implying a sort
of bitter-sweet grief. Some warrant for this belief is to be found
in the early sonnet *To Lord Byron*, which not only contains one
of Keats's extremely rare uses of 'plaintive' but is a sustained
context of delightful sorrow:

> Byron! how sweetly sad thy melody!
>   Attuning still the soul to tenderness,
>   As if soft Pity, with unusual stress,
> Had touched her *plaintive* lute . . .[25]

In short, 'plaintive anthem', along with 'waking dream'* and
'Do I wake or sleep?' returns us, in an artistically satisfying
way, to the opening chords of the poem—to the mood of
inextricably mixed pain and joy and to the sensation of
'drowsy numbness'.

There is one further thread of meaning in the last stanza too
delicate and uncertain to be laboured but deserving mention
since few critics† appear to have noticed it. The simile in the
opening lines—

>   like a bell
>   To toll me back—

has a funereal, death-association that is too strong to be discounted as a straying of undisciplined response to the poem,
and it runs very close indeed to one of Angela's lines in the
Eve of St Agnes:

> Whose passing-bell may ere the midnight toll . . .

---

* There is some ambiguity about this phrase, which may mean: 'Am
I waking from a dream?' or, 'Is this a state of day-dreaming?' The second
alternative, something of a synonym for the earlier 'drowsy numbness', is
the more likely.

† Wasserman (*The Finer Tone*, p. 219) draws attention to the association
suggested here.

Subconscious meaning is always hazardous ground to explore, but this simile, with the later description of the nightingale's song as '*buried* deep' in the valley glades, appears to confirm the impression that the *Ode to a Nightingale* is a work of a poet who, at least when he composed it, was much obsessed with death. At any rate Keats was much more concerned with death than he was with mystical ecstasy or the apprehension of the 'Eternal Moment'.

CHAPTER VIII

KEATS'S ROMANTICISM AND THE 'ODE ON MELANCHOLY'

. . . such romantic chaps as Brown and I.
                    Letter to Thomas Keats, 17–21 July 1819

I will not spoil my love of gloom by writing
                    an Ode to Darkness!
                    Letter to Haydon, 8 March 1819

Do not diet your mind with grief, it destroys
                    the constitution.
                    Letter to Fanny Keats, 23 August 1820

THERE are three poets who have been unaffected by the sharp depreciation of the Romantic period in twentieth-century criticism—Blake, Wordsworth, and, with some exceptions, Keats. The reputations of Blake and Wordsworth, both essential Romantics, have survived (and indeed increased) probably because we feel that these two poets express much of what is most significant and permanently valuable in the Romantic revolution. Keats, on the other hand, has been protected by a process of isolation: formative influences apart—and those easily disposed of—we have been encouraged to think of him as transcending his age much as the immeasurably greater genius of Shakespeare transcends the Elizabethan period. Middleton Murry's influential study represents a notable instance of this isolating kind of critical approach, and certainly a very strong case can be made for regarding Keats as the least romantic of the great Romantic poets.

Complex and baffling as Romanticism is to define, there can be little doubt that the heart of it, at least in the literature of the period to which we attach the label, was what Keats in some observation on the poetical character once described as the 'egotistical sublime'[1]—the cult of original, distinctive personality, the impassioned belief in individualism, the use of poetry primarily for self-projection, self-analysis, self-assertion, and ultimately sometimes for exhibitionism and self-gratification. The first and foremost article of the Romantic creed was the affirmation of a god-like 'I' that makes the poetic world and that, in creating poetry, creates itself.

Keats not only dissented from this article but consciously and consistently maintained an antithetical belief. Against poetry of the 'Wordsworthian or egotistical sublime', introverted writing that draws all experience into the poet's ego and insists on shaping it to those subjective attitudes and beliefs that constitute 'character', Keats upheld the ideal of a selfless, unrestricted, outflowing sensibility—a poetry of which drama is the highest form. It was because of this ideal that we find him so often censorious of fellow Romantic poets: that he wrote of Wordsworth, 'for the sake of a few fine imaginative or domestic passages, are we to be bullied into a certain Philosophy engendered in the whims of an Egotist?';* that he had no admiration for *Childe Harold* or 'the whole of anybody's life and opinions',[2] and that in the deeply considered Induction to *The Fall of Hyperion* he so contemptuously dismissed

all mock lyrists, large self-worshippers.†

The best expression of his own poetic ideal is to be found in the letter in which the phrase 'egotistical sublime' occurs:

As to the poetical Character itself (I mean that sort of which, if I am any thing, I am a Member; that sort distinguished from the wordsworthian or egotistical sublime; which is a thing per se and stands alone) it is not itself—it has no self—it is every thing and nothing—It has no character—it enjoys light and shade; it lives in

* *Letters*, p. 96. Cf. p. 107: 'I am sorry that Wordsworth has left a bad impression wherever he visited in town by his egotism, Vanity, and Bigotry.'

† L. 207 (from a passage that Keats probably intended to cancel or revise).

gusto, be it foul or fair, high or low, rich or poor, mean or elevated
—It has as much delight in conceiving an Iago as an Imogen.
What shocks the virtuous philosopher, delights the camelion Poet.
It does no harm from its relish of the dark side of things any more
than from its taste for the bright one; because they both end in
speculation. A Poet is the most unpoetical of anything in existence;
because he has no Identity—he is continually [informing] and
filling some other Body—The Sun, the Moon, the Sea and Men and
Women who are creatures of impulse are poetical and have about
them an unchangeable attribute—the poet has none; no identity—
he is certainly the most unpoetical of all God's creatures.[3]

These ideas, so saturated in heresy against the Romantic
creed of the 'egotistical sublime', are repeated elsewhere in
Keats's writing—in the famous definition of Shakespeare's
'Negative Capability',[4] the observations on Dilke's character,[5]
the fragmentary poem 'Where's the Poet?', and in Endymion's speech on happiness, where felicity (including love, its
highest form) is defined precisely as a state in which we have
no self-identity and are continually informing and filling
some other body. However, recollection of Endymion's speech
should put us on our guard against pressing the charge of
heresy too far. As we have said, Romanticism is an extremely
complex attitude, full of contradictions, and along with all its
assertive and sometimes strident individualism there was also
a novel stress on those self-obliterating states of consciousness
to which we give names like reverie, abstraction, trance, and
ecstasy. Paradoxically enough, it is Wordsworth, the poet of
the 'egotistical sublime', who offers us some of the most memorable expressions in Romantic poetry of this sort of experience,
as in *Tintern Abbey* where he writes of

> That serene and blessed mood,
> In which the affections gently lead us on,—
> Until, the breath of this corporeal frame
> And even the motion of our human blood
> Almost suspended, we are laid asleep
> In body, and become a living soul.[6]

For De Quincey 'trance' and 'reverie' are 'the crown and

consummation of what opium can do for human nature';[7] and he goes on to describe an experience that, apart from the opium stimulus, closely resembles Wordsworth's 'blessed mood': 'many a time it has happened to me on a summer night—when I have been seated at an open window . . . that from sunset to sunrise, all through the hours of night, I have continued motionless, as if frozen, without consciousness of myself as of an object anywise distinct from the multiform scene which I contemplated from above.'[8]

Besides the argument in Endymion's speech that these states of self-destroying 'oneness' constitute the height of happiness, Keats's letters show that he himself sometimes experienced this lapsing out of intellectual and appetitive consciousness. 'Indolence' is one of his words for the sensation, and his 1819 moods of indolence, not always pleasurable, have much to do with the odes. Yet while there was certainly this much of the Romantic in him, on one occasion, in that curious poem *Lines written in the Highlands*, he expressed a strikingly un-Romantic realization of the danger of trance and abstraction. He describes how, tramping through the countryside, he falls into a muse, entirely oblivious to his physical weariness and immediate surroundings. In part this muse is induced by thoughts of patriot battles that have been fought in the neighbourhood* and by typical Romantic imaginings of the 'Druids old'. But what most takes him out of himself is the long-experienced, intoxicating dream of poetic fame, this time of Burns,

> One who was great through mortal days, and died of fame
> unshorn.[9]

As he says more explicitly in one of his letters at the time: 'One of the pleasantest means of *annulling self* is approaching

---

* It is interesting to recall that in Endymion's speech on happiness one of the first kinds of 'oneness' described is produced when
Bronze clarions awake, and faintly bruit,
Where long ago a Giant Battle was (I, 791–2).

such a shrine as the Cottage of Burns.'* In this mood there is a suspension of normal faculties:

> At such a time the soul's a child, in childhood is the brain;
> Forgotten is the worldly heart—alone, it beats in vain. [10]

But then Keats suddenly perceives that such a state as this, 'half-idiot', must be very close to madness; and, displaying none of that sympathy for insanity into which Romantic writers were sometimes driven by part of their creed, he recoils in horror:

> Aye, if a madman could have leave to pass a healthful day
> To tell his forehead's swoon and faint when first began decay,
> He might make tremble many a one whose spirit had gone
> [forth
> To find a Bard's low cradle-place about the silent North!
> Scanty the hour and few the steps beyond the bourn of care,
> Beyond the sweet and bitter world,—beyond it unaware!
> Scanty the hour and few the steps, because a longer stay
> Would bar return, and make a man forget his mortal way:
> O horrible! to lose the sight of well remember'd face,
> Of Brother's eyes, of Sister's brow—constant to every place. [11]

Further—it is a curious twist in this curious poem—he sets these intimacies of ordinary human life† against, and above, the world of the painter's imagination, which, reminiscent of

---

* *Letters*, p. 175. (My italics.) See also the sonnet, 'This mortal body of a thousand days', to which *Lines written in the Highlands* are 'cousin-german' (Keats's phrase):

> My eyes are wandering, and I cannot see,
> Fancy is dead and drunken at its goal . . .
> *Yet can I think of these till thought is blind.*

† It is revealing to compare this with the references to his brother and sister in the letter to Bailey which contained this poem (*Letters*, p. 194): 'I could not have had a greater pleasure in these parts than your mention of my Sister. She is very much prisoned from me: I am afraid it will be some time before I can take her to many places I wish . . . I intend to pass a whole year with George if I live to the completion of the three next.—My sister's well-fare and the hopes of such a stay in America will make me observe your advice—I shall be prudent and more careful of my health than I have been.'

Haydon's 'heroic' art, is also slightly suggestive of Fuseli's terror and nightmare:

> More warm than those heroic tints that pain a painter's sense,
> When shapes of old come striding by, and visages of old,
> Locks shining black, hair scanty grey, and passions manifold. [12]

—An odd poem: almost a panic retreat from Romanticism into the ordinary man's comfortable 'normality'.

On the whole Keats's poetry conforms to the ideas about the poetic character that he expresses in his letters. For one thing we notice that, unlike some of the Romantic poets, he devoted only a small part of his energies to the chief poetic form of subjective writing. The inevitable prominence of the odes easily leads us to overlook the fact that lyric poetry is often a quite minor by-product of his activities, and indeed even the odes were regarded by himself as incidental work. The lyrical poems he did write are never the compositions of a 'large self-worshipper', and many of them (including, with one or two exceptions, the best) are mainly of an impersonal kind. We cannot read them, like the lyrics of Byron and Shelley, as fragments of a continuous spiritual autobiography. Certainly there is some deeply felt personal experience behind the odes of 1819; but the significant fact is that this experience is *behind* the odes, not their substance, and that the poetic 'I' is to a large extent a universalized one. This is the chief measure of difference between, say, the *Ode to a Nightingale* and *Dejection: an Ode;* between the ode *To Autumn* and the *Ode to the West Wind.* Further, when we read some of the most personal of Keats's lyrics (the ode *To Fanny*, 'The day is gone', 'I cry your mercy', for instance), we feel that while these poems are thoroughly Romantic they are only momentarily, and not typically, Keatsian. And sometimes, as notably in the 'Bright star' sonnet, there is a curious blend of objective writing and romantic confessional outpouring in the same lyric.

Similar observations hold good for Keats's longer poems, which, constituting the main part of his work, were regarded by him as steps towards his ambition in the most objective form of poetry, poetic drama. Some of these poems can be related to his personal experience, and he undoubtedly entertained a growing belief that his poetry should be expressive of his own deepest preoccupations. For all this, there is very little of the obsessions, of the projection and self-dramatization, the masks and thinly disguised autobiography, that we find in the longer poems of Byron and Shelley. Even in *Lamia*, though it is extremely tempting to interpret the Lycius-Lamia-Apollonius triangle in terms of Keats, Fanny Brawne and Charles Brown, we cannot be really sure that this is the right way to read the poem; if there is autobiography, it is certainly related with an un-Romantic obliqueness.

Closely involved in the egocentricity of Romanticism there was its non-conformity, its Prometheanism (or Satanism) that ranged from a spirit of vague unrest to loud defiance and revolt. With one exception (and that of no great consequence), there is nothing of this attitude in Keats's poetry. He was interested in politics and stood on the left of his time; when in 1819 it seemed that he would have to turn to journalism for a living, he was insistent that his writing should be 'on the liberal side of the question'.* But for all Bernard Shaw's approval of the description of the capitalist exploitations of Lorenzo's employers (*Isabella*, stanzas XIV–XVII), this strong liberalism of Keats had little effect on his poetry and none that seriously matters. So, too, in religion. The letters leave the impression of a free-thinking agnostic; but Keats was no atheist or Romantic diabolist, and we find him seriously—and informatively—advising his sister on her confirmation. Even Bailey, who, as a middle-aged Archdeacon of Colombo, felt himself compelled to say of Keats that 'On religion . . . he had . . . the most lax notions', immediately qualifies this statement with

---

* *Letters*, p. 395. Cf. the letter to Dilke (p. 394): 'Notwithstanding my aristocratic temper I cannot help being very much pleased with the present public proceedings. I hope sincerely I shall be able to put a Mite of help to the Liberal side of the Question before I die.'

the remark. 'But he was never a scoffer; and he was guiltless of irreverence'.[13] In any event, whatever Keats's private doubts about immortality, the divinity of Christ, or other parts of the Christian faith, he never used his poetry for the expression of free-thinking speculations.

Yet another of Keats's striking departures from the central creed of Romanticism is indicated by his remark, 'Scenery is fine—but human nature is finer.'[14]

Though this opinion, which sounds so much more Augustan than Romantic, is repeated several times in the letters, in remarks like 'I am getting a great dislike of the picturesque',[15] some readers may find it hard to believe that Keats really meant what he said, for it is a persisting effect of the Romantic Revolution that many of us are inclined to think of 'Nature' as an essential constituent of poetry. Yet Keats's remark has a true bearing on his poetic work, since while nature furnishes a large part of his imagery (though much less from *Hyperion* onwards), it rarely provided the direct and powerful inspiration that Wordsworth and Shelley experienced, and he wrote few poems that consisted primarily of natural description. Again, in spite of his long expedition into the Lake District and Scotland and his journey home by sea, he had singularly little of the Romantic taste for the wild and awe-inspiring manifestations of nature, for mountains,* wastes, seas, storm and tempests, or for the sort of sentiment that Byron was voicing when he wrote:

> England! thy beauties are tame and domestic
>   To one who has roamed on the mountains afar:
> Oh! for the crags that are wild and majestic!
>   The steep, frowning glories of dark Loch na Gar.[16]

---

* Though the Scottish tour had been undertaken partly to 'identify finer scenes, load me with grander Mountains' (*Letters*, p. 193) some of the attraction of mountain scenery apparently wore off during the trip: 'The first Mountains I saw, though not so large as some I have since seen, weighed very solemnly upon me. The effect is wearing away—yet I like them mainly' (p. 193).

What Keats enjoyed in nature he enjoyed with a simple, intense sensuousness; and Wordsworth's well-known comment on his 'paganism', tactless and ungracious as it was for the occasion, was not so very wide of the mark. There is nothing in his poetry of the common Romantic tendency to identify scenes and landscapes with subjective moods and emotions; nothing of the contagious Wordsworthian conviction of some spiritual significance in nature; and indeed—one or two possibly controversial passages of *Endymion* apart—no sense of mystery at all.*

The nature-religion of Romantic poetry did much to render it acceptable to the Baileys of the time. But this vague spirituality had its dark complement of Satanism, one of the chief forms of which was a daring confusion or inversion of accepted values, whether moral or aesthetic. As we shall see in our consideration of the *Ode on Melancholy*, there are certain traces of this perverse strain in Keats; but it is never a major impulse in his work, and his conscious rejection of it comes out with particular force in his reaction to Byron's *Don Juan:* 'How horrible an example of human nature is this man, who has no pleasure left him but to gloat over and jeer, at the most awful incidents of life. Oh! this is a paltry originality, which consist in making solemn things gay, and gay things solemn, and yet it will fascinate thousands, by the very diabolical outrage of their sympathies. Byron's perverted education makes him assume to feel, and try to impart to others, those depraved sensations which the want of any education excites in many.'[17] Not only is this a penetrating observation on an unspent current of Romanticism that was to spread far and wide in the poetry and fiction of the next hundred and fifty years; it was a judgment that, on the basis of his own poetic work, Keats had every right to make.

As a final example of the important un-Romantic traits in

---

* For a different opinion see Bowra's *The Romantic Imagination*: for example, the remark (pp. 159–60) that 'Byron's conception of nature lacked the mystery which Wordsworth, Coleridge, and Keats found in it.'

Keats we may mention his attitude to his own art. In spite of his fluency of expression, and in spite of his confession that the *Ode to Psyche* was the only poem 'with which I have taken even moderate pains. I have for the most part dash'd off my lines in a hurry',[18] there is abundant MS. evidence to show that he often laboured hard to achieve perfect expression. One small but interesting example of this habit of working over the initial inspiration is furnished by those endlessly quoted lines in the *Ode to a Nightingale—*

> Charm'd magic casements, opening on the foam
> Of perilous seas, in faery lands forlorn.

These lines have frequently been instanced as pure and purely spontaneous poetry, in which every word is compulsively inevitable. Perhaps that is our final impression, but it is something of a shock to see for the first time the autograph in the Fitzwilliam Museum, Cambridge (especially if M. R. Ridley is right in his belief that there was an earlier rough draft to this autograph) and to notice how the felicity of these lines has emerged through the alterations of

> Charm'd the wide casements, opening on the foam
> Of ruthless [*or*, keeless?] seas, in fairy lands forlorn.

Such alert and patient reconsideration of lines, along with the numerous acute observations on the art of poetry that are scattered through his letters, certainly justifies Garrod's contention that 'more than most of our poets Keats was truly a student of his art'.* It is this characteristic that distinguishes him from most of the Romantic poets, especially from those of his own generation, for if they occasionally philosophized generally about poetry, by and large they did not think much about its technique, nor, rating inspiration and rapture so highly, were they fond of the arduous labour of revision. They wrote most commonly on a 'hit or miss' principle, trusting that

---

* *Keats*, p. 11.

the mysterious power of poetic inspiration would ensure more hits than misses and reluctant to tamper with the products of that inspiration. Keats stands apart from them as an 'artist' who, though he may have underestimated Shelley's purely poetic qualities, had every right to advise his great contemporary to 'be more of an artist'.

However, while Keats's work contains much that is remote from the main body of Romantic poetry, it also belongs to its historical time and place. For all the large exceptions we must make, Keats *is* an English Romantic poet, and if we ignore this fact we are always in danger of lapsing into unsound and even unsympathetic criticism. This danger, as the writing of Middleton Murry often shows, is particularly insidious when we discuss Romantic features of Keats's poetry without realizing that they are Romantic.

We have recently suggested that Keats's sense of poetic craftsmanship, his consciousness of himself as an 'artist', is exceptional for his time. On the other hand, we must understand that his attitude to his art was also in several important respects a thoroughly Romantic one. Now and then he apparently had moments when he questioned and doubted the value of poetry. A letter to Bailey, from early 1818, records such a moment: 'I am sometimes so very sceptical as to think Poetry itself a mere Jack a lanthen to amuse whoever may chance to be struck with its brilliance. As Tradesmen say every thing is worth what it will fetch, so probably every mental pursuit takes its reality and worth from the ardour of the pursuer—being in itself a nothing.'* But for most of his life he wrote out of an assured Romantic belief in the transcendent value of poetry; and the Induction to *The Fall of Hyperion* is a decisive testament to this belief. Facing up to his

---

* *Letters*, pp. 111–12. See also (though Keats's thoughts are more on the question of making a living by writing): 'I have no trust whatever on Poetry. I dont wonder at it—the marvel is for me how people read so much of it' (p. 393).

most searching doubts, believing and accepting that in a world of so much misery the true poet is doomed to an exceptional burden of pain, he unswervingly re-affirmed his conviction that poetry—if not of the kind that he had mainly written, at least the poetry he would one day write—is supremely worthwhile.

With this Romantic belief in the supreme value of poetry he dedicated himself to it, absolutely. Nothing else really mattered. 'I find that I cannot exist without poetry—without eternal poetry—half the day will not do—the whole of it—I began with a little, but habit has made me a Leviathan.'[19]—That is an early statement of Keats's attitude, and perhaps an extreme one. He had not yet fallen in love. But substantially this confession to Reynolds expresses what he always felt, even when Fanny Brawne had entered to divide his life; and most of the other Romantic poets would have endorsed it with their approval and sympathy. To all of them, except Byron, poetry was the new religion and all true poets its high dedicated priests.

These remarks to Reynolds (to say nothing of their suggestion of addiction to poetry as to a drug) imply something of a spirit of self-indulgence. Such a charge would be an unjust and absurd one to level at Keats's work as a whole, yet in one very important sense he is a Romantic egotist, notwithstanding his completely sincere rejection of poetry of the 'egotistical sublime'. Measure him by his most deeply considered and responsible statement on the nature of poetry, the Induction to *The Fall of Hyperion*, and we discover that all his preoccupation is with what poetry means to him, with poetry as the mode of his own spiritual development. To realize this is not to doubt the greatness or profundity of the Induction; but it is to appreciate that the poem is in one important respect an essentially Romantic utterance—another breach in the traditional assumption that the writer is bound by a sort of social contract that always directs him, first and foremost, towards his audience. What by implication Keats is asserting in the Induction to

The Fall of Hyperion is the revolutionary Romantic claim that the poet creates primarily to create himself. Elsewhere he makes the claim quite consciously and explicitly, as when the confesses, 'I never wrote one single Line of Poetry with the least Shadow of public thought'.[20]

From this attitude to poetry follows the one outstanding note of Romantic rebelliousness and defiance in Keats and his typical Romantic feeling of the poet's proud isolation. The public is his enemy; and there are even times when he appears to take up the later Romantic war-cry, 'Epater la bourgeoisie'. This mood is strongest in him during the late summer of 1819, when no doubt it was exacerbated by the special condition of that time, especially by his desperate and unsuccessful attempt to make money from his pen. But we have only to examine the suppressed Preface to *Endymion* and the letters he wrote about it to see that he always regarded the public as 'a thing I cannot help looking upon as an Enemy, and which I cannot address without feelings of Hostility'.[21]

There may be some doubt about the significance of these attitudes for Keats's poetry; there can be none about his belief in the supreme value of the imagination, which, perhaps more than anything else, stamps him as a poet of the Romantic movement. At the centre of his first important poem of any length, *Sleep and Poetry*, there is the question:

> Is there so small a range
> In the present strength of manhood, that the high
> Imagination cannot freely fly
> As she was wont of old?[22]

and in this manifesto poem, castigating eighteenth-century verse mainly for its lack of imaginative qualities, Keats dedicates himself to the revival of imagination in English poetry. Again, towards the end of his short poetic life, in September 1819, we find him making this critical distinction between Byron and himself: 'There is this great difference between us. He describes what he sees—I describe what I imagine.'[23]

Yet though we must certainly think of Keats as a Romantic poet of the 'imagination', it is by no means easy to decide just what we mean by such a description. For instance, the differentiation that he makes between the poetry of Byron and himself is valid and obvious enough so long as we understand 'imagination' as a loose antithesis to 'realism'. But if we follow the definition of Keats's own *Sleep and Poetry*, where poetic imagination, symbolized by the Charioteer, is conceived as a comprehensive and steady contemplation—a Shakespearean vision—of all the complex pageant of human life, then it is arguable that Byron's *Don Juan* is a profoundly imaginative work, notwithstanding Keats's dismissal of it as a 'flash poem'.[24] On the other hand, though there are deep intuitions of this Shakespearean type of imagination in Keats's letters and a wonderfully impressive delineation of it in the Induction to *The Fall of Hyperion*, none of his poems can be regarded as the product of such imagination creatively operative. What he might have written if he had lived longer, in drama or a new kind of narrative poetry, is another matter entirely.

Again, in our twentieth-century criticism we have heard a great deal about Keats's concept of imagination as a power, closely associated with sensation, intuition, and visionary insight, by which we may apprehend (and, if poets, create) a certain kind of philosophic 'truth' that is correlative with 'beauty'—'What the imagination seizes as Beauty must be truth—whether it existed before or not.'[25] Admittedly this idea of imagination is echoed, as idea, in several of the poems; but apart from the Induction to *The Fall of Hyperion*, possibly *Hyperion* itself, and possibly (but by no means certainly) one or two of the odes, Keats's poetic work as a whole cannot be regarded as the expression of a significant body of truth that has been apprehended, or created, by the poetic imagination. In the reaction against the nineteenth-century idea of Keats as a poet merely of the senses, a worshipper of beauty, there has been far too much legerdemain between brilliant speculative passages in his letters and the poems he actually wrote;

and the same qualification applies to his idea of the 'philo-sophic' imagination as to his conception of the 'Shakespearean': that what he perceived as a possibility in poetry is quite distinct from what he was able to carry out in his own short work.

The 'imagination' of which Keats's poems are truly the fruit takes two main forms. In the first place the world of his poetry—of the long and narrative poems in particular—is predominantly an artificial one, or, to use the word in its familiar sense from his differentiation between Byron and himself, one that he *imagines* rather than reflects from direct experience. Further, in this simple sense of 'imagining', he has all the Romantic fondness for the unfamiliar and strange and for the remote in place and time. One of the most obvious manifestations of this is his medievalism: it was an intoxicating draught from *The Faerie Queene* that first turned him into a poet, and from the *Calidore* verses to the *Eve of St Agnes* and *La Belle Dame Sans Merci* his work is filled with attempts to express the

> shadows haunting fairily
> The brain, new stuff'd, in youth, with triumphs gay
> Of old romance.[26]

No less pronounced, from *Endymion* to the *Ode on a Grecian Urn* and *Lamia*, was his attempt to body forth a dream of the Grecian world and its mythology,

> Of deities or mortals, or of both,
> In Tempe or the dales of Arcady;[27]

and this combination of classical and medieval dream in his poetry makes it unique among the work of the English Ro-mantics, who usually confined themselves to one or the other. In the second place, Keats's poetry is of the imagination in the sense that a great deal of it, even of the odes, is a vision of what he would like human life to be—an expression of desires, longings, and aspirations stimulated by, and as time went on more and more in conflict with, his own experience of pain and misery.* This does not mean—contradicting what we have said earlier—that his work is filled with direct confessional outpourings in the common Romantic manner. Almost always his dreaming is objectified or universalized; and we can appreciate this important distinction if we compare his *Eve of St Agnes*, a day-dream of happy, fulfilled love, with Shelley's love-poem *Epipsychidion*. In the *Eve of St Agnes* Keats is speaking for all of us in love; in *Epipsychidion* Shelley is speaking (and dreaming) chiefly for his own highly individual self.

No doubt those who place Keats on the highest level of poetic achievement would object to these descriptions of his 'imagination' on the grounds that they reduce his work to a poetry of 'fancy'. This is not the occasion to thrust into that complicated and tangled antithesis. But at least it may be emphasized here that we have no cause to be embarrassed by the word 'fancy', for Keats uses it himself in summarizing the chief impulse of one of his greatest poems—

> Adieu! the fancy cannot cheat so well
> As she is fam'd to do, deceiving elf.[28]

Also, we may recall the poem *To Fancy*, not only for the significance of its title but because its creations and central movement—

> Let, then, winged Fancy find
> Thee a mistress to thy mind—[29]

probably take us closer to the nature of Keats's other poems than most of the metaphysical speculations to be found in his letters.

---

* In his *Prefigurative Imagination of John Keats* (p. 39) Ford has a quotation from Bertrand Russell's *Mysticism and Logic* that might almost have been written with Keats in mind: 'For the young there is nothing unattainable; a good thing desired with the whole force of a passionate will, and yet impossible, is to them not credible. Yet, by death, by illness, by poverty, or by the voice of duty, we must learn, each one of us, that the world was not made for us, and that, however beautiful may be the things we crave, Fate may nevertheless forbid them' (p. 52).

Finally, to round off this short account of the Romantic in Keats, we may briefly note several other features that are treated more fully elsewhere in this book: the abundance of imagery drawn from nature, the recurrent theme of destructive love and the Fatal Woman, the continued note of 'joy of grief', and the deep obsession with sleep, dreams, and death.

The *Ode on Melancholy* brings home with special urgency the need for an appreciation of Keats's Romanticism. Almost all modern critics have agreed in placing this poem low, and often lowest, among the odes in the 1820 volume; and the chief reason for this estimate appears to lie in its Romanticism. Further—all comparative assessments apart—our direct evaluation of the poem is likely to turn on our discrimination between what is superficially Romantic and what essentially Keatsian in it.

Before we consider the ode in detail there are two very general points to be made. First, the broad subject of the poem is typically Romantic, for melancholy, the Hamlet mood, and all the various shades of unhappy sentiment, are fundamental constituents of the Romantic temper. Most of the major poets of this period produced at least one important poem that can be grouped with the *Ode on Melancholy*, and this ode was written by one who, on his own confession, had luxuriated in a *'love of gloom'* and who later felt it necessary to warn his sister against dieting the mind with grief.

On the other hand, while it is certainly characteristic of our Romantic writers that they struck roots in Elizabethan and early seventeenth-century poetry (though not in the work of the metaphysicals), we cannot say that the *Ode on Melancholy* is romantic for the reason that it was inspired and influenced in any notable way by the writings that have at various times been suggested as Keats's 'sources'—Burton's *Anatomy of Melancholy* (including the prefatory stanzas), Fletcher's song in *The Nice Valour*, 'Hence, all you vain delights', or Milton's *L'Allegro* and *Il Penseroso*. Keats's treatment of his subject owes nothing whatever to his reading of these authors, unless the imagery of his last stanza was suggested by Burton's statement that 'in the Calends of January Angerona had her holy day, to whom in the Temple of Volupia, or Goddess of Pleasure, their Augurs and Bishops did yearly sacrifice.'* This is not to deny that his reading of Burton, Fletcher and Milton may not have given him some general impetus towards melancholy as the subject for a poem, while in Burton's book, much read by him in 1819, there are several observations like, ''Tis most absurd and ridiculous for any mortal man to look for a permanent tenor of happiness in this life',[30] that must have confirmed an attitude that we find emerging several times in his letters. We recall remarks like: 'You perhaps at one time thought there was such a thing as Worldly Happiness to be arrived at, at certain periods of, time marked out . . . I scarcely remember counting upon any Happiness—I look not for it if it be not in the present hour.'[31] Or again: 'Gorge the honey of life. I pity you as much that it cannot last for ever, as I do myself now drinking bitters.'[32]

However, these age-old cries of Ecclesiastes are far away from the limited and Romantically conditioned gloom with which Keats originally opened his ode:

> Though you should build a bark of dead men's bones,
>   And rear a phantom gibbet for a mast,
> Stitch creeds together for a sail, with groans
>   To fill it out, blood-stained and aghast;
> Although your rudder be a dragon's tail
>   Long sever'd, yet still hard with agony,
>   Your cordage large uprootings from the skull
> Of bald Medusa, certes you would fail
>   To find the Melancholy—whether she
>   Dreameth in any isle of Lethe dull.[33]

* *Anatomy of Melancholy*, ed. A. R. Shilleto, Vol. 1, p. 301. Gittings, who usually exaggerates the influence of Burton on Keats, states that the ode 'takes hardly any verbal inspiration from the pages of Burton'. On the other hand, he asserts that the stanza form of the ode was inspired by one of Burton's quotations and that its 'philosophy' was borrowed from the section, *Against Melancholy it self* (*John Keats: The Living Year*, pp. 142–3).

This stanza, which Houghton, with an appropriate reference to the dream-paintings of two great Romantic artists, called 'as grim a picture as Blake or Fuseli could have dreamed and painted',* has all the typically Romantic thrill of horror and of the cult of the frightful and repulsive. More than that: if we read these lines attentively, we sense that Keats was not merely disposing his images, so many Romantic counters of the horrific, in a superficial and uncommitted way. He may have composed a large part of the stanza in this temper, but the lines—

> Your cordage large uprootings from the skull
> Of bald Medusa

—(a reminiscence of anatomical demonstrations in his medical student days?) leave us with a impression that he was himself directly familiar with this sort of Romantic shudder.

Of course, in making an aesthetic evaluation of the ode, we should try, as far as possible, to blot this stanza from our minds: first, because Keats himself cancelled it for his 1820 publication of the ode, and secondly, because even if we allow it to stand, his consciously intended meaning is that the sort of melancholy he is celebrating in the poem is not to be stimulated by the terrible and ugly. On the intellectual level he is rejecting this kind of Romantic sensation.

Yet the fact remains that Keats did write these lines and—as we may suspect—wrote them with some gusto. Artistically considered, the ode unquestionably gains from their suppression, and we may be satisfied with Houghton's guess that Keats cancelled them because he was 'conscious that the coarseness of the contrast would destroy the general effect of luxurious tenderness which it was the object of the poem to produce.'† At the same time we have no reason for thinking that he

* *Life and Letters of Keats* (Everyman ed.), p. 170.
† *Ibid.* p. 170.

expunged the stanza because it was in itself displeasing to him, and since he put it down on paper in the first stage of composition, we should certainly take it into account in any attempt to understand (though not to evaluate) the poem.

Further, in any general appreciation of Keats's poetry the stanza is certainly significant for his attitude towards the 'unhealthy and o'er-darkened ways Made for our searching.'[34] It is true that in one of his earliest poems, *Sleep and Poetry*, which is largely a statement of his own poetic intentions, he deliberately sets his face against the Romantic cult of the repulsive and horrific: he rejects the fashionable poetry of

> trees uptorn,
> Darkness, and worms, and shrouds, and sepulchres. . .[35]

Yet even if there is deeply considered conviction in this part of *Sleep and Poetry*, it is one thing to formulate a conviction and quite another to follow it consistently in one's creative work, especially if one is setting oneself against something that is powerfully and insidiously active in the cultural atmosphere of the time. For example, against this pronouncement in *Sleep and Poetry* we have to set such a passage as:

> all the pleasant hues
> Of heaven and earth had faded: deepest shades
> Were deepest dungeons: heaths and sunny glades
> Were full of pestilent light; our taintless rills
> Seem'd sooty, and o'erspread with upturned gills
> Of dying fish; the vermeil rose had blown
> In frightful scarlet, and its thorns out-grown
> Like spiked aloe.[36]

In these lines Keats uses Endymion's misery at the departure of Cynthia to overlay images of natural beauty with a perverse and dominant impression of plague-stricken horror, so that their total effect is not unlike that of Shelley's description of the earth after the great curse of Prometheus. We may also recall much of *Isabella*, such as the sensation evoked by the lines where Isabella is pictured cherishing the severed head of her lover:

She calm'd its wild hair with a golden comb,
  And all around each eye's sepulchral cell
Pointed each fringed lash; the smeared loam
  With tears, as chilly as a dripping well,
She drench'd away:—and still she comb'd, and kept
Sighing all day—and still she kiss'd, and wept.[37]

No one would question Bridges's praise of *Isabella* for the manner in which Keats sublimates much of the gruesomeness of the original Boccaccio story. But this sublimation is not achieved by vague suggestion; nor is it, as Bridges goes on to suggests, the dreamlike remoteness of some Pre-Raphaelite painting. On the contrary, the poem is filled with a strong Romantic sensation of the exquisitely and beautifully horrible, and as the above quotation, with its concrete physical references and its exact detail ('Pointed each fringed lash') shows, this sensation is often evoked with a powerful immediacy.

Setting these two quotations, from *Endymion* and *Isabella*, beside the cancelled first stanza of the *Ode on Melancholy*, we may believe that there was in Keats a good deal of latent sympathy with the Romantic thrill of the beautiful-horrible, though whether, had he lived longer, this would ever have emerged into an open strain of Beddoes-like poetry is highly questionable. One guesses that with such healthy instincts in his make-up, and so much sturdy common-sense, the tendency would have been finally repressed. But it might have crept out from time to time, just as in the grave and unromantic poetry of T. S. Eliot, there are occasional passages, like one of the choruses in *Murder in the Cathedral*, that seem to express nothing but a fascination for nightmarish horror.

One further detail in the cancelled first stanza calls for notice, the phrase 'Stitch creeds together for a sail'. Textual consideration apart, there can be no doubt that Garrod is right in preferring 'creeds' in the Woodhouse transcript to 'shrouds' in Houghton's 1848 text, for though in one way 'shrouds' goes better with the context—and pleasingly strengthens the alliteration—its funereal meaning would to some extent be negated by the nautical. If, therefore, we may take 'creeds' as the authentic reading, the phrase gives an interesting and unusual Shelleyan touch to the stanza in the thought of conflicting religious beliefs as a source of violence and bloodshed.

Even when we ignore the original first stanza of the *Ode on Melancholy* the opening of the 1820 published version remains thoroughly romantic. To begin with, in spite of the iterated negatives and the concluding comment, our main and immediate response is an imaginative one in which positive and Romantic suggestions of death and suicide are uppermost. Of these suggestions the suicidal are the most tenuous. If we could read the obscure line, 'For shade to shade will come too drowsily', in the sense of, 'For ghost will come to Lethe, Hades, too drowsily', the idea of self-destruction would be firmly established by the time we reached the end of the stanza. But this is only a possible way of interpreting the line, which more probably means, 'For a succession of drowsy, shadowy states of consciousness will follow one upon the other'. Again, we cannot be completely certain that there is a suicidal implication in the lines

> nor [let] the death-moth be
> Your mournful Psyche.

But there can be no mistaking the drift of the opening—

> neither twist
> Wolf's-bane, tight-rooted, for its poisonous wine,

while our immediate response to nightshade, described as the grape of the goddess of death and the underworld, must be the one Keats intended.*

---

* It is possible that Burton's prescriptions for *head*-melancholy may have suggested the rather curious idea of nightshade applied to the forehead. But from the context Keats can hardly be thinking of nightshade simply as a soothing application.

Incidentally the phrase 'thy pale forehead', evoking a sickly and typical

However, if the suicidal strain is somewhat nebulous, at least we cannot miss the characteristically Romantic association of melancholy with brooding over death, night, and darkness, this being created by the allusions to nightshade, yew-tree, the death-moth* and owl. Further, the perverse Romantic confusion of opposites is very much in evidence in this stanza. Wolf's-bane, though poisonous, is represented desirably as a wine, nightshade as a 'ruby grape'; and the paradox of these lines, of life with death, the desirable with the abhorrent, is heightened when we recall that for Keats wine was always something of intense sensuous gusto. In the same category of wilfully confused sensations there is the black-mass juxtaposition of 'rosary'† and 'yew-berries'—the hint of some dark religion of death.

But—it may be said—Keats is after all rejecting this Romantic sort of melancholy that takes the form of brooding over death and suicide, just as in the cancelled stanza he rejected the melancholy associated with the frightful and repellent.

There are two answers to this objection. First, we are concerned with the ambiguous language of poetic utterance in which, where all the complex layers of 'meaning' are valid, unconscious intention may run counter to conscious and imaginative implication to intellectual statement. True enough, with his negatives leading into the conclusion

---

romantic countenance, recalls many such descriptions in Keats's poetry, like that of Lorenzo with his 'forehead high . . . waxing very pale and dead' (*Isabella*, ll. 52–3).

* Garrod's identification of this death-moth with 'mournful Psyche' is very questionable, though, if the identity holds, his conclusion certainly follows: 'This death-moth, this "mournful Psyche", who typifies melancholic love, even if we conceive the melancholic pattern wrought to that degree that it is symbolized by the *death-moth*, is no partner in the mysteries of that deeper and truer melancholy which the Ode celebrates' (*Keats*, p. 97). But surely stanzas II and III show that love is very much a partner in 'sorrow's mysteries'?

† It is just possible that this detail was suggested by the allegorical picture in the front of the *Anatomy of Melancholy*, where the Superstitious Man is shown holding a rosary.

> For shade to shade will come too drowsily,
>   And drown the wakeful anguish of the soul,

Keats is affirming that it is not a melancholy of being 'half in love with easeful death' that he is celebrating. But the imaginative drift and emphasis of the stanza is such that as we read it our senses are powerfully stirred by the Romantic luxury of the love of death and darkness. For a similar poetic effect we may recall Book IV of *Paradise Lost* where Milton rounds off his description of Eden with a number of classical and literary references, including the famous 'fair fields of Enna' lines. These allusions are formally contained by a negative statement: none of these earthly beauties, Milton declares

>   might with this Paradise
> Of Eden strive.³⁸

Yet for all this negative statement these classical references do in fact colour and enrich the description of Eden as we read the poem. So, in the first stanza of Keats's ode, what is rejected is, imaginatively speaking, almost as significant as the intellectual motion of rejection. Moreover, the amplitude and poetic appeal of the writing lead us to feel that there was a side of Keats that was drawn to the sort of Romanticism that he is dismissing at a conscious level.

Secondly, even if we give full consideration to the conscious intent of the stanza, its ideas remain thoroughly Romantic. However we interpret the penultimate line in detail, it is evident that what Keats is rejecting is his characteristic mood of 'drowsy numbness', and there is an extremely close parallel to the opening of the *Ode to a Nightingale:*

> My heart aches, and a drowsy numbness pains
>   My sense, as though of hemlock I had drunk,
> Or emptied some dull opiate to the drains
>   One minute past, and Lethe-wards had sunk.

In these lines the poet's state of a Lethean 'drowsy numbness' is exactly the condition suggested by

For shade to shade will come too drowsily,

while the references in the *Ode on Melancholy* to the poisonous wine of wolf's-bane and to 'nightshade, ruby grape of Proserpine', have their obvious counterparts in the allusions to hemlock and 'dull opiate'. The essential difference between the two passages is that whereas in the *Ode on Melancholy* Keats is deprecating a condition of 'drowsy numbness' in which the 'wakeful anguish of the soul' is 'drowned', in the *Ode to a Nightingale* the poet's 'drowsy numbness' *is* accompanied by a 'wakeful anguish'. His heart aches, there is pain; and the reason for this feeling is that he is too happy in the happiness of the nightingale. As is described in the last stanza of the *Ode on Melancholy*, excessive joy has turned to its opposite, and in one sense the *Ode to a Nightingale* records the actuality of such an aesthetic and emotional experience as Keats is advocating in the *Ode on Melancholy*.

There is of course nothing specifically Romantic in the rejection of 'drowsy numbness' that is expressed in the first stanza of the *Ode on Melancholy* or in the implied desire to feel —intensely. What is truly Romantic is the prizing and cherishing of fully conscious *painful* feeling—the 'wakeful anguish of the soul'.

This Romantic attitude (or perversion, as some may think) is fully elaborated in the second and central stanza of the ode. This stanza begins with a long simile:

> But when the melancholy fit shall fall
>   Sudden from heaven like a weeping cloud,
> That fosters the droop-headed flowers all,
>   And hides the green hill in an April shroud.

F. R. Leavis, though admirably responsive to the irrepressible sensuous vitality that enters the ode in these lines, describes the simile as 'formal'.* But surely it is significantly relevant to the main thought of the poem. What Keats appears to imply

---

* *Revaluations*, p. 261.

by his evocation of green April and of rain fostering the flowers is that melancholy is a fertilizing, creative emotion.* 'I have the same Idea of *all* our Passions as of Love: they are all in their sublime, creative of essential Beauty.'[39]

However we regard the opening simile, the main intention of the stanza is quite clear: it is a plea and a poetic recipe for the conscious, exquisite cultivation of melancholy. When the fit falls on us we should not resist it; on the contrary, we should sustain it and work ourselves into a state of wakeful anguish by contemplation of the brief, transient beauties of nature† and by feeding deep upon the eyes of a mistress who is doomed to die. Nevertheless, for all this intention, the mood communicated by the stanza is not a thin-blooded, aesthetic pose of some Yellow-Book poet of the 'nineties, for the invigorating sensuousness of the opening simile is sustained by words like 'glut' and 'globed', by the rich melodic appeal of the middle lines, and by the characteristic physical immediacy of

> Emprison her soft hand.

There is a further Romantic suggestion about this stanza that is frequently glossed over, or ignored, by critics who presumably still feel the need to alleviate the nineteenth-century anxiety about a certain 'unhealthiness' in Keats. The mistress of the last three lines, with her 'peerless eyes', is there **pri**marily because she is a supreme manifestation of the 'Beauty that must die'. But there is also something else in these lines, a perversity, a pleasure in a masochistic sort of love-making:

> Or if thy mistress some rich anger shows,
>   Emprison her soft hand, and let her rave,
>   And feed deep, deep upon her peerless eyes.

* There may be an echo of Collins's *Ode on the Death of Mr Thomson*:
    Now waft me from the *green Hill's side*
    Whose cold Turf hides the *buried Friend* (ll. 31–2).
These lines (and his own cancelled stanza) may have suggested
                                        Keats's 'shroud'.
  † Keats's illustrations—roses, peonies, and the 'rainbow of the salt sand-wave'—are carefully chosen to create this impression.

Nor is this perversity of erotic sensation (including the Romantic confusion that is packed into 'rich anger') something that is to be dismissed as marginal or accidental. On the contrary, it indicates an aspect of Keats that links him with the darker side of general Romantic sensibility, even though he does not qualify for an important place in Mario Praz's *Romantic Agony*. This masochism, with its associated opposite, is plain enough in the letters to Fanny Brawne, and it also emerges in other parts of his poetry, notably (for there is a close parallel with the *Ode on Melancholy*) in *Lamia:*

> He thereat was stung,
> Perverse, with stronger fancy to reclaim
> Her wild and timid nature to his aim:
> Besides, for all his love, in self despite
> Against his better self, *he took delight*
> *Luxurious in her sorrows*, soft and new.
> His passion, cruel grown, took on a hue
> Fierce and sanguineous . . .[40]

The second stanza of this ode of unpausing continuity leads straight into the paradoxical conclusion of the third. Because beauty is death-doomed, because joy is essentially transient, and pleasure (significantly described as 'aching') turns to poison, the intensest sort of melancholy, the desired 'wakeful anguish',* is only to be found in the intensity of sensuous delight: it is only experienced by the man

> whose strenuous tongue
> Can burst Joy's grape against his palate fine.

Once more, in this powerful image, we feel the vital sensuousness that is behind the ode. But here it brings a certain shift in meaning. In the second stanza the melancholy mood that

---

* It is interesting to notice that where the 1820 text has the penultimate line,
> His soul shall taste the sadness of her might,
the autograph reads:
> His soul shall taste the anguish of her might.

Keats is commending is somewhat contemplative, slightly detached and intellectual. Now, in this conclusive image of the strenuous tongue bursting joy's grape, as well as in the earlier reference to 'while the bee-mouth sips', he seems to be carried farther into the suggestion that the desired melancholy is to be found solely in intensely sensuous experience.*

However, the last stanza does more than reaffirm the Romantic theme of the desirability of melancholy's 'Wakeful anguish of the soul'. There is also a grand Romantic gesture—the final impression of the poem—as Keats exults in the idea of being a sacrifice to melancholy, 'among her cloudy trophies hung'.

Possibly it may appear to some that we are reading the ode too literally if we say that Keats is finally caught up in a deathwards impulse, in the Romantic luxury of 'half in love with easeful death'. But, as we have already shown, there is certainly a deathly, suicidal suggestion in the first stanza, while before hastily dismissing this impression of a self-destroying impulse we should recall again Keats's later, and no doubt considered, observations on his 'love of Gloom': 'Do not suffer your Mind to dwell on unpleasant reflections—that sort of thing has been the destruction of my health . . . Do not diet your mind with grief, it destroys the constitution.' [41]

It is the last stanza of the ode in particular that calls for a clear discrimination between what was fundamental and what superficially Romantic in Keats's attitude. For Middleton Murry, following Bridges, who considered that the ode expressed profound and experienced thought, the final stanza is of the highest significance as poetic philosophy: he leads into

---

* Incidentally, there may be a germ of the Induction to *The Fall of Hyperion* in this stanza. Saturn's temple is certainly no temple of Delight. But Moneta is essentially a figure of melancholy, she is veiled and beside a shrine, and the Poet does not see her before he has eaten 'deliciously' and drunk from 'a cool vessel of transparent juice'. Gittings (*John Keats: The Living Year*, p. 178) draws attention to this resemblance between the two poems.

his quotation of it with the observation, 'This consequence—
this "love of good and ill"—is manifest in all Keats's poetry in
this period of sudden opulence. As it is in the *Ode to a Nightingale*, so it is in the *Ode on Melancholy*.'* For Leavis, on the other
hand, the ode displays Keats in his 'most Swinburnian mood'.
It is a poem, he declares, of 'perverse and debilitating indulgences', representing one of 'the most obviously decadent developments of Beauty-addiction—of the cult of "exquisite passion" and "finest senses".'†

Between these two critical estimates there is clearly the
widest of divergencies, and some further consideration of the
Romanticism of the ode may perhaps enable us to see how
such diverse judgments arise, as well as to assess their relative
truth.

The foregoing analysis of the ode—if valid—certainly
supports Leavis's contention that the poem is largely one of
'perverse and debilitating indulgences', this mood being
tempered, as Leavis thoroughly perceives, by Keats's 'characteristic vitality'. All that need be said further is that in de-
fining these indulgences as Romantic (and implying that they
are superficial, the consequences of an imaginative infection)
we are not employing a merely contingent description. All
through Keats's poetry there is abundant evidence that he
felt the appeal, in a superficial way, of the Romantic 'joy of
grief'. As G. Wilson Knight says: 'Melancholy is with him
from the beginning both sincerely felt and luxuriously enjoyed.'‡ This note enters prominently in one of his earliest
poems, a poem that is doubly interesting in that it reveals the
Romantic writer from whom he in all probability first learnt
the perversion of a desired, cultivated melancholy. This is the
unpublished sonnet *To Lord Byron*, where the older poet is
rhapsodized as a teller of the enchanting 'tale of pleasing
woe':

* *Keats and Shakespeare*, p. 129.
† *Revaluations*, p. 260.
‡ *The Starlit Dome*, p. 274.

> Byron! how sweetly sad thy melody!
>   Attuning still the soul to tenderness,
>   As if soft Pity, with unusual stress,
> Had touch'd her plaintive lute, and thou, being by,
> Hadst caught the tones, nor suffer'd them to die.
>   O'ershading sorrow doth not make thee less
>   Delightful: thou thy griefs dost dress
> With a bright halo, shining beamily . . .[42]

Of course this sonnet is a very early poem, and the enthusiasm for Byron's tales of 'pleasing woe' was soon spent. But, marking one of many such bridges from it, for instance the lines in 'I stood tip-toe' describing the desolate Pan—

>   how he did weep to find,
> Nought but a lovely sighing of the wind
> Along the reedy stream; a half-heard strain,
> Full of sweet desolation—balmy pain—[43]

we may pass on to a much later poem, that shows how in 1818 Keats still responded to the superficial Romantic cult of melancholy and to 'the sweetness of the pain'.[44] This is the fragment, 'Welcome joy, and welcome sorrow', which has often been suggested as a germ of the *Ode on Melancholy*. The contrasts that form the substance of this lyric are crude and highly artificial, while the emblems of sorrow are the stock Romantic properties:

> Infant playing with a skull;
> Morning fair, and shipwreck'd hull;
> Nightshade with the woodbine kissing;
> Serpents in red roses hissing;
> Cleopatra regal-dress'd
> With aspic at her breast[45]

On the other hand, side by side with this conventional Romanticism of the 'joy of grief' there runs through Keats's writing, from the time of *Endymion* onwards, a much more serious awareness of the juxtaposition of joy and sorrow in human experience:

> woe! woe; is grief contain'd
> In the very deeps of pleasure?*

This heart-felt awareness is surely behind such lines as those in which Mnemosyne describes the effect of Apollo's music:

> all the vast
> Unwearied ear of the whole universe
> Listen'd in pain and pleasure at the birth
> Of such new tuneful wonder;[46]

and it is this same awareness that produces such a memorable and un-Byronic reflection in the letters as: 'While we are laughing the seed of some trouble is put into the wide arable land of events—while we are laughing it sprouts, it grows and suddenly bears a poison fruit which we must pluck.'[47] And if, in the infection of superficial Romanticism, he could write a poem like 'Welcome joy, and welcome sorrow', he could also write in the same year one like *On visiting the Tomb of Burns*, in which there is a deep, authentic feeling, not fully achieved as poetry perhaps, for the pain in beauty:

> The Town, the churchyard, and the setting sun,
> The clouds, the trees, the rounded hills all seem,
> Though beautiful, cold—strange—as in a dream,
> I dreamed long ago, now new begun.
> The short liv'd, paly Summer is but won
> From Winter's ague, for an hour's gleam;
> Though sapphire-warm, their stars do never beam:
> All is cold Beauty; pain is never done:
> For who has mind to relish, Minos-wise,
> The Real of Beauty, free from that dead hue
> Sickly imagination and sick pride
> Cast wan upon it?[48]

As poetry this sonnet cannot of course compare with the effortless power, the rich imagery and melody of the *Ode on*

---

* ɪɪ, 823–4. The closeness of these lines to *Melancholy* is brought out by the draft version:

> is grief contain'd
> In the very *shrine* of pleasure?

Melancholy; the writing is subdued, halting. But it is arguable that it reflects, however brokenly, a maturer—and healthier—attitude of mind: a moment of true visionary insight against the enraptured fever-fit of the ode.

Again, later than the ode, there are those lines that form part of the description of Lamia—

> of sciental brain
> To unperplex bliss from its neighbour pain;
> Define their pettish limits, and estrange
> Their points of contact, and swift counterchange.[49]

Here, though of course Keats is writing of a non-human personage, he appears to envisage a state of existence in which joy and grief are mercifully distinct and separate; but in *The Fall of Hyperion*, written about the same time, he declares that part of the inevitable burden of the 'dreamer' poet is that he can never know unadulterated happiness:

> Every sole man hath days of joy and pain,
> Whether his labours be sublime or low—
> The pain alone; the joy alone; distinct:
> Only the dreamer venoms all his days,
> Bearing more woe than all his sins deserve.[50]

Such passages as these cannot be ascribed to a superficial Romantic cult of the deliciousness of sorrow. Behind them is Keats's own fundamental psychological constitution, which appears to have been one liable to sudden and extreme fluctuations of mood between depression and joy. There is some indication of this from time to time in the letters,* but for our chief evidence we must rely on Severn's account of the poet: 'even when in a mood of joyous observance, with flow of happy spirits, he would suddenly become taciturn, not because he was tired, not even because his mind was suddenly wrought to some bewitching vision, but from a profound disquiet that he could not or would not explain.'[51] All the

---

* See, for example, *Letters*, p. 402: 'With my inconstant disposition it is no wonder that this morning, amid all our bad times and misfortunes, I should feel so alert and well-spirited.'

experience of Keats's life went to strengthen this inherent disposition: he was not romanticizing, he was expressing the simple, painful truth when he wrote: 'I have never known any unalloy'd Happiness for many days together: the death or sickness of someone has always spoilt my hours.'[52] Nor was it a Romantic pose that prompted him to write, in the spring-time of his twenty-second year, 'I scarcely remember counting upon any Happiness.'[53]

No doubt F. R. Leavis would reprehend any response to the *Ode on Melancholy* that was consciously conditioned by reference to other poems of Keats or to passages in the letters. But if, once we become familiar with the work of a poet in its entirety, this way of reading a poem is legitimate, not to say inevitable, we may perhaps feel that there is, after all, something of this deeper attitude to joy and pain in the ode, particularly in the lines:

> She dwells with Beauty—Beauty that must die;
>   And Joy, whose hand is ever at his lips
> Bidding adieu.

On the other hand, neither the last stanza nor the ode as a whole can be taken as expressing something philosophically significant about beauty or melancholy or the relationship of joy and grief, as they are by Murry, and by Garrod when he writes: 'I suppose [Keats] to say . . . that the top of poetry, its supreme mood, is precisely that mood in which the beauty, of which the poet is priest and worshipper, is so apprehended that the awareness of it is *anguish*.'* Essentially the ode is a plea for 'wakeful anguish' as a desirable state (so much so that it might almost have been entitled an *Ode to Anguish*) and a poetic exhibition of how this state is to be experienced through a deliberate cultivation of a certain kind of melancholy. On one occasion at least this exhibition runs close to psychological perversity. And the climax of the poem is not in those lines

---

* *Keats*, p. 98.

'She dwells with Beauty' etc., but in the image, exultantly toned, of the devotee of melancholy immolated to the goddess —'among her cloudy trophies hung'. If the deathwards trend is consciously rejected in the first stanza it re-emerges again, unsuppressed, in the close.

Like the *Nightingale*, *Grecian Urn*, and *Indolence* odes, the *Ode on Melancholy* springs ultimately from a sense of human misery that, owing to Keats's personal experience, was particularly strong in him at the time. All of these odes are essentially explorations of ways in which this misery might be endured, and in the *Ode on Melancholy* Keats gave himself up to that Romantic sensation of 'pleasing woe' that had attracted him to some extent from the youthful days of his admiration for Byron. In this sensation sorrow and unhappiness were cherished partly because they are (or were felt to be) stimulants to an intensified aesthetic experience, and partly because any sort of feeling was preferable to indolence, emptiness, ennui, or 'drowsy numbness'. The *Ode on Melancholy* is chiefly an expression of this sensation, fully manifest; and though, as Leavis rightly points out, the poem is also infused with Keats's characteristic, vital sensuousness, though there may be some slight movement in it towards a maturer acceptance of the pain in human life, we probably rate it below the other odes because we feel that the cult of 'pleasing woe' is one of the shallowest and—if the word is not too puritanical—unhealthiest parts of the Romantic attitude.

CHAPTER IX

THE 'ODE ON A GRECIAN URN'

In spite of all,
Some shape of beauty moves away the pall
From our dark spirits.

Endymion

. . . the yearning Passion I have for the beautiful . . .
Letter to George and Georgiana Keats, October 1818

THE more we know of Keats, of his sensibility, attitude, interests and experience, the more inevitable seems the composition of some such poem as his *Ode on a Grecian Urn*. Yet while the work is one that some acquaintance who had read *Poems* (1817) and *Endymion* carefully and sympathetically might have been prescient enough to foreshadow in rough outline, it is also the most divergently interpreted of the five main odes;* and one line in particular, the notoriously disputed 'Beauty is truth, truth beauty', has become a sort of Holy Grail of Keatsian criticism, luring its interpreters on the most diverse journeys and leaving them, as often as not, in remote, mistily confused places of speculation.

It is possible that the ode is indeed an obscure or deeply ambiguous poem rightly eliciting a wide variety of responses. On the other hand, since serious criticism of Keats is comparatively young, a product mainly of the last fifty years, it is also possible that some of the interpretations proposed (including of course what follows) may be misguided or flatly mistaken. For this reason we should continually remind ourselves of some of the simplest and most obvious facts about the poem.

In diction, rhythm, metrical form, kind and organization of

---

* See Appendix VI.

imagery, it is obviously linked very closely with the four other odes that were probably written in the space of not much more than a month (late April and May 1819). From this fact two consequences of interpretation follow. First, our reading of it is always likely to be illuminated by the other odes; and since these poems, coming so closely together in time, stem from a common body of experience,* these illuminations will often go deeper than merely formal or superficial correspondences. Secondly, any interpretation of the *Ode on a Grecian Urn* that treats it as markedly and essentially different from the *Ode to a Nightingale*, the *Ode on Melancholy* and the *Ode on Indolence* should be regarded with the greatest reserve. The *Grecian Urn* may be different in essential kind from these three odes, as the *Ode to Psyche* certainly is; but probability is against this.

Nearly four-fifths of the ode (the three middle stanzas and parts of the first and last) is devoted to a description of frieze-like pictures on the urn. The urn itself is an imaginary one, for the pictorial decoration on the neo-Attic type of urn that Keats evidently had in mind consisted of one continuous scene, not two or more as are found in the ode. But though the urn is imaginary, the pictures that he represents on it certainly owe something to works of art with which he was familiar, chiefly through illustrations. For the scenes in the first three stanzas he probably derived some inspiration from the Borghese Vase and the Bacchic pictures of Poussin, while the scene in stanza IV is partly a compound of Claude's 'Sacrifice to Apollo' and of the Sosibios vase that he had himself at one time drawn.† Besides these main inspirations there may have been others like the Townley vase; and Sir Maurice Bowra, following

* This fundamental point about the odes has been admirably emphasized in an essay by John Holloway ('The Odes of Keats', *Cambridge Journal*, April 1952): 'What unites these poems is essentially a singleness in experience' (p. 416).

† See Colvin, *Life of John Keats*, pp. 416–17. (Colvin includes a reproduction of the Sosibios and Borghese vases.) See also Bowra, *The Romantic Imagination*, pp. 128–31. But Bowra rather curiously ignores the influence of Claude and Poussin.

perhaps an earlier remark of Colvin, has recently suggested that the 'heifer lowing at the skies' in stanza IV may be a recollection of the southern frieze of the Parthenon.* At the same time no critic has ever contended that these 'sources' constituted anything more than stimulating suggestions to the visual imagery of the ode. In their organization, elaboration, and in the emotions and modes of sensibility associated with them, the scenes on the Grecian urn are primarily of Keats's own making. This fact should always be central in any true interpretation of the ode.

Most of the other inspirational forces behind the ode and of the filaments that join it to the rest of Keats's work will be best treated in our direct discussion of the poem. But there is one matter that may most conveniently be dealt with at this point. This is the remarkable resemblance in phrasing, and to some extent in imagery, between the ode and a passage in Collins's *The Passions:*

> Last came Joy's *Ecstatic* Trial,
> He with viny crown advancing,
>   First to the lively *Pipe* his Hand addrest,
> But soon he saw the brisk awak'ning Viol,
>   Whose *sweet* entrancing Voice he lov'd the best.
> They would have thought who heard the Strain,
> They saw in *Tempe's Vale* her native *Maids,*
> Amidst the festal sounding Shades,
> To some *unwearied Minstrel dancing.*†

In spite of some striking parallels, notably between 'Tempe's Vale' and 'Tempe or the dales of Arcady' and 'unwearied Minstrel' and 'happy melodist, unwearied', we cannot of

---

* *The Romantic Imagination*, p. 131.

† Ll. 80–88. My italics; and I have included 'dancing' among the words echoed in the ode because of the cancelled l. 9—'What mad pursuit? what love? what dance . . .' De Selincourt in the notes to his edition (p. 563 a) draws attention to ll. 85–8.

It is also to be noticed that four lines before the quoted passage Collins has 'sylvan Boys'. Though 'sylvan' is a favourite epithet with eighteenth-century poets, Keats uses the word rarely.

course be certain that this passage, lodged in Keats's subconscious mind, formed an embryo out of which a considerable part of his ode evolved. But there is much beside the obvious similarities that points to this probability. We know that Keats had read the poetry of Collins; there is his use in the last stanza of the ode of the unusual word 'brede', which Collins had employed in *To Evening* (l. 7); and the conclusion of *The Passions* suggests another reason why he may have vaguely recollected the poem in his own composition:

> Revive the just Designs of Greece,
> Return in all thy simple State!
> Confirm the Tales her Sons relate!

The first stanza of the *Ode on a Grecian Urn* is probably as good a poetic exemplification as any of the opinion Keats had once expressed to Reynolds: 'Poetry should be great and unobtrusive, a thing which enters into one's soul, and does not startle it or amaze it with itself, but with its subject.'* It begins smoothly, quietly, calmly, with two lines in that measured, deep-breathing rhythm that characterizes so much of Keats's best writing, this effect being strengthened by the repeated long 'i' sound and the two immediately-following speaking stresses that weight the end of the second line:

> Thou still unravish'd bride of quietness,
> Thou foster-child of silence and slów tíme . . .

Led unobtrusively into the poem by these two lines of effortless, subdued strength, we are borne along irresistibly. The invocation to the urn merges almost imperceptibly—for the question, 'What leaf-fring'd legend haunts about thy shape?', is in no way arresting—into the first picture, which is one of Bacchic revelry;† the slow opening rhythm is gradually

---

* *Letters*, p. 96. I quote this sentence for its spirit, not for its actual reference in the letter.

† Some contemporary critics have discovered a good deal of meaningful complexity in this picture, and its alleged creation of paradox has been

modulated into shorter, more broken cadences that communicate the breathless excitement of the scene; and the
opening monotone changes into a dance, not much patterned,
of varied vowel sounds. In the last line there is a satisfying
return of the long 'i' of the opening—

What pipes and timbrels? What wild ecstasy?

—but now, in a different rhythmical context, the sound has
a piercing intensity.

Because of this irresistible development (to say nothing of
our over-familiarity with the lines from school-room days) it is
not surprising if we miss some of the important detail of this
opening stanza.* Notably, though critics rarely so much as
mention it, there is that surprising phrase in the first line,

heavily stressed—motion, restlessness, ecstasy, against the immobility of
the urn, sound against silence, the mortal against the immortal, activity
in time against timelessness, etc. Wasserman (*The Finer Tone*, pp. 14–20)
goes even further in this kind of interpretation than Cleanth Brooks did
in his essay in *The Well Wrought Urn*, insisting, for example, on a subtle
antithesis of meaning between 'Tempe' and 'the dales of Arcady' (p. 17).
For an illustration of what Wasserman makes of the scene the following
will serve: 'Like the humanity and/or (sic) divinity of the figures, like the
marriage-chastity of the urn and the virginity-ravishment of the maidens,
the immortality of the urn and the temporality of the figures are delicately
poised on each side of heaven's bourne, yearning towards that area of
mystic interfusion to which solitary thinkings can mount—"but no more" '
(p. 19).

I prefer to regard the scene as something not so much made by Keats
(as his images in stanzas II and III are) but generally recollected from
illustrations of vases and possibly pictures—the starting point of his poem.
There is some contradiction certainly between what he has said about the
urn, especially 'unravish'd bride of quietness', and what he imagines upon
its frieze; but this contradiction is to a large extent accidental and not
particularly prominent. For our first glance at such a classical scene, not
immediately identifiable, the interrogative note is entirely natural, and
this note may have been further prompted by Keats's need to reconcile
what he knew to be descriptive elements drawn from several sources.

* I do not include 'sylvan historian' which Cleanth Brooks (*The Well
Wrought Urn*, p. 143) finds complicated in meaning. By 'historian' Keats
probably meant no more than 'story-teller', especially one whose tale was
about the past; and the urn was a '*sylvan* historian' because of the 'leaf-
fring'd legend', the 'happy boughs', etc.

'still unravish'd bride'.* This is arresting both for its highly (and at this point of the poem, isolated) sexual nature and also for its bold paradox that comes close to a contradiction of terms. Presumably, in the word 'unravish'd' at least, Keats is referring among other things to the way the urn has survived intact† through so many centuries, and if the last part of the stanza was already in his mind when he composed the opening line, 'unravish'd' may have been prompted, without much conscious thought, by his 'maidens loth' and 'mad pursuit'. But though the phrase is a puzzling and surprising one that, once we are fully aware of it, takes away some of the unobtrusive quality in the opening lines, it strikes an effective prelude note to the last part of the stanza. Further, as we shall see shortly, the paradox of the 'unravish'd bride' serves to announce one of the basic themes of the second and third stanzas.

This prelusive effect is by no means confined to the phrase 'still unravish'd bride'. Admittedly the two opening lines, if we choose to dwell on their meaning, are a little vague and obscure: they are typically Romantic in expression, an antithesis of Augustan explicitness. But they are not meaningless,‡ and if we read them carefully, against the rest of the poem, it is not difficult to see that they constitute a packed initial statement of main themes that is unique among the odes. It is hardly an exaggeration to say that the whole of the *Ode on a Grecian Urn* exists, in embryo, in its two opening lines.

One of these themes announced in the opening is developed in some isolation from the others and may therefore be discussed separately. For Keats a primary association of his imagined urn is with silence: in his invocation he describes it as the 'foster child of silence', and this significance is repeated in the

---

* Wasserman, however, gives considerable attention to the phrase (*op. cit.* pp. 14–20).

† It is curious that this word too has a sexual significance. With urns and vases as familiar womb symbols, the psychologist should have a happy holiday with the first line.

‡ As Murry suggests when he writes (*The Mystery of Keats*, p. 165) that Keats 'says whatever it is that he says'.

last stanza through the summary phrase 'silent form'. Between these points of reference we have two developments of the theme. The first, prompted by the picture of the happy melodist, is a delighted description of that kind of music we can hear only in our minds:*

> Heard melodies are sweet, but those unheard
>> Are sweeter; therefore, ye soft pipes, play on:
> Not to the sensual ear, but, more endear'd,
>> Pipe to the spirit ditties of no tone.

The second, slighter, development is a contrasting one, a pathetic fancy of the little town deserted by all its folk:

> And, little town, thy streets for evermore
>> Will silent be.

In these direct ways—not to mention remoter suggestions—the urn is continuously associated with silence. In the second line of the ode 'silence' should probably be read in closest conjunction with 'slow time': originally, of course, the urn was created by some forgotten artist, was his 'child'; but it has survived because it has been fostered and cherished by time. Of what happened to it through the long centuries since its creation we know nothing: its history is enigmatically silent. Thus time, and the silence that goes with it, may be regarded as its foster-parents. Possibly, too, there is something in the line of that simple, almost inevitable human response to some relic of the remote past: 'If only it could talk!' But also it is extremely probable that this association of the urn with silence is an

---

* For Cleanth Brooks (*The Well Wrought Urn*, p. 144) this is one of the many paradoxes in the poem. But many composers have declared that they have heard music 'in their heads' more beautiful than anything they have composed or heard in the concert room. And this phenomenon of the imagination is not confined to musicians. Cf. *'Tis Pity She's a Whore*, II, i, 13–14—a play Keats had read (see *Letters*, p. 436):
> Music as well consists
> In the ear as in the playing.
It is characteristic of Keats that what we do imaginatively hear in the poem is soft and subdued—of the pipes.

expression of Keats's individual sensibility. As we have described elsewhere he was exceptionally delighted by gentle and delicate sounds, hush and silence; and alongside the first four lines of stanza II (not of course expressing quite the same idea but evidence of the same sensibility) we may set such a description as that of lips that speak

> In ripest quiet, shadows of sweet sounds.*

Further, in this fascination that silence always had for him there was a curious sense of the 'hush of natural objects'[1] and of inanimate things, and several critics have drawn attention to that germ of part of the ode that is to be found in *Endymion*— 'silent as a consecrated urn'.[2] Also, much nearer in time to the ode, there is the reference in the sonnet *To Sleep* (April 1819) to 'the hushed casket of my soul', while in the *Ode on Indolence* he addresses his urn figures with the line

> How came ye muffled in so hush a masque?

In the first line of the ode the urn is described as the bride of 'quietness'. Though the primary reference of this word is almost certainly to a spiritual state of tranquillity, repose (and possibly passivity), in its context it can hardly be read without some intrusion of its sound denotation.† This double meaning is worth noticing here because if we are to appreciate the full significance of the silence theme (particularly as it connects with the other themes) we must understand that it is not confined to a state of aesthetic sensibility. No doubt it would be wrong to claim that Keats ever had the mystic's deep experience of silence—as, for instance, it has been described by Simone Weil: 'At the same time, filling every part of this infinity of infinity, there is silence, a silence which is not an

---

* 'Unfelt, unheard, unseen', l. 9.
† Cleanth Brooks appears to take this associated meaning of 'quietness' as the primary one: 'The silence of the urn is stressed—it is a "bride of quietness" ' (*op. cit.* p. 142). But this would create a bad redundancy with 'foster-child of silence'.

absence of sound but which is the object of a positive sensation, more positive than that of sound.'³ On the other hand he certainly longed all his life for that 'quietness' which is of the spirit. As early as *Endymion* we find him identifying quietness with spiritual health and serenity: a thing of beauty, he wrote,

> still will keep
> A bower quiet for us, and a sleep
> Full of sweet dreams, and health, and quiet breathing;⁴

while his Cave of Quietude, symbolizing a state of spiritual recuperation, is a place of profound, healing silence:

> within ye hear
> No sound so loud as when on curtain'd bier
> The death-watch tick is stifled . . .
> . . . where silence dreariest
> Is most articulate.*

More to the point of the ode, his writings in 1819 show him deeply concerned about the 'feverish' state of being that, he felt, had always been his. The clearest and fullest expression of this concern occurs in one of his letters to his brother and sister-in-law: 'Some think I have lost that poetic ardour and fire 'tis said I once had—the fact is perhaps I have: but instead of that I hope I shall substitute a more thoughtful and quiet power. I am more frequently, now, contented to read and think—but now and then, haunted with ambitious thoughts. Quieter in my pulse, improved in my digestion; exerting myself against vexing speculations—scarcely content to write the best verses for the fever they leave behind.'† His

---

* IV, 529–31 and 539–40. Admittedly these lines are complicated by associations with death.

† *Letters*, p. 421–2. Though this letter was written in September, after a period of exceptionally violent 'fever' and when Keats seems to have achieved at least a momentary quietness of spirit, it has a bearing on his mood when he was composing the odes. Like other letters (see p. 340 and 345) it indicates that poetic composition involved a particularly heavy expenditure of nervous energy for Keats, and what D. H. Lawrence once

poems, too, bear witness to the same concern: there is his
second sonnet on Fame ('How fever'd is the man'), the reference to 'the fever and the fret' in the *Nightingale* ode, and to
the 'heart's short fever-fit' in *Indolence;* and above all, there is
the heart-stabbing accusation of Moneta in *The Fall of Hyperion:*

> Thou art a dreaming thing,
> A fever of thyself.[5]

'Fever' is unquestionably a key-word to Keats's mood in the
year of his poetic maturity, and the longing to escape fever,
even, paradoxically, when he is inducing it, is one of the main
impulses behind the *Ode on a Grecian Urn*. Whatever else the
urn represents, it is a 'bride' of that 'quietness'* of spirit that
is the opposite of 'fever'.

The first four lines of stanza II, 'Heard melodies are sweet',
etc., constitute a transition passage of direct comment.
Rhythmically, in pace, length of cadence, and in the two
instances of end-weighting ('play on' and 'no tone'), they
recall the opening lines of the Ode, though their strong
median pauses gives them a distinctive quality. They are
followed by a description of the second picture on the urn,
with a certain repetition that is one of the weaknesses of the
Ode, to the end of the third stanza.

It is possible that Keats intended this second description as
a continuation of the first, that he was now concentrating his
attention on some selected details from it. This is certainly
suggested by the transition lines, where 'soft pipes' both refers

wrote to Middleton Murry may not be so wide of the mark, though some
might find the observation applicable to Lawrence himself: 'To kill
yourself like Keats, for what you've got to say, is to mix the eggshell in
with the omelette' (4 January 1926).

* When the Ode was first printed in *Annals of the Fine Arts* there was a
comma after 'still' in l. 1, making the word an epithet. If this was really
Keats's intention (and since neither the transcripts nor the text of the
1820 volume give us an hyphenated 'still-unravish'd' there is no absolute
certainty that 'still' is an adverb), this would greatly strengthen the impression of quietness—even if with some tautology.

back to 'What pipes and timbrels?' and introduces the youth who is piping beneath the trees. But the change of focus is all-important: what was general and uncertain, implied through questions, becomes particular and explicit. More significant still, whereas the scene in stanza I is simply descriptive, with some erotic suggestion—a straightforward, composite recollection of vase-illustrations and paintings that Keats had seen—the images in stanzas II and III are much more of his own making,* deliberately chosen, one cannot doubt, in order to communicate something that he was feeling intensely about human experience. At any rate they certainly involve attitudes to that experience. Further, Keats is now himself passionately, and increasingly, identified with his images. For these reasons it is best to regard the scene that is represented in stanzas II and III as a second, and separate, picture.

This second scene has three constituents—leafy trees, a youth who is playing a pipe,† and two lovers. Of these images the least complicated is the trees, clothed in their fresh spring-time foliage:

> Ah, happy, happy boughs! that cannot shed
> Your leaves, nor ever bid the Spring adieu.‡

---

* This is not to say that Keats owed nothing here to Greek vases and to paintings with which he was familiar.

† It is perhaps just possible to conceive the 'fair youth' and 'happy melodist' as two separate figures on the frieze. But as stanza III repeats the subjects of the trees and the lovers, it is reasonable to assume that the 'happy melodist' is a repetition of the 'fair youth'. The 'song' of the 'fair youth' is merely a synonym for music, as the later phrase 'piping songs' makes clear.

‡ There is no reason why (as Wasserman argues, in *The Finer Tone*, pp. 22 ff.) we should take the iterated 'happy' as a hint of the 'pleasure-thermometer' and read the stanza in the light of Endymion's speech on happiness. Keats's turn of expression here, and its implications, is essentially the same as that in the opening of 'In a drear-nighted December':

> In a drear-nighted December,
> Too happy, happy tree,
> Thy branches ne'er remember
> Their green felicity.

Here the trees are 'happy' because they are insensible to change, the loss

326

As we have described elsewhere, Keats's sensibility was obsessed by vegetation, and there can be little doubt that these trees on the urn symbolize sensuous beauty. Keats is indulging in the age-old poet's dream of a beauty that is physical and yet beyond change and dissolution: these trees that can never be bare are the opposite of the 'morning rose' and 'globed peonies', with their brief moment of beauty and perfection; and he is escaping for a while from that sorrowful realization in the other ode of 'Beauty that must die'.

The second image, the 'fair youth' and 'happy melodist' piping under the trees, most probably stands for another key-reference in the odes—'poesy', and, closely linked with this, fame or ambition. But what of Keats's particular interpretation of the figure here?—that he cannot leave his song and that he is happy because he is

> *unwearied*,
> For ever piping songs *for ever new*.

One critic, Cleanth Brooks, suggests that there is a certain sadness in Keats's attitude to the 'fair youth'. He writes: 'in the case of "thou canst not leave Thy song", one could interpret: the musician cannot leave the song even if he would: he is fettered to it, a prisoner.'* Yet, not to emphasize the tentative, uncommitted manner in which Brooks hints at 'darker implication' in stanza II, this interpretation is contradicted by Keats's phrase 'happy melodist' in his second reference. It is much more likely that when he wrote 'thou canst not leave Thy song'—in conjunction with 'nor ever can these trees be bare'—he meant that nothing could tear the youth away from his happy song. In this elysium dream poesy is as eternal as beauty, and the stimulus to this particular imagining was

---

of summer beauty, 'passed joy', etc. In the Ode the trees are 'happy' because they enjoy an everlasting spring-time. But though the pathetic fallacy remains, there is the difference in the Ode that the poet's own happiness is involved.

* *The Well Wrought Urn*, p. 145.

almost certainly Keats's fear, and possible premonition, that death would soon snatch him away from song. It is not irrelevant to remember that when he was writing his odes he was far from well: on 14 June, and again on 17 June, we find him excusing himself for not walking over to his sister at Walthamstow, while he was at the time considering the idea of a voyage for health reasons, possibly as a surgeon on an East Indiaman.

Keats's second comment on the image, that the melodist is 'unwearied', piping songs 'ever new', has been explained by relating it to the earlier 'Heard melodies are sweet' lines and arguing that Keats is expressing the platonic ideal of poetry.* Again, as we have already shown, the 'melodist, unwearied' with 'songs for ever new' as a natural elaboration, may to some extent be a recollection of 'some unwearied Minstrel' in Collins's *The Passions*.† But it is much more probable that Keats was imagining an ideal poetic state of perpetual tireless creation—this dream intensified by the fact that he had only just emerged from a trying period of sterility and was far from satisfied by what he was doing in this period of the odes.‡ Probably, too, 'unwearied' carries a hint of his exhausting distractions from song—ill health, money-troubles, his absorption in Fanny Brawne.

There is one further possible significance of the piper to be touched on. He is a 'fair youth'. The phrase may be merely decorative, written down without much thought; but it may also be a conscious contradiction of what Keats had said in the *Nightingale* ode of the human life.

---

* See Sir Maurice Bowra, *The Romantic Imagination*, p. 141—'The ideal song beyond all existing songs has an eternal freshness because it is not actual song but the essence of song presupposed in any music which we make or hear.'

† This possible recollection from a wholly joyous passage is another reason for questioning the 'darker implication' that Cleanth Brooks finds.

‡ His letters at this time contain several references to his 'indolence', and on 9 June he wrote to Miss Jeffrey, 'I have been very idle lately, very averse to writing' (*Letters*, p. 347).

> Where youth grows pale, and spectre-thin, and dies;

and certainly, along with the love that is 'for ever young', it helps to suggest that the elysium of Keats's imagination is one of perennial youth as well as of unfading beauty and eternal song.

In the odes (and in one or two other poems belonging to this period, like 'Why did I laugh') there are three matters around which Keats's thoughts are perpetually turning—love and beauty, 'poesy', fame and ambition. It is the lovers who furnish the third subject in the imagined urn scene, and this theme is the one that is most extensively and complexly treated.

Here Keats's 'blissful imaginings'* are sharpened by an explicit contrast with the experienced reality that stimulates them—

> All breathing human passion far above,
> That leaves a heart high-sorrowful and cloy'd,
> A burning forehead, and a parching tongue.

As we read these lines, the most powerful immediate effect is probably created by the last, with its intense image of physical discomfort and sickness. Literally translated, the 'burning forehead' and 'parching tongue' spell fever, like the appearance of the love-destroyed Knight in *La Belle Dame Sans Merci:*

> I see a lilly on thy brow,
> With anguish moist and fever dew;[6]

and though Keats may have been enjoying one of his rare spells of happiness with Fanny Brawne when he wrote this ode, he is certainly confessing that the 'breathing human passion' that he has known is physically and emotionally exhausting, a ravage of his being and a potent source of his fever. Nor, as we have shown elsewhere, is this by any means

---

* Newell Ford's expression from one of his definitions of Keats's 'prefigurative imagination'—'a feelingful faith in the prefigurative veracity of blissful imaginings' (*The Prefigurative Imagination of John Keats*, p. 88).

an isolated note in his poems and letters. For instance, there is that revealing wish at the close of the first version of the 'Bright star' sonnet, written only a short while before the ode:

> To hear, to feel her tender-taken breath,
> *Half passionless*, and so swoon on to death.

This 'breathing human passion' of actuality is not only feverishly exhausting; it is also cloying,* and one assumes from line 29 that this is chiefly why the heart is left 'high-sorrowful'. The poem *Fancy*, so close to the *Ode on a Grecian Urn* in its main impulse, communicates just the same impression:

> Every thing is spoilt by use:
> Where's the cheek that doth not fade,
> Too much gaz'd at? Where's the maid
> Whose lip mature is ever new?
> Where's the eye, however blue
> Doth not weary? Where's the face
> One would meet in every place?
> Where's the voice, however soft,
> One would hear so very oft?
> At a touch sweet Pleasure melteth
> Like to bubbles when rain pelteth.[7]

If the ground of reality, sketched in the last three lines of stanza III, is straightforward and familiar enough, the dream of love that Keats embodies in his imaginary scene on the urn is much more difficult to grasp, or to accept. One thing at least is clear: in the place of the beauty who 'cannot keep her lustrous eyes', we have the vision of a beloved who 'cannot fade', who is part of the eternal, unchanging beauty. But

---

* This word is an important and significant one in Keats's poetry at this time, and it is not only to be found in a love context. See *To Fancy* (ll. 13–15):

> Autumn's red-lipp'd fruitage too,
> Blushing through the mist and dew
> Cloys with tasting . . .

and in *Bards of Passion* (ll. 27–8):

> Where your other souls are joying,
> Never slumber'd, never cloying.

beyond this we are tangled in contradictions that are hard to reconcile. With all his sense of the cloying and debilitation of passionate sensuous love, Keats reveals no wish to transcend it for something more spiritual: his ideal, 'happy' love remains

> For ever warm and still to be enjoy'd,
> For ever panting, and for ever young.*

Yet somehow, he implies, this love that is unchanged in substance is no longer cloying. Again, while his description of 'breathing human passion' implies a yearning for love that has a 'quietness', is no more feverish, he is at the same time rhapsodizing a love in which pleasurable sensation is persistent and persistently *intense*—'for ever warm' and 'for ever panting'. 'Panting', a particularly revealing word, reminds us of a sonnet to Reynolds that he had written a year before. This poem not only closely resembles the ode in its general mood but expresses the very aspiration we are discussing, especially the longing that we might 'keep our souls in one eternal pant'. Further, if this sonnet has an illuminative bearing on the ode, it is important to note the autograph conclusion, so much more candidly truthful than the transcript version that Garrod prints:†

> This morn and yester eve, my friend, has taught
> Such Greediness of Pleasure.⁸

These contradictions, which particularly justify F. R. Leavis' critical stricture on the ode—'Getting it both ways—the poem *is* essentially that'‡— may perhaps be loosely reconciled. Possibly there can be a love that is passionately and sensuously intense without being feverish; but it is hard to believe that

---

* It is most unlikely that there is any ambiguity—even unconscious—in 'still' here, as Wasserman maintains (*The Finer Tone*, p. 36). The meaning must be 'yet' to correspond with 'Bold lover, never, never, canst thou kiss' and 'panting'. If 'still' also means 'forever', then the love *is* enjoyed: the lover has his 'bliss', and there is no longer expectation.

† This morn, my friend, and yester evening taught
  Me how to harbour such a happy thought.

‡ *Revaluations*, p. 253.

the 'quietness' of spirit that Keats longed for could ever exist in, or along with, such love, and harder still—with that crucial word 'panting'—to believe that he at this time really perceived a satisfying compromise and reconciliation. In an anxiety to explain away contradictions we are in danger of reading into the poem something that is not there.

However, the first contradiction (and possibly the second) is to some extent reconciled in the poem itself, for the ideal love of Keats's happy dream is an anticipation that stops, perpetually, just short of fulfilment and satisfaction. Unlike the sea-drowned, resurrected lovers who take on immortality in the more naïve *Endymion*, the Lover and the Maiden do not embrace; their 'happy, happy love' is 'still to be enjoyed':

> Bold Lover, never, never canst thou kiss,
> Though winning near the goal—yet, do not grieve;
> She cannot fade, though thou hast not thy bliss . . .*

So too with the beauty that is symbolized by the 'happy boughs': it is not full-flush summer of roses and 'globed peonies', but stirring, expectant spring-time. In this way, in anticipation rather than consummation, the love that is still very much a 'breathing human passion' may avoid cloyment; and for the same reason perhaps 'quietness' may be found in a love that is warm and panting. As Cleanth Brooks has conclusively put it, the urn maiden, even more than the urn itself, is the 'still unravish'd bride of quietness'.† Keats's treatment of his lovers has fully elaborated the paradoxical theme succinctly announced in the opening line.

In the sonnet to Reynolds that we have mentioned the condition of the wish that we could 'keep our souls in one eternal pant' is the annihilation of time—or rather a trans-

---

* Cleanth Brooks (*The Well Wrought Urn*, pp. 144–5) finds a 'darker implication' in these lines. But, as I read them, Keats is not comforting the Lover in actual grief: he is reassuring him that, in his situation, he never has any reason to grieve.

† *Op. cit.* p. 144.

formation of our sense of time so that a day or week would be immensely prolonged—'So could we live long life in little space'. In the opening of the ode Keats addresses the urn as the foster-child of 'slow time', by which he means that it belongs to a dimension of time that is different from that of our own brief individual lives: it has survived centuries and so can speak to the successive 'generations'* in turn. However, neither of these imaginings is strictly relevant to his vision of the trees, the melodist, and the lover, for their ideality and felicity lie in the fact that they are beyond time, in an eternally arrested moment.

There can be no question that this eternal moment, out of time, is an indispensable *condition* of Keats's 'blissful imaginings' in the ode. But though, since he is feigning to write about a work of art, he may very well be implying that art has the power of making the fugitive permanent, there is no reason for thinking, any more than in stanza vii of the *Nightingale* ode, that he is chiefly trying to express some visionary or mystical apprehension of timelessness. It is all a matter of appreciating his stress. Out of his own actual unhappiness he is indulging in a dream of supreme felicity, and the constituents of this are such as no true mystic would for a moment accept: sexual passion, undecaying physical beauty, and an eternity of songs and poesy. The arrested moment is a necessary condition of his vision because happiness, as here conceived, is a fresh, throbbing state of expectancy, and unhappiness the exhaustion and disillusionment of consummation. He had said exactly the same thing in *Fancy*, where 'fancy' had been celebrated as freedom from time and a means of escape from the inevitably cloying pleasures of nature and love. The *Ode on a Grecian Urn* is an immeasurably finer poem of course, but it is no less a

---

* Cleanth Brooks (*op. cit.* p. 150) writes admirably on the impact of this word, which of course also appears in the *Nightingale* ode: 'The word "generation" ... is very rich. It means on one level "that which is generated"—that which springs from human loins—Adam's breed; and yet, so intimately is death wedded to men, the word "generation" has become, as here, a measure of time.'

'luxury' and no more serious, philosophically speaking, than *Fancy*—or, for that matter, than the sonnet to Reynolds. Further, since Keats is drawing solace from a work of art (though imaginary), the ode has a great deal in common with the *Epistle to Reynolds*.

A smooth line of steady rhythmical beat, cast in a dramatic interrogative form—

Who are these coming to the sacrifice?

—leads us effortlessly into the third imagined scene on the urn. It is as though we are moving our eyes forward along one continuous frieze; and what we see is wholly enchanting. But, apart from the silence of the little town, the scene has no apparent connexion with what has gone before, and at some point a feeling of discontinuity, or of the stanza as a detached passage, arises. Clearly this picture of pagan sacrifice and a deserted town cannot be immediately related to such obviously personal experience as lies behind the two preceding stanzas. Has the description then any meaning, any relevance in the general pattern of the ode, or is it, with all its loveliness, merely decorative like the last lines of the first stanza, something of a digression that would go to justify Bridges's comment on the 'unprogressive'* nature of the poem?

Though this is perhaps the chief critical problem that the ode raises, critics have been curiously unconcerned about it.† Even Cleanth Brooks in his close analysis goes no further in general interpretation than to state that the stanza 'emphasises, not individual aspiration and desire, but communal life'.‡ Sir Maurice Bowra, in another recent study, says little more than

---

* *Collected Essays*, Vol. IV, p. 132.

† For all his microscopic general explication of the ode (including stanza IV) even Wasserman fails to ask why this particular scene emerges at this point. I might add that Wasserman's analysis of this stanza strikes me as particularly misguided, as when he argues that the significance of its questions is to remind us of dimensions of time and space.

‡ *Op. cit.* p. 147.

that the stanza expresses 'luminous order'—* the Apollonian element in the poem that is the antithesis of the earlier Dionysian element.

Yet the problem we have posed is by no means unanswerable. It so happens that this picture of pagan sacrificial rites, which almost certainly owed a good deal to Claude's 'Sacrifice to Apollo', exhibited at the British Institute in 1816, occurs on three other occasions in Keats's poetry. This fact not only proves that the image bore some special significance for him, but enables us to perceive, to some degree at any rate, what this significance was.

Just over twelve months before the ode, in March 1818, he had sent Reynolds a letter in verse that included the following lines:

> The sacrifice goes on; the pontiff knife
> Gleams in the sun, the milk-white heifer lows,
> The pipes go shrilly, the libation flows . . .'

Though these lines are immediately preceded by a reference to 'Titian colours' and followed by a fancifully adapted description of Claude's 'Enchanted Castle', which is mentioned by name, they are almost certainly a reminiscence of the 'Sacrifice to Apollo'. But much more interesting than their origin is their close resemblance to the opening lines of stanza IV in the ode:

> Who are these coming to the sacrifice?
> To what green altar, O mysterious priest,
> Lead'st thou that heifer lowing at the skies?

Further, though the 'little town', which is vaguely suggested in the background of Claude's picture, does not occur in that part of the *Epistle to Reynolds* where Keats is recalling the 'Sacrifice to Apollo', references elsewhere in the poem to the sea, mountains, lakes and 'neighbour rills' build up very much the same sort of Claude-like background as is evoked in the ode by the lines,

---

* *The Romantic Imagination*, p. 128.

What little town by river or sea shore
Or mountain-built . . .

However, the *Epistle to Reynolds* not only demonstrates that this picture in the ode of a priest at a sacrificial altar, against a background of sea and mountainous landscape, was deeply impressed on Keats's mind. Notwithstanding its humorous touches, the poem is the expression of serious and complex emotions, and in these the Claude landscapes were deeply involved. For one thing Keats was sending the poem to divert and comfort his friend 'while sick and ill he lies'; and this was no mere conventional politeness, for he felt intensely about Reynolds's ill-health, which, occurring at the same time as Tom's, seemed part of a malign conspiracy of sickness surrounding his life.[10] Again, if the descriptive medley of Claude's paintings had this conscious purpose, the implication of the poem is that the composition of it also served as a relief for Keats himself from 'detested moods', such as the vision of the 'eternal fierce destruction' in nature that he so vividly depicts. Further, the Claude recollections constitute a beautiful, if deliberately contrived, day-dream to counterbalance another sort of day- and night-dream—

Of Shapes, and Shadows and Remembrances
That every other minute vex and please.[11]

—while the last part of the poem is principally concerned with the theme of happiness.

It is likely then that whatever it was that in the first place suggested to Keats this sacrificial scene for his third picture on the urn, he admitted the inspiration because the scene was associated for him with solace and ministration, even perhaps through some obscure memory of his poem to Reynolds. Here was one sort of picture that would make his imagined urn 'a friend to man' in the midst of woe—if, that is, we may assume that the thought of the concluding stanza was in Keats's mind from the outset.

Of course these connexions establish nothing more than a private sort of significance for stanza IV of the ode—one that, as readers, we can never apprehend except remotely and intellectually as 'information'. We did not write the *Epistle to Reynolds*, and it was in the writing of this, for Keats himself, that the solacing associations of the sacrificial scene were established. However, if we pursue our investigations of the scene a little farther, we shall discover that this picture in stanza IV is after all something that we can richly and directly share once we have found the key to it: what emerges is that the scene had come to possess a special symbolical significance for Keats.

The key to this symbolism lies in *Endymion*. Here, in the first half of Book I, Keats gives us his most unmistakable and fully elaborated version of the 'Sacrifice to Apollo'. There is the same background of distant sea and thickly wooded, mountainous country, the same lawny clearing on which stands a marble altar. Into this scene, when

> Apollo's upward fire
> Made every eastern cloud a silvery pyre
> Of brightness,[12]

enter first a troop of children and then the Latmian folk accompanied by their venerable priest. Rites, including a hymn to Pan, are celebrated at the altar, and the rest of the day is spent in a joyous festival of games, singing, dancing, and story-telling. On this occasion there is no sacrificial heifer 'lowing at the skies', and the folk are shepherds, not the inhabitants of some small town. But, apart from these small variations, the scene is the same one that Keats was to depict both in his verse letter to Reynolds and in the ode. He had also sketched something like it, a few weeks before he made a start on *Endymion*, in the dedicatory sonnet to Leigh Hunt that introduces *Poems* (1817).

Now if we read the description of the Festival of Pan in *Endymion* attentively, several points emerge that have an important bearing on the re-appearance and significance of the scene in the *Ode on a Grecian Urn*. First, as we have already demonstrated in the earlier study of *Endymion*, Keats treats the occasion as one of universal joyousness. To some extent no doubt this atmosphere was a deliberate artistic contrivance, for the second half of the Book goes on to deal with the contrasting woe of the hero, Endymion. But the happiness that Keats suggests is not entirely for such an aesthetic effect, and it is evident from several passages that these 'fair living forms', who unconscious 'cull Time's sweet first-fruits', represent for him a Golden Age of simple, happy, satisfied living, one of the things of beauty that are a joy for ever. That his hellenism did include some such belief in a Golden Age in early Greek times is apparent from other poems. The belief is present, by implication at least, in the opening line of his dedicatory sonnet to Leigh Hunt,

> Glory and loveliness have passed away,

which is pointed by a picture of primitive Greek worship of Flora; while in his fragmentary *Ode to May* he had dreamed of being one of the old Greek bards,

> Rich in the simple worship of a day.[13]

It is important to notice these phrases like 'simple worship of a day', 'their old piety', and (in the ode itself) 'pious morn',* since, whether or not as an obscure compensation for his agnosticism, Keats certainly appears to have regarded this simple piety and pagan nature-worship as an essential part of the happiness in this Golden Age. Probably that is why his vision of it so frequently takes the form of a scene of worship and sacrificial rites.

Finally in the description of the Pan festival in *Endymion* we may trace an expression—a fugitive one, it is true—of his belief that this Golden Age of the early Greeks is immortalized in their art. These 'fair creatures', he declares, are

---

* See also: Yet even in these days so far retir'd
                 From happy pieties . . . .   (*Ode to Psyche*, 40–1)

> not yet dead,
> But *in old marbles* ever beautiful,[14]

and in writing 'old marbles' he almost certainly meant marble urns, not statuary.

If in reading the ode, we bear in mind these implications of the 'green altar' scene in *Endymion*,* we are in a position to appreciate the relevance and full significance of the fourth stanza. Keats's image of sacrificial rites on a 'pious morn' is certainly not digressive or merely decorative. Deriving from his belief in a Golden Age at the time of the ancient Greeks, it stands for communal happiness,† and is thus complementary with his picture of ideal individual felicity in the two previous stanzas. Further, just as the earlier scene conveys the impression of youth, springtime, and of expectancy rather than consummation for the individual, so this one represents the Greek folk‡ in their youth and primitive freshness—this general impression being particularly suggested by the morning setting and perhaps by the force of the phrase 'green altar'. If one may point this by a further reference to the *Endymion* passage (though on this occasion quite without the warrant of anything in the text of the ode), one guesses that these folk are also those

> whose young children's children bred
> Thermopylae its heroes.[15]

But what of Keats's emphasis on the deserted 'little town', and what in particular of the last lines of the stanza?—

---

* The altar in *Endymion* is decked 'With a tress Of flowers budded newly'.

† While Keats's picture is mainly a backwards-looking, idealizing dream, there may be one touch of realism in it. 'Peaceful citadel' indicates that the folk are free from the miseries of war, and behind this detail may be something of his strong anti-militarism.

‡ Wasserman's comment is quite beside the point—'unlike the men-gods, those eternal youths who have been the actors in the drama up to this point, the inhabitants are only humble "folk" ' (*The Finer Tone*, p. 44). Keats's word is a natural one in the context.

> And, little town, thy streets for ever more
> Will silent be; and not a soul to tell
> Why thou art desolate, can e'er return.*

This is undoubtedly a passage that may be said to give the ode a 'darker implication', and most of us will concur with Cleanth Brooks when he writes: 'The little town . . . is endowed with a poignance beyond anything else in the poem.'† Almost every critic who has written on the ode has testified to the haunting sadness of these lines—to their quiet, plaintive music and their deeply moving image of desolation. Yet once more, what of their relevance? Is the sadness they convey gratuitous, fanciful?

On the contrary. Bearing in mind the significance of the preceding lines of the stanza, and observing the striking parallel effect of 'faery lands forlorn', which comes at exactly the same point in the development of the *Nightingale* ode, we see that the little town, 'emptied', 'silent', 'desolate',‡ represents the intrusion of disenchantment, another breath of reality blowing against the dream. As in the *Ode to a Nightingale* 'forlorn' communicates an ultimate realization that the Spenserian world of wonder and romance is past and unattainable, so in the *Grecian Urn* the silent, desolate town expresses Keats's sorrowful realization that there is no way back, except through the glimpses afforded by art, to the Golden Age of the Greeks. In truth, 'Glory and loveliness have passed away'. The parallel passage in *Endymion* also contains a mournful hint of Grecian beauty swallowed up in time's oblivion:

> Aye, those fair living forms swam heavenly
> To tunes forgotten—out of memory;[16]

---

* Bowra (*The Romantic Imagination*, p. 133) makes the interesting suggestion that Keats's idea may have been a recollection from the Bacchic ode of *Endymion* IV—especially of the lines,
> Why have ye left your bowers desolate,
> Your lutes, and gentler fate?
† *The Well Wrought Urn*, p. 148.
‡ 'Desolate' is the obvious direct link with 'faery lands *forlorn*'.

and there is surely the same lament for yet another poetry-rich dream world of the past in *Robin Hood:*

> No! those days are gone away,
> And their hours are old and gray,
> And their minutes buried all
> Under the down-trodden pall
> Of the leaves of many years . . .[17]

If at this point we may hazard a brief summary of Keats's intention in the ode, what he has been concerned with is not mystical insight or empathic experience* but a vision of felicity that is presented through a group of images with which he is closely, and at times rhapsodically, identified. So far as his aspirations turn towards individual bliss (as they mainly do) his dream takes its direction from the actuality of 'woe' that is continuously implied throughout the poem and explicitly referred to in the concluding stanza. This way of reading the ode is strongly supported by the *Ode on Indolence*, which also employs an urn—a 'dreamy urn'—for the embodiment of a dream, and, in its attempt to exorcise love, ambition, and poesy for their 'fever-fits', deals primarily with the poet's quest of happiness. The difference in scope between the two odes is that the *Ode on Indolence* is more negative, more limited and subjective, and less related to the woe of the generations than the *Ode on a Grecian Urn*. Further, this reading of the ode is entirely consistent with the opening invocation to the urn—

> Sylvan historian, who canst thus express
> A flowery tale more sweetly than our rhyme

for if we give these lines any serious heed at all, their reference to a sweet, flowery tale sounds much more like the prelude to a poem of delightful beauty than to some profound spiritual or metaphysical utterance. The opening line of the final stanza,

---

* This is the heart of Wasserman's interpretation.

which is unique among the odes for its emphatic, summarizing conclusion, leaves the same impression—

> O Attic shape! Fair attitude!

This apostrophe leads into a short, recapitulatory description, slightly reminiscent of the first stanza, that once more enables us to see the pictorial design of the urn generalized and as a whole.* Then come the rather obscure lines,

> Thou, silent form, dost tease us out of thought
> As doth Eternity.

To understand what Keats is saying here we must appreciate that for him speculative thought always had an inevitable bias towards the 'miseries of the world'; hence its pain. One of his most memorable expressions of this conclusion is his description of the 'chamber of Maiden-Thought', which, intoxicating at first through its novelty, finally has the effect of 'convincing one's nerves that the world is full of Misery and Heartbreak, Pain, Sickness and oppression—whereby this Chamber of Maiden Thought becomes gradually darken'd'.[18] Nearer in time to the *Ode on a Grecian Urn* there is the third stanza of the *Nightingale* ode, in which, in a context describing our various mortal woes, occur the lines,

> Where but to think is to be full of sorrow
> And leaden-eyed despairs.

Another indispensable clue to his meaning is to be found in a passage from the *Epistle to Reynolds:*

> Things cannot to the will
> Be settled, but they tease us out of thought.[19]

---

* Cleanth Brooks (*op. cit.* p. 149) pounces on '*marble* men and maidens' for another paradox. In my opinion 'marble' is merely descriptive and no more significant than in the *Endymion* phrase, 'in old marbles beautiful'. However, 'forest branches' may have had some association with 'old pieties': see *To Psyche*, l. 38, 'When holy were the haunted forest boughs'.

Here, by implication, he is again considering the 'thought' that is concerned with the world and life as they actually are, especially in their painful and distressing aspects. But chiefly he is saying that such thinking is brought to a perplexed, defeated stand by our realization that life in actuality is not as we would have it—'Things cannot to the will be settled'.* For a concrete illustration of this 'teasing' nature of thought, a breeder of 'vexing speculations' as he elsewhere calls it, we may turn to what he says in one of his letters to Bailey: '"Why should Woman suffer?" Aye. Why should she? . . . These things are, and he who feels how incompetent the most skyey Knight errantry is to heal this bruised fairness *is like a sensitive leaf on the hot hand of thought.*'[20]

With these clues it is much easier to understand what Keats meant in the ode when he wrote:

> Thou, silent form, dost tease us out of thought
> As doth Eternity.

Admittedly, he has not been directly concerned with the problem of the things that 'cannot to the will Be settled'. Rather he has been engaged in asserting that 'will' and demonstrating its power to imagine a state of ideal felicity. Yet the imagination of this bliss, through the pictures on the urn, cannot but raise the vexing speculation why human life is so unlike our dreams and aspirations. Hence, among other effects, the urn 'tease[s] us out of thought'.

This explanation still leaves the phrase, 'As doth Eternity', unaccounted for. Possibly the simile commended itself to Keats

* Bowra's interpretation of this and the two previous lines—'Keat expresses his unwillingness to leave his own special approach to experience through imagination for something like philosophy, and his refusal is based on the belief that the mystery of things cannot be mastered by an act of will but forces us "out of thought", that is, from ordinary ways of thinking into the approach of the imagination' (*op. cit.* p. 143)—seems to me wrong at every point. The reasons for my objections will be plain from what I have written. But I should like to take up his first point. Surely Keats is not refusing philosophy but regretting that, as 'the love of good and ill', the philosophic attitude is not yet his—'and to philosophise I dare not yet'?

because his dream of perpetual youth, poesy, and uncloying love was dependent on timelessness—or eternity. On the other hand, there is no strong reason for believing that the urn has anything of consequence to say about eternity. After all, the phrase is a simile, and we may take 'Eternity' merely as one of numerous ideas Keats might have mentioned that have the effect of bringing our thoughts to a state of baffled arrest.

No doubt this suggested reading of the fourth and fifth lines gives the last stanza something of a jolting, to-and-fro effect, first, because—one or two passages apart—the urn has been predominantly an embodiment of delight, and secondly, because shortly afterwards it is represented as a supremely solacing 'friend to man' amid the woes of each generation. But the last stanza of the *Ode to a Nightingale*—as would be generally admitted—produces exactly the same effect, and in both poems the cause is identical: it is fancy clashing with the thought that cannot after all be suppressed, enchantment (reluctantly to be surrendered) with disenchantment—a fundamental uncertainty of spirit.

And amid these alternations, what are we to make of 'Cold Pastoral!'?

Many critics have done their best to justify the contradiction that is commonly felt to be created by this apostrophe and to explain in what senses the urn could after all be a 'cold' thing for Keats. But the contradiction is an extremely difficult one to sustain, and in spite of all the exegetic ingenuity that has been expended on the phrase,* the reader is to be forgiven if he still finds it obscure. To begin with, in the immediate context, 'cold' strikes as an odd epithet to apply to something that is such a profound source of solace. Again, however we choose to interpret the main body of the poem, we shall all agree that

* See Brooks (*The Well Wrought Urn*, pp. 149–50). But Brooks seems to be persuading himself with his own metaphors when he writes: 'The recognition that the men and maidens are *frozen*, fixed, arrested . . . the central paradox of the poem . . . comes to conclusion in the phrase, "Cold Pastoral".' Other critics—Garrod, for example—have taken this phrase for a false note like 'plaintive anthem' in the *Nightingale* ode.

the urn Keats depicts creates an intense impression of warm, pulsing life—at least in two of the three stanzas; and even for the third stanza, with all its sadness and silence, 'cold' is not the word. Finally, the sensation of coldness always has a peculiarly distastefulness, even abhorrence, for Keats, and is often evoked in a context of death.*

May the solution of these difficulties be that 'cold' is not Keats's own epithet at all, that he is giving us what may be the response of some men to a marble Grecian urn and then opposing to it his own belief? If this is the explanation, then he is saying—in harmony with the rest of the ode, surely—that his urn is the very antithesis of a 'cold Pastoral'.

The ode ends with two lines in which the urn, comforting the succeeding generations in their woe, is supposed to speak its own message.† In these lines, the heart of them, comes the most endlessly debated sentence in all Keats's poetry—'Beauty is truth, truth beauty'.

Now while a very large part of the analysis in this book has been based on the assumption that it is right and profitable when studying a major poet whose works are all parts of a developing homogeneous attitude to life, to use one of his poems (or a passage in a letter) to interpret another, this principle does not apply when we are trying to decide what Keats meant when he made his urn utter its aphorism, for the whole poem has been about that urn, and the aphorism is its conclusion expressed in the form of an overt statement. To elucidate that statement we must turn not to what Keats had written about beauty and truth—and their relationship—in his letters and other poems but to the four preceding stanzas of the ode—to the nature of the urn as he has presented it.

This leads to another important consideration that far too

---

* See *Endymion* II, 239–350, *passim*; *The Fall of Hyperion*, I, 107–34.
† See Bowra (*The Romantic Imagination*, pp. 145–6) for a sound discussion of the textual difficulty here, especially concerning the printing of the epigram in inverted commas.

many critics have overlooked. Keats's epigram is not a comment on some given work of art—*King Lear* or West's picture 'Death on a Pale Horse',* for instance. It is a conclusion on an imaginary work of art that he has preferred to invent for himself and that he has fashioned to embody his own dreams.

Further, it will be noticed that 'beauty' falls at the two places of main emphasis in a sentence—at the beginning and at the end. Not all readers will be in agreement on this point, but it is possible to feel that, as Keats has expressed his conclusion, the stress is rather more on 'beauty' than it is on 'truth'.

In the light of these considerations the urn's message is perhaps not really difficult to understand. Throughout the ode its frieze (the most important aspect of it so far as Keats is concerned) has been used to express a vision of ideal bliss—*if*, that is to say, things could be settled to the will. These aspirations and yearnings are 'beauty' or 'things of beauty', which in Keats's language means that they are not merely aesthetically pleasing but intensely to be desired and a source of ecstasy. Just before his conclusion he has admitted that this beauty, by reason of the contrast with actual human unhappiness that it forces on us, brings us to a baffled arrest of thought. However, in spite of this admission, he now asserts that such beautiful imaginings have their own validity and reality and so represent a kind of 'truth'—the only truth we can know on earth where 'thought' leads us into teasing and feverish perplexity. In brief, the urn's message is an affirmation, direct from the body of the poem, that beautiful dreams are not a vanity. If any further gloss is needed, we may perhaps find it in one of his remarks to Bailey, though admittedly this was written in mood of scepticism: 'probably every mental pursuit takes its reality and worth from the ardour of the pursuer.'[21]

* The point of these illustrations will be clear to those who read Murry's commentary on the ode (*The Mystery of Keats*, pp. 162–77). These two works are mentioned in one of the places in the *Letters* (p. 71) where Keats is discussing truth and beauty.

This, or something very like it, is what F. R. Leavis must have had in mind when he spoke of the 'obviousness' of Keats's aphorism, and when, with a gust that should have swept away the cobwebs of hyper-subtle speculation that still thickly overlay this ode, he added that the concluding pronouncement 'should cause no metaphysical tremors of excitement or illumination, and need no great profundity or ingenuity of any kind to elucidate it'.*

* *Revaluations*, p. 254.

CHAPTER X

SOME CONCLUSIONS

Thou art a dreaming thing;
A fever of thyself . . .

The Fall of Hyperion

Though this book has been primarily concerned with various particular aspects of Keats's work, several general conclusions have inevitably suggested themselves.

Of these the main one is that the bulk of his poetry, including most of what he wrote in 1819, is predominantly an expression of two activities—of 'luxury', or an intense, richly varied, and sometimes deliberately cultivated, relish of sensuous experience, and of a 'fancy' that is most commonly stimulated by what Leavis has called 'warm imaginings of an ideal life'.* Frequently these impulses run together, for his yearnings and dreams always take their substance and colour from his sensuous delight in living experience; but sometimes his writing is purely an expression of an unfailing sensuous gusto.

Such poetic creation is aptly and succinctly described by his own favourite word—'poesy'.†

'Luxury', 'fancy', 'poesy' . . . There remains one further keyword, also much used by Keats himself, that must be taken into account in any summary description and evaluation of his work; and, in view of the debate, and confusion, that has eddied round it, we may perhaps best approach it through a distinction that Maritain makes in his *Creative Intuition in Art and Poetry:*

---

* *Revaluations*, p. 254.

† Cf. *ibid.* p. 248: 'poetry was Poesy to the Keats of *Endymion* and the Odes.'

In the eyes of God all that exists is beautiful, to the very extent to which it participates in being. For the beauty that God beholds is transcendental beauty, which permeates every existent, to one degree or another. This is not the beauty that our senses perceive, and here we are obliged to introduce an new idea, the idea of aesthetic beauty, as contradistinguished to transcendental beauty. For when it comes to aesthetic beauty, we have to do with a province of beauty in which senses and sense perception play an essential part, and in which, as a result, not all things are beautiful. The presence of the senses, which depend on our fleshly constitution, is inherently involved in the notion of aesthetic beauty . . . In the eyes of God all things are more or less beautiful, none is ugly.[1]

In several of his letters Keats touches on something that he calls 'the principle of beauty in all things',[2] and it is arguable that what he had in mind was a conception that comes very close to Maritain's 'transcendental beauty', by which 'all things are more or less beautiful, none is ugly'. Again, it is certain that the Induction to *The Fall of Hyperion* embodies some intimation of this God-like comprehensive vision that is 'transcendental beauty':

> My power, which to me is still a curse,
> Shall be to thee a wonder; for the scenes
> Still swooning vivid through my globed brain
> With an electral changing misery
> Thou shalt with those dull mortal eyes behold,
> Free from all pain, if wonder pain thee not.*

But these are the exceptions, and in all the rest of Keats's writing, including the odes, the 'beauty' that he cherishes and cultivates as one of his three or four absolutes ('poesy', fame, and love being the others) is certainly what Maritain describes as 'aesthetic beauty'. By definition this 'aesthetic beauty' is self-evidently the quality of his 'poesy' when it is expressing his sensuous delight and gusto in warm, breathing life. But it is no less the quality of his writing when he is soaring on the

---

* I, 243–8. And, of course, the vision of Moneta's face (I, 256–71).

wings of 'fancy', for since this fancy is most commonly impelled by longings, aspirations, dreams—a dissatisfaction with actuality—it necessarily carries the implication that 'not all things are beautiful'. For this reason the *Ode to a Nightingale* and *Ode on a Grecian Urn* belong as much to the province of 'aesthetic beauty' as *Endymion* does.

There are of course other, quite different opinions about the nature of Keats's poetry. A generation ago, in his *Keats and Shakespeare*, Middleton Murry maintained that in much of his writing besides the Induction to *The Fall of Hyperion* Keats achieved a Shakespearean vision and comprehension of human life ('Ripeness is all') that would certainly fall within Maritain's category of 'transcendental beauty'. More recently, as we have shown, several critics have been intent on demonstrating a profoundly metaphysical Keats whose subtle insights and speculations extend far beyond the alleged neoplatonic allegory of *Endymion*. For Wasserman, who has taken this sort of interpretation the furthest to date, even *The Eve of St Agnes* is made to yield an elaborate metaphysical meaning; and when we find him talking of the 'ideological system'* of Keats's poetry and of 'the oxymoronic ontology within which he thinks',† we realize that we have travelled far from the once widely supported conclusions of Arthur Symons, who roundly stated that Keats 'was not troubled about his soul, the meaning of the universe, or any other metaphysical questions, to which he shows a happy indifference, or rather, a placid unconsciousness'.‡

Several of the studies in this book, directly or by implication, have challenged these contentions that Keats was a poet of Shakespearean 'ripeness' or acceptance, a mystic, or a deeply metaphysical writer; and there would be no point in repeating what has already been said. However, before breaking off from this debate, which will no doubt continue

---

* *The Finer Tone*, p. 185.
† *Ibid.* p. 180.
‡ *The Romantic Movement*, p. 303.

for a long time yet, something further must be said about a poem that has never been more than glanced at in these pages—the Induction to *The Fall of Hyperion*.

Obviously this important and, in some respects of detail, obscure poem cannot be discussed in a few sentences. But if one thing may be said briefly and simply, it is that the work is the imagination (and to some extent the achievement) of a complete transformation of Keats's poetic nature—nothing less than a dying into life. This new sort of poetic utterance that is Moneta's gift to him is not only immeasurably finer than the old one; it is of a different order. All that he has written up to this time is merely 'a feast of summer fruits' and a 'cloudy swoon',[3] and if he fails now to make the transforming ascent of the steps to Moneta's altar

> thy bones
> Will wither in few years, and vanish so
> That not the quickest eye could find a grain
> Of what thou now art on that pavement cold.[4]

How, in the light of such self-condemnation as this, more severe and penetrating than anything the most hostile critic is ever likely to write, can we believe Keats's poetry was of the profound kind that Murry and Wasserman in their different ways allege it to be?

On the other hand, if what Keats had written up to the autumn of 1819 was mainly a creation of luxury, aesthetic beauty, and fancy, then the dying into life that is symbolically enacted in the Induction, and the strong self-criticism that this ascent carries with it, is perfectly understandable. As he lays hold of the truth that

> None can usurp this height . . .
> But those to whom the miseries of the world
> Are misery, and will not let them rest,[5]

he is at last decisively turning, much sooner than he had anticipated in *Sleep and Poetry*, from the joys of ten years of 'poesy'

to
                                             a nobler life,
                        Where I may find the agonies, the strife
                        Of human hearts.[6]

   Again, while the higher conception of poetry that is embodied in the Induction still envisages the poet as a 'dreamer',
distinguished from those who labour actively for human good,
it is fairly certain that Moneta's condemnatory words,

                        Thou art a dreaming thing;
                     A fever of thyself,[7]

refer principally to Keats's poetry up to this time—to the bad
or inferior sort of dream-poetry, so to speak. The proof of this
reading lies in Moneta's charge of 'fever', for, as Keats himself
fully realized, the 'poesy' that he had hitherto cultivated was
inseparable from a continuously feverish condition, and the
letters plainly show that he was striving towards a serener,
quieter, more balanced kind of writing and imaginative life.
His ultimate ideal of poetry certainly involved a terrible burden, and it may be that even the admirable type of dreamer-
poet, never able to keep pain and joy distinct,

                           venoms all his days,
               Bearing more woe than all his sins deserve.[8]

But in view of what he says at various places in the letters of
1819, it is quite impossible to believe that he accepted 'fever'
as an inevitable part of the true poet's destiny. Further, there
is the same condemnation of his past poetry as a thing of inferior dreaming and feverish agitation in the later speech of
Moneta that he intended to cancel or at least radically revise:*

   * Murry is probably right in his repeated contention that Keats wanted
188–210 deleted. But he is quite wrong in asserting that the lines 'conflict with the real argument of the poem' (*The Mystery of Keats*, p. 192). The
passage is consistent with the rest of the Induction. Keats's main reason for
wishing to delete or revise it was almost certainly because the poet-
dreamer antithesis confused the terminology of the poem. He had already
accepted his ideal poet as a 'dreamer'. In the antithesis he is thinking of
the inferior 'dreamer'.

Art thou not of the dreamer tribe?
The poet and the dreamer are distinct,
Diverse, sheer opposite, antipodes.
The one pours out a balm upon the world,
The other vexes it.[9]

If the greater part of Keats's writing—with the notable exception of the Induction to *The Fall of Hyperion*, and possibly the ode *To Autumn*—is regarded as 'poesy', it follows that he is emphatically *not* with Shakespeare and not in the very first rank of our poets. That such high claims have been made for his poetry is due partly to the romantic tendency to measure him by his promise instead of his achievement (and there is no question that his work, including the letters, reveals immense potentialities),* partly to the full and necessary swing of the pendulum away from the nineteenth-century estimate of a hedonistic, aesthete-poet, with some regrettable and unhealthy tendencies, and partly to the false assumption that the maturity, intelligence, and ranging speculations so often displayed in the letters are automatically carried over into the poetry. On the other hand, the 'poesy' of his writing does not make him a minor poet; nor are we by any means forced to return to the Victorian evaluation.

Not that it is easy, at this point in the middle of the twentieth century, to establish a firm and acceptable judgment, for he is a poet who suffers particularly, in distorted interpretation as well as evaluation, from the unbalance of contemporary criticism. Largely (one suspects) because we are inclined to regard poetry as a substitute for religion and philosophy—Arnold's prophecy fulfilled—we have forgotten, or ignore, the fundamental commonplace that the poet's business is to delight as well as to teach. A disciplined seriousness has come into our reading of poetry, joy has gone out. We throw an excessive stress on the significance of what a poet has

---

* On the other hand, as Gittings reminds us (*John Keats: The Living Year*, p. 191), there is the possibility that Keats had burnt himself out as a poet through the immense productivity of 1819.

353

to say, with the result that most of our current estimates are heavily biased in favour of poetry that expresses deep, complex, meaningful experience. This explains why some modern critics have shown little regard for Keats's 'poesy', apart from an approving word for its integrity, or even dismissed admiration for it as a sign of adolescent immaturity. On the other hand, this same bias may sometimes tempt us to read into a poet's work more than is actually there, especially when we wish to defend his reputation; and one cannot help feeling that some of the recent attempts to create a 'metaphysical' Keats have been unconsciously prompted by this motive. When we do address ourselves to poems as creations out of words, images, sounds, and rhythms, our attention tends to concentrate heavily on mechanism and efficiency and such verbal qualities as lend themselves to close semantic discussion. This inclination has led critics like Cleanth Brooks and Wasserman to apply to Keats's poetry a kind of analysis that is not really suited to Romantic writing, while both of them rigorously eschew anything that might encourage an unanalytical delight.

Once we succeed in bringing pleasure back to its rightful place in the reading of poetry, Keats's 'poesy' in such works as *The Eve of St Agnes*, *Lamia*, the odes, and even part of *Endymion* will assuredly be recognized as belonging to the highest order of its kind. Many poets afford us great sensuous delight, but very few of them have the vitality and bounteous variety of Keats's sensuousness, the power of rendering sensible experience with such intense palpable immediacy. Again, while many enchant our ears with their music, few, if any, surpass him in his full rich melodiousness and rhythmical satisfaction. And out of all this continuous delight, emerges as we have shown, that comparatively rare thing—a distinctive, fully created, poetic 'world'.

His attitude, dominated by dreams and longings, surrendering to easy flights of fancy, is immature, feverish, often naïve, and ultimately unsatisfying, as he himself came to realize. Yet for several good reasons it is not to be dismissed out of consideration with the fashionable and over-used label 'escapist'. For one thing, while his poetry will probably always appeal much more to the young than the middle-aged or old, it remains permanently and generally valuable because, like Marlowe's, it offers one of the most memorable expressions in the language of many of the passionate, irresistible desires and aspirations of youth. 'Ultimately' unsatisfying it may be; but who except the most rigidly disciplined and austere of readers can remain unmoved by the warm and colourful enchantment of Keats's imaginings of what life might be—if only things could 'to the will Be settled'? Though often naïve, it is not simple or shallow, for as we have indicated in several of the previous chapters it is ravelled with complex impulses and ambivalences, like the love of death and the 'gordian complication of feelings' about women, that fascinate and take us deep into the secret places of the human heart. Above all, the fine intelligence that is so evident in the letters is by no means absent from his poetry. When Leavis writes, with excellent perception, 'Keats never takes his dreams for reality or . . . remains lost in them',* he is paying implicit tribute to this quality of intelligence. It also ensures that even when Keats is writing at his most rhapsodic, in the *Ode to a Nightingale* or *Ode on a Grecian Urn*, for instance, he never loses sight of actuality, while intelligence is certainly behind his steady awareness, from *Endymion* onwards, of the inextricably mixed joy and sorrow of human experience.

One of the chief regrets of his early death is that this awareness never became the constant centre of his poetry as it almost certainly would have done had he lived a few years longer.

---

* *Revaluations*, p. 262.

NOTES

CHAPTER I (pp. 1–43)

1 Abraham Cowley, *Essays, Plays, and Sundry Verses,* ed. A. R. Waller, pp. 457–8.
2 *Letters of John Keats,* ed. M. B. Forman, p. 347. (To Miss Jeffrey, 9 June 1819.) All quotations from Keats's letters are taken from the third edition of this collection.
3 *Letters,* p. 20.
4 Pp. 58–9.
5 *Endymion,* I, 394. All quotations from Keats's poetry in this book are taken from H. W. Garrod's *The Poetical Works of John Keats.*
6 *The Tempest,* I, ii, 408.
7 *Pericles,* III, ii, 99–101.
8 L. 61.
9 Ll. 14–15.
10 VII, 438–40.
11 Ll. 10–11
12 *To Autumn,* l. 22.
13 *Ode on Melancholy,* ll. 27–8.
14 *Letters,* p. 130. (To Reynolds.)
15 *Autobiography and Journals,* ed. Malcolm Elwin, p. 65.
16 Ed. 1932 (*Hogarth Letters,* No. 8), pp. 9–10.
17 *The Lay of the Last Minstrel,* II, xi. (Logie Robertson's Oxford edition of Scott's poems, 1926.)
18 *Ibid.* viii.
19 *Ibid.* xvii.
20 *Ibid.* xx.
21 *Ibid.* xxiii.
22 *The Eve of St Agnes,* ll. 24–7.
23 *Ibid.* ll. 377–8.
24 *The Lay,* Introduction, ll. 1–4.
25 *St Agnes,* ll. 16–18.
26 *The Lay,* VI, xxiii.
27 *Ibid.* II, iii.
28 *Ibid.* vii.
29 *Ibid.* xviii.
30 *St Agnes,* ll. 112–13.
31 *The Lay,* II, xxv.
32 *St Agnes,* ll. 320–1.
33 *The Lay,* II, xxxiv.
34 *St Agnes,* l. 198 and l. 333.
35 *Ibid.* l. 355.
36 *The Lay,* VI, vi.
37 *St Agnes,* ll. 30–1.
38 *The Lay,* V, v.
39 *St Agnes,* l. 227. (Cf. *Christabel,* ll. 64–5.)
40 *The Lay,* II, xii.
41 Ll. 8–12.
42 III, 567–9.
43 Stanza XIII.
44 Stanza XVIII, l. 1.
45 Stanza XIV.
46 *Letters,* p. 248.
47 *Ibid.* p. 97.
48 *Ibid.* pp. 87–8.
49 *Ibid.* p. 259.
50 Sonnet *To Byron.*
51 Note to *Letters,* p. 521.
52 *Letters,* p. 391.
53 *Ibid.* p. 440.

CHAPTER II (pp. 44–80)

1 *Endymion,* I, 6–7.
2 *To Some Ladies,* l. 4.
3 *Endymion,* III, 142 ff.
4 Ll. 9–12.

356

5   I, 591–3.
6   L. 4; ll. 10–12.
7   III, 16–17.
8   Ll. 63–7; 101–6; 113–21.
9   *Letters*, ed. M. B. Forman, pp. 156–7.
10 *Calidore*, ll. 26–8.
11 Ll. 117–21. See also 'I stood tip-toe', ll. 29–30, 131–36, 166.
12 II, 700.
13 I, 899–901 and III, 935–7. See also I, 665 and II, 425–7.
14 I, 429–41.
15 I, 665–71; I, 861–72; I, 939–41.
16 II, 407–14.
17 IV, 670–7.
18 L. 85.
19 Ll. 9–11.
20 Ll. 58–61.
21 Ll. 25–7.
22 'To one who has been long in city pent', ll. 5–7.
23 II, 289–90.
24 II, 330.
25 III, 109.
26 II, 441.
27 II, 466.
28 IV, 102.
29 IV, 59.
30 Ll. 9–10.
31 L. 52.
32 *Endymion*, IV, 679–710.
33 II, 717–19.
34 II, 737–8.
35 I, 63–6. See also I, 240–1.
36 Ll. 53–4.
37 Ll. 12–14.
38 *Endymion*, II, 905–9.
39 Ll. 32–3.
40 L. 12.
41 *Calidore*, ll. 1–50, *passim*; *Sleep and Poetry*, ll. 5–6; *Endymion*, I, 427–35.
42 II, 274–5.
43 III, 24–7.

44 Ll. 10–11.
45 II, 670–1.
46 *Calidore*, ll. 51–2; *Endymion* I, 102–3; II, 52; II, 133–4.
47 *Calidore*, ll. 50–4.
48 *Endymion*, II, 339–42.
49 *Lamia*, I, 27–9.
50 Ll. 209–10.
51 Ll. 611–16.
52 II, 125–41.
53 III, 270–4.
54 III, 798–800. See also III, 187–8.
55 *Endymion*, II, 444 and 450–1.
56 Ll. 27–8.
57 *Endymion*, II, 449–50.
58 Second sonnet *On Fame*, ll. 5–6, 11.
59 *Endymion*, I, 215.
60 *Ode on Melancholy*, l. 17.
61 Ll. 7–8.
62 II, 396–407.
63 Ll. 13–14 and ff.
64 *Calidore*, Induction, l. 49.
65 *Sleep and Poetry*, ll. 119–21.
66 *Endymion*, I, 271; II, 880.
67 *Otho the Great*, I, I, 13.
68 III, 102–3.
69 I, 932; II, 99.
70 IV, 695–6.
71 *Endymion*, I, 458–60.
72 'I stood tip-toe', ll. 3–5.
73 Ll. 109–10.
74 L. 73.
75 Ll. 59–60.
76 *Endymion*, II, 511–14.
77 *Calidore*, ll. 152–3.
78 L. 15.
79 *Sleep and Poetry*, l. 11.
80 *To Sleep*, l. 1.
81 Ll. 10–11.
82 *Ode to Psyche*, l. 18.
83 Ll. 221–4.
84 L. 7.
85 Ll. 33–6.

86 *Endymion*, I, 829; II, 804:
   Ode to Psyche, l. 13: *Hyperion*, III, 55.
87 'I stood tip-toe', ll. 225-6.
88 *Calidore*, l. 6.
89 *Endymion*, II, 289–90.
90 II, 305–6.
91 I, ii, 1–2.
92 *Hyperion*, III, 18–19.
93 *Endymion*, I, 945–6.
94 II, 53–5.
95 II, 325–6.
96 *Lamia*, II, 191–3.
97 Ll. 21–2, and 81–2.
98 I, 16–18.
99 I, 4.
100 I, 107.
101 Ll. 4–6.
102 I, 446–52.

103 L. 9.
104 'I stood tip-toe', ll. 10–12.
105 *Ode on a Grecian Urn*, ll. 11–12.
106 *Ode to Psyche*, l. 58.
107 Ll. 38–41.
108 Ll. 89–92.
109 *Letters*, p. 20.
110 II, 79–82.
111 Ll. 9–14.
112 L. 21. See also ll. 14–22 and 57–60.
113 I, 352–6.
114 *The Eve of St Agnes*, ll. 258–9.
115 I, 4–5.
116 III, 40 and II, 280.
117 Ll. 9–13.
118 Ll. 9–14.

CHAPTER III (pp. 81–122)

1 *Letters*, p. 507.
2 *Ibid.* p. 108.
3 *Endymion*, II, 396–400.
4 I, 309–11.
5 Ll. 8–11.
6 *Poetical Works of Keats*, ed. H.W. Garrod, *op. cit.* p. 116.
7 I, 311.
8 Garrod, *Poetical Works of Keats, app. crit.* p. 74.
9 *To Autumn*, l. 15.
10 *Endymion*, IV, 377.
11 Ll. 16–17.
12 II, 15–17.
13 Ll. 56–7.
14 This and the following quotations are taken from the copy of Bailey's Letter in Rollins's *The Keats Circle*, Vol. II, pp. 227–8. (See Appendix II.)
15 *To Homer*, l. 7.
16 *Isabella*, l. 99.
17 *The Eve of St Agnes*, l. 221.
18 *Ibid.* l. 211.

19 *Ode on Melancholy*, l. 4.
20 *To Autumn*, l. 29.
21 *Lamia*, I, 75.
22 *Ibid.* 9–10.
23 *Endymion*, IV, 200–1.
24 *Ibid.* 254–6.
25 IV, 209–17.
26 *Letters*, p. 381.
27 II, 122–31.
28 Ll. 208–16.
29 From a photostat of the autograph MS. in the Harvard College Library.
30 P. 269 (1860 ed.).
31 Ll. 262–70.
32 Ll. 193–4.
33 Ll. 219–20.
34 Garrod, *Poetical Works of Keats, app. crit.* p. 276.
35 I, 251–62.
36 'Bright star', l. 2.
37 *On first looking into Chapman's Homer*, ll. 13–14.
38 *Endymion*, I, 232–3.
39 *To Ailsa Rock*, ll. 5–6.

NOTES

40 *Hyperion* I, 74.
41 *The Eve of St Agnes*, l. 274.
42 *Ode on Melancholy*, l. 20.
43 *Ode on a Grecian Urn*, ll. 1–2.
44 *Lamia*, I, 379.
45 'Bright star', l. 1.
46 Ll. 271–5.
47 I, 74 and II, 35.
48 I, 279–83.

49 I, 154.
50 I, 297–9.
51 Garrod, *Poetical Works of Keats*, *app. crit.* p. 277.
52 I, 17–20.
53 *The Eve of St Agnes*, l. 230.
54 L. 109.
55 I, 30.
56 I, 203.

CHAPTER IV (pp. 123–145)

1 *Letters*, p. 12.
2 Ll. 205–6.
3 Ll. 10–11.
4 Ll. 209–10.
5 Ll. 201–4.
6 L. 110.
7 Ll. 122–5.
8 Ll. 86–180.
9 *Letters*, pp. 67–8.
10 *Ibid.* pp. 90–1.
11 *Tintern Abbey*, ll. 105–7.

12 *Letters*, p. 91.
13 I, 808–9.
14 I, 841–2.
15 IV, iii, 327–33.
16 *Letters*, p. 52.
17 *Poetical Works of Keats*, ed. Garrod, p. lxxxix.
18 *Ibid.* p. lxxxviii.
19 *Ibid.* p. 64.
20 *Letters*, p. 507.

CHAPTER V (pp. 146–202)

1 I, 34–5.
2 I, 214–222.
3 I, 129–30.
4 I, 372–3.
5 I, 317–21.
6 *Ode on Melancholy*, ll. 25–6.
7 I, 608–22.
8 I, 651–64.
9 I, 655–7.
10 I, 966–9.
11 I, 822–3.
12 I, 807–8.
13 I, 826–7.
14 I, 835–42.
15 I, 813–15.
16 I, 653–5.
17 I, 825 and I, 823.
18 I, 795–7.
19 I, 797–801.
20 I, 812–13.

21 I, 777–81.
22 *Poetical Works of Keats*, ed. Garrod, *app. crit.* p. 88.
23 II, 6–7.
24 II, 28–9.
25 See. II, 38.
26 I, 701–3.
27 II, 280.
28 II, 332; IV, 312.
29 II, 267.
30 II, 271–3.
31 II, 321–3.
32 II, 274–6.
33 II, 274–6.
34 Ll. 59–60.
35 II, 337–47.
36 II, 376–86.
37 II, 385.
38 II, 407–18 (quoted p. 51).

39   II, 490–2.
40   II, 461–4.
41   II, 549–50.
42   II, 590.
43   *Letters*, p. 44.
44   II, 594–5.
45   II, 615–20.
46   II, 663–79.
47   II, 506.
48   II, 671–2.
49   II, 711–13.
50   II, 770–2.
51   II, 827–9.
52   II, 904–9.
53   II, 868–9.
54   II, 943–8.
55   II, 823–4.
56   II, 986–7.
57   II, 984–5.
58   III, 81–5.
59   III, 74–7.
60   III, 92–6.
61   III, 162–6.
62   III, 175–7.
63   III, 180–1.
64   I, 826–7.
65   III, 933–4.
66   III, 398–9.
67   III, 300.
68   III, 315–18.
69   III, 470–2.
70   III, 702.
71   III, 735–6.
72   III, 983–5.

73   III, 1013–18.
74   III, 877–8.
75   III, 798–800.
76   III, 927–37.
77   IV, 20–5.
78   IV, 30–5.
79   IV, 188–92.
80   IV, 494–5.
81   IV, 614.
82   *Milton's Poetical Works*, Oxford (1941), Appendix II, p. 576. (Translation of the Seventh *Elegy*).
83   *Ibid.*
84   *Within a Budding Grove*, Part II *(Remembrance of Things Past)*, translated by Scott-Moncrieff.
85   *Ibid.* p. 121.
86   *Ibid.* p. 244.
87   I, 653–4.
88   Thomas Hardy, *The Temporary of All.*
89   IV, 636–8.
90   *Lamia*, I, 328–33.
91   IV, 649–50.
92   IV, 300–1.
93   IV, 543–5.
94   IV, 546–52.
95   IV, 531–4.
96   IV, 542.
97   *Letters*, p. 336. (Keats's italics.)
98   IV, 537–42.

CHAPTER VI (pp. 203–250)

1   *Letters*, p. 193.
2   *Ibid.* p. 152.
3   *Ibid.* p. 202.
4   *Ibid.* p. 217 and 218. (To Reynolds.)
5   *Ibid.* p. 217.
6   *Ibid.* p. 233.
7   *Ibid.* p. 234.
8   *Ibid.* p. 192.
9   *Ibid.* p. 233.

10   *Ibid.* p. 233–4.
11   Written late December 1818 or early January 1819.
12   February–April ? 1818.
13   *Letters*, p. 391.
14   Ll. 16–20.
15   Ll. 5–16.
16   IV, 101–4.
17   *Letters*, p. 304.
18   Ll. 13–14.

NOTES

19 *Letters*, p. 356.
20 *Endymion*, III, 567–9.
21 *On a Dream*, ll. 9–14.
22 *Letters*, p. 326.
23 *Letters*, p. 326.
24 Ll. 39–40.
25 Ll. 43–6.
26 *Letters*, p. 362.
27 Ll. 7–12.
28 *Letters*, pp. 339–40.
29 Ll. 44–9.
30 Ll. 23–4.
31 Ll. 29–30.
32 Ll. 29–30.
33 L. 32.
34 Ll. 18–20.
35 *Letters*, p. 436.
36 *Ibid.* p. 436.
37 *Ibid.* p. 362. (My italics).
38 *Ibid.* p. 353.
39 *Ibid.* p. 372.
40 *Ibid.* p. 241.
41 *Ibid.* p. 374.
42 *Ibid.* pp. 240–1.
43 *Ibid.* p. 371.
44 *Ibid.* p. 436.
45 *Ibid.* p. 362.
46 *Ibid.* p. 465.
47 *Ibid.* p. 440.
48 I, 55–6.
49 III, 494–5.
50 I, 290–7.
51 I, 102–3.
52 I, 191–4.
53 I, 394–7.
54 I, 145.

55 II, 1–4.
56 II, 9–10.
57 II, 11–16.
58 II, 31.
59 II, 72–7.
60 *Poetical Works of Keats*, ed. Garrod, *app. crit.* p. 205.
61 *Ibid. app. crit.* p. 205.
62 I, 377.
63 II, 125–6.
64 II, 181–2.
65 I, 126–8.
66 II, 39.
67 II, 22–5.
68 II, 28–33.
69 II, 34–9.
70 *Letters*, p. 366.
71 III, ii, 5–8.
72 III, ii, 13–14.
73 'I cry your mercy', ll. 9–10.
74 *Letters*, p. 461.
75 I, i, 141–3.
76 II, ii, 22–3.
77 III, ii. 209–10.
78 III, i, 7–8.
79 *Endymion*, I, 826–7.
80 Ll. 1–3.
81 Ll. 5–9.
82 Ll. 12–14.
83 Ll. 18–23.
84 Ll. 34–43.
85 Ll. 48–53.
86 *Letters*, p. 353.
87 L. 54.
88 *Letters*, p. 460.

CHAPTER VII (pp. 251–281)

1 I, 777, ff.
2 *Letters*, p. 69.
3 Ll. 7–11.
4 *Letters*, p. 315.
5 Ll. 15–18.
6 *Letters*, p. 147.
7 III, 86–9.
8 IV, 817–19.

9 Ll. 25–30.
10 II, 383–6.
11 IV, 202–3.
12 L. 270.
13 Ll. 1–4.
14 II, 483–6.
15 Amy Lowell, *John Keats*, II, p. 528. Also quoted in

Letters of Fanny Brawne to
Fanny Keats, p. 28.
16 Ll. 9–14.
17 Ll. 55–9.
18 I, 653–5.
19 Letters, p. 151.

20 Ibid. p. 178.
21 Ibid. p. 362.
22 II, 280.
23 The Fall of Hyperion, I, 201.
24 IV, 372–3.
25 Ll. 1–4.

CHAPTER VIII (pp. 282–315)

1 Letters, p. 227.
2 Ibid. p. 97.
3 Ibid. pp. 227–8.
4 Ibid. p. 72.
5 Ibid. p. 426.
6 Ll. 42–7.
7 The Opium Eater (Oxford World Classics ed.) p. 205.
8 Ibid. pp. 205–6.
9 L. 12.
10 Ll. 23–4.
11 Ll. 25–34.
12 Ll. 36–8.
13 Quoted in Rollins, Keats and his Circle, vol. II, p. 261.
14 Letters, p. 111.
15 Ibid. p. 370.
16 Lachin Y Gair, ll. 37–40.
17 Quoted in a footnote in the Letters, p. 521.
18 Letters, p. 339.
19 Ibid. p. 21.
20 Ibid. p. 131.
21 Ibid. p. 130.
22 Ll. 162–5.
23 Letters, p. 413.
24 Ibid. p. 405.
25 Ibid. p. 67.
26 The Eve of St Agnes, ll. 39–41.
27 Ode on a Grecian Urn, ll. 6–7.
28 Ode to a Nightingale, ll. 73–4.
29 Ll. 79–80.
30 Anatomy of Melancholy, ed. A. R. Shilleto, vol. I, pp. 165–6.
31 Letters, p. 69.
32 Ibid. p. 217.
33 Poetical Works of Keats, ed. Garrod, p. 502.
34 Endymion, I, 10–11.
35 Ll. 242–3.
36 Endymion, I, 691–8.
37 Ll. 403–8.
38 IV, 274–5.
39 Letters, p. 67. (My italics.)
40 II, 69–76.
41 Letters, p. 516.
42 Ll. 1–8.
43 Ll. 159–62.
44 'Welcome joy, and welcome sorrow', l. 22.
45 Ibid. ll. 12–17.
46 Hyperion, III, 64–7.
47 Letters, pp. 315–16.
48 Ll. 1–12.
49 Lamia, I, 191–4.
50 Ll. 172–6.
51 Quoted in Colvin, Life of John Keats, p. 80.
52 Letters, p. 353.
53 Ibid. p. 69.

CHAPTER IX (pp. 316–347)

1 The Poet, l. 5.
2 III, 32.
3 Waiting on God, p. 24.
4 I, 3–5.

5   I, 168–9.
6   Ll. 9–10.
7   Ll. 68–78.
8   *Poetical Works of Keats*, ed.
    Garrod, *app. crit.*, p. 465.
9   Ll. 20–2.
10 *Letters*, p. 114.
11 Ll. 3–4.
12 I, 95–7.

13 L. 14.
14 I, 318–19.
15 I, 317–18.
16 I, 315–16.
17 Ll. 1–5.
18 *Letters*, p. 144.
19 Ll. 76–7.
20 *Letters*, p. 84. (My italics.)
21 *Ibid*. p. 112.

CHAPTER X (pp. 348–355)

1   Pp. 163–4.
2   *Letters*,
    p. 468.
3   L. 29; l. 55.
4   Ll. 110–13.

5   Ll. 147–9.
6   Ll. 123–25.
7   Ll. 168–9.
8   Ll. 175–6.
9   Ll. 198–202.

INITIAL CONSONANTS
IN KEATS'S POETRY

T HE somewhat impressionistic account of the general nature of Keats's melody given in Chapter III may be supplemented by a little analysis. For example, if we examine the initial consonants of the nouns, adjectives, root verbs, and adverbs in a selection of passages (a restricted test, of course), some interesting conclusions emerge. About 17 per cent of English words start with the letter *s*, this being by far the largest group. Keats does not exceed this percentage: his figure is approximately 16 per cent. But it is illuminating to find that he at least makes an extensive use of this easy, smooth-sounding, and usually soft consonant; that in some poems the proportion is exceptionally high (16 out of 54 in the 'Bright star' sonnet); and that an impressive number of his favourite words belong to this group: *sleep, slumber, swoon, sorrow, shade, shadow, soft, sweet, silent, silver, smooth, swell, sigh, soothe.*

Much more remarkable, but thoroughly characteristic, is Keats's fondness for words that begin with another soft consonant, *f.* While in the language approximately 5 per cent of our words start with *f*, in Keats's poetry this proportion rises to no less than 10 per cent. Once again the group includes many characteristic words: *forest, fruit, flower, fever, fair, full, fragrant, faery, fade, faint.*

The labial *b*, which begins another group of favourite words (*bloom, bud, bower, balm, beauty, bard, bright, brim, blush*) is also well above the norm as an initial letter, and there is a slight increase in the two soft consonants *h* and *w.*

Of the initial consonants that appear to fall substantially below the figure of average usage the most surprising is *m.* We might imagine that this consonantal sound would appeal to Keats's ear, but an analysis of sample passages gives only

5 per cent against 11 per cent in the *Shorter Oxford Dictionary*. The other marked falls are as we should expect, and confirm the impression of a melody that avoids the stronger, harsher, or more emphatic sounds—*p* from 10.5 per cent to 6 per cent, *t* from 8 per cent to 4.5 per cent, and *r* from 6 per cent to 4 per cent.

KEATS'S THEORY OF MELODY
IN POETRY

The following extract is taken from Bailey's letter to Milnes, October 1848. (Rollins, *The Keats Circle*, Vol. II, pp. 227–8.)

ONE of his favourite topics of discourse was the principle of melody in Verse, upon which he had his own notions, particularly in the management of open and close vowels. I think I have seen a somewhat similar theory attributed to Mr Wordsworth. But I do not remember his laying it down in writing. Be this as it may, Keats's theory was worked out by himself. He was himself, as already observed, a master of melody, which may be illustrated by almost numberless passages of his poems. As an instance of this, I may cite a few lines of that most perfect passage of *Hyperion*, which has been quoted by more than one of your Reviewers—the picture of dethroned Saturn in his melancholy solitude. Keats's theory was, that the vowels should be so managed as not to clash with one another so as to mar the melody,—and yet they should be inter-changed, like differing notes of music to prevent monotony. The following lines will, I think, illustrate his theory, as I understood him:

> Dēep in thĕ shădў sādness ŏf ă vāle,
> Fār sūnken from the hĕalthy brēath of mōrn—
> Fār frōm thĕ fiĕry mōon* and ēve's ōne stār—
> Sāt grey haired Sāturn, quïet as a stōne,
> Stĭll as the sĭlence round about his lāir:
> Fōrest on fōrest hung about his hēad
> Like clōud on clōud.

* A misquotation for 'noon' [E.C.P.].

These lines are exquisitely wrought into melody. They are beautifully varied in their vowel sounds, save when the exception proves the rule, and monotony is a beauty; as in the prolonged breathing, as it were, of the similar vowels in 'hēalthy brēath of morn', in which we almost inhale the freshness of the morning air; and in the vowel sounds repeated in the words—

> 'Sāt grey haired Sāturn'—and
> Fōrest on forest—'like clōud on clōud'

—In all which the sameness of the sound increases the melancholy and monotony of the situation of the dethroned Father of the Gods. The rest is beautiful by its skilful variation of the vowel-sounds: as these are touching by their sameness and monotony.

You mention Keats's taste for painting and music. Of the first I remember no more than his general love of the art, and his admiration of Haydon. But I remember his telling me that, had he studied music, he had some notions of the combinations of sounds, by which he thought he could have done something as original as his poetry.

APPENDIX III

'AT MORN, AT NOON, AT EVE,
AND MIDDLE NIGHT'

FINNEY'S account of this early sonnet as an expression of neo-platonic ideas (see *The Evolution of Keats's Poetry*, p. 175–6) has recently been followed by Wasserman: 'All things may be symbolic in proportion to the intensity with which one is engaged in them, for this sensuous intensity is the magic that opens the husk of natural objects to the core and reveals their spiritual essences' (*The Finer Tone*, p. 53).

But there is no reason to read anything specifically metaphysical into the opening lines, which closely resemble the description of the Charioteer (the spirit of Poetry and Imagination) in *Sleep and Poetry*. Lines 4–8, with their account of the poet's visionary, intuitive penetration into 'essences' that reveal the 'good and fair' (the platonic good and beautiful?) may conceivably bear some metaphysical significance, though as we have shown in Chapter IV 'essence' is a dangerously misleading word. But before following Finney in his contention that 'the mystical flight into the sky in the sestet connects the sonnet with the neo-platonic and mythological sources' of *Endymion*, we must pause for several considerations. First, these aerial flights, which are closely linked with Keats's fancy of some sort of Elysium for poets, are common enough in his early verse, and our usual impression (see *Written on the Day Mr Leigh Hunt left Prison*, 'Oh, how I love, on a fair summer's eve', and 'As from the darkling gloom') is of Keats indulging in a traditional sort of metaphor rather than attempting to describe the authentic ecstasy of mysticism and neo-platonism. Secondly, before we read anything neo-platonic into the lines

and with its destined skies
Hold premature and mystic communings,

368

we should remember the long description of such 'communings' in *To My Brother George*, where the 'destined skies' turn out to be mainly a Spenserian pageant of chivalry and fair ladies.

The slighting reference to 'the gross and palpable things Of this diurnal sphere' may be a vaguely neo-platonic sentiment; but if the reference is of this kind, it probably represents nothing more than a passing reminiscence of Spenser's *Hymnes*.

Most significant of all, Keats himself attached no particular importance to this sonnet, which, though it is not noticeably inferior to some of the published ones, was excluded from the 1817 volume.

NOTES ON 'ENDYMION', BOOK IV

'I have a triple soul!' (*l.* 95)

QUOTING and stressing this line, Bridges asserted that Endymion's love for the moon-goddess has a dual significance: as the Moon she 'represents "Poetry" or the ideality of desired objects, the principle of beauty in all things'; as Cynthia, 'ideal beauty or love of woman' (*Collected Essays*, vol. IV, pp. 85–7). Thorpe also insists on a similar duality in Endymion's love for Cynthia (see *The Mind of John Keats*, pp. 187–8).

But there is not the slightest hint in the context that Endymion's love for Cynthia is a twofold one, and all the emphasis is simply on the hero's being rent in two between Cynthia and the Indian Maid (ll. 96–7):

> For both, for both my love is so immense,
> I feel my heart is cut for them in twain.

Presumably the meaning of 'triple soul' is that the hero's heart is partly his own and partly divided between Cynthia and the Indian Maid.

The ode to Bacchus (*ll.* 182–272)

Whatever else may be said about this ode, which forms a substantial part of Book IV, certainly no sort of allegorical meaning can be wrung from it. But though Keats was no doubt chiefly occupied in a delighted picturing of the Progress of Bacchus when he wrote it, it has some bearing on the main themes of the poem and is not purely decorative like the later wedding ode (ll. 563–610). It is concerned with grief and with wine as an escape from grief; and if this seems a prosaic paraphrase of some enraptured poetry, it should be remembered that the second stanza of the *Ode to a Nightingale* bears just this same 'meaning'.

'*And I Have no self-passion or identity*' (*ll.* 476–7).

The context of this line should elucidate some of its obscurity. What Endymion is feeling strongly at this moment is a devastating conflict within himself, this arising not only from the apparently twofold nature of his love ('would I were whole in love') but from the fact that he can love the Indian Maid without any feeling of treachery towards Cynthia (ll. 473–4):

> Can I prize thee, fair maid, all price above,
> Even when I feel as true as innocence?

He also has a dark foreboding of retribution.

The link between this general context and line 477 (hinted, though only obliquely, in '*self*-passion') is surely Keats's fairly settled notion that it is consistency, firm convictions and beliefs, that give us 'self' or 'identity'. There are several well-known passages in his letters (where self-identity is usually discussed as 'character') that may be used for illuminating commentary. Perhaps the most immediately relevant is a remark to Woodhouse: 'It is a wretched thing to confess; but is a very fact that not one word I ever utter can be taken for granted as an opinion growing out of my *identical nature*—how can it, when I have no nature' (*Letters*, p. 228).

However, Endymion is wretched in his outcry, while Keats—in spite of the tone of the isolated sentence just quoted—rejoices, as always, that he is the sort of poet without 'self' or 'identity'. This contrast may of course be dismissed by arguing that we must not confuse Endymion with Keats himself. But even if we accept this distinction, a certain degree of contradiction appears to remain in Endymion's lament, for earlier, in the speech on happiness, 'self-destroying' had been proclaimed as the essential conditon of felicity.

Probably Keats meant here that a divided love like Endymion's was a wrong kind of 'self-destroying': it was not the 'oneness' that comes from fusion with a single love.

NOTES ON SOME FURTHER 'DISTILLATIONS' IN THE 'ODE TO A NIGHTINGALE'

Stanza i

(1) *Lethe.* Always a favourite word with Keats.

(2) Ll. 7–10. See *Epistle to G. F. Mathew* (ll. 45–7), and *Endymion*, i, 828–9, which seem to indicate an established association—nightingales; trees (rather than bushes); leaves; shadowy coolness.

Stanza ii

(1) Ll. 11–12. Cf. 'please heaven, a little claret-wine cool out of a cellar a mile deep' (*Letters*, p. 295). And note the reference to Flora twenty words further on.

(2) *Flora.* A personification of Keats's obsessing love of flowers, fruits, trees and vegetation that is often mentioned in his early poetry.

(3) Ll. 16–18. Two earlier wine-descriptions (*Endymion*, ii 441–4; *Hyperion*, iii, 18–19) contain the same complex of red or purple colour, bubbling and sparkling, and coolness.

(4) *Forest dim.* Keats's general fascination for forests, and *Isabella* (l. 175):

> For they resolved in some forest dim . . .

Stanza iii

(1) For the stanza generally see the passage on the 'Chamber of Maiden-thought' (Letter to Reynolds, 3 May 1818).

(2) *Fever.* A recurrent word at this time. For example, 'How fever'd is the man', written two or three weeks before.

(3) *Where palsy*, etc. A strong association between old age, decrepitude, palsy, and—rather oddly—hair (cf. *Endymion*, iv,

956–7; *Hyperion*, I, 93–4). Angela in *The Eve of St Agnes* is a 'palsy-stricken' thing (l. 155), who dies 'palsy-twitch'd' (376) and part of Lycius's curse on Apollonius is one of 'trembling dotage' (Lamia, II, 283).

(4) *Where youth grows pale*, etc. Cf. *La Belle Dame Sans Merci*, 37–8.

(5) Ll. 29–30. Cf. *Fancy*, ll. 69–73.

Stanza IV

(1) *Viewless wings of Poesy*. Cf. 'Oh, how I love' (l. 12).

(2) Ll. 38–40. See Chapter II for the significance of breezes, moss, and the word 'verdurous' in Keats's imagery. Note also the sonnet 'Happy is England!' (ll. 1–4).

(3) *Glooms*. This word (for a suggestion of atmosphere rather than to denote a mental state) appears to have been running in Keats's head a good deal at this period. See *Song of Four Fairies*, *La Belle Dame Sans Merci*, and 'How fever'd is the man'.

Stanza V

(1) The details of this bower image appear to owe something to some of Keats's earlier poems and also point to some interesting associations. In a bower description in 'I stood tip-toe' (ll. 32–7) grass, violets, moss, leaves, wild briar, woodbine, and a soft wind all occur. Later there is a passage (ll.133–7) where we find a combination of 'dewy roses', 'sweet briar', 'at our feet', and 'bloomy'. 'Bloomy' is notable because Keats's first draft for line 42 in the ode was: 'Nor what blooms soft . . .'

(2) *Musk-rose*. Probably the most frequently mentioned flower in Keats's poetry. For the association of roses with dew see especially 'Had I a man's fair form' (ll. 10–11) and *Old Meg* (l. 7). The musk-rose is frequently associated with descriptive details that reappear in the ode: *Sleep and Poetry* (ll. 5–8) links it with 'green', 'far', 'leafiness', 'nightingales'; in *Endymion* (I, 18–19) there is a connexion of 'musk-rose' with

'mid-forest brake'; and in the *Epistle to George* (ll. 89–93) the musk-rose and violet appear together.

(3) Behind this stanza there was probably a strong memory of one of Shakespeare's plays that Keats appears to have read most often, *A Midsummer Night's Dream*, especially II, i, 249–5ᵒ.

Stanza VI

(1) Ll. 53–6. Cf. *To Hope:* 'To sigh out sonnets to the mid-night air' (l. 28).

(2) *Requiem.* To be noted, along with 'incense' and 'anthem', as examples of Keats's fondness for religious phraseology. See G. Wilson Knight's comment on *Endymion* (*The Starlit Dome*, p. 269) and also his commentary on the *Ode to Psyche*.

Stanza VII

(1) Ll. 69–70. Probably another recollection of Claude's 'Enchanted Castle'. See the *Epistle to Reynolds*. 'Charm'd magic casements' may be a compression of

> The doors all look as if they oped themselves,
> The windows as if latch'd by fays and elves.

Possibly, too, some recollection of the conclusion of the *Ode to Psyche*.

(2) *Foam.* A reminder of what was always one of the most fascinating features of seascape to Keats. See particularly the *Epistle to Reynolds* (ll. 90–2).

NOTES ON
SOME INTERPRETATIONS OF THE
'ODE ON A GRECIAN URN'

The traditional interpretation

THE traditional view has been that the ode is essentially a poem about art. Exponents of this—Colvin, Bridges, Garrod, Finney, etc.—have agreed on two central points of interpretation: that Keats is expressing the solace of art amid the pain of life, and that art is solacing because of its timelessness and achievement of permanence. A fair summary of this reading would be Finney's comment (*The Evolution of Keats's Poetry*, p. 637): 'Saddened by the mutability of natural beauty, he [Keats] sought consolation in the more permanent beauty of art.'

This widely supported view has some validity, and certainly stanzas II and III may be read as an expression—if an oblique one—of the conquest over flux and time achieved by all important artistic creation. However, there are several objections to the belief that the ode is chiefly and at its deepest level concerned with art:

(1) Keats has not chosen to focus his attention on some important and actual work of art, as he does in the Elgin Marbles sonnets and the *Epistle to Reynolds*, and as he usually does in his letters when he is speculating on art. Most of stanza I and stanzas II–IV, the body of the poem, consist of images that cannot be regarded—apart from the piper—as primarily and directly symbolizing the essential nature of art.

(2) This view has failed to account for stanza IV and has been forced to regard it as a beautiful digression.

(3) There is little in the ode to support the belief that 'beauty' in the concluding aphorism is chiefly, or even at all, the beauty of art.

*Cleanth Brooks**

In one of his rare generalizations Brooks links himself with the exponents of the traditional view: 'the poem is obviously intended to be a parable on the nature of poetry, and of art in general' (p. 140).

Unfortunately Brooks makes no direct or sustained attempt to justify this assertion, and his arguments have to be dug for. What emerges is something like this—the traditional view with a decidedly new look: (1) art is the imposition of significant order and vital (not lifeless) pattern on the chaotic flux of human experience; (2) the urn expresses this sort of ordered 'life beyond life'; (3) therefore the ode is a parable of art.

But does this syllogism really take us very far? Could it not be used to demonstrate that most poems of consequence are in some measure 'parables' on the nature of poetry and art?

However, the chief defect of Brooks's interpretation, which offers several excellent insights into the ode, is that he assumes a controlled, conscious ambiguity in Keats's use of language that is entirely alien to Romantic practice. This assumption leads him into a great deal of needless complication and to the fabrication of non-existent paradoxes. Further, his ideas of paradox encourage him to resolve into an artistic harmony what are really expressions of confusions and conflicts in Keats—his contradictory attitudes to love, for instance.

Another weakness of the study is that while Brooks at one time defends the 'truth' of the last stanza on the grounds that it is a *dramatic* utterance of the urn, to be appreciated primarily within the context of the poem, at another he speaks of the ode's 'insight into essential truth' (p. 151). But he cannot have it both ways. If the ode really expresses some insight into essential truth, then he cannot lock that insight away inside the poem and refuse to test its validity against the 'scientific and philosophical generalizations which dominate our world'

* *The Well Wrought Urn*, pp. 139–52.

376

(p. 151). He has merely evaded Eliot's charge of the untruth of the final aphorism, not met it.

J. Middleton Murry*

Murry's is one of several recent attempts to read into the ode a profound metaphysical significance. In Murry's view the poem is essentially an apprehension of spiritual renunciation and detachment: 'To attain the vision which Keats describes as the knowledge that "Beauty is Truth, Truth Beauty" we are required to put away all our human desires and beliefs and anxieties. We have to forget all those cares, delightful or painful, which appertain to our animal existence' (p. 175).

Unhappily the study is quite unworthy of this critic who has in the past often written on Keats with considerable illumination. Even if we are sympathetic to the ideal of detachment that he propounds, it passes understanding how any reasonable critic could ever find this ideal in the words Keats actually wrote. Such a typical observation as—'The Beauty of the Real . . . lies in the perfection of uniqueness which belongs to every thing, or thought, simply because it *is*' (p.174)—may be true, but it has nothing whatsoever to do with the ode. Almost all the intricate web of religious and metaphysical significance that Murry weaves over the poem is spun out of purely subjective speculations.

Sir Maurice Bowra†

This second strongly metaphysical interpretation of the ode has some kinship with the traditional view—for example, 'The main subject of the *Ode on a Grecian Urn* is the creative ecstasy which the artist perpetuates in a masterpiece' (p. 142). But Sir Maurice Bowra's reading is clearly distinguished from the traditional one, for he regards the ode as less of an expression of aesthetic doctrine and more of a mystical intuition of ultimate reality through art. He writes of a 'sense of timeless

* *The Mystery of Keats*, pp. 162–77.
† *The Romantic Imagination*, pp. 126–48.

rapture' in the ode (p. 142), of the urn's 'special order of reality' (p. 136), and of its being 'a concrete symbol of some vast reality' (p. 137).

Though the ode is often buried under a discussion of 'origins' and 'influences' and of statements in the letters and other poems, this argument for a metaphysical reading is much more sensible and deserving of consideration than Murry's. Personally, I consider its suggestion of elements of platonic thought in the ode highly questionable, and I think Sir Maurice has not sufficiently realized that the essential making of the poem lies in the scenes and figures that Keats depicts on the urn—one result of this being that the study fails to give serious and close attention to stanzas II–IV. Further, I do not find the exposition of the 'special order of reality' that the urn is supposed to embody very convincing—particularly when Sir Maurice writes that Keats's 'ideal world was not a scheme of abstractions but a source of living powers beyond the senses' (p. 141). How, when we read the dream of uncloying sensuous delight in physical beauty and of a love 'for ever warm' in stanzas II and III, can we believe that Keats is concerned with living powers deriving from an ideal world 'beyond the senses'? The world Keats represents in his urn frieze is earthly and physical and sensuous still—'ideal' only in the sense that he has shaped it 'to the will' and rid it of all the inevitable distresses of actuality.

B. *Wasserman**

As Wasserman represents the ode there are three primary, closely interwoven, themes. First, the ode is an apprehension of 'heaven's bourne' (reached in stanza III), followed by the inevitable falling away from it—this 'heaven's bourne', 'mystic oxymoron', or 'essence' being a region 'where earth and the ethereal, light and darkness, time and no-time become one' (p. 16). Secondly, Keats attains to heaven's bourne through

* *The Finer Tone*, pp. 13–62.

an empathic relationship with the symbols on the urn frieze—'empathic entrance into the life of the frieze, the vital core of the urn'—'the act of freeing the self of its identity and its existence in time and space, and consequently the act of mystic absorption with the essence of outward forms' (p. 24). Thirdly, the urn's message (which is dramatically exhibited through the poem) is not so much 'Beauty is Truth', etc., but that heaven's bourne is to be reached through art: 'what the symbolic drama ultimately discovers is the way in which art (the urn) relates man to that region' (p. 16).

This study, regarding the poem as 'religious experience' that is 'almost terrifying' to Keats (p. 56), is certainly the most elaborate metaphysical interpretation of the ode that has yet appeared, and in it Wasserman gives such an impressive demonstration of semantic and philosophical analysis that one hardly dares to disagree with him. Nevertheless, I am convinced that most of his interpretation is wrong and much of his method of analysis out of place.

As the essay is a very long one my disagreement will have to be indicated by the most summary of statements.

Setting aside what seems to be a highly dubious reading of Endymion's speech on happiness, a failure to define the constantly used word 'essence', and the problem (which I am not metaphysician enough to discuss) whether it is possible for a poet to enjoy a truly empathic experience with something he is creating, I consider that Wasserman only achieves his reading of the first three stanzas by ignoring the 'woe', mutability, and mortality that are always so strongly present by implication. Because he ignores this implication he makes the unwarranted statement that Keats 'has stumbled' (p. 34) into the last three lines of stanza III, where what has been implicit becomes explicit. His interpretation of the first three stanzas also leads him to the highly questionable opinion that 'Beauty is Truth', etc., only applies to these stanzas.

He supports his reading of Keats's empathic experience by the discovery (once more) of the 'pleasure thermometer'. This discovery is not convincing, and at one place it is quite at fault. When Keats writes '*More* happy, happy love' he is not implying that love is higher on the thermometer scale than nature or art; he is simply speaking of a love that is more happy than the actuality that he describes in the last three lines of the stanza.

It is hard to believe that the lines 'More happy, happy love', etc., represent the climax of empathy as Wasserman defines it (see my first paragraph), while Keats's state is certainly an extraordinarily subtle one if 'it threatens to disintegrate upon the least incaution, even an incaution in choice of syntax' (p. 40).

Largely because of his interpretation of the first three stanzas Wasserman misreads the fourth as an antithesis to them—'To put it bluntly, stanza three has said that at "heaven's bourne" beauty is truth; and stanza four has said that in this world beauty is not truth, truth is not beauty' (p. 48); and much of his comment is footling. What grounds, for instance, has he for asserting that 'the sacrifical altar towards which the procession goes is . . . dedicated to heaven, to a realm of pure spirit' (p. 42)?

Had Keats written a poem of the metaphysical penetration and complexity with which Wasserman credits him he would never have condemned himself as he does in *The Fall of Hyperion*.

A word or two will have to suffice on Wasserman's method, which far outdoes Cleanth Brooks in over-complication and hyper-subtlety. Who really believes that 'the paradoxical vagueness [?] of the words "haunts about" makes that relationship (between the urn and its frieze) fluid, malleable, instead of fixed' (p. 19); that 'In its Keatsian sense the repetition of "happy" conveys an empathic experience that is nervously taut' (p. 28); or that 'the suggestion of disorder in the rhymes of the first sestet . . . persists in those of the second; but the sestet of the third stanza conveys the . . . sense of the unfolding of a spiritual harmony . . .' (p. 28)?

*'Silent as a consecrated urn'**

Murry, Sir Maurice Bowra, and Wasserman all note this line in their studies and (in various way) treat its context as a metaphysical utterance. It would take some space to deal with these interpretations and to insist that the 'thousand powers' are simply gods and goddesses, some of whom do, and some do not, exercise a benevolent influence on the world below. Perhaps the discussion can be abbreviated by pointing out that none of these critics pays any attention to Keats's original line, which ran

> And silent, as a corpse upon a pyre.

Coming as a second thought—and after such a first—'silent as a consecrated urn' can hardly be seriously regarded as a vital link between the alleged mystical or metaphysical vision of this part of *Endymion* and the ode.

* *Endymion*, III, 32.

INDEX

'After dark vapours', and association of love and death, 271.
visual, tactile and sound imagery, 62 n., 70, 79.
'Ah! ken ye what I met the day', metrical form compared with *La Belle Dame Sans Merci*, 30.
Alastor and parallels with *Endymion*, 140–1, 161 n., 163 n., 190 n.
'Amena' letters, and *La Belle Dame Sans Merci*, 36–7.
Arabian Nights, imagery derived from, 100, 161.
Arnold, Matthew, on *Endymion*, 143.
and modern criticism, 353.
'As from the darkling gloom', absence of neoplatonic feeling in, 368.
'As Hermes once', and *La Belle Dame Sans Merci*, 217–19; and *Ode to a Nightingale*, 270.
'At morn, at noon, at eve', Finney's account of as expression of neoplatonic ideas, 368–9.
quoted as example of Keats's delight in quietness, 73.
Auden, W. H., Spender on influence of memory in his poetry, 7–8.
verbal echoes in his poetry, 8 n.

Bailey, Benjamin, correspondence with John Taylor concerning *Endymion*, 143–5.
Keats's discussion in letter to Bailey of truth through imagination and 'consequitive reasoning', 131 ff.
on principle of melody in Keats's verse, 90 ff., 366–7.
Ballad of Thomas of Ercildoune, and *La Belle Dame Sans Merci*, 32–5.
Bards of Passion, quoted for significant use of 'cloys', 'cloying', 330 n.

Baudelaire, his sensibilities paralleled in Keats, 20, 162 n.
Beattie, James, 3.
Keats's reference to his poetry, 40.
Beyer, W. W., on influence of Wieland's *Oberon* on *Eve of St Agnes*, 22 n.; on *La Belle Dame Sans Merci*, 32 n., 36; on *Lamia*, 231, 234.
Blackstone, B., on Keats and imagery of William Blake, 48 n.
Blake, William, 300.
Keats and his imagery, 48.
position in Romantic revolution, 282.
Bowra, Sir Maurice, on *Ode on a Grecian Urn*, 317–18, 317 n., 328 n., 334–5, 343 n., 345 n.; and recollection of *Endymion* Book IV, 340 n.; his metaphysical interpretation, 377–8, 381.
on *Ode on Melancholy*, 290 n.
on *Ode to a Nightingale*, 260 n., 276.
Brawne, Fanny, Keats's love for her, 207, 224–7, 245–50; and *Hyperion* Book III, 208; and *Eve of St Agnes*, 212; and *La Belle Dame Sans Merci*, 215–16; and Paolo and Francesca, 218; and *Ode to Psyche*, 222; and *Lamia*, 228, 233, 242; and *Ode on a Grecian Urn*, 328, 329.
her independence, 205 n.
parallels in vocabulary between early poems and those written to her, 69.
Bridges, Robert, on *Endymion* Book II, 125; Book IV, 370.
on *Isabella*, 208, 302.
on Keats's power of imitation, 9 n.
on *Ode on a Grecian Urn*, 334, 375.
on *Ode on Melancholy*, 309.
on *Ode to a Nightingale*, 276, 279 n.